STRATEGIC HUMAN RESOURCE MANAGEMENT

STRATEGIC HUMAN RESOURCE MANAGEMENT

CHARLES J. FOMBRUN
NOEL M. TICHY
MARY ANNE DEVANNA

JOHN WILEY & SONS

New York   Chichester   Brisbane   Toronto   Singapore

Library of Congress Cataloging in Publication Data:

Fombrun, Charles J.
      Strategic human resource management.

      Includes index.
      1. Personnel management. I. Tichy, Noel M.
II. Devanna, Mary Anne. III. Title.

HF5549.F587   1984   658.3   84-15223
ISBN 0-471-81079-7

To Burton H. Meltzer
whom we remember as our sponsor,
colleague and friend.

CONTRIBUTORS

CHESTER C. BORUCKI is Research Assistant at the Graduate School of Business, University of Michigan

CORTLANDT CAMMAN is Program Director at the Institute for Social Research, University of Michigan

GLENN D. CHILDS is Manager of Executive Communications in the Public Systems Company, Westinghouse Electric Corporation

MARY ANNE DEVANNA is Research Coordinator of the Center for Research in Career Development and Associate Director of the Strategy Research Center at the Graduate School of Business, Columbia University

CHARLES J. FOMBRUN is on the faculty of the The Wharton School, University of Pennsylvania, and Visiting Associate Professor at the Graduate School of Business, New York University

JOHN A. FOSSUM is Associate Professor at the Industrial Relations Center, University of Minnesota

STEWART D. FRIEDMAN is Assistant Professor of Management at The Wharton School, University of Pennsylvania

JAY R. GALBRAITH is President, Management Consultants, Ltd.

THOMAS N. GILMORE is Associate Director of the Management and Behavioral Science Center, The Wharton School, University of Pennsylvania

DOUGLAS T. HALL is Professor at the Graduate School of Business, Boston University

STANLEY HARRIS is Research Associate at the Institute for Social Research, University of Michigan

vii

LARRY HIRSCHHORN is Senior Associate at the Management and Behavioral Science Center, The Wharton School, University of Pennsylvania

ALAN F. LAFLEY is Executive-in-Residence and Adjunct Professor at the Graduate School of Business, University of Michigan

ROBERT L. LAUD is Vice President and Director of Group Outplacement Counselling, Drake Beam Morin, Inc.

GARY P. LATHAM is Adjunct Professor at the School of Business Administration, University of Washington

EDWARD E. LAWLER III is Director of the Center for Effective Organization, Graduate School of Business Administration, University of Southern California

GERALD E. LEDFORD is Research Scientist, The Center for Effective Organization, Graduate School of Business Administration, University of Southern California

THEODORE P. LEVINO is Senior Vice President of Executive Management Staff, General Electric Company

PETER LORANGE is Professor of Management, The Wharton School, University of Pennsylvania

ANDREW R. MCGILL is Research Associate at the Institute for Social Research, University of Michigan

EDWIN L. MILLER is Professor at the Graduate School of Business, University of Michigan

DECLAN MURPHY is Research Assistant at The Wharton School, University of Pennsylvania

VLADIMIR PUCIK is Assistant Professor at the Graduate School of Business, University of Michigan

NOEL M. TICHY is Professor of Organizational Behavior at the Graduate School of Business Administration, University of Michigan

PREFACE

In recent years we have witnessed a burgeoning of interest in the development of managerial skills. It is manifested in the renewed popularity of productivity management and quality circles and is most visible in the widespread popularity of so-called Japanese Management.

While the current concern with management technique has all the characteristics of a "fad," there is good reason to believe that it reflects an underlying transformation in the organization of work in modern society, one which is expressing itself in the broad concern with general management and the full utilization of human resources in the workplace. On the one hand, economic pressures born of increasing resource scarcities and interdependence on a global scale are provoking a scramble for market share, competitiveness, and the efficient use of resource inputs in the production process. Based on sound economic logic, then, the untapped contributions of the human resources in organizations could make the difference between efficiency and inefficiency, death and survival in the competitive marketplace.

At the same time, the increasing professionalization of the workforce and its involvement in white-collar activities is changing the fundamental systems which organizations have traditionally relied upon to control employee behavior—namely, the bureaucratic structure along with its attendant job ladders, promotion opportunities, power distribution, and reward and evaluation processes. These structural shifts are strongly buttressed by the declining proportion of unionized labor in the United States among blue-collar workers.

Such trends suggest that the century-old conflict between worker and manager is shifting to new levels that call for a new approach to industrial relations, one focusing increasingly on the management of professionals.

This is the broad environmental landscape which Part I of the book sets out to describe and address. It presents the contextual forces to which organizations are struggling to respond and suggests that a concern with increasing productivity through improved human resource management will continue to dominate the managerial outlook of most organizations in the near future.

The 13 chapters of Part II of the book expand on each of these four human resource systems by focusing, in detail, on how selection, appraisal, reward, and development practices can be systematically used to support the strategic outlook of the basic business or set of businesses the organization is involved in.

Part III develops in detail the human resource issues likely to be of greatest strategic importance to organizations in the near future; the different facets of the environment are drawn out in terms of their implications for the strategic management of human resources.

Altogether, this book is designed to begin the necessary dialogue between planners and human resource professionals in large organizations. The traditional isolation of human resource concerns from the planning process in most organizations is a strong barrier to the effective mobilization of employees needed in the implementation of strategic plans. The neglect of human resource concerns also encourages the formulation of unrealistic plans that recognize neither the fundamental constraints nor the tremendous opportunities that inhere in the human capital of the organization. We hope that as communication and understanding increase, organizations will be better equipped to draw on the vast reserve of talent available to them and will be strong enough to rise to the challenges of the environment in the years ahead.

Philadelphia, Pennsylvania
Ann Arbor, Michigan
New York, New York
August 1984

CHARLES J. FOMBRUN
NOEL M. TICHY
MARY ANNE DEVANNA

ACKNOWLEDGMENTS

The ideas described in this book were born in the nurturing atmosphere of the Center for Research in Career Development at Columbia University's Graduate School of Business. The early financial and emotional support of the Center's Director, Kirby Warren, encouraged the formulation of a research program which, with Burt Meltzer's support at Exxon, developed into an action research strategy devoted to exploring the link between theory and practice in the management of human resources.

This book brings together a large number of remarkable individuals who agreed to participate in a project for which we had specified dramatically short deadlines. That the quality of the work has not suffered is a clear indication that excellence and productivity do sometimes go hand in hand. In this respect, the corporations that agreed to participate in describing some of their strategic practices deserve special mention for their patience and active support throughout, especially Ted LeVino of General Electric, Alan Lafley of Chase Manhattan, Tom Murrin and Glenn Childs of Westinghouse, and Larry Smith and Warde Wheaton at Honeywell.

As with all academic tasks, none of this would have been possible without the diligent support of some remarkable administrators along the way. At ISR, that means Carole K. Barnett, at Wharton, Elizabeth Andy helped through some difficult moments, and the final preparation of the manuscript was ably supervised by Evelyn Massar, with the help of Elizabeth Warren, at Columbia University.

C. J. F.
N. M. T.
M. A. D.

CONTENTS

xiii

PART IV   HUMAN RESOURCES: THE CEO's PERSPECTIVE

STRATEGIC HUMAN RESOURCE MANAGEMENT

PART

I

ENVIRONMENT, STRATEGY, AND ORGANIZATION

Part I lays out the framework for the human resource management issues which are discussed in the remainder of the book. Chapter 1 describes the broad environmental issues which affect organizations in this area. It presents the contextual forces to which organizations are struggling to respond and suggests that a concern with increasing productivity through improved human resources management will continue to dominate the managerial outlook of most organizations in the near future.

Chapter 2 brings the analysis down to the organization level and describes some of the current responses that leading-edge corporations are making to the environmental forces impinging on them. The results of a survey of strategic planners and senior human resource executives in a sample of Fortune 500 companies are presented as evidence of the perceived need for a more systematic integration of planning and control in ndustry.

Chapter 3 brings together a set of conceptual frameworks for understanding the nature of the four principal human resource systems in organizations: selection, appraisal, reward, and development. These systems are discussed as structures of control, and the chapter also stresses their role in encouraging the individual pursuit of strategic objectives, managerial goals, and operational activities. In so doing, it emphasizes that the coherence of these systems and their integration into the other control systems of the organization—the planning, budgeting, and information systems—is precisely what makes for effective management.

1

CHAPTER

1

THE EXTERNAL CONTEXT OF HUMAN RESOURCE MANAGEMENT

Charles J. Fombrun

Throughout time people have been concerned with prediction. Witch doctors, oracles, crystal balls, tarot cards, and tea leaves—all reflect the timeless preoccupation of decision-makers with the consequences of their choices. The right forecast could mean power and wealth; the wrong forecast could mean ruin and death.

The quest for certainty has changed little over the years. As social institutions have grown increasingly sophisticated, leaders have replaced the sorcerer with his apprentice, the planner, and mysticism with environmental scanning. For most, prediction is no less hazardous than it used to be. Although summarized in sophisticated probabilities, the future remains as shrouded in the mists of uncertainty as it was for the Greek courtiers consulting the Delphi Oracle. Today sector forecasts, trends analysis, and the formulation of alternative scenarios are the modern crystal balls many organizations use to gaze into the future in their frantic attempt to unlock the doors of time. As it did for the Hellenists of old, it gives them the assurance they need to commit to a course of action and to struggle with the outcomes of their frequently untimely decisions.

3

For a significant number of organizations today, however, predictive accuracy is less a concern than the systematic control of the environmental forces themselves. Through the positions they occupy, their centrality in the economic system, and their large-scale employment, these organizations have become pervasive institutions for whom the environment is far from simply "external" or "a constraint." Rather, the commitment of these "core" organizations to a course of action largely creates the circumstances to which they, and the periphery firms that surround them, are obliged to respond.[1] For these institutions, much of the future, then, is an open book waiting to be written by their commitments in terms of physical assets, financial resources, and human resources.

As we attempt to frame some of the socioeconomic forces that are transforming the environmental landscape, it is well to keep in mind the vital role large institutions across the business, labor, and governmental domains play in actively shaping and landscaping the environment itself. It is with these large organizations that this book is principally concerned.

This chapter sketches some of the environmental trends in terms of four principal sectors:

1. *Technological Sector.*   The set of established technologies used in the production of goods and services; the rate and locus of innovation in products and processes.
2. *Economic Sector.*   The costs of the factors of production and their impact on the market system; the leading indicators of the macroeconomy.
3. *Sociocultural Sector.*   The changing values and attitudes of society and in particular the labor force.
4. *Political Sector.*   The influence of the controlling overlayer, its manifestation in the social system; the nature of societal decision-making.

Although each of these sectors unfolds independently, they are dynamically interrelated.[2] Thus the changing composition of the workforce affects the distribution of income across social groups which, in turn, mobilizes concern and action in the political sector. These transformations take place with leads and lags which move the social system from one configuration to another. Numerous theorists of society have argued the primacy of one or the other of the four sectors in the dynamics of social change.[3] This is not the subject of our discussion. Rather, we focus on the interrelatedness of these sectors and tease out their joint implications for organizations.

[1] Averitt (1968) and Edwards (1979) discuss the "core-periphery" model at great length and present empirical evidence to support it.

[2] This approach is based on Talcott Parsons' analysis of social systems. Diesing (1968) also discusses the particular "rationality" of each of the four sectors of society.

[3] See Daniel Bell's (1976) analysis of the independence and primacy of the different sectors, and their internal dynamic, each a response to a distinct "axial principal."

TECHNOLOGICAL SECTOR: THE IMPACT OF AUTOMATION

Organizations and their employees are experiencing technological change on several fronts that will need their immediate attention. First is the increasing sophistication of information technology. As most computer networks come to link scattered sectors of society, workers are increasingly required to manipulate information and to engage in activities of a service nature rather than the handling of physical goods. Perhaps, as Alvin Toffler suggests,[4] this will increase the organization's ability to decentralize decisions. Whatever the case, it will probably mean less personal interaction and more isolation for workers.

At the same time, technological advances in production techniques have fostered the emergence of robotics. In the auto industry, an increasing proportion of assembly-line work is being done by robots that are both more efficient and more resistant to monotony. This is a direct response to concerns over the declining productivity of labor (shown in Table 1.1), particularly in the goods producing sector of the economy.[5]

The increasing popularity of CAM (Computer-Aided Manufacturing), CAD (Computer-Aided Design) technologies, and their integration in CIM (Computer-Integrated Manufacturing) is revolutionizing the manufacturing process in the traditional sector of U.S. industry. CIM integrates the functionally segmented areas of inventory control and the physical distribution of inputs and throughputs with the cost accounting and purchasing systems of the organization. It is coordination through information flows across the enterprise, with highly flexible decision-making as a result.

Among the managerial ranks, the revolution is felt both in terms of its origins in shop-floor technology as it alters the substance of decision-making, and in the office itself in terms of work processes. Office automation is changing the daily activities of most managerial and office staff, facilitating data storage, retrieval, and communication. As with the automation of production, office automation calls for new ways of thinking about work, retooling in terms of work methods, and hence new jobs with different degrees of interdependence requiring new reward systems, evaluation systems, and training to support them.

As the dynamic of cost-minimization and competitiveness drives further automation into the fundamental work processes of society, the reactions of displaced labor, whether fired or retrained, or of unemployed workers and their families, are likely to provoke or support social unrest and political militancy. As society struggles with these problems, organizations will prob-

---

[4] See Toffler (1979) for a provocative projection of social trends that stresses the role of continually evolving technology.

[5] The underlying causes of the declining productivity of labor are not agreed upon. Nonetheless, falling productivity encourages organizations to substitute capital for labor in order to increase efficiency.

TABLE 1.1. Labor Productivity Growth Rate.

Sector	Labor Productivity Growth Rate (Annual Average %)		
	1948–1965	1965–1973	1973–1978
Overall	3.2	2.1	1.6
Agriculture, forestry, and fishes	5.5	5.3	2.9
Mining	4.2	2.0	−4.0
Construction	2.9	−2.2	−1.8
Manufacturing	3.1	2.4	1.7
Durable goods	2.8	1.9	1.2
Nondurable goods	2.8	1.9	1.2
Transportation	3.3	2.9	0.9
Communication	5.5	4.8	7.1
Electric, gas, and sanitary services	6.2	4.0	0.1
Trade	2.7	3.0	0.4
Wholesale	3.1	3.9	0.2
Retail	2.4	2.3	0.8
Finance, insurance, real estate	1.0	−0.3	1.4
Services	1.5	1.9	0.5
Government	−0.8	0.9	−0.7

SOURCE: Adapted from Hayes and Abernathy. "Managing Our Way to Econmic Decline." *Harvard Business Review*, July–August, 1980.

ably be asked to play a key role in the retooling of workers, in maintaining motivation, managing psychological strife, and reshaping decision-making for the information age.

ECONOMIC SECTOR: GLOBAL COMPETITION AND SCARCITY

The vitality of the economies of Western Europe and especially Japan have challenged common assumptions about U.S. supremacy and have attacked the hypothesis of a unity of interests among the industrialized nations of the West. In fact, the recent decline in the automobile, steel, and rubber industries in the United States reflects a broader shift in the sectoral importance of manufacturing in the economies of the industrialized nations. Some estimates suggest that by the year 2000, manufacturing will account for only 20% GNP in most of the industrialized nations, a specific manifestation of the ongoing march of the division of labor on a global scale with the transfer of goods production to the less developed nations and the growth of the service sector in the postindustrial nations.*

*For instance, Leontief, W. et al. *The Future of the World Economy*. New York: United Nations, 1977.

As the industrialized nations vie for control of the leading manufacturing industries of semiconductors, electronics, communications, automobiles, and computers, global competition provokes an increasing concern for efficiency and fuels the application of evermore sophisticated technology. For all firms it means a greater concern with the control of costs, the extraction of maximum productivity from the different factor inputs, and a need for flexibility and responsiveness in organizational systems and structures to address competitive pressures on a global scale.

The susceptibility of the international economic system to disruptions occasioned by political activity in the furtherance of regional claims has been abundantly vocalized by critics, academics, and practitioners everywhere.[6] The world is still reeling from the economic impact of the 1973 oil embargo, and this is manifest in the persistence of high levels of inflation in most of the industrialized nations and the large accumulated deficits of the less developed nations. Both East and West have suffered from the dislocations, and this has shifted the traditional East–West political axis of confrontation to a more pluralistic configuration of global politics.

The real and artificial scarcities in natural resources, investment capital, and disposable income, when combined with global competitiveness, have accentuated the inflationary problems and increased the economic distortions and uncertainties for all organizations, and especially multinational firms. They undoubtedly have encouraged the overcautious stance and short-run orientation of many U.S. firms in their strategic investment policies and research activity, and frequently made "retrenchment" a necessity. These pressures are likely to remain as the United States struggles to redefine its position in the new global order of highly interdependent activities.

SOCIOCULTURAL SECTOR: THE KNOWLEDGE WORKERS

At the same time, the economic transformation of industry in the United States away from manufacturing and into services has progressively altered the mix of occupational groups employed in large organizations. Table 1.2 describes the increase in white-collar employment across industrial sectors in manufacturing. Combined with the rapid growth of such ancillary service sectors as transportation, trade, and professional services, in recent years the United States has witnessed an explosion in the employment of white-collar workers, a reality that has given some advantage to women, blacks, and other minorities. As Table 1.3 shows, between 1958 and 1974 the most rapidly growing occupational groups were the professional and technical white-collar workers.[7] With these professionals come a new set of work standards, a

---

[6] See, for instance, Nixon (1979).

[7] Daniel Bell (1973) discusses the general societal impact of a shift from industrialism to the professional service economy he labels the "postindustrial" society. Peter Drucker (1979) draws out some of the managerial implications of this trend.

TABLE 1.2.   The Ratio of White-Collar Workers to Blue-Collar Workers by Industry.

Industry	1947	1955	1965	1975
All manufacturing	19.5	26.8	34.4	40.6
Tobacco	7.3	9.0	16.1	23.5
Chemicals	32.2	48.4	66.4	78.3
Petroleum and coal	29.9	45.5	61.8	56.1
Rubber	22.7	26.6	28.5	30.9
Primary metals	14.6	18.4	22.4	28.9
Fabricated metals	18.9	24.1	29.1	34.2
Nonelectrical machinery	26.2	35.1	42.9	54.4
Electrical machinery	30.0	36.7	45.9	55.6
Transportation equipment	21.7	30.2	40.2	42.9

SOURCE: Adapted from Richard Edwards *Contested Terrain*. New York: Basic Books, 1979, Appendix Table A-8.

cosmopolitan value orientation that facilitates interfirm mobility, and a workforce freed from the tedium of supervision and oriented to coordination, organization, and planning.

The most striking characteristic of the new labor force in the United States is its level of education. In 1975, 15% of the U.S. labor force had completed four years of college or more and 36% had completed high school. Only 11% of the labor force had less than an elementary school education. Such statistics support the view that the human resource problems of organizations in the future are not likely to be those of the past. Where managerial attention in the first half of the twentieth century was focused on the problems of managing a blue-collar labor force where unionization had its strongest appeal, the managerial concerns of the year 2000 are the problems of motivating and rewarding a highly professional and educated group of workers. In the next 10 or 20 years, these problems will be particularly exacerbated in the United States by the burgeoning of the ranks of the 28–45-year cohort, the coming of age of the post–World War II baby boom. Thus, in 1990 there will be an estimated 60 million workers of promotion age compared to only 39 million in 1975.

Born after the Depression, after the wars, this group of workers grew up in an affluent society where infinite growth seemed more substantial than a dream and guaranteed the viability of liberal *laissez-faire* attitudes to lifestyles, decision-making, and politics. Pressured by achievement-oriented parents, they pursued educational credentials to such an extent that the cohort itself is now the most educated group in the history of America. More than 40% of that group will have been to college by the age of 30.

Such trends have strong implications for organizations. Facing a plentiful labor market of highly educated workers, organizations can easily disregard

TABLE 1.3.   Occupational Distribution 1958–1974.

Occupational Group	1958 Numbers (in thousands)	1974 Numbers (in thousands)	% Increase 1958–1974
Total	63,000	85,935	36.4
White-collar workers	26,835	41,740	55.5
Professional and technical	6,950	12,340	77.5
Managers and officials	6,785	8,940	31.8
Clerical	9,115	15,000	64.6
Sales	3,985	5,400	35.5
Blue-collar workers	23,350	29,775	27.5
Craftspersons and forepersons	8,460	11,470	35.5
Operatives (semiskilled)	11,400	13,920	22.1
Laborers (unskilled)	3,485	4,380	25.6
Service workers	7,490	11,370	51.8
Private household	1,975	1,230	(37.7)
Others	5,500	10,140	84.3
Farm workers	5,360	3,050	(43.1)
Farmers and farm managers	3,070	1,640	(46.6)
Farm laborers	2,280	1,400	(38.6)

SOURCE: Adapted from Daniel Bell, Table 2.5.

the needs of their employees. Stressing efficiency in such a slack labor market is made simple: organizations can readily alienate, confident in the excess supply available to replace the disillusioned worker.

Consequently, on the basis of numbers alone, it is clear that the workforce of the future faces increasing competition for jobs, especially as mandatory retirement moves from age 65 to 70. What this means is that society and, consequently, organizations will increasingly have to address the frustrated expectations and dissatisfaction of workers. Consistent with Christopher Lasch's sketch of the narcissistic personality,[8] the depersonalization of human interaction will call for increasing attention to the losers in the game of

---

[8] Christopher Lasch (1980) describes the set of individual attitudes, expectations, and preoccupations as "narcissistic," emphasizing their self-centered orientation and arguing that these measures are manifested at a societal level.

corporate politics and the effective organization will, ironically, be asked to pay detailed attention, more than ever before, to programs that motivate achievement, reward success, and cope with failure.

POLITICAL SECTOR: REGULATION, INTERVENTION, AND PARTICIPATION

The growth of the public sector in the second half of the twentieth century is one of the largest structural changes in the occupational structure of the United States. Today over 12 million people (or 16% of the labor force) work directly for the government (local, state, or federal).[9] As a legacy of the New Deal philosophies of Franklin Delano Roosevelt, this segment of the labor force works to design and implement the regulatory framework of the welfare state and manage the network of interrelated policies and guidelines for controlling the activities of individuals and organizations throughout society. The regulatory burden on organizations is apparent in the weight of compliance standards required of organizations in employment, compensation, health and safety, tax, pricing, and pollution. Recognizing the "externalities" of the economy, the divergence of "private costs" from the "social costs" which would lead to the optimal social allocation of resources, government has moved to control the activities of organizations large and small at great cost to those organizations in terms of time and resources needed to ensure compliance.

At the international level, government intervention is manifest in the increasing protectionism of state governments such as Japan, and in the activities of such regional groups as the European Community or the OPEC nations. High import taxes, quotas, and embargos are fractionizing the global markets and distorting the efficient allocation of production and distribution on a global scale. Under the current nation-state system of accounting this is likely to continue, particularly in a period of world recession and increasing scarcity, as nations struggle to balance their national accounts and increase their standard of living. To do this, joint partnerships of the major social actors within nation-states and across limited regions in terms of social planning are emerging as an essential process long practiced in West Germany and Japan, and manifested more recently in the call for the "reindustrialization" of America.

As countries respond to economic turmoil by collective decision-making at the national level, so are organizations pressured towards cooperative policies. The quality of work life movement in the United States, like industrial democracy in Western Europe, is in part a bid for co-determination within the enterprise. In many developing nations, as in some countries of Europe,

---

[9] As Eli Ginzberg (1981) points out, however, such estimates do not include the indirect employment government generates through the private sector. When taken into account, the not-for-profit sector as a whole is estimated to employ an astounding 32% of the labor force.

participation is taking the form of a shared ownership by workers and managers in the equity capital of the firm. Such trends suggest that questions of equity in the distribution of gains and participation in the determination of outcomes are likely to be major issues confronting organizations, particularly as minorities enter the competitive workforce in the slow growth world economy of the foreseeable future.

THE COMING OF AGE OF HUMAN RESOURCE MANAGEMENT

It is in the broad context of a global recession with increasing competition and scarcity, and a professional, highly educated, and abundant labor supply that the modern corporation operating in core activities has begun to address itself to the better management of its human resources. The recent focus on human capital as an underutilized resource is in part a response to the environmental context outlined in Figure 1.1. It is also an aggressive strategy designed to tighten the belt on corporate slack. For the human resource

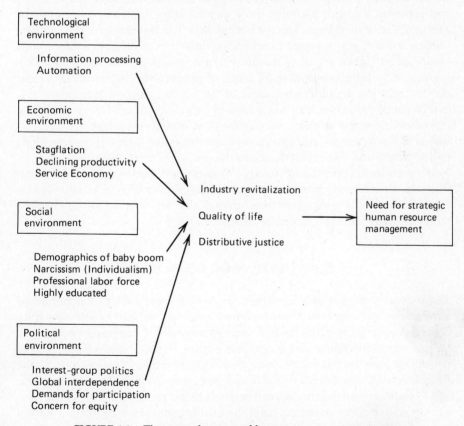

FIGURE 1.1.   The external context of human resource management.

management function—the former personnel function—it is a coming of age that is long overdue.

The organizational landscape is littered with the remains of personnel practices born in earlier stages of development. Still preponderant in the small periphery firms of the nation are those personnel departments devoted to operational servicing and the maintenance of files and records. In these firms, the personnel function is the repository of documents and forms, a library of historical materials all too often filed to be forgotten.

In the middle layer of organizations significant enough to be called upon to account to governmental agencies on the guidelines set forth by the Civil Rights Act of 1964 and the legal statutes and guidelines of ERISA, OSHA, and EEOC, the personnel function has emerged as a managerial tool for organizations, one charged with the proper administration of employee procedures and responsiveness to government, in addition to adequate file maintenance.

But it is principally in the core firms of the private sector, where large-scale employment is both a constraint and an opportunity, that we are seeing the birth of the strategic human resource management function whose inputs and activities are on a par with those of marketing and finance in terms of a recognition of their impact on the bottom line. The emergence of the strategic human resource management function is a reflection of the converging trends identified in Figure 1.1. It is manifest in the recent popularity of Japanese management techniques and in all forms of productivity improvement across the organization. In addressing some of the fundamental environmental demands for participation, the motivation of professionals, and the frustrations of competition, the strategic management of human resources is a concern that is likely to remain and spread through successive layers of organizations in the years ahead. Figure 1.2 diagrams the evolution of the personnel function from operational servicing to strategic management. As the following section suggests, the strategic human resource management function is actively engaged in attempts to support the strategically oriented organization as it struggles with the environmental trends of Figure 1.1.

COOPERATION OR CONFLICT?

The pervasive impact of the current context on organizations has provoked a varied set of responses from the three principal sectors of the operating core: business firms, labor unions, and government. Concerned with maintaining competitiveness and acceptable profits, business organizations have petitioned government for protectionism against foreign imports, tax credits for reinvestment in outdated plants and equipment, depreciation allowances, and a host of selective measures designed to buttress their attempts at regaining lost market share, particularly in the manufacturing sector. At the bargaining table these same firms have sought a decreasing cost burden, asking

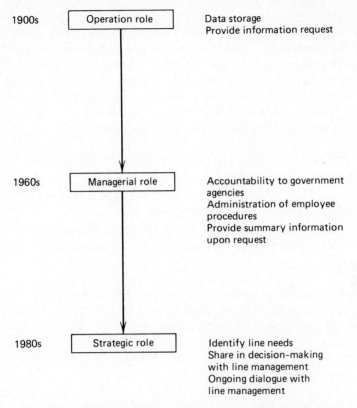

FIGURE 1.2.   From personnel to strategic human resource management.

and frequently winning wage concessions and other cost-economies from their workers.

For labor, the early 1980s was less than enthralling. Faced with high inflation and decreasing employment alternatives, the worker has witnessed a steady erosion of bargaining power in the early 1980s, a fact that has provoked considerable turmoil for the union leadership and their increasing involvement at the national level. Unable to reap immediate monetary gains, labor has traded off economic advantage for increased involvement in decision-making both within organizations and in collective bodies across industrial sectors.[10] As unemployment continues at dizzying levels, there is no evidence that this is a satisfactory solution at the worker level, and it is vividly described in the strikes by workers at Chrysler and U.S. Steel, among others.

For government, this has been a difficult period of shifting priorities that

[10]Recent discussions of "concessionary bargaining" emphasize this point. See *Business Week* (1982) and Mills (1983).

claim to address the economic concerns of the underpriviledged masses of workers struggling to survive in the ailing economy while implementing policies that buttress the defense apparatus and return disposable income to the upper-income classes of the nation. A plethora of books and articles describing the paralysis of the pluralistic process of decision-making in the modern economy have recently been published, and an even more abundant set of suggestions made for the "redesign" of America. Taken as a whole, they can be discussed in terms of these broad agendas:

1. *Industrial Revitalization.* A focus on the decaying industries and the necessity for rebuilding infrastructure.

2. *Quality of Life.* A continuing concern with the conditions of work, the tradeoff between family, leisure, and career.

3. *Distributive Justice.* An awareness of the inequities in the social system in the distribution of the two primary scarce resources: money and power.

Together, these three sets of concerns are responses at the national level that mirror the dismal environmental backdrop against which organizations are currently operating. They are strategic issues all actors in the operating core of the nation are struggling with in one form or another. They push the three sectors of business, labor, and government into alternating modes of conflict and cooperation.

An Economic Agenda: Industry Revitalization

A recognition of the decaying infrastructure of the traditionally dominant manufacturing sector of the economy has motivated a variety of economic proposals to reindustrialize America.[11] Whether through a carefully formulated industrial policy that involves picking "winning" industries and writing off the "losers," or through general policies that favor investment, these proposals address the modernization of the industrial heartland, and mark the refusal to accept any inevitability in the increasing service orientation of the post-industrial U.S. economy.

Insisting on the long-term benefits to all, revitalization calls for trilateral cooperation between organizations, labor, and government in political structures resembling those of Japan and West Germany. In its impact on the labor force it calls for technologies that all too frequently increase the capital/labor ratio through automation, and provoke a need for retraining workers into new sets of skills. Here labor typically has been at odds with government and its policy of noninvolvement in the retooling of workers or the support of workers displaced by technology.

---

[11] Numerous programs have been proposed, for instance, Etzioni (1982).

As competition and innovation trends continue to erode the industrial core, the pressures from revitalization are likely to grow stronger and more insistent than ever before.

A Social Agenda: The Quality of Life

Ever since the early years of industrialization, America has been politically concerned with improving the quality of life. Indeed, in the twentieth century its economic system as a whole has been praised far and wide for its success in increasing the national standard of living at an astronomical pace.

With the increasing affluence of the average American has also come a changing social fabric. The work ethic that long supported industriousness and a growing labor productivity has given way to what Christopher Lasch has labeled a culture of "narcissism," one dominated by an ethos of individual welfare instead of collective well-being, oriented to work as a means to the purchase of leisure rather than an intrinsic source of fulfillment.

Today this is manifest in the demands for a decreasing work week, flexible hours of work, new options for individualizing benefits packages, and early retirement. As legislation has ensured that organizations satisfactorily address the safety and health concerns of most workers, job conditions fall lower and lower in the bargaining priorities of unionized workers. They are replaced by the continuing demand for high wages, and increasing requests for flexibility, autonomy, and opportunity in the estimated 2000 organizations involved in "Quality of Work Life" interventions in 1975,[12] and discussed by the numerous groups devoted to its study, such as the National Quality of Work Center, The Quality of Work Center, and the Work in America Institute. Given the contextual trends, the increasing mechanization of work, the displacement of workers and competition, the concern for the quality of life as a whole and its manifestation in the work environment are likely to continue. Under a global recession they are also likely to exacerbate the conflict between the individual and the organization, causing considerable personal and social strife.

A Political Agenda: Distributive Justice

In a provocative analysis of the American economy, Lester Thurow describes the national paralysis in decision-making brought on by the splintered pluralism of the political system and the unquestioned legitimacy of interest group politics in which the demands of the few can overwhelm the preferences of the many.[13] For Thurow, the problem lies in the system's reluctance and inability to acknowledge the redistributive implications of all decisions in a

---

[12] See Chapters 21 and 22 for a detailed discussion of quality of work life programs.

[13] Thurow (1980) expands on equity and the politics of interest groups at great length.

A similar concern has long been voiced by radical theorists of organization who see the problem of organization as a problem of "control." For them, organizations are battlefields in which workers and managers vie for the scarce resources of power, income, and opportunity.[14] Collective bargaining in this light is an institutionalized system for addressing distributive justice in the organization, and hence in society as a whole. The call for more power to the workers in organizations has taken two forms: industrial democracy and participative management.

Participative management is the request by workers for a say in the making of decisions that affect their daily work-lives. It asks for involvement in managerial and strategic decision-making, and is typically addressed through suggestion boxes, joint labor–management committees that review worker grievances, and, infrequently, in rotating membership on the board of directors.

Industrial democracy, on the other hand, is a political structure long institutionalized in Western Europe, one that shares decision-making through formal and often equal representation of labor at all levels of the organization. It ensures that within organizations the distributive implications of decisions are addressed.

At the other extreme, of course, stands Japan, where an institutional structure of industrial groups locks workers into a system of paternalism that identifies worker interests with organizational interests, and defuses the latent conflict between labor and management. Thus despite a high cost of living, wages are low and the labor force is submissive to the institutional demands placed on it. The attempts to bring Japanese management to America, when seen in this light, are likely to fail since there is no institutional matrix of protectionism, paternalism, and chauvinism[15] to support it in the United States. On the contrary, the continued influx of women and minorities into the competitive workplace is likely to put increasing pressure on U.S. organizations to address the distributive equality concerns of the labor force, and its manifestation in national decision-making.

Managerial Strategies

Figure 1.3 summarizes the various kinds of practices and policies organizations are implementing in one form or another. As the figure suggests, these practices have made at base: (1) fundamentally different assumptions about the nature of the employment relation, and (2) targeted different hierarchical groups in the organization.

---

[14] Edwards (1979) presents this view cogently.

[15] By chauvinism is meant the pattern of hiring full-time male workers, and maintaining a large part-time slack labor pool of women. In Japanese society, the woman's place is still in the home.

Assumption about employment relationship

	CONFLICT	COOPERATION
Executive	Lobby groups Federal regulations	Tripartite advisory groups Joint labor-management committee Worker directorships
Supervisory	Professional unionization	Organization development Participative management "Japanese" management Succession planning
Rank and file	Concession bargaining Collective bargaining	Quality-work life Industrial democracy Owner-managed enterprise Quality circles
	↓ Mobilization of power	↓ Fragmentation of power

FIGURE 1.3.   A framework for human resource management.

Where a basic conflict between organization and individual is assumed, the stress is on practices that mobilize political power and make salient the competing interests of the parties. *Negotiation* is the hallmark of all interventions under this world-view, and distributive bargaining or collective regulation the only way to achieve this.

In contrast, a wide range of approaches assumes an underlying exchange relationship between employer and employee, one which emphasizes their commonality of interests. Power in such organizations is to be shared as equally as possible, and structural interventions are intended to fragment the political power of any single group. We note in this regard the claim of radical theorists that such interventions are only mechanisms for dissimulating the "real" power of strategic decision-making which remains centralized at the top, a process of *cooptation* rather than cooperation.

Although we do not settle the issue in this book, Part III presents some convincing summaries and examples of activities taking place across the environmental landscape that call for cooperative activity in the context of a conflictual system of bargaining relations. These examples and others suggest that much benefit for all parties to the organization in the future will come from strategically balancing conflictual and cooperative approaches. Excellent human resource management may well mean developing strategies for mobilizing power where conflict is unavoidable, and sharing power when cooperation is possible. The national structure of collective bargaining and collective regulation in the United States is here to stay. What we need to understand is how to strategically identify areas in which we can benefit from defining organizations as systems of cooperative exchange.

CONCLUSION

The turbulent context of global recession and interdependence sets the stage for strategic activity in organizations of all sizes as the United States struggles to manage the pressures of postindustrialism. The declining manufacturing industries and the increasing service orientation of the economy call for national priority setting that makes core business and labor organizations central partners in the collective endeavors of government. Their strategic stance externally also translates into the management systems they articulate to reinforce their strategic goals. The pressure to automate in order to maintain competitiveness is only one of many contextual influences that will affect the labor force. In the coming years the large influx of highly educated professional workers will create significant managerial dilemmas for management as they are pressured to respond to national demands for distributive justice in the allocation of power and opportunity in the workplace. To these demands, the cutting-edge organization concerned with innovation, productivity, and competitiveness will want to respond with a well-developed and systematic process of strategic human resource management.

CHAPTER

2

THE ORGANIZATIONAL CONTEXT OF STRATEGIC HUMAN RESOURCE MANAGEMENT

Noel M. Tichy
Charles J. Fombrun
Mary Anne Devanna

Managing in turbulent times requires organizations to return to basic questions about their nature and purpose. This chapter argues in favor of including human resource management in the strategic management process. The role of human resources in strategy formulation and implementation is discussed in terms of survey and anecdotal data that illustrate the extent to which major U.S. companies have integrated human resource management in their strategic planning process.

THE CHALLENGE OF STRATEGIC HUMAN RESOURCE MANAGEMENT

In 1981 the Strategy Research Center at Columbia University surveyed a set of human resource executives and strategic planners in 224 large corporations. The purpose of the study was to ascertain how the heads of these functions

19

viewed the role of human resource management in strategy formulation and implementation for their firms. Responses were received from 252 executives representing 168 companies.

Because there were no significant differences between the responses of the strategic planning and human resource executives, we report them below as a single group. The sample represents a cross section of American industry and includes a representative number of companies in the aerospace, chemicals, automotive, banking, life insurance, food and beverage, and leisure time industries.

Strategic Planning Activities

In Figure 2.1, 53% of the respondents report that formal strategic planning activities were used to a great extent in their company, whereas 39% report that a moderate amount of strategic planning goes on in their organizations. Although formal strategic planning processes seem very much a part of corporate activities today, 52% of the executives report that they have been in use for less than six years. Strategic planning can, therefore, be viewed as a somewhat recent addition to corporate activity.

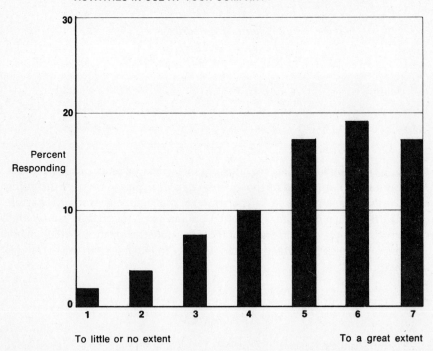

FIGURE 2.1(a). To what extent are there formal strategic planning activities in use at your company?

The respondents vary in their judgment as to the specific contribution that strategic planning makes to overall corporate performance. Figure 2.1 shows that 31% of the respondents feel that the process was moderately effective, and 48% feel it was more than moderately effective in contributing to the overall effectiveness of their companies. There is obviously room for improvement.

The Role of Human Resource Management in Strategy Formulation

Respondents were asked the following questions concerning the utility of human resource data in strategy formulation:

1. Is human resource data systematically available?
2. To what extent does it influence the process of strategy formulation?

As seen in Figure 2.2, executives responded to these questions for six categories of human resource data. They are listed on the vertical axis of the chart. Based on these results, it is possible to conclude that at least some information is available to planners, in particular, (1) an inventory of man-

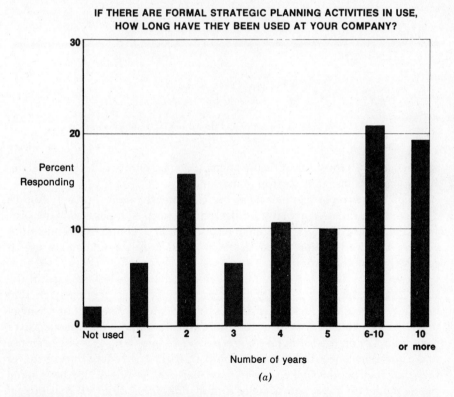

IF THERE ARE FORMAL STRATEGIC PLANNING ACTIVITIES IN USE, HOW LONG HAVE THEY BEEN USED AT YOUR COMPANY?

(a)

FIGURE 2.1(b). If there are formal strategic planning activities in use, how long have they been used at your company?

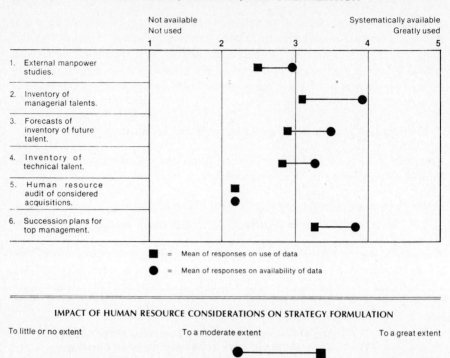

FIGURE 2.2.   Availability and use of human resource data.

agerial talent, (2) forecasts of future talent, (3) an inventory of technical talent, and (4) succession plans for top management.

Respondents reported that there are consistently more human resource data available than are actually utilized in the various decision making processes. The one exception is a human resource audit of considered acquisitions because this information tends to be collected only for immediate use in considering an acquisition.

Executives wish to see more human resources information utilized in the strategic planning process. Fifty-three percent of the respondents felt that human resources considerations had less than a moderate effect on strategy formulation, while 47% percent felt that this information had a moderate or greater impact on the formulation process. More important was the response to the question concerning the desired impact. Eighty percent of the executives said that they would like to see human resource considerations have more than a moderate impact on strategy formulation. Only 20% felt that human resource information should play a minor role in formulating corporate strategy. In general, it seems that both human resource executives and strategic planners see a need to use more human resource data in strategy formulation.

The Role of Human Resource Management in Strategy Implementation

Strategic management is a process that can be broken down into a formulation stage and an implementation stage. The third phase of the survey focused on strategy implementation issues. The following questions were asked:

1. To what extent are human resource activities used in strategy implementation?
2. To what extent should human resource activities be used in strategy implementation?

There were seven types of human resources activities considered as potentially useful for strategy implementation. These seven tools are listed on the left-hand side of Figure 2.3.

For the first five out of seven activities, the majority of respondents report moderate utilization in strategy implementation. The last two activities (conducting development programs designed to support strategic changes and career planning to help develop key personnel for strategic plans) were regarded as less than moderately utilized in the implementation process at this time.

It seems from these results that formal training and development programs have not been nearly as prevalent in corporations as assessment activities. Until recently corporations have relied primarily on job rotation and teaching executives the skills they need to aid in strategy implementation. With today's constrained economy and with the decreasing mobility of younger employees, job rotation and transfers are a less practical human resource tool.

Figure 2.3 shows a consistently large difference between the use of human resource activities and the extent to which the executives feel they should be used in implementing strategies. Respondents clearly indicate a desire to see higher utilization of human resource activities in strategy implementation. The greatest difference between the actual and desired use of personnel tools can be seen in the last two activities. It is interesting to note that even though both of these activities are currently the least utilized, they are seen as equally desirable to the other five in the future. This seems to verify the fact that formal training programs are becoming a necessity in the corporate world.

In the final analysis the respondents report that they wish to see a much larger use of human resource activities in the strategy implementation process. Eighty-three percent of the respondents felt that human resource tools were currently less than capitalized upon in the implementation phase of the strategic planning process. When asked to what extent they would like to see human resource activities utilized, 95% of the respondents reported that they would like to see a greater use of human resource tools in implementing strategies.

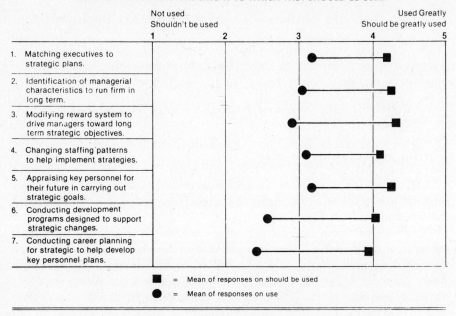

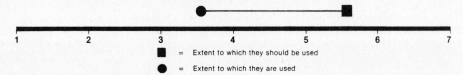

FIGURE 2.3. The extent to which human resource activities are used in strategy implementation and the extent to which they should be used.

The need for a strategic human resource role appears to exist. The dilemma is to figure out how to accomplish this role. The remainder of this chapter highlights some of the attempts organizations are making to close the gap. Much remains to be done, but the illustrations that follow are indeed encouraging as they indicate that steady progress is being made.

FORMULATING STRATEGY: THE ROLE OF HUMAN RESOURCES

The role of human resource management in strategy formulation represents a true frontier for human resource management. As we indicated in the previous section, most firms would like to use human resource data in the strategy formulation process, but few have successfully carved out an appropriate role for their human resources. Traditionally, human resources have been considered a factor only after the strategic business decisions are made. One human resource executive put it succinctly when he said, "The line's job is to tell us where the business is going and then it is up to us to find the people to develop." Unfortunately, human resource executives are not always able to deliver even on this restricted mandate. A large chemical company recently watched a $50 million acquisition go sour because they had not considered the human resource implications of their purchase. Neither of the parties to the merger had the management capability needed to run the business. Yet human resource issues were not even discussed during the deliberations that preceded the decision to purchase the business.

Examples of the use of human resource management as an integral part of strategy formulation are found in such companies as IBM, GE, and Intel. Indeed, many companies have begun to require a human resource component in their plans. These include, among others, Chase Manhattan Bank, General Foods, Xerox, and parts of Honeywell. Where it has begun, a great deal of experimentation and problem-solving is required to decide what data are required, what issues should be included, and how they should relate to the various aspects of the business.

For instance, IBM and GE both require a human resource section in their strategic plan. These firms not only have decided what data they need but also have put targeted control systems in place to ensure that the plans have high quality human resource components. A major question to ask in this regard is: How can you get line and human resource staff to collaboratively integrate human resources into the strategic plan? This is an area which is given serious priority at IBM, in part because the personnel manager is required to sign off on the business unit's strategic plan before it goes forward. If there is disagreement, the personnel manager can register nonconcurrence, in which case if the difference is not resolved with the business unit's management, IBM's contention system is activated. Regular procedures exist for differences to get kicked up a level for eventual resolution. The importance of this personnel role is that political pressure exists on both the line and personnel to take the human resource portion of the strategic plan seriously. The personnel manager's professionalism is on the line in signing off on the plan. If there are inadequacies in the human resources area, his or her career is at stake. On the other hand, line management cannot take the human resource issues lightly since consensus is expected, and a line manager who cannot reach agreement with the personnel manager is probably not doing the job adequately. The result has been an active involvement of personnel managers in the strategy formulation process.

At GE the plans have also had a required human resource component for

---

[1] See Chapter 17 for a discussion of the issues that should be included in requiring human resource components in strategy formulation.

the strategic plan since the late 1970s. In order to accomplish this several steps were taken. First, the strategic planning guidelines include a specific human resource side along with marketing, finance, technology, and so on. Second, the human resource staff is given training in strategic planning and human resource planning. Third, human resource planner roles were created and assigned to the business units responsible for providing the staff support to the human resource portion of the strategic plans. The process is still evolving at GE but is an accepted part of the management process.

IMPLEMENTING STRATEGY: THE ROLE OF HUMAN RESOURCES

To date, the major emphasis in strategic planning has doubtless been on formulation. This led to the conclusion by the early 1980s that much time and thought had gone into analyzing and planning strategy yet very little into its implementation. The result has been an indictment of the whole strategic planning field, one which was well documented in a critique published in *Fortune* in December, 1983. The challenge of the 1980s, in our view, is the effective implementation of strategy—getting people to do the right things to make strategies happen. In this respect, the human resource tools become central and focus specifically on selecting the right people to run a business, rewarding them for strategic activities, and designing staffing patterns that match the strategic plans, as well as creating more strategically motivated development and labor relations policies. To this end, the human resource systems will need to become more flexible so that they can be aligned to drive strategy. In this section we present some illustrations of how this is already occurring in some companies. These are discussed in terms of the four generic human resource activities of all organizations: (1) selection/promotion/placement process, (2) reward process, (3) development process, and (4) appraisal process.

Selection/Promotion/Placement Process

The selection, promotion, and placement process includes all those activities related to the internal movement of people across positions and external hiring into the organization. The essential process is one of matching available resources to jobs in the organization. It entails defining the organizations human needs for particular positions and assessing the available pool of people to determine the best fit.

Corning Glass Company

At Corning an extensive effort is underway to assess the company's top 100 executives for such qualities as entrepreneurial flair. The goal is to have a clearer profile of the organization's pool of executive talent specified in terms of capabilities for managing different parts of the BCG matrix. An example of this in practice occurred in December 1979 when:

> Corning reshaped its electronic strategy, deciding that the market was starting to expand again, and that it needed a growth oriented manager. It placed a manufacturing specialist who had shown a great deal of flair in working with customers in the top marketing slot for electronics, and says Shafer, "It looks like he's turning it around." [*Business Week*, February 25, 1980]

Chase Manhattan Bank

During the period between 1975 and 1980 the bank underwent major managerial changes. A key to the bank's successful turnaround from a troubled bank in the mid-'70s was careful strategic level selection and placement of executives. Historically, in banking in general and specifically at Chase, senior level positions were decided based on historical precedent with old-boy networks playing a major role. Also, the tradition in banking was to reward those with banker skills, not those with managerial skills which were implicitly considered to be of less importance. Under the stress of serious performance problems, Chase Manhattan Bank had to reexamine these practices. As a result, a very systematic effort was launched to strategically manage senior selection and placement decisions. Thus,

> When the trust manager retired, corporate management decided that the department, whose operation had been essentially stable, should focus on a more aggressive growth strategy. Instead of seeking a veteran banker, Chase hired a man whose experience had been with IBM. [*Business Week*, February 25, 1980]

because it was felt he brought a strong marketing orientation to the trust department which the new strategy required.

> Similarly, when Chase reorganized its retail banking business from a low margin operation in which the stress was on keeping down costs to a more expansionary business offering broader consumer financial services it hired, because of his entrepreneurial skills, an executive who had been a division chief for a small industrial firm and had a track record of entrepreneurial management experience. The former head of retail banking, who was viewed as a strong cost cutter, was matched with the bank's European strategy calling for tightening up expenses and getting the operation in better financial shape. [*Business Week*, February 25, 1980]

Reward Process

Good selection is a *sine qua non* of performance. Once people are in jobs and perform, however, they should also be rewarded for good performance. These incumbents should also be developed to improve performance and/or prepare them for a new position.

A major strategic issue involves using the reward system to overcome the tendency toward short-sighted management. The rewards for this year's profits generally turn out to be both financial incentives and promotions. Thus, motivation of senior executives toward long-term strategic goals tends to be difficult since the reward system encourages short-term achievement at the expense of long-term goals. As *The New York Times* (April 24, 1980) points out:

> Though bonuses based on achieving sales or earnings goals have long been common, the emphasis on long-term is a new element. Top corporate executives, under pressure from Wall Street and stockholders have been rewarded with bonuses and stock options when immediate profits spurt. The auto industry, for example, is notable for its short-term rewards.

It is unreasonable and unwise to recommend that managers only be rewarded for long-term strategic goals as businesses must clearly perform in the present to succeed in the future. Thus the reward system should provide balanced support to short and long-term strategic goals.

Texas Instruments

One company which has thought long and hard about the use of reward systems for driving the company's short and long-term goals is TI.

A major part of TI's strategy since the early 1960s has been to rigidly adhere to the "learning curve theory." Simply put, it states that "manufacturing costs can be brought down by a fixed percentage depending on the product, each time cumulative volume is doubled" (*Business Week*, September 18, 1978). The strategy involves constant redesign improvement of the product and the processes of production so that prices can drop as fast as possible. This strategy was implemented by organizing into Product Customer Centers (PCCs) which were essentially divisions of the company. This created decentralized profit centers that could be closely monitored for performance. The reward system was tied to the PCCs so that managers worked hard to make the "learning curve theory" operative. However, there were some problems.

The PCCs and associated reward systems worked at cross-purposes to another organizational strategy, however, namely the development of innovative products. The rewards were structured to drive managers to be overly concerned with short-run efficiencies and not with long-term strategic goals.

The solution to this dilemma was to design a new organization which was draped over the existing PCC structure. It was called the Objectives, Strategies, and Tactics (OST) organization at TI. It was created to supplement the PCC which remained intact. The OST structure is concerned with the formulation and implementation of long-range plans. The same people belong to both organizations. The company's total expenditures are systematically divided between the PCC structure and the OST structure. The top managers at TI wear two hats. With one hat they are bottom-line, efficiency-focused managers working to drive the PCC structure and are rewarded and evaluated for accomplishing the efficiency objectives. With the other hat (the OST hat) they are involved in working toward a strategic objective which may have a 10–20-year time horizon. There are separate monitoring and appraisal systems tied to the OST and these are used to drive performance in the long-term strategic arena. For example, a manager may be responsible for a PCC while at the same time work in the OST toward a strategic objective for products in the computerized auto industry of the future. If 60% of the manager's time was allocated to the PCC and 40% of the time to OST, the manager's compensation would be split to reflect the short and long-term aspects of the job.

TI has also used the reward system to encourage another set of desired strategic behaviors. Having discovered that managers tend to set low risk objectives so as to enhance their chances of receiving a bigger bonus (thereby stifling creativity and innovation), TI altered the reward system to attack this problem. Through a "wild hare" program, TI provided funding for more speculative programs that were being underfunded in the initial OST system. Managers are asked to rank speculative projects on a separate basis, and the bonus system is then tied into this process.

Another TI reward mechanism used in fostering organizational innovation is to provide any member of the organization with a chance to obtain a grant from a pool containing several million dollars. The result has been the emergence of informal groups who apply for grants from the innovation pool, called IDEA, that they then attempt to turn into viable products.

Development Process

Ensuring that the organization has an adequate supply of human resource talent at all levels is no easy task especially when organizations are undergoing rapid strategic changes. The key is to have a human resource planning system that makes accurate forecasts. Such systems are not easily built and even though most large companies have manpower planning systems, they are very inadequate. Doubtless there are many reasons for the failure of most human resource planning systems. Critical among these is the fact that the data about people which are input into the system have frequently been unreliable. Managers have generally not appraised employees well enough to ensure that valid data about current performance levels are available, let alone data on future potential. In order to plan for the future, an accurate inventory of the current human resource stock is important. This should include both an assessment of current individual performance and future potential of these individuals. The appraisal process is the ideal vehicle to provide these data. As we point out in Chapter 3, the appraisal process is the weakest of all the human resource systems; hence, the planning systems built on these data are also going to be inadequate.

A second basic flaw in strategic development has been its lack of linkage to the business strategy. Although many organizations have given lip service to such a link, the reality is that it has been an afterthought usually delegated to the human resource staff without any line management involvement in the process. As a result, the human resource plan frequently remains a paper exercise that is not used in the strategic decision process.

In our opinion, only a handful of U.S. companies have strategically managed the development of senior executive talent. Among them are General Motors, Exxon, General Electric, Texas Instruments, IBM, and Proctor & Gamble.

Exxon

The Compensation and Executive Development (COED) system at Exxon is designed to ensure a disciplined approach to the development of managerial talent for the company. The system is driven from the top of the corporation where a senior-level committee headed by the CEO, and made up of members of Exxon's board, is charged with reviewing the development and placement of the top 250 Exxon executives. This committee (called the Compensation and Executive Development, or COED for short) meets every Monday of the year with few exceptions. A senior staff group collects data on the company's top executives for use in these meetings. The COED committee carefully reviews the performance of executives, examines the developmental needs of each individual, compares them with each other, and makes decisions about future development so as to ensure the flow of managerial talent and back-up candidates for all positions.

The COED system also exists within each of the Exxon subsidiaries where the president of each subsidiary runs a COED committee similar to the one operating at the corporate level. Each subsidiary also has a senior level staff for the COED committee. This enables the COED system to cascade down to the top 2000 or so managers at Exxon.

In discussions with senior Exxon managers it is striking to hear the universal acclaim given the system. Most state unequivocally that the system accounts for Exxon's overall success as a company and is unbeatable as a system for developing managers.

Appraisal Process

The key to an effective appraisal process at the strategic level is the commitment of quality managerial time to systematic examination and evaluation of executive talent. The descriptions of the Exxon and GM development systems are in part descriptive of their appraisal systems as the two processes are interrelated. Perhaps the company with the most strategic appraisal system is General Electric where a great deal of time and staff work goes into appraising the top 600 executives. Chapter 12 discusses GE's process at great length.

General Electric

The diversification of GE makes the appraisal of managers more complex than most other companies. Unlike GM or Exxon which have one major line of business, GE has more than 200 businesses. As a result, GE has developed elaborate approaches to handling the appraisal of key managers.

One very important strategic activity is the slate system. The top 600 positions at GE are carefully managed and monitored by the chairman of GE. A special staff group under the direction of a senior vice president reviews these key executives. This staff works with line managers to develop slates of acceptable candidates for key personnel positions at GE. Positions can only be filled from among those on the approved slate. Thus, a business head cannot select a vice president of marketing unless the individual is among those on the official slate list for the position. The slate is approved by the human resource staff. If a manager wants to push strongly for an individual not on the slate, the decision must ultimately be kicked up the hierarchy at GE to the Chairman. Since this is frowned upon, few people not on the slate are ever selected for these positions.

CONCLUSION

Managing strategically is increasingly a way of life for organizations faced with the turbulent economic, political, and cultural forces of the 1980s. In order to be successful, organizations and their managers will have to confront basic questions regarding the formulation and implementation of strategy in their organizations.

The area that will be getting much attention in the 1980s is human resource management because it has been the most neglected strategic area and also because it will be central to implementing the needed cultural and political changes in organizations. A process for changing the human resource management of an organization in the future will need specific strategic frameworks for dealing with the challenges before them. This is the task we set for ourselves in the next chapter.

3

A FRAMEWORK FOR STRATEGIC HUMAN RESOURCE MANAGEMENT

Mary Anne Devanna
Charles J. Fombrun
Noel M. Tichy

Discussions of the current state of American industry tend to center on two issues: the declining productivity of the American worker and the declining rate of innovation in American industries. Theories abound as to the cause of these declines and solutions to put it right are no less numerous. Although the causes of these problems are much too complex for us to consider in this discussion[1] and the systems we are about to present only a small part of the solution that may be needed to revitalize the economic infrastructure in the United States, it is our belief that more effective systems for managing human resources within companies will lead to increased effectiveness in organizations.

[1] The productivity issue has been addressed in some detail in books such as Amitai Etzioni's *An Immodest Agenda,* and articles such as Robert Hayes and William J. Abernathy's "Managing Our Way to Economic Decline" which appeared in the *Harvard Business Review.* A challenge to these views was put forth in an article written in the *New York Times,* January 13, 1983, by Richard B. West and Dennis E. Logue.

To bolster this argument, this chapter presents a set of frameworks for conceptualizing human resource management and explores the link between human resource management and the formulation and implementation of strategic corporate and/or business objectives.

MANAGEMENT AND ORGANIZATIONAL MODELS

Chapter 1 has made the point that the environment most organizations face has become increasingly complex and that it tends to change at an ever more rapid rate compared to a decade ago. Managers faced with the problem of processing increasing amounts of information need some way of organizing these data so that they can focus on the critical factors that impact on their organization's effectiveness. To this end, we present in this chapter a set of conceptual frameworks that will help managers understand not only how the status quo operates but how required adaptations in organizational strategy will have an impact on existing systems, and which systems will have to be modified if the new strategy is to work.

Most of the frameworks discussed in this chapter are essentially descriptive. They focus attention on issues that managers might want to think about under differing conditions such as the implementation of increasingly complex organizational structures. Other models, such as the human resource cycle, have dynamic implications to the extent that the process involves feedback loops that provide for increasing organizational effectiveness through successive iterations of the human resource management cycle.

In both cases, however, the models or frameworks are abstractions of a highly complex reality and managers should expect to have to adapt them to the particular circumstances that they face in their own organizations. In addition, the authors look upon these models as evolving, and it is our hope that they will become more refined as our own understanding of human resource management increases.

More specifically, strategic management involves consideration of the following.

(1). *Mission and Strategy.*   An organization needs a reason for being (mission), and a sense of how to display materials, information, and people to carry it out (strategy).

(2). *Formal Structure.*   People and tasks are organized to implement the organization's strategy. The organization's formal structure includes its systems of financial accounting and information dissemination.

(3). *Human Resource Systems.*   People are recruited and developed to do jobs defined by the organization's formal structure; their performance must be monitored and rewards allocated to maintain productivity.

These are discussed at length in the following sections.

STRATEGIC MANAGEMENT

Organizations exist to accomplish some mission or set of objectives. Over time, the reason for any organization's existence may change so completely that it is difficult to identify the current organization with its historical predecessor except in name, that is, its continued existence as a legal entity. American Telephone and Telegraph, for instance, is undergoing a much-publicized metamorphosis of this sort. More frequently, the change in mission or corporate objectives is of a more incremental nature as the organization adapts to changing consumer tastes or competitive threats. Thus at any point in time the organization has a reason for being, an *objective* that it tries to accomplish through the use of money, material, information, and people.

To accomplish its mission or objectives, the firm must decide what optimal structure is needed to carry out its objectives. Once the nature of the structure is decided upon, it must attract and retain sufficient numbers of people to carry out the tasks needed to see that its objectives or strategies are effectively implemented. Figure 3.1 presents the basic elements of mission and strategy, formal structure, and human resource management as interrelated systems that are embedded in a turbulent environment. This framework elaborates the traditional view of how a firm should think about strategic management by including human resource management as an integral tool that managers can use in the strategic arena of their organizations.

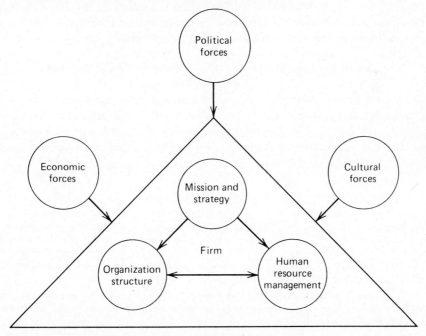

FIGURE 3.1. Strategic management and environmental pressures.

In this framework we define strategy as both the process by which the objectives of the organization are chosen from the set of all feasible objectives available to the organization, as well as the process by which the organization uses its resources to carry out those objectives.

The formal structure is viewed as the way in which the organization is designed to carry out its objectives and includes the fundamental division of labor and description of jobs to be done, their aggregation into groups, projects, functions, or businesses as well as the degree of centralized or decentralized control that top management chooses to exercise over the operating units.

The Link Between Strategy and Structure

In this early historical analysis, Alfred Chandler (1962) argued that the structure of an organization followed from its strategy.[2] He classified growth strategies that resulted in structural modifications in organizations as being of the following types: (1) expansion of volume, (2) geographic dispersion, (3) vertical integration, and (4) product diversification. As organizations grew larger and became more complex, he argued, they underwent structural transformations from functional to product to multidivisional forms. Thus Chandler's marriage of strategy and structure addressed the need to adapt the basic control structure of the organization to its objectives at successive stages of its evolution. Firms that failed to adapt their structures to the new strategies were plagued with inefficiencies until the pressure for adaptation either forced the adoption of a new structure or drove them out of business.

Strategy, Structure and Human Resource Management

Chandler's thesis has influenced two decades of scholarship and practice in business strategy. But it was not until Galbraith and Nathanson (1978) addressed the issues of strategy implementation that scholarly attention was focused on a complementary managerial tool that could be used to facilitate the implementation of strategy: human resource management.[3] Galbraith and

---

[2] In this analysis we leave out the question that Chandler asked as to why the strategy which required the structural adaptation arose in the first place. Readers who are interested in the issue can refer to Chandler's argument that shifts in conditions external to the firm presented either opportunities or threats that the firm responded to with a new strategic direction or to Penrose's competing view that strategies are born in the minds of managers independent of external conditions and that the changes in corporate strategy were simply an *ex post facto* recognition of these individual initiatives on the part of managers.

[3] This is not to imply that the importance of the human element in organizations had not been previously recognized. It received considerable attention from behaviorally oriented researchers from Elton Mayo to the present and plays a central role in management texts such as Newman et al.'s (1982) *Process of Management*. However, Galbraith and Nathanson (1978) focused attention on human resource systems as an extension of Chandler's analysis of strategy and structure.

Nathanson focused on such issues as fitting performance measures to the strategy and structures as well as to rewards, career paths, and leadership styles. In Table 3.1 we have expanded this framework to describe the four generic human resource systems that are consistent with the different stages of growth that Chandler argued all organizations pass through from birth to maturity.

The argument we make is that just as firms will be faced with inefficiencies when they try to implement new strategies with outmoded structures, so they will also face problems of implementation when they attempt to effect new strategies with inappropriate human resource systems. The critical managerial task is to align the formal structure and the human resource systems so that they drive the strategic objectives of the organization.

HUMAN RESOURCE SYSTEMS: THE UNDERLYING HYPOTHESES ABOUT PEOPLE

An analysis of the human resource systems of large companies should yield information about what assumptions the designers of those systems hold about people. Are they Maslow's self-motivators who primarily seek opportunities to develop their competencies, or do they more closely resemble a conditioned prototype seeking to avoid punishment and obtain rewards? Although most managers probably do not consciously articulate their beliefs, these can be deduced from the control systems that they fashion to motivate human resources in their companies. And since they were typically designed in an evolutionary piece-meal, catch-as-catch-can fashion, there are frequent incompatibilities in the subsystems. For example, it is not at all unusual to find that the compensation and promotion system is predicated on the notion that people will turn in higher levels of performance if those levels of performance are tightly linked with monetary and promotional rewards. On the other hand, people responsible for the management development and/or organizational development strategies in the same companies see people as basically self-motivated individuals and seek to create cooperative environments for them in an essentially competitive world.

Peters and Waterman (1982) point out that excellent companies have clearly articulated their management philosophy and its relationship to the specific policies of the organization. Some of the dimensions that senior management might want to consider in the design of their human resource systems include the following.

Nature of the Employment Contract

What is the nature of the "psychological contract" that we hold with our employees? At one end of the spectrum is the notion of "a fair day's work for a fair day's pay," where the employer emphasizes the extrinsic rewards

TABLE 3.1 **Human Resources Management Links to Strategy and Structure.**

Strategy	Structure	Human Resource Management			
		Selection	Appraisal	Rewards	Development
1. Single product	Functional	Functionally oriented: subjective criteria used	Subjective: measure via personal contact	Unsystematic and allocated in a paternalistic manner	Unsystematic, largely job experiences: single function focus
2. Single product (vertically integrated)	Functional	Functionally oriented: standardized criteria used	Impersonal: based on cost and productivity data	Related to performance and productivity	Functional specialists with some generalists: largely job rotation
3. Growth by acquisition (holding company) of unrelated businesses	Separate, self-contained businesses	Functionally oriented, but varies from business to business in terms of how systematic	Impersonal: based on return on investment and profitability	Formula-based and includes return on investment and profitability	Cross functional but not cross-business

4. Related diversification of product lines through international growth and acquisition	Multidivisonal	Functionally and generalist oriented: systematic criteria used	Impersonal: based on return on investment, productivity, and subjective assessment of contribution to company	Large bonuses: based on profitability and subjective assessment of contribution to overall company	Cross functional, cross divisional, and cross corporate/divisional: formal
5. Multiple products in multiple countries	Global organization (geographic center and world-wide)	Functionally and generalists oriented: systematic criteria used	Impersonal: based on multiple goals such as return on investment, profit tailored to product and country	Bonuses: based on multiple planned goals with moderate top management discretion	Cross divisional and cross subsidiary to corporate: formal and systematic

Source: Table adapted from J. Galbraith and D. Nathanson, *Strategy Implementation: The Role of Structure and Process.* St. Paul, MN: West Publishing, 1978.

associated with performance and design systems that link these rewards to short-term performance. Many U. S. blue-collar jobs fit this description and, indeed, managerial work in some organizations can also be characterized by this philosophy. At the other end of the spectrum is a contract that stresses "challenging, meaningful work in return for loyal, committed service." Most of the companies that Peters and Waterman describe as truly excellent are bunched at this end of the spectrum, although not all of the companies that received high marks in a recent *Fortune* survey would be characterized in this way.

Degree of Participation in Decision-Making

A second policy decision that senior managers make about their people is the extent to which they are willing to share decision-making and power through the organization. Firms could be ranked on a continuum depending upon the degree to which they are driven by *top-down* as opposed to *bottom-up* decision making. In a top-down organization the human resource system centralizes all key selection, appraisal, reward, and development decisions. A bottom-up system encourages widespread participation in these activities.

Internal versus External Labor Markets

Organizations also vary on the degree to which they promote from within versus hire from external labor pools. In many mature companies these options are a matter of choice for management. In some companies that are growing rapidly or diversifying into unrelated areas the choices about the develop or hire decision may be more limited. In most companies, however, there is an expressed preference for one strategy of selection over the other and this tends to influence the context in which human resource systems are developed and operated. In companies with a strong "promote from within" orientation there will be an associated stress on development as a strong human resource tool. In companies at the other end of the spectrum, we would expect to find a strong recruiting function and a relatively weak development function.

Group versus Individual Performance

Human resource systems can be geared toward collective, group-based performance, individual performance, or toward some mixture of the two. In some cases these choices are dictated by the technology involved, with group-based performance systems being required when it is difficult or even impossible to evaluate the contribution of individual performers to the overall effort. In other cases the system is a matter of choice and is meant to support a cultural orientation toward a cooperative rather than competitive climate.

In either case the issue of social compatibility becomes important in the selection process.

THE HUMAN RESOURCE CYCLE

Once management has articulated a philosophy about people, it can begin to focus on the design of the human resource system. Figure 3.2 shows the four generic functions that are performed by human resource managers in all organizations. This cycle represents sequential managerial tasks. The dependent variable is behavior according to a dominant value and the system is ideally designed to have an impact on performance at both the individual and the organizational levels.

Performance is a function of all the human resource components: *selecting* people who are best able to perform the jobs defined by the structure, *appraising* their performance to facilitate the equitable distribution of rewards, motivating employees by linking *rewards* to high levels of performance, and *developing* employees to enhance their current performance at work as well as to prepare them to perform in positions they may hold in the future.

If we return to Figure 3.1 we understand, of course, that performance is not only a product of the human resource systems but of the other components as well. Thus strategy and structure also influence performance through the

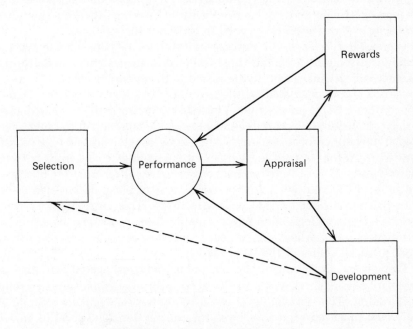

FIGURE 3.2. The human resource cycle.

way in which jobs are designed, the way in which the organization is formally structured, and the choice of strategy meant to respond to environmental threats and opportunities.

LEVELS OF MANAGERIAL ACTIVITY

The remainder of this chapter deals with the human resource systems as they affect the strategic activities of the organization. To define our focus it is necessary to add one more degree of complexity to the frameworks already presented. To do this we use Robert Anthony's definition of the three levels of managerial work: strategic, managerial, and operational.

The *strategic level* deals with policy formulation and overall goal setting; its objective is to position the organization in the best possible way to deal effectively with its environment. The *managerial level* focuses on the processes by which the organization obtains and allocates the resources needed to carry out its strategy and objectives. For example, to effectively compete in the businesses specified in the strategic plan, the organization must assess the capital, information, technology, and talent it will require to execute the strategic plan. At the *operational level*, the day-to-day management of the organization is carried out. Although the process just described seems to be a top-down system, it obviously implies feedback loops that allow the organization to formulate strategy more effectively by using data about the current availability of the resources needed to carry out the strategy.

Figure 3.3 and Table 3.2 describe the reciprocity between the types of activities associated with the three levels of management and the human resource subsystems. The activities listed in the operational category are the day-to-day tasks discussed in all personnel texts and carried out in most organizations. Managerial activities include evaluating current practices to see if they are meeting client needs and address the integration of the subsystems so that the entire human resource system is philosophically and operationally consistent. At the strategic level organizations should be concerned with two issues: How will our future business or businesses differ from the businesses we are in today, and what environmental pressures should we plan to deal with that we do not have to deal with today. This latter category would include changes in legislation influencing the human resource aspects of any jurisdictional area where the company operates, as well as changes in the work or social values of the labor market.

Professional execution of the operational and managerial activities is a necessary but, in our view, not sufficient basis for an effective human resource organization. The strategic level activities, however, begin to separate the truly well-managed companies from the competition. This level of analysis provides the focus for most of the discussion in this book.

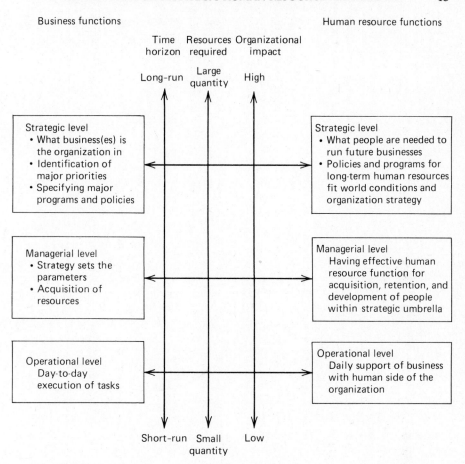

FIGURE 3.3. Three levels of activity for business and human resource functions.

Strategic Selection

As we have argued, the selection process includes all activities related to the internal movement of people across positions as well as to hiring. The process matches available human resources to jobs in the organization. Three strategic concerns are particularly important. The first involves the design of a selection system that supports the organization's strategy. For example, if a company plans to diversify in the next decade, a careful analysis should be made of the types of people who will be needed to staff the new business or businesses. A parallel analysis should be made of the general availability of such personnel. Some illustrations of the different problems that organizations face in this area are readily forthcoming from the recent diversification efforts in two industries: oil and chemicals.

TABLE 3.2. Human Resource Activities.

Management Level	Selection	Appraisal	Rewards (Compensation and Fringe Benefits)	Development
Strategic	Developing characteristics of people needed to run business in long term Designing internal and external systems to reflect future businesses	In long term, what should be valued? Developing means to appraise future dimensions Early identification of potential	In world as it might be in long term, how will force be rewarded? Linking rewards to the long-term business strategy	Planning developmental experiences for people running business of the future Designing systems with flexibility to adjust to change Developing career paths
Managerial	Validation of selection criteria Development of recruitment marketing plan New markets	Designing systems to link current and future potential Assessment centers for development	Five-year compensation plans for individuals Cafeteria-style fringe packages	Organizing management development program Organization development activities Fostering self-development
Operational	Staffing plans Recruitment plans	Annual appraisal system(s) Day-to-day control systems	Wage and salary administration Benefit plans	Delivering job skill training On-the-job training

Most of the oil companies have launched major diversification efforts that will reduce their involvement with petroleum production and marketing as a single product business. The direction of the diversification has not been homogeneous across all companies in the industry. Mobil's initial efforts have brought businesses as diverse as Marcor, a labor-intensive retailing operation, into their portfolio whereas Sun Oil has chosen to steer clear of labor-intensive diversification and concentrate on capital-intensive acquisitions. Both need to analyze the extent to which these businesses will dominate the company in the next 20 years and to analyze the skills needed to operate such ventures as opposed to an oil company. They may need less technically trained personnel and more financially oriented or market-oriented talent in the future. This may have an impact on their hiring mix at entry levels now, inasmuch as the people who will be running these companies in 20 years will be drawn at least partly from a pool of individuals who are being hired now.

The chemicals companies face a different dilemma. Most do not plan to diversify significantly out of chemicals but they share a need to get out of the commodities chemical business if they do not own their own petroleum feedstocks. This has both short and long-term implications for these companies. In the short term this means more marketing-oriented people and more innovation to create products that can be sold as differentiated goods with the value-added profit accruing to the company. In addition to this classic vertical integration solution to the problem of rising petroleum costs, many chemical companies are pushing ahead on another front, and that is to convert from current dependence upon petroleum feedstocks to new technological approaches such as the use of biomass. Human resource concerns in this area pose a significant challenge because it is well acknowledged that an insufficient number of people are being trained in the scientific disciplines associated with those technologies to meet the projected demand for their services.

Obviously, companies engaged in such strategic shifts need to systematically examine current policies *vis-à-vis* their technical personnel since they will be facing a seller's market in these labor markets for some time to come. Practices such as dual career ladders and shared decision-making with technical staff on technical decisions need to be evaluated and modified to ensure that the company will be able to hire and retain needed personnel. Truly strategic companies will also be investing funds and time on campuses to encourage more people to pursue the fields of study that meet their own future needs.

Some companies have voiced a concern that this kind of planning may not yield a sufficient return on their investment of time and energy to be worthwhile. They take the position that they will go out and hire the appropriate people from the competition, if necessary, when they are needed. The desirability of this sit-back-and-wait approach is brought into question by much recent research suggesting that good managers, from an individual corporation's point of view, are not born but made. They were developed over some 15 to 20 years within the organization, and the obvious implication is that it takes a long time for them to learn the intricacies of managing a specific complex organization (Kotter, 1982).

The second concern is to monitor the internal flow of personnel to match emerging business strategies. AT&T's move into the competitive electronics business forces a reappraisal of the types of managers they will need to run the company into the year 2000. The primary challenge for them is to revalue certain managerial characteristics in such a way that people with good marketing skills and those most capable of marketable innovation now are judged to have higher potential for promotion than those with good operating skills. This, of course, is a significant shift in the traditional career path orientation at AT&T.

The third strategic concern is with matching key executives to business strategies. In large companies where businesses are thought of as portfolios as opposed to single product ventures, there has been an increasing interest in matching people to types of business. One of the more commonly discussed approaches is promoted by the Boston Consulting Group, in which businesses are categorized as to the stage of the product lifecycle they are currently in and managerial characteristics appropriate to those businesses are identified and used as selection criteria for assigning managers to the different businesses. This work is still in its infancy and much remains to be done both in terms of assessing the validity of the approach and the reliability of various techniques used for assessing managerial potential.

Strategic Appraisal

The performance appraisal process is the key to an effective human resource system and yet it is frequently given little more than lip service. Much has been written on why managers dislike conducting performance appraisals, and several approaches have been devised to put a sugar coating on what is perceived to be an unpalatable task. Thus many companies talk about doing a performance appraisal only for developmental purposes. If one were to ask whether they had a merit pay system (not to mention the criteria used for promotion), one would discover that a merit pay system did indeed exist but that the decision was made in a different time-frame from the performance appraisal feedback. By separating the events in time the employee is not supposed to realize that if his or her appraisal indicates that performance is not up to par, the salary adjustment will be small or nonexistent. Obviously, this scenario is much more reminiscent of a walk with Alice through Wonderland than it is of an effective control system in an organization. Despite problems such as poorly designed procedures, psychological resistance on the part of managers to giving negative appraisals, and resistance on the part of employees to being evaluated as average, it is important to devote significant amounts of managerial time to effectively appraise performance because it contributes to the following organization processes.

1.   The most important ingredient in the distribution of scarce rewards in organizations is the perception on the part of the employees that the decision process around their distribution is equitable. If employees believe otherwise, it is impossible to link organizational rewards to performance.

2.   Rewards can be allocated on the basis of performance only if that performance can be measured. In the absence of the ability to measure performance, whether it be group or individual level performance, the organization has no control system to evaluate performance. Performance in some situations can be measured by objective criteria such as profitability, return on investment, or market share and these measures should be used whenever possible. In situations where these measures are inappropriate the organization must rely more heavily on personal judgment by other managers. Control systems to ensure that these judgments are as accurate as possible are discussed in detail in the chapters on performance appraisal.

3.   Human resource planning depends upon valid appraisals. A current inventory of talent can be made only through a valid appraisal process that gives visibility to those who have been performing well and points out those who have not. In addition, future human resource projections depend upon assessments of the performance potential of existing personnel so that plans can be made for future personnel shortages or surpluses. Without good performance appraisal data such forecasting is impossible since there is no basis for making predictions.

4.   The development process also depends upon accurate data generated by the performance appraisal system because the aggregated data on individual strengths and weaknesses point up areas requiring training and development. These data also permit the organization to examine different strategic alternatives in terms of their personnel feasibility.

Lorsch and Allen (1973) conducted a study that indicates that companies must develop a performance appraisal system that is supportive of their business strategy because there is a link between such a system and total performance for the firm. The study compared the appraisal systems in diversified companies with those in integrated companies and found that effective diversified companies placed more emphasis on objective and results measures such as productivity, profit, or volume, whereas the integrated companies relied more on subjective evaluations of the manager's ability to plan, control, lead, and organize. Although the diversified companies' approach is intrinsically more appealing, it does not work well in integrated companies where there is greater interdivisional contact and sharing of resources which makes it hard to judge who gets credit for what share of the end result.

Repeated conversations with human resource executives in companies with well-respected performance appraisal systems such as Exxon and General Electric reveal that the key to effective appraisal is the willingness of management to devote time and resources to the process not only for the review of performance but also for the continued coaching or training of those responsible for doing the performance appraisal. Government challenges are increasingly being made on the basis of the criteria which are brought to bear, and organizations must respond to this reality. The fact remains, however, that a good performance appraisal system is probably less dependent on the technical aspects involved than it is on the process issues. Excellent managers and companies simply recognize that an integral part of management is the process of evaluation performance.

Strategic Rewards

Organizations tend to think of rewards in a fairly limited way as pay, promotion, and benefits. Yet in studies with diverse populations we have found that there are many other rewards that the organization has to offer that individuals value. A partial list of the rewards that are deemed to be important are the following:

Pay in its many forms such as salary, bonuses, stock options, benefits, and perquisites.

Promotion, both upward mobility and lateral transfers into desirable positions.

Career opportunities, a long-term chance for growth and development.

Positive feedback from customers or clients.

Personal sense of well-being for doing a job well.

Opportunity to learn, to develop new competencies.

Job security, especially important in tight economic times.

Responsibility

Respect from co-workers.

In a survey of Columbia MBAs who had been working for a decade, Devanna (1983) discovered that pay did not rank among the top three rewards that motivated this group when they took either their first job or their present job. The most important reward for new MBAs was the opportunity to learn new skills and the most important reward for the group after 10 years in the labor force was responsibility. Studies of engineers (Devanna et al., 1981) and computer specialists (Roth et al., 1983) show that pay rarely ranks among the top three rewards valued by technical, professional, or managerial employees.

Most organizations do not do a very good job of managing these rewards and, as a consequence, the reward system in many organizations remains among the most underutilized managerial tools for driving organizational performance. We have already pointed out that the organization must do a good job of evaluating performance to be able to use the reward system. Assuming this is done, the organization has good reason for allocating rewards based on how well people perform. From a performance viewpoint this is a superior strategy to managing pay alone.

A major strategic issue is how to use the reward system to overcome the tendency toward short-sighted management. When organizational rewards are tied too closely to this year's performance, it is difficult to motivate senior executives to devote their time and energy to long-term objectives whose effect on the bottom line may not show up for several years. Although it is unreasonable to suggest that managers be rewarded only for progress toward long-term strategic objectives, inasmuch as organizations must perform in the present if they are to be around to perform in the future, the converse of rewarding solely for present performance is equally deleterious since it encourages managers to mortgage the future for present performance.

Another practice that has achieved much attention is the current trend in organizations to make a significant bonus pool available for distribution to a small percentage of the employees, those whose performance is perceived to be in the top 10 or 15% of all managers in a certain group. Although this system provides tremendous incentive to succeed, it also provides tremendous incentive to engage in practices that would be more appropriate in a Las Vegas casino than in a *Fortune* 500 company. It also heightens the sense of competition that exists in all organizations as achievement-oriented managers understand that not everyone will be promoted to the next level. Perhaps the most troubling aspect of this type of bonus system is that it brands the majority of the employees as failures since, if only 15% will share the bonus pool, 85% will obtain no rewards despite the fact that they may have worked hard and made a valuable contribution to the organization. For organizations who feel that the benefits of this bonus system outweigh the risks, there is a need to control unwanted behavioral outcomes.

Strategic Development

Activities designed to ensure that individuals are properly equipped with skills and knowledge to carry out their jobs fall into the management development category. Most of the development that occurs in organizations takes the form of on-the-job training. To be effective, this method requires the organization to think about job rotation as a developmental sequence aimed at producing as many people capable of filling key positions in the company as is feasible.

The second aspect of development is formal training or educational programs conducted either by the organization or with the aid of outside institutions whose function it is to offer programs for executive development. The final developmental tool is one which occurs informally in most organizations but which is being formally instituted in some companies: mentoring. Although the importance of having a mentor continues to be debated, a study conducted by the authors at the Columbia University's Strategy Research Center shows that more than two-thirds of the top executives who were interviewed in six major companies reported they had had a mentor and that this relationship had played an important role in their development as strategic decision-makers.

In most organizations this relationship occurs spontaneously and there is some debate as to whether a system of mentoring can be formalized within organizations. What is clear is that companies which do not have highly structured systems with checks and balances around performance appraisal and advancement may lose highly qualified people at early stages in their careers simply because they were not assigned to influential superiors who could advance their careers. Tushman and Katz (1983) have shown a significant difference in the career advancement of high-tech personnel depending upon their position in the laboratory. Those who had been assigned to project managers who were highly influential both inside and outside the laboratory were more likely to have achieved greater success than those who were assigned to less influential project managers.

IMPLEMENTING STRATEGIC HUMAN RESOURCE MANAGEMENT

Once a manager has used these frameworks to identify the scope of the human resource function in a particular organization the task becomes one of implementation. The following steps should prove helpful as a guideline for that task.

1.   The tasks that the organization needs to support its strategic objectives should be identified at the strategic, managerial, and operational level.

2.   Gaps in the delivery of service to clients at the present time should be identified. Just as it is not possible to reward managers solely for how well they meet long-term goals, so a human resource system must have its operational house in order before it can afford the luxury of concentrating on the formulation and implementation of a human resource strategy.

3.   If the organization has no process by which it engages in strategic planning at the corporate or business level, it will not be possible for the human resource function to develop a strategic thrust since the human resource strategy flows from the corporate or business strategy.

4.   In terms of staffing the function, the organization will need to provide for people trained as business generalists so they can better respond to line management concerns.

5.   The reward and control systems should be altered to support the strategic human resource function. Just as managers need to be rewarded for both performance of operational and managerial short-term objectives as well as for progress against strategic goals, there should be a similar system to drive the human resources function.

6.   Systematic links should be designed between the human resource function and the line organization. Although the debate rages on over where

responsibility for human resource management should reside—within the function or in the line—it is probably more important for the organization to admit the need to manage human resources and then to decide the structural question of how to manage them based on existing organizational precedents, on what arrangement is most supportive of the culture, or on where the expertise resides.

SUMMARY AND CONCLUSIONS

Human resource management is increasingly recognized as an important force in driving organizational effectiveness. This chapter provides a series of frameworks to help managers think about the role and structure of the human resource systems in their own organization. The major beliefs underlying this structure are the following.

1.   Human resource activities have a major impact on individual performance and hence on productivity and organizational performance.

2.   The ability of organizations to innovate depends upon creating an organizational context supportive of innovation. The foundation of this system lies in the systems designed to manage innovative human resources.

3.   The quality of the strategic decisions made in organizations is linked to the quality of the human resource data that feeds into the decision-making process.

4.   Success in the implementation of strategic objectives depends to a great extent on how well the organization has carried out its human resource cycle and selected the right people, measured the proper behaviors, rewarded progress against the strategic objectives, and developed the skills needed to ensure the success of the strategy.

PART

II

THE STRATEGIC ROLE OF THE HUMAN RESOURCE SYSTEMS

Part II defines the strategic role of each of the four human resource systems: selection, appraisal, rewards, and development, and goes on to use the concept of "corporate culture" to integrate the four systems in support of a set of dominant values in the organization. The final two chapters in the section deal with the human resource management audit, a systematic change process for defining the strategic role of the human resource management function in the organization and the use of the audit in a change effort undertaken at Honeywell's Aerospace and Defense business.

In Chapter 4, Ed Miller discusses the strategic staffing issues facing organizations and examines the alternatives that organizations may choose to implement appropriate staffing strategies. The dilemmas and solutions chosen by one organization that took a zero-based approach to solving its staffing problems is described vividly in an interview with Alan Lafley, Executive Vice President of Chase Manhattan Bank in Chapter 5.

The performance appraisal component of the human resource cycle is covered in Chapters 6, 7, and 8. In Chapter 6, Gary Latham advocates the use of behaviorally anchored measures to track the progress of line managers and senior staff against strategic corporate and business objectives. Chapter 7 deals with the performance measures that face organizations at the corporate, functional, and individual levels, and deals with the issue central to the use of performance appraisal as a motivational tool, namely, the perception of equity on the part of employees in the choice of measures and the links between those measures and the distribution of organizational rewards. Chapter 8 reports on an extensive survey conducted by Drake Beam Morin, Inc. on the performance appraisal practices of the largest companies in the United States.

In Chapter 9 Ed Lawler discusses the role that rewards play in helping an organization realize its business and corporate objectives. In addition to addressing the issues of linking rewards to performance, the chapter also focuses on the role that rewards can play in leading change efforts in organizations and in helping to implement new strategies. Andy McGill presents us with some of the real-world problems that will pressure organizations to ignore theory (although they may pay a price for doing so) when he describes in Chapter 10 the situation that General Motors was forced to confront in 1982–1983. The conflicts that arose when the company simultaneously needed to obtain concessions and cooperation from the UAW and to address the issue of excessive attrition of valued employees in the exempt ranks following a period of negative earnings demonstrates the need to evaluate the effects of compensation policies in the context of several scenarios.

In Chapter 11 Tim Hall points out that development is, perhaps, the most neglected of all the human resource systems and that its importance in organizations attempting to deal with current human resource problems from more effective strategic planning and implementation to the introduction of new technologies into existing businesses is rapidly increasing. Chapter 12 presents us with a case description of the EMS system at General Electric, a company that recognized the importance of strategic appraisal and development for its top-level management and has spent decades honing the process that is used to identify and prepare managers needed to run General Electric.

Chapter 13 discusses the popular concept of a corporate culture as an emergent property of all organizations, one which reflects specific configurations and overlays of the human resource systems of the organizations, and which also corresponds to the industrial and societal context in which the organizations is embedded. Within these boundaries, an organization's culture can then be seen as a competitive strategy in which all the internal systems are designed to support a set of carefully articulated dominant values.

Chapter 14 presents a description of the process by which one company, Hewlett-Packard, has successfully implemented and maintained a culture leading to high morale and effective human resource management.

Part II of the book concludes with two chapters on the theory and application of the human resource management audit. Chapter 15 maps out the issues and the pitfalls centered around conducting an audit and provides human resource managers with a guide designed to help ensure success for those interested in systematically assessing the functioning of their human resource systems. Chapter 16 is a case discussion of an audit conducted at Honeywell's Aerospace and Defense Systems division and shows the types of data and preparation involved in an audit process.

All together, Part II elaborates on the human resource cycle presented in Chapter 3 by describing the generic systems of selection, appraisal, rewards, and development in detail. Each of the conceptual chapters is then followed by a corporate example demonstrating the applications presented in the previous chapter. The culture chapter and the audit chapter attempt to integrate the subsystems in the context of organizational objectives and goals.

CHAPTER

4

STRATEGIC STAFFING

Edward Miller

At this point, the message has been heard clearly and taken seriously that "treating people not money, machines or minds as the natural resources may be the key to it all" (Peters and Waterman, 1982). Now executive leaders are thrown into the struggle of attempting to translate this concern for people into policies and action that go beyond the traditional annual speech. The quest for excellence means getting the right people in the right spots at the right time. For decades organizations have been espousing lofty staffing objectives, but most of them are mired in practices that:

1. contribute to managers hoarding good people at the expense of the total organization;
2. foster promotions from within a manager's own department or network of acquaintances without consideration of organization-wide candidates;
3. limit individual's opportunities for other jobs in the organization due to the individual's boss' opinions and knowledge of other opportunities;
4. do not provide individuals with feedback as to whether they were candidates for jobs in the organization and if they were, why they were not selected;

5. foster individual self-doubt about organizational career opportunities thus leading to quitting (Alfred, 1967).

These practices prevail because most organizations have not developed the countervailing forces needed to overcome cronyism, comfort, and parochialism. Unchecked, these forces prevent large-scale strategic staffing which must be based on detailed information about candidates, policies, and systems for selection and movement of people and supporting human resource practices in the appraisal, reward, and development areas.

This chapter views strategic staffing in the context of an overall integrated corporate staffing system that includes effective operational staffing which feeds managerial level staffing and which, in turn, links with the strategic level. Such an integrated system requires clarity around major organizational policy and the kinds of philosophical issues addressed in Chapter 3 such as the balance between promotion from within versus external staffing, the firm's position on employment security, and the degree of cross-functional development deemed important for strategic staffing. These issues provide the backdrop for this chapter, which begins by presenting a strategic framework for integrating strategic organization design and staffing. Specific tactics and techniques for supporting strategic staffing are discussed along with means for carrying out internal and external staffing activities. The chapter ends with a discussion of the requisites at the managerial and operational levels for an integrated human resource staffing system.

A STRATEGIC ORIENTATION OF THE STAFFING PROCESS

This section builds on the work of Fombrun and Tichy (1984) and discusses the relationship between strategic staffing, business strategy, and organization design.

Organizational Strategy

The organization's purpose plays a critical role in the staffing process. Redefinition of the company's business domain has strategic implications for its human resource management system. Thus serious thought must be given to defining the qualifications that are mandatory for managing the new organization. Specification of the qualifications, identification of persons possessing those skills, and moving people into the jobs should be guided by the organization's strategic plans and its overall staffing strategy.

Strategic organization realignment similar to that at AT&T influences career expectations and the ability of the workforce to respond to the altered organizational purpose and business domain. Career paths may be radically changed, career expectations may be frustrated, uncertainty and disappointment may appear, and the organization's commitment to its employees put in doubt.

It has been suggested that there are three different approaches for viewing organizational change: technical, political, and cultural elements. (Tichy, 1983) From a technical orientation, organizational realignment will have an impact on the staffing process in terms of an emphasis on the proper matching of people to jobs, specification of performance criteria, and the means for measurement of the criteria.

Organizational realignment will probably have an impact on the culture of the organization, its values and traditions. This is clearly the case for those at AT&T moving into the competitive position of the business. The staffing process will be affected by this realignment because in many cases older values and traditions may no longer suffice. Where are individuals possessing the desired values to be located? Are they currently employed or must the organization expect to search for such persons elsewhere? The organization's values will influence its image and, consequently, its ability to recruit and hire the desired kinds of people (Henderson, 1979). Furthermore, management succession as well as management development programs will be directly affected because these two processes will be the vehicles for socializing managers.

The political ramifications for organizational changes are familiar to most of us. Organizational realignment may cause readjustments in the organization's power structure and the strategic planning process. Informal discussions and speculations among employees concerning who will be promoted into key management jobs, readjustments in the power relationships between functional groups, and an attempt to identify key jobs or experiences for future promotions are the consequences of realignments affecting the political dimension. Based on this analysis of the new political milieu, employees seek to reposition themselves with respect to jobs, functions, and newly ascending executives. A shift in basic strategy, therefore, must be coupled with a basic shift in staffing strategy.

Strategic Planning and Staffing

The organization's strategy for managing its various businesses is a critical factor that also influences the staffing process. Earlier we stressed the importance of meshing executive skills and qualifications with strategic planning. This integration of strategic planning and staffing can be developed in the simplest case for organizations using a product portfolio analysis approach to strategic management.

Table 4.1 defines the staffing implications of the BCG's product portfolio. This table suggests the staffing criteria that are most important in different types of businesses. Perhaps the most valuable contribution the lifecycle approach can make to the development of a strategic approach to staffing occurs because it raises the possibility of developing a differentiated staffing

TABLE 4.1. Business Life Cycle.

	Start-Up Business	Growth Business	Mature Business	Declining Business
Selection placement	Recruitment for activities Recruit entrepreneurial style	Recruit for future business	Lateral moves for enhancing efficiency	Transfers to different businesses, outplacement, early retirement
Dominant cultural value	Entrepreneurship	Sales	Competitiveness	Cost control

*Source: Adapted from Fombrun, C. and N. Tichy *Strategic Planning and Human Resources Management: At Rainbow's End.* In R. Lamb(ed.) Competitive Strategic Management, pp. 319–332, Englewood Cliffs, NJ: Prentice-Hall, 1984.

approach. Management's strategic plans for a specific business should drive the staffing decisions associated with the management of the product or business.

For instance, if senior management, plans to divest and withdraw from a particular business, such plans should have significant ramifications on the selection of managers responsible for managing that business during its last days. Top management of the organization should be concerned with identifying and selecting persons capable of implementing the organization's divestment plans. The question to ask is: What skills, experience, and personality attributes are required to successfully divest ourselves of a losing business? Table 4.1 suggests some of the possible criteria useful in a divestment situation. Among other things, the general manager will be expected to maintain employee morale and performance, to nurture customer goodwill, and to control costs. The assignment of managers considered to be organizational failures or who are superfluous to oversee the divestment of a business unit has been a common staffing decision when, in fact, the opposite approach should be taken. The organization must also have procedures to bring the manager back in after the divestiture takes place or the assignment has little allure.

Although product portfolio analysis has leverage and appeal for developing staffing criteria, we must not be misled by its simplicity. For example, an organization planning to build up a "question mark" business needs a successful manager with entrepreneurial spirit, and a willingness to take risks. Reaching the conclusion that only these qualities will be necessary because the decision has been made to build the business would not be totally correct. A closer look at the contextual circumstances of the unit might show that the manager must also have good managerial skills in planning and coordinating as well as the ability to control costs. Thus no single selection criterion is sufficient.

The product portfolio will make an important contribution to the development of an organization's staffing strategy if it becomes the driving force in the recruitment, selection, development, and promotion plans and programs. Coordination between the organization's strategic plans and its staffing practices can improve the organization's ability to adapt to environmental circumstances.

Organization Design and Staffing

The major structural variations of the organization also bear on the organization's staffing process. The organization tends to staff with individuals who have characteristics similar to those managers who are currently performing within it. Little conscious attention is paid to identifying the characteristics most congruent with different organizational configurations.

In order to illustrate how staffing can vary due to organization design three common forms are discussed: the functional, divisional, and matrix structures (Galbraith and Nathanson, 1978).

Functional Staffing

A functional design divides organizations into groups that perform the specialized functions necessary to accomplish the overall organizational goals. Functionalization is the organizational counterpart of specialization and mirrors the differentiated activities of many individuals. A functional organization generally consists of both managerial and technical functions, the traditional staff and line breakdown.

What are some of the consequences for an organization's staffing process if it is organized according to a functional model? First, specialization provides a straightforward and easily visible line of promotion and advancement. Employees are clearly aware of the possibilities and requirements for advancement. For example, an employee in the marketing department would know the various rungs on the department's promotion ladder as well as the requirements for promotion. At the same time, grouping people with similar backgrounds and interests also tends to foster a high degree of cohesion, the backbone of a functional culture.

The functional organization design has shortcomings, as well. The manager who has come up the managerial hierarchy through a specialist function is probably unsuited to fill a position that requires a balanced view of all aspects of the organization. Flexibility and integration of strategic management with the organization's staffing strategy is likely to be constrained. Are the very best people being chosen to move into the organization's key management positions? It is not likely to be the case. Functional organization lends itself to a lockstep promotion from within practice and, in many cases, the individuals emerging into the key management positions are not adequately prepared to lead the organization. This occurs because the training and preparation of managers is too narrow to meet the generalist demands of high-level management jobs.

Functional organization seems to work against the imperative of identifying and choosing the best people for general management level assignments. A functional organization design tends to insulate the staffing process and the staffing plans and practices from external concerns or strategic plans. Although the functional organization produces highly qualified persons for technical assignments, they are ill-prepared to cope with the more ambiguous contextual issues facing the firm. In this respect managers who ascend to key executive positions and succeed in these assignments do so *in spite* of their previous training and development unless the organization has developed a cross-functional training program for those with a high potential for top-management succession.

Divisional Staffing

In the *divisional organization* functions are combined into product groups, customer groups, or area groups. Members of an organizational unit are identified not by specialty, as in functional organizations, but by their relationship to a product, customer, or location. Divisional organization takes advantage of natural synergies as well as work specialization by combining various specialties into one organizational unit.

The most obvious advantage of the divisional organization is that it tends to stimulate the training and development of generalists for top-level management positions. The manager in charge of a product or service unit is encouraged to learn to balance many functional considerations—a task that only the top management learns to do in a functional organization. This is frequently done by job transfers through various functions. The result of this type of organization, and most important, is the breadth to take on general management positions.

Divisional organization places different demands upon the organization's staffing strategy. Given that the product structure requires that the managers possess a broadly balanced perspective, the challenge becomes that of identifying the kinds of people that have the basic managerial qualifications and the means for developing and capitalizing upon those attributes. In contrast to the functional organization, where expertise prevailed, a different set of experiences and criteria for promotion will be developed.

Product organization has its disadvantages, however, and some of those include the struggle for scarce resources, the ambiguity of promotion ladders, and the conflicts over power. The struggle for control by individuals and units is more acute in a divisional organization. Decentralization often creates autonomous groups who try to enhance their organizational power and opportunities by influencing the strategic plans. Which group is considered the star? Is the strategic plan building up one product at the expense of another? Some jobs or experiences become stepping stones to top management positions whereas others lead nowhere. In a similar vein, certain functions are considered to be critical on the pathway up the managerial hierarchy. The problem is to identify those avenues for advancement and to be perceptive enough to realize that certain types of jobs or functions may be relevant today but irrelevant tomorrow.

The ambiguity and fluidity of the career path to top-management positions becomes increasingly complex for individuals faced with assessing advancement opportunities. Trying to identify and decide on the nature of the next assignment can be a challenge. Quite apart from job contract or salary level, the prospects for advancement largely influence people's career decisions. They ask: which jobs will bring exposure, visibility, and the opportunity to build strong political alliances? Kanter (1977) has written insightfully on the relationship between organization, power, and the staffing process.

Matrix Staffing

Finally, the *matrix organization* attempts to capitalize on the strengths of the functional and divisional forms while avoiding their weaknesses. The matrix or project form seems appropriate where circumstances require the organization to make rapid changes because of market conditions, pressures for rapid information processing, or the need to deal with shared resources when neither the product nor the functional design suffice (Davis and Lawrence 1979). Whereas successful performance within a specialty becomes the basis for promotion in a functionally organized structure, the matrix organization design calls for a balanced perspective of the organization, a need for both specialists and managerial breadth, and an appreciation for conflicting demands. In addition, matrix organizations require that managers coordinate functional and product requirements simultaneously. The result can be intensely stressful but it provides a significant series of managerial experiences at reasonably low levels in the management hierarchy, valuable insights for the manager regarding the meaning of managing, and important data pertaining to the quality of the prospective candidate's managerial skills.

From a strategic perspective, matrix organization seems to be a costly response to long-term organizational requirements. Current projects dictate the necessary skills required but those same skills may not be needed on the next project, and individuals are apt to become frustrated with the lack of continual support. Finally, because a matrix organization seeks to capitalize on both specialization and coordination, it promotes conflict and requires an ability to deal with multiple bosses and to accept the instability associated with working on projects having a limited life. Matrix is obviously not for everyone.

Linking the organization's strategic plans with its employee staffing process will result in a more sophisticated and valuable approach to managing. Organizational performance is presumably enhanced by having the "right" people in the "right" spots, and a consistent system for developing employees for succession to the key managerial positions. A major challenge facing the human resource function is that of developing and implementing the procedures that will produce a continuous upward flow of highly qualified managerial personnel who are relevant to the organization's managerial requirements. This will require a high degree of creativity, attention to coordination, and a commitment to energize the various frameworks designed to achieve the strategic staffing plans.

Indeed, organizations that are in a growth cycle probably should not be wed to a promotion from within philosophy as it may limit their rate of growth or, more seriously, promote unqualified people to positions where they cannot succeed. Assuming the choice of strategy is correct, human resource management's function is to develop and administer the mechanisms to ensure that the best people are continuously identified and chosen to fill jobs at all levels within the organization.

SUSTAINING INTERNAL HIRING

The principal techniques or procedures used to promote internal mobility are job posting, management development, and succession planning.

Job posting is an arrangement under which each job vacancy is advertised throughout the company. The abilities and experiences necessary to qualify for the vacancy are typically identified, and employees interested in the job can then make their interests formally known to the organization. Based on a democratic belief that full information on job vacancies is a desirable practice, job posting opens an information channel to employees about what jobs are available, what the job requirements will be, and what steps they must take in order to move to another job in the organization. In this respect job posting becomes an internal recruiting technique as well as a tool for increasing the organization's likelihood of choosing the best individual for a job opening.

Management development is concerned with the preparation of the individual employee for increased managerial responsibilities. Development programs are meant to provide a planned sequence of education, training, and work experience for employees, and help foster a dynamic interaction between the organization's human resource needs or requirements and the individual's career objectives.[1] Management development programs offer a means for upgrading an individual's technical and managerial skills and, accordingly, the quality of the human resources pool will be upgraded. Job moves can be viewed as developmental experiences rather than simply promotions.

Succession planning is another important activity that helps sustain a continuous flow of managerial personnel. This process supports an internal selection

[1]Schein (1979) discusses the necessary integration between the individual's career objectives and the organization's planning needs (Ed.).

procedure because it is intended to evaluate managerial personnel on the basis of their job performance and qualifications relative to the job requirements of increasingly responsible positions. Job assignments, formal education, and on-the-job training are among the more typical means for enhancing, appraising, and developing managerial skills.

Job posting, management development, and succession planning provide the human resources management function with an opportunity to bring a measure of integration to the staffing process and to exert control over the internal movement of the organization's human resources. It is particularly important that recruitment for entry-level jobs and the internal movement of personnel be coordinated with the strategic concerns of the organization.

SUSTAINING EXTERNAL HIRING

The organization will turn to external sources when it doesn't have available qualified people to promote from within. Obviously, the frequency with which an organization turns to external sources will vary depending on the nature of the job, its position in the organization hierarchy, the availability of qualified persons, and the rate at which the organization is growing.[2] Recruiting and executive search firms have been two of the more common and familiar means of attracting and ultimately hiring personnel.

Traditionally, it has been assumed that recruiting required nothing more than just making it known that an organization had job vacancies and a large number of eager, highly qualified applicants would appear. Most organizations, however, do not hire undifferentiated labor. Rather, they hire persons with specialized skills and the potential to move into responsible professional or managerial positions. Since these types of skills and qualifications are difficult to locate, the organization will frequently seek out prospective employees through external recruitment. As a whole, the recruitment process must attract those types of applicants who, because of their qualifications or potential, will perform successfully in that organizational setting. It must also provide an adequate number of qualified applicants to ensure the competitiveness of the job offer package.

Executive search firms are frequently used in the search for qualified persons for higher level management positions. The value of the search firm is that it can offer an organization expertise and resources which it does not have. Nationwide contacts, familiarity with specific industries, and a systematic search process are among the attractions of search firms. The executive search firm will seek out highly effective executives who have the skills to do the job, who can adjust to the organization, its climate, and idiosyncracies, and who are looking for new challenges and opportunities.

[2] It could also depend on the organization's strategy. Frequently, at critical strategic junctures the organization will hire from the outside as a symbol that "things are changing." For instance, AT&T brought in senior level IBM and P&G personnel to head its business sectors when it announced its new "marketing" orientation (Ed.).

Outside searches are likely to have an impact on the organization's human resource system as well. Skepticism or antagonism toward the new manager sometimes occurs because of disappointment among employees who considered themselves to be desirable candidates for the job. Organizations must weigh the costs and benefits of each hiring strategy.

Strategic Staffing

This final section identifies some of the basic underpinnings needed for an integrated strategic staffing system. Human resource planning is at the heart of the managerial level of the human resource management function's involvement in the organization's staffing process. From our perspective, human resource planning becomes the means for developing and implementing an organization's staffing strategy. In this regard, it has its roots in the strategic as well as the managerial levels.

Human resource planning is a combination of needs forecasting and the specification of the various human resource activities designed to meet the needs forecasted. In the words of Eric Vetter (1967), the human resource planning process is the means:

> by which management determines how the organization should move from its current "manpower" position. Through planning, management strives to have the right number and the right kinds of people, at the right places, at the right times, doing things which result in both the organization and the individual receiving long-run benefits.

Many organizations rely on an array of human resource activities to meet their forecasted human resource requirements. However, the rationale and interrelationship between the organization's strategic plans, strategic level staffing plans, and the development of various programs to satisfy the organization's human resource requirements are less than clearly specified in most organizations. At the managerial level, the early identification of management potential, the design of management development programs, and developmental job assignments are some of the more important elements of the human resources management function's involvement.

Let us examine some of these human resource activities in greater detail, keeping in mind that these techniques are not ends in themselves, but should be related to the strategic aspects of the organization's staffing plan.

For many organizations the *early identification of high potential* individuals is a very significant and highly controversial activity. To meet this need many firms have developed systematic programs.

Typically, the identification program is intended to locate those individuals who possess the qualities assumed to be necessary for successful performance in higher level management jobs. It is also intended to give an estimate of the available managerial resources who have the qualifications for the higher level positions within the organization's managerial hierarchy. (Mahler and Wrightnour, 1973) Finally, an early identification program also improves the quality of staffing decisions by identifying the developmental needs of employees.

An identification program is essentially an internal recruiting activity designed to contribute significantly to the probability of more accurate promotion decisions. It does this by trying to enlarge the internal pool of qualified candidates for each management position, and thus avoiding those situations in which the promotion decision is made solely on the basis of tenure, friendship, or availability.

Based on the succession plans and early identification, *management development programs* provide employees with new perspectives and knowledge to improve managerial skills. Concurrently, management development efforts emphasize job assignments, educational experiences, coaching on the job, and specific skills training. In this respect management development is directly related to the enhancement of the organization's objectives and the quality of its human resources.

Preparing employees to occupy increasingly responsible management positions is an overriding concern of a management development program. For it to be effective, it must be closely related to the organization's strategic plans and an evaluation of human resource stock.

Management development programs typically consist of a wide range of educational options, work experiences, and job assignments. In this respect the development of the employee represents an individualized development program based upon an assessment of the person's qualifications and the organization's requirements.

Job assignments are a valuable means for developing managerial personnel because they provide a way to satisfy organizational human resource requirements while at the same time gathering information about the employee's ability to perform. In an interesting study of the multinational overseas staffing process, Edstrom and Galbraith (1977) identified certain basic reasons for assigning an expatriate to an overseas location, and these reasons were congruent with a strategic orientation to their staffing process. First, many transfers of managerial personnel are made to fill positions when qualified local nationals are not available or easily trained. This type of transfer occurs when a firm is investing in developing countries. Second, a firm may transfer managerial personnel for purposes of developing expatriates for positions of increased responsibility within the parent company or its international business activities. Third, the assignment of managerial personnel abroad is for the purposes of organizational development. In this case transfers are used as a means of modifying and sustaining the organization's structure and decision processes, and it develops expatriate managers who have a sense of organizational loyalty, varied overseas experiences, rich organizational communication links, and a global perspective. They suggest the value of a carefully crafted link between staffing and various organizational processes.

Operational Level Activities

Operational level activities represent the bulk of the human resource function's involvement in the staffing process, and it is the most fully understood and developed aspect of staffing. Nevertheless, for an integrated staffing system it is essential to see that development of annual budgets and the implementation of specific programs and activities are carefully aligned to the managerial and strategic level staffing policies and activities.

CONCLUSION

Approaching the staffing process from a strategic perspective requires an integrated interpretation of the relationships between the various levels of human resource concerns in the planning process. Identifying and choosing people who will best run the organization and its businesses in the long run requires a broad set of programs and activities required to find those people. The development of the specific activities to satisfy the organization's forecasted human resource requirements will largely ensure the implementation of the strategic plans and the availability of individuals capable of running the organization at all levels.

The challenge is to develop a long-run perspective within the human resource organization's staffing process. Staffing decisions made today will have consequences on the organization's performance in the future. If the organization is to have the very best people in all positions, all staffing activities, programs, and structures must be oriented to make this happen. A strategic approach to staffing linked to the business plan is essential.

CHAPTER

5

STRATEGIC STAFFING AT CHASE MANHATTAN BANK

Chester C. Borucki
Alan F. Lafley

A review of the recent literature on staffing practices (Devanna et al., 1982; Miller et al., 1980; Tichy et al., 1982; Vetter, 1980; Walker, 1974, 1980) suggests that many organizations are departing from traditional staffing methods that tend to fill vacant or newly created positions based on short-term organizational needs and time horizons. Reactive staffing practices are increasingly found to be inadequate and obsolete in organizations facing uncertainty and stiff competition in today's global marketplace. Consequently, several corporations are adopting a proactive approach to human resource management, and with good reason. The changing economic times, workforce demographics, high technology, struggle for market share, and other variables have necessitated the development of strategic staffing practices, which is defined here as careful selection and placement of the appropriate, highly

Alan Lafley wishes to acknowledge the contributions of his Human Resources staff to Chase's approach to strategic staffing, particularly the efforts of Doug Barile, Jerry Dols, and Tom O'Reilly.

qualified individual possessing the experience, skills, and potential required to fulfill the longer-term needs and objectives of the organization.

One corporation actively employing strategic staffing practices and widely considered a forerunner in strategic human resources management is The Chase Manhattan Bank. This case is designed to reveal the strategic staffing concepts and practices that Chase incorporates as viewed by the principal architect of the bank's strategic staffing approach, Alan Lafley, Executive Vice President of Human Resources.

This case is outlined as follows. The first section presents a summary of key events in Chase's recent history in table format as background. The emphasis in this section is on significant events that have occurred over the past 10 years. It is during this period that major fundamental changes have occurred in strategy, policy, execution, culture, and other elements of human resources management. The second section provides a summary statement of Chase's human resources management philosophy with an emphasis on the bank's approach to staffing. The last section provides the substance of the bank's strategic staffing philosophy, concepts, and methodology as described by Lafley. Also discussed in this section is the role of the human resources executive, strategic staffing policy formulation and implementation, handling staffing issues under adversity, and Lafley's comments on the future direction of strategic staffing.

KEY EVENTS IN THE CHASE HISTORY

Gauged by today's standards, The Chase Manhattan Bank is a highly successful financial institution with a prestigious international reputation. With operations in over 100 countries and transactions in scores of currencies, Chase plays a vital role in international trade and investment. The bank is one of the very few financial institutions in the world capable of anticipating customer needs and responding to them quickly and effectively from any one of the world's major financial centers. Following Citicorp and BankAmerica, Chase Manhattan is currently a comfortable third in a list of the nation's largest banks. Following is a summary of significant events that have had an impact on Chase's position in the global marketplace, and in some respects, the shaping of its human resources management philosophy.

In the beginning . . . 1955	The Chase Manhattan Bank is born from the merger of Chase National and The Bank of The Manhattan Company, the third and the fifteenth largest domestic banks of the time.
The Champion years 1961– 1969	George Champion served as Chairperson and CEO, and is the chief architect of the Chase's business strategy. Chase is the first

A series of firsts

bank to fully automate check-handling operations, and is one of the first banks nationally to provide computer-based services in the form of tax return processing, airline ticket handling, and rent collection. With changes in state regulations, Chase moves into the suburbs—17 branches opened up in Westchester county. Champion's focus is on domestic banking.

A constrained president

An overseas thrust

David Rockefeller, as President during this period, pushes to expand business overseas and introduce modern management methods, but is constrained in his goals by the more conservative Champion. Some headway in international banking in the European and Latin America areas is made. Modern management methods are introduced in Chase under Rockefeller's leadership.

Changes at the top 1969–1980

David Rockefeller becomes Chairperson and CEO upon Champion's retirement. Herbert Patterson is appointed President and COO.

Rockefeller at the helm 1972

Patterson's accomplishments fall short of what is expected of him. The board encourages Rockefeller to act. Patterson resigns and Willard Butcher, a 25-year Chase veteran, is appointed the new president.

Veering off course 1972–1975

"Bank in Trouble"—Chase experiences a series of setbacks. The board again presses Rockefeller to act. "Trimming the Fat" results in a 30% reduction in operations personnel, a "quick fix" that later results in more problems.

Loan volume begins to weaken. Chase, in response to Citicorp's bold 15% per annum earnings goals, aggressively pushes into domestic real estate lending, sponsoring its own REIT. Loan problems are the result.

Internal problems

Comptroller of Currency's Office conducts bank examination—"every closet the examiners opened, something fell out."

A bond trading account is found to be a problem. Executives said to suppress problems during the considerable number of meetings that occurred during this period.

Reorganization	A top to bottom reorganization occurs to convert the corporation from a geographically oriented bank to a market oriented financial services company.
A change in the culture	In a departure from tradition, Chase goes outside and brings in Alan Lafley with over 20 years of personnel experience in GE (via a year with Clark Equipment Company) to work with Rockefeller and Butcher in the position of EVP-Human Resources.
Going outside for managerial talent	Lafley forms a strong team with Wright Elliot, who has been brought in from outside to head Chase's external and internal communications, government, and community affairs.
	Gerald Weiss is brought on board from General Electric to head corporate planning. He is another of a number of executives brought in from the outside to strengthen key corporate functions and businesses during this period.
A new human resources approach	Chase's management takes a number of bold and necessary actions in the human resources area—an overhaul of compensation plans, searches to bring people in from the outside, and highly disciplined staffing reviews and development efforts.
Ambitious plans for recovery 1976	The bank turnaround begins. Rockefeller and Butcher lay out ambitious plans for the future; their three-year projection calls for tripling the 1976 earnings figure of $105 million by 1979.
	Key management changes are made. Thomas Labreque is added to the management committee. Fred Hammer and Ed Allinson are brought in from the outside to become general managers of the retail banking and trust businesses, respectively. Chase works its way out of real estate problems.
The turnaround 1977–1980	A new strategic focus for human resources management, with improvements in implementation, results in stringent selection and placement criteria for executive staffing. Higher performance standards result in several hundred managers leaving Chase under

an equitable termination policy developed by the human resources function.

Continuing emphasis is placed on strengthening management throughout Chase. An advanced management program is developed specifically for senior management, focused on strategic planning, marketing, and general management.

To the surprise of many in the banking industry, Chase begins an aggressive policy of foreclosing on properties deemed unlikely to attain earning status. These actions saved the bank several million dollars.

Record profits

Chase Manhattan experiences a 45% annual growth rate for the three-year period and surpasses earlier projections.

Willard Butcher as new CEO 1980–1981

Willard Butcher is appointed CEO of both the Chase Corporation and the Bank on Jan. 1, 1980, and becomes Chairperson and CEO upon Rockefeller's retirement on April 1, 1981. His appointment reflects a well-planned and orderly approach to executive succession planning.

Despite a volatile global environment and turbulent domestic interest rates (wildly fluctuating between 10¾% and 21½%) Chase closes fiscal 1980 again with record earnings.

A new management team and new record results

More executive changes evolve during the year. Thomas Labreque is appointed president and COO, William S. Ogden is appointed vice chairperson. These changes are viewed as catalytic considering the recovery the bank had made from beatings it had taken due to real estate losses, loss of market share, and behind it all, unsure and weak managers.

Record earnings in 1981 are realized.

The Drysdale affair May 1982

Drysdale Government Securities defaults on $160 million of interest payments owed to nearly 30 of the nation's top brokerage firms. Chase, as intermediary, initially insists that it has no obligation, creating anxiety for two days in the financial markets. Realizing the full implications of its position, Chase agrees

	to cover the full amount and to liquidate Drysdale's portfolio.
Wall Street is critical . . .	Wall Street is critical and by week's end, Chase's stock drops by $6.75/share.
	In an address to Chase employees, Butcher demonstrates leadership with a note of optimism:
	"I liken this to a superbly trained boxer . . . who momentarily dropped his guard (and) got slugged. I am convinced we will pick ourselves off the canvas and fight." [*Newsweek,* May 31, 1982]
The Penn Square debacle June 1982	Penn Square Bank collapses on June 5, leaving customers holding $190 million in uninsured deposits and at least six banks, including Chase, with $2 billion in problem loans. Chase posts a $16.2 million loss for the second quarter of 1982 as a result of Drysdale and Penn Square.
Decisive action taken on managers involved	Butcher announces changes in senior management to remove those responsible for Drysdale and Penn Square. Results: the problem-riddled domestic banking was placed under proven managers. An executive vice president and a senior vice president resign, another EVP is transferred to a position with other responsibility, and seven lower ranking officers resign.
	Reaction on Wall Street is positive: (Stock rises 2½ points)
	"It's a positive sign that management took firm, decisive action in dealing with a problem." [*Wall Street Journal,* July 21, 1982 p. 40]
Back to profitability October 1982	Third quarter 1982 results are the second highest in the bank's history . . . $124 million in earnings before securities transactions.

HUMAN RESOURCE MANAGEMENT AT CHASE MANHATTAN

Recognizing the problems in human resource management, the chairperson and CEO (David Rockefeller) and the President (Bill Butcher) broke with tradition in a big way by bringing in an experienced and respected human resource executive from outside Chase to help address the issues. With a new mandate, the human resource executive, Alan Lafley, placed a primary emphasis on strengthening management throughout the bank. The strong members of senior management were reinforced by selective internal promotions from an identified pool of talented managers and, as necessary, from aggressive recruitment of top-level talent from outside Chase. In addition to the staffing actions, new management development efforts were focused both on senior managers and middle managers who, in a more diversified banking institution, carry the responsibilities critical to its success. These efforts evidently paid off.

The core philosophy of Chase for managing its people is to assure its employees that they will be respected and treated as individuals and enjoy individual dignity at all times. This declaration of what employees can expect of Chase is paralleled by an equally clear declaration of what the organization has a right to expect of the employees in return. This kind of mutual understanding is fundamental to effective human resource management within Chase, as top executives are convinced that human resource capacity, even more than financial capacity, is critical to meet the bank's short and long-range objectives. Staffing has played an instrumental role in human resource management, as discussed in the following interview with Alan Lafley, a principal architect of the Chase human resource strategy.

Interview with Alan Lafley

Q. Mr. Lafley, what brought you to the human resource executive position at Chase?

A. I was offered an opportunity at Chase Manhattan to build and lead a worldwide corporate human resource function that would have a major impact on the business results of a leading international bank. The functional scope would be broad. It would include organization structuring and management process; executive staffing and succession planning; compensation plans design and implementation; recruiting, selection, training, and development of Chase's human resources; affirmative action program leadership; and employee relations policy and practices development, communication, and monitoring. The position would report to the president and chief operating officer on succession planning and other critical human resources matters. It would be a key executive position involved in the planning and policy-making deliberations and decisions of the corporation.

Q. What impact can the human resource executive have on an organization?

A. The human resource executive can have a major impact on an organization's success. The degree of impact depends on a number of factors. It depends mostly on the CEO and president's view of what a human resource function can contribute to the development and achievement of business plans and results, and on the credibility and performance of the person in the human resource executive position. The ability of the human resource executive to add value in determining the strategic direction of the corporation with particular focus on the human resource issues is very important. It is my opinion that most corporate executive officers recognize the important contribution to be made by the human resource function, and are seeking this level of contribution from their human resource managers and professionals capable of meeting their standards for this critical business function.

Q.   What is required of today's human resource executive?

A.   The requirements begin with the fact that human resource capacity will be a critical factor for most corporations in the attainment of business objectives in the years ahead. That capacity is being stretched today and the demands on it can be expected to grow. There is an increasing need for human resource executives to bring into question both the adequacy and relevance of recruiting, selection, appraisal, development, and reward systems, as the breadth and depth of managerial and professional skills required to compete effectively in our markets continue to grow and change. In this context, it is crucial for them to highlight priorities and guide human resource planning and development efforts as we go forward. As we assess our strategic positioning in relation to the anticipated environment of the '80s, human resource capacity more than financial capacity lies on the critical path to meeting our business objectives in the years ahead.

Q.   When you entered this position at Chase, it appears that you were advocating breaking away from the Chase tradition of developing and promoting people from within. Now it's my understanding that you would like to develop people from within the Chase organization to satisfy the management needs of the corporation. Will you please comment on this apparent contradiction?

A.   When I joined Chase it soon became apparent to me that we must go outside the corporation to search for and attract particular managerial and professional talent of the highest quality to correct identified deficiencies. This was necessary because we had not recruited at the entry level the quantity, quality, or type to satisfy certain needs, had failed to develop the competencies required, made some poor placements as a result of our selection process, and had not achieved the performance results required because of our performance evaluation process and our reward systems.

The CEO and president were convinced that the success of the Chase, both short and long-term, depended on the identification and placement of the very best people available in the particular positions at that point in time. And if that necessitated going outside the corporation to achieve the best placements, then we should do so.

There are significant problems, however, in assimilating outside hires into an organization at other than the entry level. Individuals within the organization are disappointed when there is no opportunity for promotion from within. Higher salaries that often need to be paid to attract outstanding talent from a competitor can cause inequities. Furthermore, it takes time and considerable managerial attention to assimilate an individual into a new organization. And the failure rate of outside hires is high no matter how well the selection and assimilation of the individual is done. We realized these risks inherent in external recruiting and fortunately managed the situations with considerable success.

Today our external recruiting is focused primarily on the entry level, with much improved human resource planning and development efforts. And our policy is clearly to promote from within whenever possible. There has not been a change in our belief about the positive influence on employee morale of promotion from within, but it still must not be accomplished by sacrificing quality and suitability when filling the position. Because of the critical importance of strength and depth relative to key general manager and key professional positions, we will continually stay in the external market on a very selective basis to identify and attract top talent with the experience and competencies suited to our corporate-wide needs.

Q. You have been quoted as saying, "In order to get the best, you've got to pay for the best." Would you please expand on this comment?

A. Chase at one time made the mistake of cutting salary budgets as a part of expense reductions to a level where they were not competitive with the market, and they could not attract or retain the most competent and highly qualified individuals. In many cases they got what they paid for—adequate people for adequate salaries, but not the best managers or professionals. Compensation plans and salary structures must be competitive with your major competitors in each business. In Chase, we are in that position today, we will make certain that we remain there. At the same time, the compensation paid, both salaries and incentive payments, is managed so as to significantly differentiate the amounts paid to the better and lesser erformers.

Let me add a comment that not only must pay be competitive, but the total reward system must be equal to or better than the competitors'. The opportunities for personal development and promotion, challenging work, a satisfying work environment, a good manager, a successful and well-respected company, are all important factors in attracting and retaining the highest quality employees.

Q. The staffing of senior level positions within many corporations is often a troublesome, political process. How does Chase deal with politics in selecting individuals for senior level positions?

A. We have taken the staffing of senior level positions out of any political process without question and, I believe, have a very effective approach to making decisions for staffing key managerial positions throughout the corporation worldwide. Staffing decisions for general managers and other key managerial positions are the responsibility of the president or chief executive officer. They are made after consideration of the sector executive's recommendations and a discussion of candidates identified and evaluated relative to the open position's agreed-upon specifications. The candidates are discussed relative to the position requirements in a very open and forthright manner in the meetings of the sector or equivalent executive with the human resource executive and president and/or CEO depending on the level of the position. The individuals recommended have been identified and evaluated previously as candidates for the position during the quarterly management resource review sessions with the president and his direct reports, and at the annual management resource review sessions with the chief executive, president, vice chairperson, and executives at the sector level. The human resource executive is the coordinator and an active participant in all management resource review sessions.

Q. What are the important components or elements of strategic staffing?

A. To answer your question on strategic staffing and to bring some of our previous comments on staffing into focus, let's discuss the linkage of staffing with development as key elements of human resource management to provide the strength and depth of talent required to meet the needs of the corporation in a timely fashion.

Based on some fundamental assumptions about Chase's development needs, a framework has been developed around a concept of "core" and "specialized" development streams. A development stream depicts a progression pattern for a particular "population" or family of jobs. "Core development streams" represent the job families which have the broadest application across the corporation and typically lead to general management roles; "specialized development streams" relate to more specialized job families and most often lead to functional management roles or the management of a more specialized business.

Each development stream is made up of the following elements:

A recruiting profile which represents the "starting point" in development.

Development stages, relating to one's position in the career cycle and general organizational level.

Developmental activities, including both on-the-job experiences and formal training, for each developmental stage.

A series of developmental targets, or outcomes, representing attainment of the "core competencies" required of the fully qualified professional or manager at various stages in the developmental stream.

Once defined, development streams must be supported by a number of staffing and development practices if the overall development job is to get done. They include:

Manpower needs forecasts linked with longer-range business plans.

A selection process focused to ensure the appropriate qualitative inputs.

Assessment processes and manpower reviews to identify the most promising and their developmental needs.

The placement process to match the development needs of the most promising with the best development opportunities.

Reward systems to reinforce development objectives.

We see the development task requiring agreement on the critical competencies needed in our key professional and managerial populations today and in the years ahead. With agreement on these profiles, we can then use them to drive our staffing, recruiting, selection, and placement and our development strategies and practices.

A number of Chase's fundamental concepts underlying our development framework relate to staffing strategy, (for example):

- We will continue to draw most of our general managers from our professional ranks. Consequently, in order to adequately broaden the professionals who are deemed to be the best suited for general management roles, we will need to identify these people early enough in their careers to get the broadening job done.
- General management depth is dependent upon adequate professional depth.
- We should place our development emphasis on the competencies we cannot recruit for effectively and attempt to recruit for those competencies which others develop particularly well.
- Given the increased complexity of many managerial and professional roles today, it is becoming less feasible in recruiting entry level talent for these roles to seek the "blank template" and grow all of the skills that we require in-house. Consequently, it is becoming more important that we examine our "development target" to determine which of the competencies we can recruit for (e.g., knowledge of a particular function, technology, or customer segment) and which we must develop ourselves, either because the skills or knowledge are not available in the market (e.g., familiarity with the Chase network, knowledge of Chase products) or because we want to shape the learning process ourselves (e.g., the approach to assessing credit risk).
- It is important to ensure recognition of the *interdependencies* between various elements in the developmental process, and staffing is one of those key

elements. For example, the skills we recruit for or the stage in the career cycle at which the individual enters the organization strongly influence the nature and the amount of development required. Further, our effectiveness in assimilating the individual into our organizational culture and the individual's resulting commitment level will be as important to performance as the skills brought to the job. And since most learning occurs on the job, job content and the manager under whom we place someone are more important in meeting our development objectives than formal training.

Q. You have previously referred to strategically staffing a business manager position to meet the needs of the strategic plan for the business. How do you feel about using the Boston Consulting Group matrix, or a similar method, in identifying and fitting a general manager to the strategic phase of a business? For example, the use of the star, cash cow, question mark, and dog categories to identify growth phases, and have complementary growers, caretakers, harvesters, and undertakers. Is this type of matrix used in Chase?

A. I think that such an approach is an oversimplification of the general manager staffing process. Successful staffing of a position is highly dependent on arriving at a clear understanding and agreement on what the job is, that is, what needs to be accomplished in the particular general manager position over the next two to five years. And then it is necessary to interpret those needs into staffing specifications in terms of competencies, experience, and individual characteristics required. More staffing failures, in my opinion, come about because of lack of careful thought and agreement on the position requirements than are caused by poor assessments of an internal candidate's strengths and weaknesses. The strategy for a business and knowledge of where we want to take it are important in determining the staffing requirements for the manager, but it's much more than assigning a generic strategic category. There may be a need to rethink the strategic direction of the business, and the position, therefore, requires a general manager who has outstanding ability to think strategically. You may need both an excellent strategic thinker and one who can bring costs in line. Does the business require strong marketing experience, or is the focus on technical strengths regardless of the growth phase? Do we need product development leadership or production strength? A business may have need for an unusual inspirational leader because of the circumstances in the organization, regardless of the strategic direction.

So my point is that although strategic direction is an important consideration in making the staffing decision, many other factors about the business are important in determining the position specifications and individual requirements.

Q. Is there some mystique about the perfect manager?

A. In my opinion there is no perfect manager or singular model of a successful manager. I think that it is now very clear, since it has been proven over the years in numerous situations, that professional managers for all seasons do not exist. Companies have found that the concept of professional managers who can successfully manage any business is unsound, and it has resulted in numerous failures. There is a need to know the particular business and have sufficient experience in it to become a successful general manager. It is true for a functional manager as well. Unless you have knowledge of the function, you cannot successfully manage it. The concept of the professional manager was overstated and over-taught at one time. Fortunately, some of the companies who preached and taught the role of the professional manager have had their book burnings and the concept has passed.

It is, therefore, important in a development framework that we view recruitment and selection, assimilation, job experiences, performance appraisal, and formal development experiences interdependently.

Q. Recent literature suggests that culture is strongly related to organizational performance. How should it be considered in the staffing strategy and the selection process?

A. Before specifically answering your question, I would like to express a word of caution about all of the focus on culture of an organization. I have a concern that too much time can be spent on assessing the corporate culture and becoming so overly sensitive to the organization's faults that the corporate management becomes immobile. It's somewhat analogous to a person worrying about all their little pains and aches to a point where they can no longer physically or mentally handle life's problems.

Certainly, the culture of the corporation has an impact on all elements of human resources management. It affects the approaches to selection, appraisal, development, reward, and the total work environment. It is an important consideration in determining staffing strategy and the selection process, and in deciding on needed changes in approach.

Q. What selection criteria do you use at Chase for recruiting and selection at entry level?

A. The selection process is crucial. It involves careful planning and effective implementation to ensure that we not only recruit the quality of individuals we want in Chase, but that we recruit for enough of the core professional competencies we require and a sufficient number of individuals who appear to have the qualities needed to grow into key managerial positions. The human resource development job is manageable if a sufficient number of entry-level hires have the basic qualities to be effective in broad managerial roles. Chase's entry-level selection criteria include certain *core criteria.* These are the qualities which, if found in sufficient measure, will provide the raw material for general management, and are in most cases equally relevant for our functional and professional populations. The core criteria include: interpersonal skills, that is, the ability to communicate ideas persuasively, understand the viewpoint of others, and relate effectively to a broad range of people; mental abilities, the intellectual breadth and versatility in addition to the depth of mental capacity; achievement motivation, the high individual achievement needs involving the "desire to do better" are the foundation of strong on-the-job performance; adaptability, to change and cross components (the rapid rate of change in our markets and in technology makes this quality extremely important; cross-cultural adaptability is becoming increasingly important as more of our businesses become "global" in scope); leadership ability/potential, a significant proportion of our entry-level hires should rate high against this criterion, since in many cases our assessment will prove to be incorrect and in others it will prove irrelevant due to individual's career interests and the problems of fit to position needs as careers develop.

The other entry-level selection criterion is *population and component-specific criteria*. These are the additional criteria which, if consciously recruited for, will make the development job more manageable and enable us to focus our early-career development on the special professional skills and abilities which will give Chase a competitive edge. These are: functional skills/knowledge, the indepth academic training and/or experience in a functional discipline (e.g., finance, information systems) which is fundamental to the work of a professional population (this can mitigate our development investment in a raw recruit substantiality); market knowledge experience, knowledge or experience related to a particular customer segment or geographic market, can considerably reduce orientation time and permit us to bring someone "online" more rapidly; special qualifications, which would include special skills (e.g., competency in a particular language) or knowledge areas (e.g., specialized product or technology) desired by a particular component at a point in time.

Q.   How are people selected as candidates for higher level positions within Chase and how does one "move", that is, develop and advance in the corporation?

A.   Chase's strategy for selection and development is to focus on the most promising for both managerial and professional roles.

Initial judgments are made about the long-term promise of the individual as early as possible in their Chase careers. While these initial judgments are necessarily tentative and need to be reviewed continuously throughout an individual's career, it is critical that the most (and least) promising be identified early to permit focused assessments and individual attention. Among those identified as "most promising," assessments have differing development implications. In the case of the promising future general managers, we begin broadening within and across core development streams early in their careers. The promising professionals are given more intensive development within specialized development streams.

Discussions with the individual are particularly important to ensure compatibility of individual goals with the company's manpower development plans. In addition, it is important for the corporation to identify and maintain an inventory of "key development jobs" which are seen to be most effective in developing and testing those competencies required in greatest measure in our general managers. Senior management concurrence with corporate human resources involvement is required in staffing them to maximize their development value. And, as with the development of key professionals, the selection of strong "mentoring" managers is important right along with job content.

Chase's disciplined approach to management resource reviews and candidate slates for key positions help to ensure worldwide consideration of the most promising and best qualified individuals for open positions. The recruiting, selection process is focused to ensure the appropriate qualitative inputs. Assessment processes and manpower reviews are focused on identifying the best performers, the most promising in each development stream, and giving individual development attention to those with the greatest potential. The placement process is geared to matching the development needs of the most promising with the best job development opportunities. And the reward systems reinforce the manager's responsibility for development of quality talent to meet the corporation's needs.

Q.   What is your opinion about career ladders and their importance to individuals?

A.   I am concerned about many of the approaches to career planning and some of the references to career ladders or career paths. An individual moving along a defined or planned career path, or up a career ladder which connotes vertical, upward progress as ideal development and the way to promotion and increased responsibility disturbs me.

Sound individuals' development planning and successful moves to positions of increased responsibility must optimize the fit between individual career goals, solid assessments of strengths and weaknesses based on performance, and the organization's needs.

Too many individuals get all hung up over unrealistic career plans developed by them. Seldom does a career progress as one plans, particularly in the job sequence and on the time schedule expected. Some of the best individual development moves are to lateral or even lower position levels. Too many failures are a result of climbing straight upward on a career ladder without sufficient experience, development, and testing at each rung. This has resulted in large numbers of executives falling off when they reach the top.

One of the situations that we had to turn around at Chase was the problem of too many people on career paths where they would spend two or three years on each job in a sequence of positions, each at a higher level, until they reached an executive position and a senior officer title, only to then find their performance unsatisfactory because the job moves neither provided the development experiences or the assessments required for sound growth and promotion.

Q.   How far into the future are your staffing plans made?

A.   Staffing strategy and plans must be an integral part of the Chase business strategies and plans. A corporate staffing strategy and plan cannot stand alone. Staffing and other human resource issues must be part of the particular business plans, but modified accordingly and summarized in a corporate staffing plan to ensure that the long-term staffing requirements of the corporation are met in terms of numbers, skills, and management competencies.

Chase staffing plans are reviewed on a 6-month rolling basis with a focus on requirements 12–18 months in the future. I believe that staffing strategy and planning is much more dynamic than we tend to recognize, because the environment, both internal and external, is much more difficult to forecast than we admit in our business planning, particularly in banking and finance services.

Q.   Handling staffing issues in troubled times can be problematic. Experts in the banking industry have commented favorably on your handling personnel associated with Drysdale and Penn Square in a firm, decisive manner. Can you elaborate on the actions you have taken to resolve these issues? Is this the normal approach you take when such circumstances occur?

A.   I do not believe that we would have made different decisions, or handled the personnel actions differently were we to replay the same scenario tomorrow. We calmly investigated the situations before we took any personnel actions. We deliberately and thoughtfully gathered the facts. We carefully reviewed them, and then moved quickly. We made our decisions on each personnel case on one day, communicated the decisions, and took action the next day. We did not dribble out our findings and leave our people wondering whether or not another shoe was going to drop. Our approach was consistent with the way we normally handle difficult personnel situations.

Q.   What is the role or responsibility of human resource management when poor performance of this nature surfaces and becomes problematic?

A.   When business performance is not up to reasonable expectations, we must focus on the core elements of human resource management: (1) staffing—the recruiting, selection, and placement process; (2) training and development; (3) performance appraisal and measurement; (4) reward systems and practices; (5) the work environment. If the problem is poor staffing, and particularly in key manager positions, the poor placements have to be corrected in an uncompromising manner as soon as the evidence is clear. Related organization structure and staffing actions must be taken without delay, accompanied by appropriate discussions and communications. We must not contribute to increasing the anxieties of individuals by dragging out the process unnecessarily. This is where the culture of the organization is a factor in successful implementation. Staffing actions that have a negative impact on individuals must be handled with sensitivity and fairness to the people affected. Transfer, out-placement, and termination policies and practices must provide alternatives for the positive support that individuals need under these circumstances. It has been my experience that necessary staffing changes due to performance or future business needs can be made with firmness in a decisive and timely manner so that most individuals feel that they have been treated fairly by the company and have located a new position much better suited to their interests and strengths. I sincerely believe that the greatest injustice that we can do to an individual, as well as the company, is to let a person remain in a position for which he is unqualified and where he becomes increasingly unhappy.

Q.   What do you consider to be the lessons that human resources at Chase has learned from the Drysdale and Penn Square events?

A.   These events have caused us to reflect on selection, placement, compensation, and training issues, and on management culture. Should we have made staffing changes sooner? Should we allow an incentive plan to be put into place if it can be mismanaged? We have been reminded that there are some things we need to do better in manager training. We are putting all of our present managers and those appointed in the future through a newly designed manager awareness program. Its purpose is to provide the knowledge that a manager must process before he or she is placed in a position of significant managerial responsibility. And there are management culture issues to reflect on. Can we improve management communications upward and horizontally, and the way in which managers "manage" their subordinates? These are some of the areas where human resource lessons may be learned. The conclusion is that the best of human resource systems under poor management are doomed to failure.

Q.   How have the Drysdale and Penn Square events affected the culture of Chase?

A.   The impact on the bank's people has been different than that experienced as a result of problems in the mid-'70s. There was more anger and disappointment because individuals bankwide were performing well; the bank was meeting or exceeding its performance goals in nearly all its businesses in a very difficult external environment. Morale was high, employees were proud of their performance; they were with a winner. Unlike the mid-'70s, these were isolated incidents involving a handful of people out of more than

30,000. Their actions, however, had a significant negative impact on Chase not only on its profitability, but its reputation. It was a very different kind of situation. It's fortunate that Chase people today view themselves as part of a winning team and have gone back to work with even greater resolve. They have a positive attitude and are working hard to demonstrate that we at Chase will come back stronger than ever. I believe Chase people have been able to handle adversity considerably better than others who have had to face similar problems.

Q.   Looking toward the future, what changes in direction do you see Chase taking in terms of strategic staffing?

A.   Before we focus too quickly on the need for change in strategic staffing to meet future needs, let me emphasize that most important need in Chase and most companies is to do what we've been talking about much better. There is greater need to improve our implementation of current staffing strategies and plans than to change our course.

I am not suggesting, however, that we should not be continually assessing the future staffing requirements of our businesses and modifying our recruiting, selection, training, and development strategies, plans, and methods to meet changing needs.

Increased emphasis on selection, training, and development of the most capable and best performing specialists or professionals is one change I see taking place in Chase and other companies. There is greater realization that this population is increasingly important to the success of the business. It has also become more evident that the best source for potentially successful general managers is from within the group of high-performing professionals and specialists who have demonstrated excellent results over a significant period of time. We should not be identifying and selecting the candidates for general manager development who have not demonstrated outstanding performance as individuals in challenging assignments.

[1]The authors wish to thank A. Wright Elliott, Senior Vice President, Corporation Communications for his valuable contributions to this case. In addition, we wish to thank Dr. Noel M. Tichy of The University of Michigan and Dr. Charles J. Fombrun of The Wharton School for their assistance and support in the preparation of this case.

CHAPTER

6

THE APPRAISAL SYSTEM AS A STRATEGIC CONTROL

Gary P. Latham

Strategic planning—the words themselves connote a sense of importance, dynamism, and excitement. Perhaps this is because strategic planning is forward-looking in nature. As pointed out in the first Part of the book, strategic planning is the process through which the basic mission of organization is identified, its objectives are set, and the allocation of resources to achieve these objectives are specified.

The words performance appraisal for many people connote paperwork and drudgery. Performance appraisals are often viewed as retrospective in nature because the emphasis is placed on what has occurred in the past. Yet the success or failure of a strategic plan rests, in large part, with top management's ability to properly identify the key actions that must be performed to formulate and execute the necessary steps leading to the attainment of the organization's long-range goals. Thus performance appraisal should be the process through which the critical job behaviors of the management are identified, the specific objectives of each individual manager are set, and the steps or resources needed to attain each of them are agreed upon.

Few companies have formal appraisal systems to evaluate top-level managers on how well they perform against the organization's strategic plan. In most organizations, no attempt is made to develop good measurement indicators. The prevailing attitude is that they simply do not exist. An emphasis is placed on managerial style rather than substance, and/or on whether a given result was achieved with little or no questioning as to *how* it was achieved. Thus a CEO may appraise a senior vice president primarily on whether a set of objectives was pursued in a manner similar to the way in which he or she would have pursued them (Latham and Wexley, 1981). Divergence of thinking and activity are consequently stifled. Similarly, it is quite common to find appraisal measures that reward managers for attending to the "bottom line" of their respective functions without regard to how their actions or those of their people affected the bottom lines of other divisions. No formal assessment is made to determine whether they and their subordinates behaved in a unifying way with colleagues so that the organization's overall mission could be achieved. Knowing this, one better understands why many strategic plans are not carried out successfully.

The purpose of this chapter is to illustrate the central role that performance appraisal should play in strategic planning. Specifically, examples are given of measurement indicators for assessing adherence to and implementation of a strategic plan, maximizing objectivity and minimizing subjectivity in making a performance appraisal, and ways to increase the effectiveness of the appraisal process by focusing on the future rather than the past.

APPRAISAL PURPOSES

The purpose of performance appraisal is twofold. First, the performance appraisal instrument defines what is meant by implementation and adherence to the strategic plan at the level of an individual employee. Thus when the strategic plan changes, the instrument must be reviewed for necessary modification and revision. It is through the use of this instrument that the second objective of performance appraisal is attained, namely, to bring about and sustain effective and/or efficient job performance. This can be done through self-management or through coaching and counseling of others. Each of these methods is discussed in a subsequent section of this chapter.

It has been argued elsewhere that performance appraisal is the *sine qua non* of human resource systems. This is because, as noted previously, a performance appraisal system makes explicit what constitutes effective and efficient behavior on the part of an individual employee that is critical to implementing the strategic plan. Just as the engineering department is concerned with the design of equipment, the maintenance department is concerned with the running of equipment, and manufacturing is concerned with turning out a quality product at minimum cost, the human resource department should be concerned with the identification of what it is the people in engineering, maintenance, and manufacturing must do (behavior) to be proficient in their respective functions. Similarly, they should determine what top management must do to implement the strategic plan once it has been formulated. The outcomes of these analyses are translated into a valid appraisal instrument. *Validity* refers to the fact that people are being measured on areas that are truly important to the attainment of their departmental and/or organizational objectives. To the extent that valid appraisals are made, valid decisions can be made regarding who should be rewarded monetarily or with a promotion. To the extent that valid appraisals are not made, valid selection decisions and reward practices are impossible.

Valid performance appraisals are also critical to training departments because they identify people who lack the ability to perform the job effectively. Because a valid appraisal instrument defines what needs to be done, the appraisal process not only identifies who needs training, but the type of training that is needed.[1]

THE APPRAISAL INSTRUMENT: MEASUREMENT INDICATORS OF ADHERENCE TO THE STRATEGIC PLAN

Appraisal instruments can be classified into one of three broad categories, namely, trait scales, economic indices or cost-related criteria, and behavioral measures. The basic mission or *raison d'être* of all three instruments is to provide a reliable and valid measure of job performance. Reliability here refers to whether two or more people would make the same appraisal of a person given that they had frequent opportunity to observe his or her performance. Validity, as used here, refers to whether the instrument contains a representative sampling of the critical job behaviors necessary to implement the strategic plan.

Trait Scales

The trait scale typically consists of a listing of personality attributes such as dependable, loyal, competitive, resourceful, decisive, and so on. An advantage of traits is that the same appraisal instrument can be used across jobs and departments within the organization. Everyone wants a secretary as well as a president to be dependable, loyal, decisive, and the like. A primary disadvantage is in the area of goals and objectives. The traits in themselves do not make explicit what a person has to start, stop, or continue doing to affect such areas as profitability, growth, or market share, not to mention development and training of subordinates. Feedback and goal setting in relation to this feedback is difficult if not all but impossible because of the vagueness

---

[1] This concept of "validity" presumes that there is sufficient clarity in the organization around substantive goals and the means to attain them [Ed.].

of traits. With 1.0 indicating perfect agreement, the agreement among observers when traits are used is typically .20 (Fiske, 1979).

An additional factor that makes the use of trait scales problematic is that they are frowned upon by the courts because of their lack of reliability. Specifically, the courts have ruled that traits are susceptible to the personal tastes, whims, or fancies of the evaluators (Latham and Wexley, 1981).

Performance Outcomes

Economic indices, cost-related measures, or performance outcome measures are preferred by the courts as well as the Equal Employment Opportunity Commission relative to trait scales because they are objective in nature. There is little room for subjectivity as to whether the baseball player hit a home-run, the typist typed 70 error-free words a minute, the salesperson sold 15 cars last month, and so on. Further, it is easy to determine whether the basic mission of the employee is congruent with the organizational and/or departmental strategic plan. It is easy to assess the person's performance in relation to goal attainment. The advantage of getting away from personality and focusing on results reflects, in part, the enthusiasm by some (Drucker, 1973) for embracing management by objectives (MBO) as a means of making performance appraisals. However, it must be remembered that the basic mission or fundamental strategy of the performance appraisal process is to improve or sustain an already high productivity level of the individual employee. Results measures tell the person how well or how poorly he or she is doing, but they do not in themselves tell the employee what he or she must start doing, stop doing, or continue doing to increase those results. Moreover, a sole focus on the bottom line can encourage a "results-at-all-costs" mentality that violates corporate ethics policies.

The first strategy for improving productivity is to define it in a way that it is relevant to both the appraiser and the individual employee. Only in this way will the performance appraisal have credibility for both of them. If they do not believe that the appraisal can affect productivity and hence the strategic plan positively, neither of them are likely to take the process seriously.

The credibility of performance appraisal has already been strained by an overemphasis on measures of profits, costs, units produced divided by employee hours worked and so on. This is because such macro measures are affected by technology, capital, availability of raw material, markets, and people. People appraise equipment in such terms as machine speed or rate, equipment downtime, and cost. Similarly, people who appraise others are, or should be, concerned with them as individuals, namely, their response rates, their absenteeism or downtime, their costs, and so on. In short, people who make appraisals need to be concerned with the *behavior* of the people whom they are appraising. But they also need to realize that a wide gap frequently exists between an individual employee's behavior and organizational outcome measures even when the gap between what a person does, such as cutting down a tree, and the organization's measure of productivity, such as units per employee hour, appears to be small. Equipment, terrain, and weather can have a major positive or negative effect on these important measures of productivity in the forest products industry regardless of the behavior of an individual employee.

It is ironic that the very emphasis on so-called "results" measures as the primary criterion for appraising a person's effectiveness runs the risk of impeding rather than promoting the success of an organization's strategic plan. This is especially true when appraising the productivity of upper-level management. As some authors pointed out over a decade ago, if outcome measures are the primary basis for appraising a person, many of the person's outcomes will be guided with an eye toward these results, and considerably less attention is likely to be given to the state of the system that generates the results. Such selective focusing is likely to promote deterioration of the work flow. For example, when managers must meet a quota, they will probably assign tasks, make demands, and monitor progress in such a way that the quota is indeed obtained. However, the next time the group tries to meet a quota, it may be unable to do so because the system is in a state of disarray. Excessive shortcuts may have been sanctioned. These shortcuts, in turn, may have established a set of sufficiently negative precedents and expectations so that the group is now unable to function effectively.

Furthermore, managers whose attention is directed toward outcomes rather than behavior may find themselves able to do too little too late with regard to the work processes once the results have been obtained. This often occurs by focusing primarily on work group progress (results achieved) and making immediate readjustments of personnel and tasks when the feedback is discouraging. In making these adjustments in terms of feedback regarding outcomes rather than behavior, managers may hasten the deterioration of the system they are desperately trying to improve.

In terms of strategic thinking, outcome measures are strong in that they specify desired end states in terms of goals and objectives, but, as noted earlier, they fail in terms of the basic mission of the appraisal process in that they do not provide information as to what a person has to start doing, stop doing, or continue doing to obtain or retain these goals and objectives. They are objective and are hence liked by the courts, but they also can be challenged legally if a person who has been adversely affected by an appraisal decision regarding outcome measures can show that these measures were affected by factors (e.g., equipment, territorial disadvantages, advertising concentration) beyond his or her control.

So if a primary focus on outcome measures is the problem, and a focus on employee behavior is the solution, how do we go about doing it? The answer is job analysis. And what should job analysis focus on? Probably the very outcome measures that have just been criticized, namely, the outcome measures reflecting the attainment of the strategic plan.

Behavioral Measures

The attainment of the strategic plan will not occur through osmosis. The purpose of job analysis is to identify those behaviors that are critical for employees in various positions to demonstrate in order to implement the plan successfully. A shrinking market may require job behaviors associated with holding costs down, preventing waste, and increasing market share rather than those concerned only with increasing the number of units produced divided by the number of employee hours worked. But explicit in conducting the job analysis for the purpose of performance appraisal is the realization that defining economic indices in terms of the behaviors that affect them does not necessarily imply an isomorphic relationship between behavioral and cost-related constructs. It cannot be overemphasized that in most instances the economic indices are not under the total control of the individual. A person's behavior, however, is under his or her control. Performance appraisal is concerned with the person's behavior. The strategy here is to emphasize those behaviors so as to increase the likelihood that these economic measures will be positive, or, at the very least, to minimize the probability that if the economic measures are poor, the fault is not due to what the employee did or did not do correctly.

It is beyond the scope of this chapter to outline in detail a job analysis to develop behavioral observation scales for performance appraisal purposes. The technique has been discussed elsewhere (Campbell et al., 1970). In brief, the human resources department can use a job analysis procedure known as the critical incident technique to interview people who understand the strategic plan, are aware of the aims and objectives of a given job position, and who frequently observe people performing these positions regarding the identification of observable behaviors and the contexts in which demonstrating them will be critical to the successful attainment of the organization's mission. The job analysis should be conducted every time the strategic plan is changed.

Table 6.1 presents some behavioral observation scales (BOS) that are currently used by one or more organizations to assess strategic thinking on the part of the individual employee. The items are not exhaustive, but rather serve as an illustration of what an appraisal instrument that assesses strategic activity might look like. It is likely that the items would differ for start-up, growth, mature, and declining businesses.

The advantages of behavioral observation scales for appraisal purposes are that they make explicit what is meant behaviorally and is, therefore, expected from the strategic plan. With 1.0 indicating perfect agreement among appraisers, agreement regarding observable behavior is typically between .70 and .90 (Fiske, 1979; Latham and Wexley, 1981). Furthermore, behavior is under the control of the person, and a person's behavior can be modified when it is necessary to do so. Behavioral measures assist inspection and, if necessary, correction at lower operational levels within the organization of those behaviors that are not congruent with the organization's overall cor-

TABLE 6.1. Examples of Types of Items on Behavioral Observation Scales (BOS) that Assess Strategic Planning.

I. Adheres to the basic mission
   1. Day-to-day decisions are in accordance with the organization's strategic goals and objectives.
     Almost never   0   1   2   3   4   Almost always
   2. Asks for input from managers in other divisions or departments on issues that will affect them before making a decision.
     Almost never   0   1   2   3   4   Almost always
   3. Spends time learning about other divisions and departmental manager's ongoing operations (e.g., their targets, timetables, interrelationships of targets within and between departments).
     Almost never   0   1   2   3   4   Almost always
   4. Develops ways of combining division or department objectives with the organization's overall strategic plan.
     Almost never   0   1   2   3   4   Almost always
   5. Looks for ways to support fellow managers outside his or her division or department.
     Almost never   0   1   2   3   4   Almost always
   6. Can communicate the organization's strategic plan and that of his or her division in words the listener can understand.
     Almost never   0   1   2   3   4   Almost always

II. Customer mix
   1. Specifies target markets.
     Almost never   0   1   2   3   4   Almost always
   2. Is accessible to client or customer.
     Almost never   0   1   2   3   4   Almost always
   3. Probes client with questions to ensure full understanding of, and commitment to, the problems by everyone concerned.
     Almost never   0   1   2   3   4   Almost always
   4. Generates new business by becoming aware of existing and potential client problems.
     Almost never   0   1   2   3   4   Almost always
   5. Understands the client's business.
     Almost never   0   1   2   3   4   Almost always

III. Product mix
   1. Knows the interlocking system of the client's business, and facets of his or her own division or department that influences them positively or negatively.
     Almost never   0   1   2   3   4   Almost always
   2. Shows awareness of cost implications of product development.
     Almost never   0   1   2   3   4   Almost always
   3. Chooses proper timing in implementing an idea, concept, or project.
     Almost never   0   1   2   3   4   Almost always
   4. Has realistic expectations regarding the life of a product, concept, or idea.
     Almost never   0   1   2   3   4   Almost always
   5. Has a realistic strategy for developing and expanding new or existing products.
     Almost never   0   1   2   3   4   Almost always
   6. Finds fresh angles or alternatives in dealing with subject matter and/or problems considered by others as insolvable.
     Almost never   0   1   2   3   4   Almost always

porate strategy. This is especially critical in organizations where it is difficult to discern who exactly was responsible for a specific end result (e.g., profit, volume, reduction in waste). It is also critical when cooperation and team-playing among people within and among departments are necessary for en-suring that these end results are optimal.

Interrelationship of Behavioral Measures with Selection and Monetary Rewards

Selecting people who will play a key role in implementing the strategic plan is often made on highly subjective grounds. Here "politics" often triumph over substance. A valid appraisal instrument that pinpoints a priori what constitutes critical job behavior, that is, what it is we are (should be) looking for in a person, makes it difficult to justify on an ad hoc basis the personality one wants to see in a given job position. Moreover, valid appraisals greatly facilitate valid selection and promotion procedures. Validity, with regard to selection, means that there is a correlation between how well one does on a selection instrument (e.g., interview, assessment center) and how well one does subsequently in the new job. If one knows the behaviors required on the job, specialists in human behavior can easily develop selection procedures at minimum cost that will not only predict who is likely to demonstrate those behaviors, but will minimize the probability of litigation due to charges that the selection was made on the basis of age, race, or sex.

Tying monetary rewards to performance is effective in that to the extent that money is valued, linking it to performance enhances motivation (see Chapter 9). Separating pay from performance can only raise questions as to the equity of pay decisions.

In the past, pay has either not been used or it has been used inappropriately to increase employee motivation regarding the strategic plan. Four problems inherent to pay–performance plans with managers are overcome through the use of behavioral observation scales. For example, it has been argued that tying money to performance may place an undue emphasis on individual as opposed to team performance. This problem is overcome with valid BOS that specify the cooperative behaviors that are required of each manager.

Second, it has been argued that pay-for-performance plans emphasize out-come measures to the exclusion of subjective, yet important, aspects of the job. This argument poses a problem for programs that focus solely on cost-related measures; this in not an issue with valid BOS.

Third, as noted in the introduction to this chapter, people have argued that it is difficult to measure the job performance on a single individual. This is true for non–operations-related jobs (e.g., public affairs manager) in an organization that is solely bottom-line-oriented. However, BOS can be de-veloped for any job position.

Fourth, if pay is to motivate performance, people must thoroughly un-derstand what they have to do to receive the reward. The advantage of BOS

CHAPTER

7

THE EXECUTIVE APPRAISAL

Mary Anne Devanna

In the preceding chapter the role that performance appraisal plays as a control system for monitoring progress against strategic objectives was addressed. This chapter deals with (1) the role of performance appraisal at different levels of the organizations, (2) the performance appraisal system as a means for generating strategic data, (3) performance appraisal as an integrating mechanism for the human resource system, and (4) some of the process issues that have an impact on an organization's ability to effectively appraise strategic performance and implement strategic plans.

PERFORMANCE APPRAISAL AT DIFFERENT LEVELS OF THE ORGANIZATION

We traditionally think of performance appraisal as a method of evaluating individual performance and, indeed, in this capacity it forms the cornerstone of an effective human resource system. Before discussing this aspect of performance appraisal in organizations, however, we briefly touch on appraisal at other levels which have an impact on organizational effectiveness. These are appraisals or comparisons made among organizations in the same industry, and among functions in the same organization.

In 1983 *Fortune* published the first annual reputational study of 200 companies, 10 in each of 20 industries. The response to this initial study resulted in a larger demand for that issue than any previously published. Since many of the respondents to this study are industry analysts, one would assume that financial performance would have been a good surrogate for the overall rankings in this survey. Though it did explain a large part of the variance, in reading through the survey it quickly becomes evident that financial performance in the short term was not sufficient to earn good marks for a company. The performance had to be over a period of time greater than the most recent statement of earnings. Although *Fortune* was content with reporting the results, students of organizations might well reflect on the impact that this report card had on organizational effectiveness. At a minimum, one would suspect that it affected the way in which prospective employees would evaluate an offer from the "best" and the "worst" in each industry and, indeed, would also influence entry level employees' perceptions of which industries would be better employers and more stable organizations over the long term.

Just as organizations must be concerned with the "image" they project if they wish to attract good employees, organizations should also be concerned with the "balance of power" that exists within their own companies. Many human resource functions suffer from the perception within the company that they are a powerless repository of deadwood. This frequently leads to an inability to attract good people into the function, a fact which sets in motion a self-fulfilling prophecy in which the human resource issues cannot be well represented to senior management and the feeling that little can be done in this area when compared to marketing or finance. If organizations wish to address human resource issues, they must first endow the function with the necessary power and importance that will allow it to compete for talent with other functions in the organization. Each function, in turn, should be evaluated to ensure that it is helping the organization to formulate the proper strategy and to implement the strategy chosen by the organization.

PERFORMANCE APPRAISAL AS A DATA-GENERATING SYSTEM FOR STRATEGY FORMULATION

One of the principal impediments facing organizations who have accepted the need for feeding human resources information into the strategic planning process is the quality and the availability of these data. Although most organizations have good data on the type and availability of their financial assets and their product inventory, they have less complete data on their people. The problem is compounded by the fact that the tools available to analyze human resource data are primitive when compared to those developed and implemented by the financial accounting system in organizations.

A probable reason for this lag is that regulatory agencies have kept a sharp eye on the way in which organizations manage their money but they have only recently attempted to regulate the way in which organizations manage their people. Indeed, most organizations still have better internal audit and control mechanisms to ensure that financial assets are properly administered than they have to ensure that human resources are properly used.

In Chapter 2 we describe the extent to which organizations were collecting and using human resources data in the strategy formulation process in their companies. These data show that even in companies where some effort was made to collect human resource data it was not always used in the strategy formulation process. Yet, one could argue that any organization with a reasonably sophisticated performance appraisal system should be able to generate the information it needs in areas such as an inventory of the types and numbers of technical and managerial people they have, as well as their age distribution, to enable them to make better strategic decisions. The data generated by a good performance appraisal system would also give the organization a significant leg-up on putting an effective executive succession system into place, and, if the organization has a clear model of what information was important for current operations, they would know what data they should be collecting from the outside environment to make their external personnel studies useful tools in the strategic decision making process.

Thus once an organization decides that it can make better strategic decisions by including data on its human resources, its first priority is to decide what information is useful given its objectives. For example, companies that have long-range plans to diversify whether through acquisition or by starting up new ventures internally probably would make better decisions if they established guidelines about the types of skills they have in-house and the types of skills the new business requires. These data would then be analyzed in the context of some conceptual framework that the company uses to decide how "different" the skill mix in the new business can be and still be successfully integrated into the present organization.

By aggregating data collected for performance appraisal purposes, an organization can develop a profile of its existing skill mix. For example, if the organization finds that its strength lies in the area of research and development rather than in marketing, it is faced with two basic choices to make in the strategic arena. It can attempt to dominate its competition by being more innovative than they are or, if the company perceives that the technology in the industry is becoming more mature, it can begin to shift its hiring mix so that people with marketing skills are hired and developed internally. In 1983 many of the established companies in the personal computer field were forced into the latter strategy when IBM entered the market. Industry analysts are predicting a significant shakeout as some companies are unable to adapt.

PERFORMANCE APPRAISAL AS A DATA-GENERATING SYSTEM FOR STRATEGY IMPLEMENTATION

Chapter 6 presented the case for performance appraisal as a control mechanism and persuasively argued the merits of using behavioral criteria over trait-based systems. The basic advantage, in addition to the fact that it is legally more defensible, is that it measures results, whereas trait-based systems tend to evaluate style. Behavioral criteria, however, offer additional advantages in terms of their power to generate data to facilitate strategy implementation.

First, they enable organizations to identify what managers will have to do, specifically, if a strategy is to be successfully executed. In addition, behavioral data help organizations to identify changes in skill mix that will be required to effect long-range changes in strategic direction. Some oil companies, for example, have changed their basic hiring mix to include more business-trained personnel relative to the technically trained people they have traditionally hired. The reason for this shift in staffing strategy is that their long-range goals include plans for diversification out of their current business lines and their managers of the future will need to be trained differently than the managers who run the firms today. A corollary to shifts in staffing patterns is to alter the career-planning efforts made on behalf of key personnel.

Firms that are able to specify what the managers of the future will need to "do" will be able to more realistically plan for the future than those firms who try to pin down the more elusive notion of what the manager of the future should "be."

In the shorter term, organizations will be able to implement more effective development programs to support strategic change to the extent that they can identify what managers must do to make the necessary strategic changes. A behaviorally based performance appraisal system would not only be able to assess individual strengths and weaknesses, but would be able to identify areas of organizational weakness that could be eliminated with well-designed specific programs aimed at teaching current personnel the technical and process skills they need to make the implementation of the firm's new strategy more likely to happen.

PERFORMANCE APPRAISAL AS AN INTEGRATING DEVICE FOR THE HUMAN RESOURCE SYSTEM

Chapter 3 presented a model of the human resource system containing the generic activities: selection, appraisal, rewards, and development. It stressed the role that a valid appraisal plays in generating data for strategic selection and development; in the following, the basic role of performance appraisal as a centerpiece in the human resource cycle is addressed.

Beyond its function as a tool for monitoring knowledge and ability, the appraisal system can also help in motivating individual performance. Most organizations implicitly believe that people will be motivated to do their best so that they can obtain the rewards that the organization has to offer: promotion, challenge, the opportunity to learn, and pay. To make these motivators effective, the organization must be able to distinguish different levels of performance and reward them accordingly. Thus the performance appraisal system provides a rationale for making these critical organizational decisions. To the extent that employees perceive that performance drives the reward system, they will be motivated to do their best. To the extent that employees believe that the data generated by the performance appraisal system is faulty, that is, the performance appraisal system is perceived to be inequitable, the organization will not be able to drive performance through the use of rewards because the distribution system lacks credibility. This is obviously a problem throughout the organization, but, at the strategic level, it assumes a particularly critical role. To the extent that key managers are told that achievement of organizational goals is critical but they are held accountable for a set of criteria that are not consistent with this statement, they are most likely to deliver on what they are held accountable for, and, consequently, rewarded for. A common example of what happens in many firms is that managers are told that strategic planning and corporate goals are important but their appraisal and bonus or promotion depend upon how well they do with bottom-line performance in the current year. One is not surprised to learn that most of the manager's time goes to improving the bottom line frequently at the expense of long-term goals.

One company that has recognized this problem and taken steps to ensure that necessary managerial attention is paid to strategy formulation and implementation is Texas Instruments. Top-level management at TI is evaluated for how well they accomplish two goals. One goal is to ensure that TI remains competitive in the short term and managers are evaluated on how well they accomplish their efficiency or profitability objectives. The other goal involves working toward a strategic objective that may have a 10- or 20-year time horizon. There is a separate appraisal system to monitor how well they accomplish these objectives and a set portion of their bonus is tied to this separate system.

An interesting exercise that one can engage in is to read stories about successful implementation of corporate strategies. Invariably, one discovers that most successful organizations closely monitored the progress against the strategic goals and rewarded managers for their performance in this area. For example, the May 1982 issue of *Savvy* magazine listed 16 U.S. companies that had been successful in hiring and advancing women through their middle-management ranks. The people in those companies responsible for the affirmative action programs were asked how they had managed to achieve their success. Twelve of the sixteen offered as an explanation some variation on the theme that they had set goals and tied manager's compensation to achieving those goals.

One more critical observation about the role that appraisal plays in determining the behavior of key managers can be obtained by considering the plight of the U.S. auto industry. Much of the criticism of Detroit has implied that American automakers never took the threat of Japanese competition seriously until it was too late. Somehow, this seems simplistic. It is difficult to believe that a group of intelligent managers in three separate companies were able to insulate themselves so completely from trends in their own industry that they did not understand that they were losing market share to, first, European and, finally, to Japanese competition. A more likely explanation comes from an analysis of the criteria that were used to evaluate the managers in these companies. They were evaluated and given large bonuses for their contribution to the bottom line. Thus although they may have understood the importance of designing smaller, more fuel-efficient cars and retooling their plants to produce them if they were to compete with the Japanese, they were being pulled in quite another direction by the nature of the appraisal and reward systems in their companies. The managers were not being rewarded for what was best for the company in the long run—only for what they could bring to the bottom line in the short run. When conflict exists between what is best for the organization and what is best for the manager (as defined by the organization's reward systems), the organization can expect that organizational goals will suffer.

The ability of the organization to successfully select, develop, and reward depends to a significant extent on its ability to identify the proper characteristics or behaviors of managers, to evaluate performance based on these criteria, to provide developmental opportunities to correct weaknesses identified in this process, and, finally, to distribute its rewards based on performance differentials among its managers. In other words, a successful human resource system rests on a functioning performance appraisal system.

PROCESS ISSUES AFFECTING PERFORMANCE APPRAISAL

Up to this point both the Latham chapter and this chapter on performance appraisal discuss the technical problems that organizations face in establishing a performance appraisal system that will serve management as an effective tool for the formulation and implementation of business strategy. The balance of this chapter addresses the issues that an organization faces in the evaluation process that are nontechnical—the issues that tend to involve the allocation of power in the organization. Thus an important corollary to what gets evaluated in an organization is to decide who gets to do the evaluating.

In most organizations an individual is evaluated by his or her immediate supervisor. In many organizations there is no formal process to ensure that there will be no abuse of power in this transaction. Obviously, in some cases the employee perceives that an abuse of power has occurred and this results, in extreme cases, in legal action against the company in the form of sexual harassment charges or discrimination cases based on gender, race, or age.

In other cases it may go undetected but the organization still pays a price. Potentially valuable employees may leave the company if they feel they are not being fairly treated. Frequently, the organization will not even know they have lost an employee who can make a contribution since the appraisal data that exist on the individual are not accurate.

Some organizations have developed processes to deal with these issues. They have found ways to address the imbalance of power that implicitly exists between an evaluating superior and an evaluated subordinate. The principal strategies are described in the following.

Consensus Meetings

Exxon Corporation evaluates employees in the context of consensus meetings. In these meetings a group of employees doing similar work in the same location are evaluated as a group by their superiors. As the name of these meetings implies, the group must come to agreement as to the relative position of each of the employees when compared to others in the group. The strength of the system is twofold: a manager feels constrained by the group to present a balanced view of the employee, and the manager tends to devote quality time to the evaluation process since he or she will be evaluated, in turn, by peers and their superior as to the thoroughness and accuracy of their evaluations. Since personnel are frequently rotated at Exxon, knowledge abut individuals tends to be better disseminated than it might be in other organizations and this system seems to work reasonably well.

Appeals Process

IBM addresses the issue of the lack of balance between the employee and the manager by using a formal appeal process. Any employee who feels that he or she has been unfairly treated or evaluated can make an appeal to the office of the president. Within 48 hours someone is dispatched from another site to investigate the validity of the employee's charge of unfair treatment. The employee receives the benefit of any doubt that may exist in the case. IBM also tracks the progress of the employees that have lodged a complaint to ensure that there is no significant difference in their subsequent rate of progress when compared to a comparable group of employees who have made no complaints.

Peer Review

Research has shown that peer appraisals were more accurate than those made by superiors in predicting success among graduating classes of Air Force fighter pilots. Few companies, however, use peer review as an exclusive method of appraising performance. Some companies, such as General Electric, include data collected from peers and subordinates in evaluating their top management group. There is sufficient data to indicate that the accuracy of the review process could be enhanced with the use of peer review. There is little doubt that the use of this system increases the perception on the part of employees that the system is equitable and this alone may be a justification for considering its use.

Consensus meetings, an appeal process, and peer review are organizational design solutions to deal with the imbalance of power that exists between the employee being evaluated and the supervisor doing the evaluating. They establish checks and balances in this most sensitive area. There is another area where the organization might also consider a system of checks and balances. That is in the power distribution between corporate and business units.

Much of the determination of where an employee's loyalty will be driven will rest with who controls their access to organizational rewards. Thus if the line managers in the business units appraise the performance of key staff people such as controllers and human resource managers, they may be pressured to serve the line at the expense of corporate policy. Although this may not be a problem during periods of relative stability, it may make it relatively more difficult to drive change through the organization if the line organization is resisting corporate policy changes. On the other hand, if a corporate functional boss is responsible for the performance appraisal of functional subordinates, line managers may find they have little leverage in obtaining needed adaptation of corporate policy to their special business needs.

Exxon has addressed this problem by allowing the line managers to evaluate the functional managers who report to them, but they leave the career progression and rotation power in the hands of the functional superior. This, obviously, is a system that recognizes the dual reporting relationship inherent in a matrix structure and is an effective way of balancing the power between the subsidiaries and corporate headquarters. This matching of structural requirements and performance appraisal system is at the heart of the centralization–decentralization cycle that an organization may go through. It is important to match the human resource systems to the strategic objectives along with the structural adaptations.

SUCCESSION ISSUES AND PERFORMANCE APPRAISAL

Organizations with well-developed executive succession systems are frequently confronted with the reality that they have more qualified candidates for the top positions in the company than they can promote. They will, therefore, need to manage the political processes that attend the allocation of scarce resources among qualified people. In these cases a well-defined strategic plan is a prerequisite to making the proper choice since the chief executive and his or her management team will be responsible for leading the company through the next decade or so. In turbulent times it is hard to imagine that the characteristics required will be the same as the ones needed for the previous decade.

The challenge for organizations faced with this scenario is to put together the best management team and to minimize the loss of talent to the organization when the choice has been made.

In companies where succession planning is not an integral part of the strategic management process of the firm, organizations are faced with a different problem. Rather than dealing with the issues attendant on having an excess of talent, they are faced with crisis situations in which there is uncertainty around succession. This uncertainty frequently causes a vacuum in the decision-making apparatus and lessens the energy of those who do the planning since they have no clear knowledge of who will be at the helm and what preferences that person is likely to exercise in the strategic arena.

CONCLUSION

Performance appraisal is the cornerstone of an effective human resource system. It provides the information needed to make fully informed strategic decisions by assessing the fit between current human resource systems and those systems required by a change in strategic direction. It also serves as a control system to measure performance against strategic objectives once they have been set.

In addition to the technical issues involved with effective performance appraisal the organization must also be concerned with the process of appraisal. Particular attention needs to be paid to the issue of ensuring equity by providing systems of checks and balances to offset the imbalance of power that exists between evaluator and evaluated. Organizations should also understand that they can move the organization on the centralized–decentralized continuum by redistributing the power to appraise the performance of key staff personnel.

Finally, the politics that attend appraisal-related issues such as managerial succession are critical processes that must be managed in effective organizations. To fail to do so impinges on the ability of the organization to continue to plan for its future because it adds a dimension of internal uncertainty to the environmental issues that the organization must face.

CHAPTER

8

PERFORMANCE APPRAISAL PRACTICES IN THE *FORTUNE* 1300

Robert L. Laud

Perhaps the weakest link in the human resource cycle is that of evaluating and controlling individual performance and behavior while providing an adequate supply of talent at all organizational levels on a continual basis.

In order to determine how the leading-edge practitioners in performance appraisal have reacted to environmental trends in the design of their appraisal systems, a survey of appraisal policies and practices was conducted. This chapter reports on the results gathered from a sample of firms in the *Fortune* 1000 industrials and the *Fortune* 300 nonindustrial companies.

Respondents represented all major industries including oil, food, textiles, publishing, chemicals, metal products, electronics, aerospace, pharmaceuticals, paper products, and communications. Additionally, the *Fortune* 300 sample included responses from the major nonindustrial categories: banking, life insurance, diversified financial, retailing, transportation, and utilities.

Two hundred sixty-seven questionnaires were returned for a 20% response rate. The functional area, job level, and number of respondents are presented in Table 8.1.

111

TABLE 8.1.   Number of Respondents by Level and Function.[a]

	Function			
Level	Human Resources/ Personnel	Compensation and Benefits	Management Development Training/Org. Development	Employee Industrial Relations
Vice president	17	3	—	1
Director	40	14	32	6
Manager	42	20	39	8
Supervisor	5	9	7	5
Specialist/analyst	3	2	7	—
Representative	—	—	—	3
Administration	—	—	—	4

[a]$N = 267$.

The purpose of the study was to explore the following areas.

1. *General Features of Appraisal Systems.*   An analysis of the most prevalent appraisal design by job level. In addition, attention is given to methodologies for documentation. Lastly, the legal aspects that control or influence appraisal systems are discussed.

2. *Appraisal System Link to Goals and Strategy.*   The multiple goals and uses of appraisal systems including their most current implications in strategic planning are explored.

3. *Appraisal System Link to Compensation.*   The most critical uses of appraisal systems and their use in alternative compensation methods.

4. *Appraisal System Link to Career Planning.*   The sensitivity of appraisal systems in providing meaningful career guidance to employees.

5. *Appraisal Link to Training.*   The implications of appraisal for training and improving performance.

The general responses to these five issues are discussed later.

GENERAL FEATURES OF APPRAISAL SYSTEMS

In the design of performance appraisal systems, several factors should be considered. Of primary concern is clarity of purpose. Will the system be used basically to measure performance behavior, improve performance behavior, give rewards, increase communications, identify managerial talent, isolate training needs, provide data for a human resource inventory, or improve communication?

A good place to begin the process of selecting appraisal system goals is in defining the corporate or business mission. Ambiguous understanding of the mission or corporate goals causes difficulty for workers in relating to the significance of their particular functions. Explanations of the how, what, and why of jobs as they relate to the total entity contributes to defining appropriate workplace behaviors.[1] Feedback on behavior then becomes the link between the specific job goals and the corporate mission.

In this study respondents suggest that the design of most systems is accomplished through the corporate or divisional personnel department, with some complex systems requiring the input of external consultants. Besides industrial engineers and personnel specialists, employees might also be included in the design of appraisal systems. This would help not only in developing more accurate and meaningful work standards, but would greatly contribute to a sense of acceptance, ownership, and commitment on the part of the employee.

Table 8.2 describes a variety of performance appraisal approaches. Companies varied widely in their use of these systems. Table 8.3 breaks down the nature of the systems by job level.

TABLE 8.2.   Definitions of Performance Appraisal Approaches.

Graphic rating scales	Assessing performance on line representing the range of a trait or job dimensions
Behaviorally anchored ratings	Assessing performance on a scale anchored to specific descriptions of work behavior
Work standards approach	Comparing actual performance against expected levels of performance
Essay	Writing a commentary discussing an individual's strengths, weaknesses, etc.
MBO	Setting future objectives and action plans jointly between subordinate and supervisor and then measuring outcome against goals
Objectives-based	Setting future objectives (without action plans) jointly between subordinate and supervisor and then measuring outcome against goals

Hourly and Nonexempt Appraisal Systems

An interesting finding of the study was that 29% of the hourly workers surveyed do not have a performance appraisal system. This result coupled with the productivity concerns of some organizations may reflect a need to consider the benefits of a formal performance appraisal system to enhance

[1] Chapter 6 discusses the link between strategy and the appraisal system and the importance of defining behaviorally the implications of the business plan.

TABLE 8.3. Rank Order of Performance Appraisal System Design by Job Level.[a]

Rank	Hourly (N = 160)	%		Nonexempt (N = 37)	%
1	No system	29		Work standards	33
2	Work standards	29		Essay	30
3	Graphic rating	23		Behaviorally anchored	28
4	Essay	14		Graphic rating	26
5	Behaviorally anchored	14		Objectives based	19

Rank	Exempt (N = 247)	%		Professional (Nonmanagerial) (N = 234)	%
1	Objectives based	39		Objectives based	39
2	Essay	36		MBO	36
3	MBO	34		Essay	36
4	Work standards	32		Work standards	33
5	Behaviorally anchored	24		Behaviorally anchored	24

Rank	Supervisory (N = 235)	%		Middle Management (N = 238)	%
1	Objectives based	38		MBO	44
2	MBO	37		Objectives based	42
3	Essay	36		Essay	37
4	Work standards	32		Work standards	27
5	Behaviorally anchored	25		Behaviorally anchored	24

Rank	Top Management (N = 217)	%
1	MBO	43
2	Objectives-based	39
3	Essay	33
4	Work standards	24
5	Behaviorally anchored	18

[a] Multiple responses to some questions result in percentages greater than 100.

114

internal communications and foster a more positive work environment in efforts to improve productivity. However, the reader should be aware that appraisal systems at this level may seriously conflict with union or contract arrangements that prevent discrimination between high and low performers.

Respondents indicate that only 14% of the hourly workers used behaviorally anchored rating scales. This percentage may be expected to increase as the evolving service economy gains momentum and more explicit behavioral indicators become important. Presently, the small percentage may be accounted for by the relative difficulty and expense of behaviorally anchored systems in comparison to alternative methods.

Although hourly and nonexempt workers may have similar or even identical jobs, they are treated very differently. A work standards approach dominates the nonexempt level (33%). In addition, this job level makes the most extensive use of behaviorally anchored ratings (BARS). A problem with the use of BARS at higher levels is the difficulty of breaking down complex tasks into meaningful and measurable component parts. The number of behaviors associated with broad goals in upper-level positions makes difficult an effective BARS approach. A good method to decide whether BARS is generally appropriate would be to acknowledge whether a minimum and maximum threshold of behavior is observable. If the behavior cannot be easily identified or described, as may be the case in many senior-level positions, alternate approaches should be investigated. The advantage of using BARS for nonexempt positions lies in the descriptive statements regarding more easily observed behavior. Additionally, if an equal interval scale is used, ratings will help to align more closely performance with compensation. Lastly, the descriptive statements feed back and pinpoint to the employee specifically which job behaviors are commendable and which ones need improvement. In summary, given that hourly and nonexempt jobs may be very similar, it seems reasonable that hourly systems should almost mirror nonexempt systems.

Exempt, Supervisory, and Professional Appraisal Systems

Table 8.3 suggests that objectives-based and MBO systems are collectively the most widely accepted appraisal system for these job levels. Some aspects of participative management seem apparently well entrenched, though not universal. Objectives-based and MBO systems both require joint inputs from the subordinate and manager in the goal-setting process.[2] This procedure has certain major benefits. First, it provides a stage for identifying the general goals of the work unit. This aids in establishing specific individual goals and in soliciting help for potential problem situations. Second, when the subordinates help develop and define their own goals, the organization creates a situation of involvement leading to individual and perhaps organizational

[2]See Locke and Latham (1983) for an elaboration of goal-setting as a tool for performance appraisal.

commitment. Thus the appraisal process ties into issues of loyalty, personal growth, and responsibility for actions. The workplace, as a social entity, has the potential to contribute to the psychological well-being of many of its members.

Middle and Top-Management Appraisal Systems

Somewhat similar to the exempt levels discussed, middle and top-management appraisal systems are predominantly MBO and objectives-based. Yet, unlike the ranking for the exempt levels, respondents have ranked MBO systems above objectives-based for senior-level positions. Even in view of the wide criticism that MBO or its generically related offshoot systems have received, apparently it has strengths that keep alternative systems at bay when it comes to upper-management levels.

In particular, the MBO concept remains theoretically sound. It is built on the psychological principle of active participation leading to commitment. From an applied perspective, it requires the integration of individual goals with corporate goals for a unity of purpose. Why then was it so widely criticized and what accounts for its resurgence?

To begin with, MBO systems are not geared for all levels within organizations. MBO systems assume some degree of career orientation and organizational commitment.

A second problem that managers have encountered with MBO systems is the identification of meaningful and measureable goals and objectives. Most managers are not well trained in the variety of skills needed for successful MBO implementation; that is, how to establish mutual goals, how to document work behavior, how to give feedback, how to job coach, and how to conduct the appraisal interview. MBO systems can be time-consuming, especially during the training and implementation stages.

Another aspect of pure MBO systems is that the goals and objectives are individually tailored. This often makes assessing and comparing employees for promotion, training, or compensation difficult since evaluations are based on different criteria. Some companies have ameliorated the difficulties encountered with zero-sum personnel decisions by marrying an MBO approach with some rating scale methodology so that employees are more accurately compared.

Despite the many shortcomings of MBO systems, Table 8.3 demonstrates that they certainly have survived and many MBO systems receive accolades from the practicing organizations. Managers report that although start-up time is consuming, once in place, an MBO approach becomes a shared responsibility between the supervisor and subordinate. The supervisor then actually spends less time in setting goals and less time in providing direction to subordinates since action plans have already been approved.

An important distinction between MBO and objectives-based systems is that the MBO approach requires written action plans. This apparently minor difference may account for its greater popularity in view of today's concern with quality and productivity. Action plans help direct the employee and decrease the amount of risk in accomplishing goals. Management then has a futher check on work methods which helps to minimize suboptimization (i.e., reduce conflict arising from the attainment of individual goals at the expense of organizational goals). It is not surprising that with increases in the degree of managerial accountability it would behoove managers to closely review employee action plans to help ensure goal attainment. Moreover, as corporations direct themselves towards a long-term growth orientation, the development of action plans will help managers monitor not just results, but the tradeoffs in work methods.

Who Conducts the Appraisal

When comparing data across levels, respondents indicate that the most popular method (96%) of appraisal review was evaluation by the immediate supervisor (see Table 8.4). Some companies indicated additional procedures such as peer review, but the reported use of these alternative methods was insignificant. Upward reviews were also insignificant and, for the most part, were voluntary. The small incidence of these may be due to the perceived threats for both the subordinate and the supervisor.

Legal Issues

The Equal Employment Opportunity Commission (EEOC) is responsible for interpreting and enforcing the Civil Rights Act of 1964 which guides corporations against any and all personnel practices that may be considered discriminatory with regard to race, religion, sex, color, or national origin. As mentioned earlier, the government will most likely continue to increase its authority in the corporate sector. The EEOC, being aware of inherent biases in some personnel areas, issued the *Uniform Guidelines on Employee Selection Procedures (1978)*. Given that performance appraisal is considered a selection procedure it was anticipated that most companies would have considered

TABLE 8.4.   **Rank Order of Methods of Completing Performance Appraisal Documents with Job Levels Collapsed.**[a]

Rank	Method	% (All Levels)
1	Immediate supervisor evaluates employee	96
2	Next higher level supervisor reviews document	77
3	Personnel representative reviews document	55
4	Employee evaluates self	24

[a] *N*s range from 121 to 245.

government guidelines in appraisal design. Surprisingly, less than one-half of the companies surveyed indicated that the guidelines were considered (see Table 8.5). Since one would expect that similar criteria would be used for initial selection and appraisal, it would be of interest for future research to determine how companies align these two areas. The rather small percentage of companies (44%) who did consider the guidelines may be indicative of the extensive costs, time, and difficulty of legally measuring and monitoring work behaviors. Companies indicate that when lawsuits did occur (see Table 8.6), they most often involved reliability, validity, and biased ratings.

APPRAISAL LINK TO GOALS AND STRATEGY

Strategically, the appraisal system could be used to promote a variety of goals. For instance, appraisal systems could drive employees towards increasing productivity, identify fast-trackers, punish poor work behavior, or create a psychological work union, while at the same time provide information to other human resource systems by systematically compiling data. The increased popularity of computer-based HR information systems is a case in point. Many companies are concerned with building a link between the performance appraisal system and the other human resource systems such as recruitment, compensation, career planning, and training.

As indicated in Table 8.7, appraisal systems are used by over 80% of the respondent companies for merit increases, performance feedback, and promotion. However, less than 65% of the respondents report using appraisals for termination or layoffs, evaluating potential, succession planning, or career planning. These are all key links to corporate planning and long-term growth. Unfortunately, the functions have traditionally ranked behind the day-to-day operations reflecting a short-term profit orientation. Increased efforts to strengthen the link between appraisals and human resource planning areas would contribute to the overall success of corporate strategic planning. Table 8.8 reports the effectiveness of the appraisal systems in the pursuit of various goals. On average, respondents rated six out of seven goals as less than effective. Surprisingly, one of the most critical goals for the 1980s (i.e., improve productivity) was ranked extremely effective by only 1% of the respondents in comparison to 41% who ranked it as somewhat effective or of

TABLE 8.5. Rank Order of Consideration of Government Guidelines in Performance Appraisal Design.[a]

Rank	Response	%
1	Yes	44
2	No	32
3	Uncertain	25

[a] $N = 248$.

TABLE 8.6.   Rank Order of Features Discussed in Lawsuits Involving Performance Appraisal Systems.[a]

Rank	Problem Area	%
1	Validity or reliability	44
2	Job-relatedness	44
3	Biased rating	41
4	Standardization	25
5	Other	19

[a] $N = 32$.

limited effectiveness. Again, 41% of the respondents ranked "provide an objective measure of performance" as somewhat effective or of limited effectiveness. The only goal rated above average in effectiveness was "detect and feedback actual performance," as indicated by 36% of the respondents who rated it as very or extremely effective. As Table 8.8 suggests in terms of pursuing performance appraisal goals for the company, most systems are greatly underutilized. It is startling that item g "Furnish information for other human resource systems," was indicated as not a goal for 17% of the respondents. A reevaluation of the informational links between human resource systems (selection, training, career planning, and rewards) is needed by these companies for reasons of efficiency, productivity, and probably legality. Supplying information to other human resource functions should not be a pro forma activity, but a central concern.

The study also determined that slightly more than three-quarters of the surveyed companies have enhanced strategic planning through appraisal prac-

TABLE 8.7.   Rank Order of Uses of Performance Appraisal Systems.[a]

Rank	Area	%
1	Merit increases	91
2	Performance results/feedback/job counseling	90
3	Promotion	82
4	Termination or layoff	64
5	Performance potential	62
6	Succession planning	57
7	Career planning	52
8	Transfer	50
9	Personnel planning	38
10	Bonuses	32
11	Development and evaluation of training programs	29
12	Internal communication	25
13	Criteria for selection procedure validation	16
14	Expense control	7

[a] $N = 256$.

TABLE 8.8.   Relative Effectiveness of the Performance Appraisal System in Attaining Various Goals (%).[a]

Possible Goals	Extremely Effective	Very Effective	Effective	Somewhat Effective	Limited Effectiveness	Not a Goal
a. Improve productivity	1	9	41	29	12	8
b. Promote internal control	3	18	31	26	8	14
c. Create a positive work environment	3	15	37	30	10	6
d. Stimulate and recognize achievement	4	25	40	25	4	2
e. Detect and feed back actual performance	8	28	32	26	3	2
f. Provide an objective measure of performance	3	21	32	33	8	3
g. Furnish information for other human resource systems	5	14	26	21	17	17
h. Overall, how do you think your system compares to that of other companies?	7	32	38	18	5	0

[a]$N = 241$.

tices focusing on senior management level goals. Table 8.9 lists four major appraisal uses specifically structured for strategic planning: job-matching or selection, rewards, identifying potential, and development programs. It is impressive that over 75% of the respondents show an awareness of these critical strategic activities. However, even with this awareness of these critical uses, the extent to which they have been used was indicated as less than moderate. As noted in Table 8.9, item a, "matching senior executives to long-range strategic plans," was a goal of 75% of the respondents, but was rated as not extensively used by 54% of the respondents. It suggests that strategic support of long-range goals is deficient.[3] Consistent with this finding is a less than moderate use of the appraisal system for identifying personnel for potential in carrying out strategic plans.

[3]See Chapter 2 for a discussion of data from a survey of the *Fortune* 500 industrials on issues of strategic selection and development.

TABLE 8.9.   Relative Use of Performance Appraisal in Strategic Planning (%).[a]

Possible Goals	Yes	Great Extent 5	4	Moderate 3	2	No Extent 1	Not a Goal
a. Matching senior executives to long-range strategic plans	75	6	15	18	15	21	25
b. Identifying personnel for their future potential in carrying out strategic goals	82	6	19	27	18	12	18
c. Designing the reward system to drive managers to long-range strategic planning as opposed to short-range	76	2	11	17	23	22	24
d. Designing development programs to support stategic objectives	79	3	17	24	16	19	21

[a]$N = 237$.

With regard to reward systems, Table 8.9 indicates that 46% of the respondents show less than moderate use of the appraisal system to drive managers toward long-term goals. This is not entirely surprising considering the difficulty of evaluating long-term outcomes, but it certainly suggests an area for major improvement in the design of certain reward systems. Some organizations have made attempts to correct this situation through the adoption of highly specialized long-term incentive programs including stock options, stock appreciation rights, restricted stock, or long-term cash.[4]

A last area of improvement, as reported in Table 8.9, is in the design of development programs to support strategic objectives. It is essential that selected individuals or groups of individuals within corporations receive the proper training to expeditiously and effectively replace executives who leave key strategic positions. Some major U.S. corporations have implemented elaborate selection and training procedures expressly for the purpose of maintaining a competitive edge (Tichy et al., 1982).

[4]In Chapter 9, Edward E. Lawler discusses some of the central dimensions in the design of reward systems.

APPRAISAL SYSTEM LINK TO COMPENSATION

Attracting and retaining talented personnel is a critical function of every competitive corporation. For this reason, corporations expend large sums of money in advertising, search or agency costs, and training and development costs. The establishment of a healthy workforce where members actively contribute to growth and profitability is a complex process involving a delicate relationship between desired work behaviors and anticipated rewards. The performance appraisal system is a necessary link that clarifies and measures performance and links outcomes to rewards.

Although there exist considerable conjecture and controversy surrounding the extent to which compensation influences worker motivation, it does remain an extremely effective tool in influencing behavior.[5] Its influence, however, is dependent upon several factors. To begin, workers must understand that particular forms of work behavior are tied to financial rewards. If rewards are not tied to performance, performance would be solely dependent upon internal worker motivation, an unreliable control system at best.

In order to design the most effective managerial link between performance and rewards it is necessary to return to the concept of a valid and reliable appraisal system. First, both the manager and the employee must have the same working definition of the job requirements, expected outcomes, and understanding of the criteria against which outcomes will be measured. Second, both parties must accept or modify the measurement criteria so that they become valid and reliable, that is, meaningful and consistent. Third, all employees who perform similar tasks should be rewarded in similar fashion such that any tendencies towards any form of discrimination are removed. A specific and clear understanding of this helps employees recognize and work towards those behaviors that realistically lead to rewards. It is also possible to relate particular work behaviors to different compensation components in efforts to drive employees toward specific goals. This is a relatively common procedure in the design of many jobs and as described in Table 8.10, a variety of methods exists.

The appraisal process then serves as a method for discriminating between high and low performers and the compensation link provides a logical way of distributing rewards. In Table 8.10 the most popular use of appraisal systems in compensation is as general guidelines for salary increases (89%). This method is based on specific pay grades which usually have a minimum and maximum and several interval levels. Increases are normally contingent upon the individual's place in the pay range, seniority, or performance. The advantage of this general guideline approach is that it provides leeway for the consideration of a wide range of specific individual contributions during the evaluation process.

A rather different approach is that of a forced distribution or matrix for

---

[5] See Chapter 9.

TABLE 8.10.   Rank Order of Compensation Relationships with Performance Appraisal Systems.[a]

Rank	Method	%
1	General guidelines for salary increases	88
2	Must be completed for compensation action	48
3	General guidelines for bonuses	20
4	No relationship specified for bonuses	17
5	Forced distribution for salary increases	13
6	No relationship specified for salary increases	12
7	Other fixed formula for salary	11
8	Other fixed formula for bonuses	10
9	Other	4
10	Forced distribution for bonuses	1

[a] $N = 254$.

salary increases as reported by 13% of the respondents. Although not a widely used method, its proponents note some distinct advantages. Forced distribution systems limit the amount of the compensation increase by the performance rating which is ranked on a continuum. The continuum is usually designed so that few workers fall in the top and bottom distributions and the majority fall in the middle. The design of the distribution is normally reflective of management's ultimate goal. Some systems are designed basically to rank-order performance of all workers and reward accordingly. Other management philosophies will use a forced-distribution method to conduct yearly terminations of the lowest ranked workers. This method encourages the workforce to remain competitive while constantly infusing new blood into the organization. Unfortunately, this system can undermine the potential to create a sense of company loyalty and appears to reward individual performance more than contributory efforts in team or group project work. Regardless of the compensation method chosen, it becomes clear that appraisals are necessary in linking performance to rewards and that compensation serves as a strong influence on behavior.

APPRAISAL LINK TO CAREER PLANNING

Successful career planning is dependent upon the integration and unity of individual goals and organizational goals. If the congruency is high, the individual will work towards helping the organization obtain its goals and the organization, in turn, will aid the individual in obtaining his or her goals. Individual career planning should focus upon career stages which are generally characterized by changing patterns of developmental task, activities, values, and needs that emerge as one passes through various age ranges. Central to this developmental approach is a concept of directional maturation through a series of life stages. The identification of these stages is critical in determining the career-pathing for each individual with his or her own unique personal and corporate experience.

It is advantageous for the organization to understand the developmental needs of the individual in order to work towards a supportive environment. In doing so the psychological health of the individual is enhanced which often lessens tendencies toward dysfunctional activities such as turnover, accidents, damage, dissatisfaction, and frustration.

It is encouraging, nonetheless, to find that over one-half of the sampled firms are already active in assisting employees with career planning (see Table 8.7). These organizations are linking the appraisal system to career planning through a formal documentation of individual goals, likely career options, and timing decisions (see Table 8.11). The joint communication and supervisory feedback during the appraisal interview set the stage for a discussion of long-term career moves. Although closely linked, many organizations conduct the career discussion at a point in time removed from the appraisal interview to minimize potentially conflicting interests.

APPRAISAL LINK TO TRAINING

The identification of training needs is an obvious outcome of that segment of the appraisal process which focuses on current and sometimes future employee improvement areas. It is important in the development of training programs that the appraisal process isolate reasons for performance deficiencies. Not all improvement areas will be positively affected by training. If the knowledge/skills area is identified as the case of a weak performance, it is possible to design training programs to provide the employees with the needed information. However, fit or compatibility with the organizational environment is more closely related to psychological factors. Training programs will probably have little effect in changing attitudes, but some behavior modification is possible in more sophisticated training designs. If poor performance is attributed to low aptitude, additional training may have only a marginal

TABLE 8.11.   Rank Order of Career Planning Components of Performance Appraisal Systems.[a]

Rank	Feature	%
1	Reference to strengths and weaknesses	58
2	Written development plan	45
3	Identification of future career options	39
4	Not a component	32
5	Timing for movement specified	22

[a] $N = 177$.

effect. A more suitable managerial approach would be the consideration of transfer to a position where the employee's skills level more closely matches the requirements of the job. Lastly, if motivation is determined to be the causal factor in a poor performance review, additional training will probably only be of value in the following ways. First, the actual program itself may serve as a stimulus in terms of recognition or support. However, this will most likely have only short-term impact. Second, training could affect motivation if the underlying cause for the poor performance review was actually lack of information or knowledge which caused frustration or dissatisfaction. Apart from these examples, many motivational problems may require managerial considerations of job redesign, increased control, or clarification of the important linkages between jobs.

In summary, performance appraisal systems serve as a means to identify improvement areas and then as a link to measure the effectiveness of training programs. When asked how they regarded the effectiveness of their training in appraising performance, some 45% of the respondents rated their training in appraisal practices as relatively ineffective and 10% said they had no training at all (see Table 8.12). Considering the profound impact of performance appraisal on other parts of the organization, substantial improvement is necessary in the specific appraisal process the organization uses.

CONCLUSION

Faced with the conflict between decreasing productivity and a disenchanted labor market, what opportunities does management have to rebuild a healthy work environment? One solution lies in the ability of management to control work behavior to satisfy individual goals. The concept of performance appraisal as a viable methodology seems extensively accepted by the *Fortune* 1300 as the survey results reported in this discussion demonstrate.

TABLE 8.12.   Performance Appraisal Training Effectiveness (%).[a]

	Extremely Effective	Very Effective	Effective	Somewhat Effective	Limited Effectiveness	No Training
Training Effectiveness	4	16	35	27	8	10

[a]$N = 241$.

Basic management thought regarding assumptions of human behavior have encouraged the design of systems focusing on mutual goal setting, accountability, awareness of contributions, and self-reliance. The question then should be not whether to implement an appraisal system, but to what extent the system should be participative and collaborative in instilling feelings of accountability and significance. In addition, what type of organizational climate does top management wish to create? And what functional appraisal design is best suited to the nature of the work?

As organizations come to face increased legal concerns, especially those surrounding selection and appraisal, they have the opportunity to design and implement systems that more fully meet functional and market demands.

Performance appraisal is perhaps management's most powerful tool in controlling human resources and productivity. Used effectively, appraisal systems have tremendous strategic potential for governing employee behavior and, in turn, corporate direction through the appraisal system's dynamic links to selection systems, training, career-planning systems, and reward structures.

CHAPTER

9

THE STRATEGIC DESIGN OF REWARD SYSTEMS

Edward E. Lawler III

Reward systems are one of the most prominent and frequently discussed features of organizations. Indeed, the literature on organizational behavior and personnel management is replete with examples of their functional as well as their dysfunctional role in organizations (Whyte, 1955). All too often, however, a thorough discussion of how they can be a key strategic factor in organizations is missing. The underlying assumption in this chapter is that, when properly designed, the reward systems of an organization can be a key contributor to the effectiveness of the organization. However, for this to occur, careful analysis needs to be made of the role that reward systems can and should play in the strategic plan of the organization.

OBJECTIVES OF REWARD SYSTEMS

The first step in discussing the strategic role of reward systems is to consider what behavioral impact they can have in organizations. That is, we need to

This chapter is based in part on "Reward Systems in Organizations," a chapter published in Lorsch (1983). Partial support of this work was provided by the office of Naval Research under Contract 53 N00014-81-k-0048; NR 170-923.

first address the outcomes that one can reasonably expect an effective reward system to produce. The research so far on reward systems suggests that potentially they can influence the following factors which, in turn, influence organizational effectiveness.

1. *Attraction and Retention.* Research on job choice, career choice, and turnover clearly shows that the kind and level of rewards an organization offers influences who is attracted to work for an organization and who will continue to work for it (Mobley, 1982). Overall, those organizations that give the most rewards tend to attract and retain the most people. Research also shows that better performers need to be rewarded more highly than poorer performers in order to be attracted and retained. Finally, the way rewards are administered and distributed influences who is attracted and retained. For example, better performing individuals are often attracted by merit-based reward systems.

2. *Motivation.* Those rewards that are important to individuals can influence their motivation to perform in particular ways. People in work organizations tend to behave in whatever way they perceive leads to rewards they value (Lawler, 1973; Vroom, 1964). Thus an organization that is able to tie valued rewards to the behaviors it needs to succeed is likely to find that the reward system is a positive contributor to its effectiveness.

3. *Culture.* Reward systems are one feature of organizations that contribute to their overall culture or climate. Depending upon how reward systems are developed, administered, and managed, they can cause the culture of an organization to vary quite widely. For example, they can influence the degree to which it is seen as a human resource-oriented culture, an entreprenurial culture, an innovative culture, a competence-based culture, and a participative culture.

4. *Reinforce and Define Structure.* The reward system of an organization can reinforce and define the organization's structure. Often this feature of reward systems is not fully considered in the design of reward systems. As a result, their impact on the structure of an organization is unintentional. This does not mean, however, that the impact of the reward system on structure is usually minimal. Indeed, it can help define the status hierarchy, the degree to which people in technical positions can influence people in line management positions, and it can strongly influence the kind of decision structure that exists. The key features here seem to be the degree to which the reward system is strongly hierarchical and the degree to which it allocates rewards on the basis of movements up the hierarchy.

5. *Cost.* Reward systems are often a significant cost factor. Indeed, the pay system alone may represent over 50% of the organization's operating cost. Thus it is important in strategically designing the reward system to focus on how high these costs should be and how they will vary as a function of the organization's ability to pay. For example, a reasonable outcome of a well-designed pay system might be an increased cost when the organization has

the money to spend and a decreased cost when the organization does not have the money. An additional objective might be to have lower overall reward system costs than business competitors.

In summary, reward systems in organizations should be looked at from a cost–benefit perspective. The cost can be managed and controlled and the benefits planned for. The key is to identify the outcomes needed in order for the organization to be successful and then to design the reward system in a way that these outcomes will, in fact, be realized.

RELATIONSHIP TO STRATEGIC PLANNING

Figure 9.1 presents a way of viewing the relationship between strategic planning and reward systems. It suggests that once the strategic plan is developed, the organization needs to focus on the kind of human resources, climate, and behavior that is needed in order to make it effective. The next step is to design reward systems that will motivate the right kind of performance, attract the right kind of people, and create a supportive climate and structure.

Figure 9.2 suggests another way in which the reward system needs to be taken into consideration in the area of strategic planning. It suggests that before the strategic plan is developed in an existing organization, it is important to assess a number of things including the current reward systems and to determine the kind of behavior, climate, and structure of which they are supportive. This step is needed so that when the strategic plan is developed it is based on a realistic assessment of the current condition of the organization and the changes likely to be needed to implement the new strategic plan. This point is particularly pertinent to organizations that are considering going into new lines of business, developing new strategic plans, and acquiring new divisions.

Often the new lines of business require a different behavior and, therefore, a different reward system. Simply putting the old reward system in place in

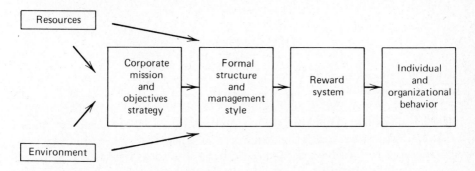

FIGURE 9–1 Reward and Strategy Implementation

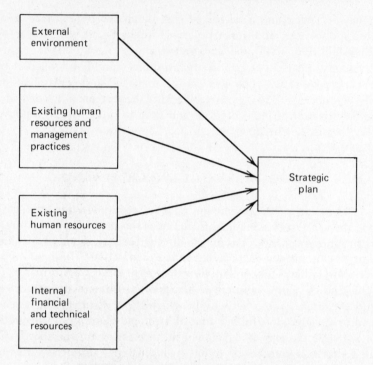

FIGURE 9–2   Constraints on Strategy Formulation

the new business is often not good enough and, indeed, can lead to failure in the new business. On the other hand, developing a new reward system for the new business can cause problems in the old business because of the type of comparisons that are made between different parts of the same organization. This is not to say that organizations should avoid venturing into new businesses, it is merely to say that a careful assessment of kinds of reward system changes that are needed should take place before organizations enter into new business sectors.

DESIGN OPTIONS

There are almost an infinite number of ways to design and manage reward systems in organizations. This is because there are a host of rewards that can be given and, of course, a large number of ways that they can be distributed. The focus in the remainder of this chapter is on the visible extrinsic rewards that an organization controls and that can as a matter of policy and practice be allocated to members on a specific basis. Included are pay, promotion, status symbols, and perquisites; little attention is given to such intrinsic rewards as feelings of responsibility, competence, and personal growth and development.

A useful dichotomy in thinking about options in the design of reward systems is the process or content one. All organizational systems have a content or structural dimension as well as a process dimension. The structural or content dimension of a reward system refers to the formal mechanisms, procedures, and practices (e.g., the salary structures, the performance appraisal forms), in short, the nuts and bolts of the system. The process side refers to the communication and decision process parts of the system. A key issue here involves the degree of openness with respect to information about how the reward system operates and how people are rewarded. A second issue is the degree of participation that is allowed in the design of the reward system and the ongoing administration of it. Many organizations, without ever choosing to, administer rewards in a top-down secretive way. As is discussed further, this is not the only way that rewards can be administered. The discussion of design choices begins by looking at some key structural choices and then turns to a consideration of some key process choices.

STRUCTURAL DECISIONS

Basis for Rewards

Traditionally, in organizations such rewards as pay and perquisites are based on the type of jobs that people do. Indeed, with the exception of bonuses and merit salary increases, the standard policy in most organizations is to evaluate the job, not the person, and then to set the reward level. This approach is based on the assumption that job worth can be determined and that the person doing the job is worth only as much to the organization as the job itself is worth. This assumption is in many respects valid since through such techniques as job evaluation programs it is possible to determine what other organizations are paying people to do the same or similar jobs. Among the advantages of this system is that it assures an organization that its compensation costs are not dramatically out of line with those of its competitors and it gives a somewhat objective basis to compensation practices.

An alternative to job-based pay which has recently been tried by a number of organizations is to pay individuals for the skills that they possess. In many cases this will not produce dramatically different pay rates than are produced by paying for the nature of the job. After all, the skills that people have usually match reasonably well the jobs that they are doing. It can, however, produce some different results in several respects. Often people have more skills than the job uses and in such cases these individuals are paid more than they would be paid under a job-based system. In other cases individuals do not have the skills when they first enter a job and do not deserve the kind of pay that goes with the job. In these cases individuals have to earn the right to be paid whatever the job-related skills are worth.

Perhaps the most important changes that are introduced when skill-based or competence-based pay is used occur in the kind of climate and motivation it produces in an organization. Instead of people being rewarded for moving up the hierarchy, people are rewarded for increasing their skills and developing themselves. This can create in the organization a climate of concern for personal growth and development and, of course, it can produce a highly talented workforce. In the case of factories where this system has been used it typically means that many people in the organization can perform multiple tasks and thus the workforce is highly knowledgeable and flexible.

In most cases where skills-based pay has been tried it tends to produce an interesting mix of positive and negative features as far as the organization is concerned (Lawler, 1981). Typically, it tends to produce somewhat higher pay levels for individuals but this is usually offset by greater workforce flexibility. This flexibility often leads to lower staffing levels, fewer problems when absenteeism or turnover occur, and, indeed, it often leads to lower absenteeism and turnover itself because people like the opportunity to utilize and be paid for a wide range of skills. On the other hand, skill-based pay can be rather challenging to administer because it is not clear how one goes to the outside marketplace and decides, for example, how much skill is worth. Skill assessment can also be difficult to accomplish. There are a number of well-developed systems for evaluating jobs and comparing them to the marketplace but there are none that really do this with respect to the skills an individual has.

There are no well-established rules to determine which organizational situations fit job-based pay and which fit skill or competence-based pay. In general, skill-based pay seems to fit those organizations that want to have a flexible, relatively permanent workforce that is oriented toward learning, growth, and development. It also seems to fit particularly well new plant start-ups and other situations where the greatest need is for skill development. Despite the newness and the potential operational problems with skill-based pay, it does seem to be a system that more and more organizations will be using especially in slow growth environments.

Pay for Performance

Perhaps the key strategic decision that needs to be made in the design of any reward system is whether it will be based on performance. Once this decision is made, a number of other features of the reward system tend to fall into place. The major alternative to basing pay on performance is to base it on seniority. Many government agencies, for example, base their rates in the job the person does and then on how long they have been in that job. In Japan individual pay is also often based on seniority, although individuals often receive bonuses based on corporate performance.

Most business organizations in the United States say that they reward individual performance and they call their pay system and their promotion system merit-based. Having a true merit pay or promotion system is often easier said than done, however. Indeed, it has been observed that many organizations would be better off if they did not try to relate pay and promotion to performance and relied on other bases for motivating performance.[1] The logic for this statement stems from the difficulty of specifying what kind of performance is desired and then determining whether, in fact, it has been demonstrated. There is ample evidence that a poorly designed and administered reward system can do more harm than good. However, there is evidence that when pay is effectively related to the desired performance, it can help to motivate, attract, and retain outstanding performers. Thus when it is feasible it is usually desirable to relate pay to performance.

There are numerous ways to relate pay to performance and often the most important strategic decision that organizations make is how they do this. The options open to organizations are enormous. The kind of pay reward that is given can vary widely and include such things as stock and cash. In addition, the frequency with which rewards are given can vary tremendously from time periods of a few minutes to many years. Performance can be measured at the individual level so that each individual gets a reward based on his or her performance. Rewards also can be given to groups based on the performance of the group, and rewards can be given based on the performance of total organizations. This gives the same reward to everyone in an organization. Finally, there are many different kinds of performance that can be rewarded. For example, managers can be rewarded for sales increases, productivity volumes, their ability to develop their subordinates, their cost reduction ideas, and so on.

Rewarding some behaviors and not others has clear implications for performance and thus decisions about what is to be rewarded need to be made carefully and with attention to the overall strategic plan of the business (Galbraith and Nathanson, 1978; Salschneider, 1981). Consideration needs to be given to such issues as short versus long-term performance, ROI maximization versus sales growth, and so on. Once the strategic plan has been developed to the point where key performance objectives have been defined, then the reward system needs to be designed to motivate the appropriate performance. Decisions about such issues as whether to use stock options (a long-term incentive), for example, should be made only after careful consideration of whether they are supportive of the kind of behavior that is desired (Crystal, 1978; Ellij, 1982).

It is beyond the scope of this chapter to go into any great detail about the pros and cons of the many approaches to relating pay to performance. Table 9.1 gives an idea of some of the design features possible in a reward system and some of the pluses and minuses associated with them.

First, each plan is evaluated in terms of its effectiveness in creating the perception that pay is tied to performance. In general this indicates the degree

[1] See Kerr (1975) for an interesting discussion of reward systems and their unintended consequences.

TABLE 9.1. Ratings of Various Incentive Plans.[a]

Salary Reward		Tie Pay to Performance	Negative Side	Encourage Cooperation	Employee Acceptance
Individual plan	Productivity	4	1	1	4
	Cost effectiveness	3	1	1	4
	Superior's rating	3	1	1	3
Group plan	Productivity	3	1	2	4
	Cost effectiveness	3	1	2	4
	Superior's rating	2	1	2	3
Organizational plan	Productivity	2	1	3	4
	Cost effectiveness	2	1	2	4
Individual plan	Productivity	5	3	1	2
	Cost effectiveness	4	2	1	2
	Superior's rating	4	2	1	2
Group plan	Productivity	4	1	3	3
	Cost effectiveness	3	1	3	3
	Superior's ating	3	1	3	3
Organizational plan	Productivity	3	1	3	4
	Cost effectiveness	3	1	3	4
	Profit	2	—	—	—

[a] On a scale of 1 to 5, 1 = low and 5 = high.

to which the approach ties pay to performance in a way that leads employees to believe that higher pay will follow good performance. Second, each plan is evaluated in terms of whether it resulted in the negative side effects that often are produced by performance-based pay plans. These include social ostracism of good performers, defensive behavior, and giving false data about performance. Third, each plan is evaluated in terms of the degree to which it encourages cooperation among employees. Finally, employee acceptance of the plan is rated. The ratings range from 1 to 5; a 5 indicates that the plan is generally high on the factor and a 1 indicates it is low. The ratings were developed based on a review of the literature and on my experience with the different types of plans.[2]

A number of trends appear in the ratings. Looking only at the criterion of tying pay to performance, we see that the individual plans tend to be rated highest, group plans are rated next, and organizational plans are rated lowest. This occurs because in group plans, to some extent, and in organizational plans, to a great extent, an individual's pay is not directly a function of his or her behavior. An individual's pay in these situations is influenced by the behavior of many others. In addition, when some types of performance measures (e.g., profits) are used, pay is influenced by external conditions that employees cannot control.

Bonus plans are generally rated higher than pay raise and salary increase plans. This is because with bonus plans it is possible to substantially vary an individual's pay from time period to time period. With salary increase plans, this is very difficult since past raises tend to become an annuity.

Finally, note that approaches that use objective measures of performance are rated higher than those that use subjective measures. In general, objective measures enjoy higher credibility; that is, employees will often accept the validity of an objective measure, such as sales volume or units produced, when they will not accept a superior's rating. When pay is tied to objective measures, therefore, it is usually clearer to employees that pay is determined by performance. Objective measures are also often publicly measurable. When pay is tied to them, the relationship between performance and pay is much more visible than when it is tied to a subjective, nonverifiable measure, such as a supervisor's rating. Overall, the suggestion is that individually based bonus plans that rely on objective measures produce the strongest perceived connection between pay and performance.

The ratings of the degree to which plans contribute to negative side effects reveal that most plans have little tendency to produce such effects. The notable exceptions here are individual bonus and incentive plans at the non-management level. These plans often lead to situations in which social rejection and ostracism are tied to good performance, and in which employees present false performance data and restrict their production. These side effects

[2]Lawler (1971) discusses this at greater length.

are particularly likely to appear where trust is low and subjective productivity standards are used.

In terms of the third criterion—encouraging cooperation—the ratings are generally higher for group and organizational plans than for individual plans. Under group and organizational plans, it is generally to everyone's advantage that an individual work effectively, because all share in the financial fruits of higher performance. This is not true under an individual plan. As a result, good performance is much more likely to be supported and encouraged by others when group and organizational plans are used. If people feel they can benefit from another's good performance, they are much more likely to encourage and help other workers to perform well than if they cannot benefit and may be harmed.

The final criterion—employee acceptance—shows that, as noted earlier, most performance-based pay plans have only moderate acceptance. The least acceptable seems to be individual plans. Their low acceptance, particularly among nonmanagement employees, seems to stem from their tendency to encourage competitive relationships between employees and from the difficulty in administering such plans fairly.

It should be clear that no one performance-based pay plan represents a panacea. It is, therefore, unlikely that any organization will ever be completely satisfied with the approach it chooses. Furthermore, some of the plans that make the greatest contributions to organizational effectiveness do not make the greatest contributions to quality of work life and vice versa. Still the situation is not completely hopeless. When all factors are taken into account, group and organizational bonus plans that are based on objective data and individual level salary increase plans rate high.

Many organizations choose to put individuals on multiple or combination reward systems. For example, they may put individuals on a salary increase system that rewards them for their individual performance while at the same time giving everybody in the division or plant a bonus based on divisional performance. Some plans measure group or company performance and then divide up the bonus pool generated by the performance of a larger group among individuals based on individual performance. This has the effect of causing individuals to be rewarded for both individual and group performance in the hope that this will cause individuals to perform all needed behaviors.

A common error in the design of many pay-for-performance systems is the tendency to focus on measurable short-term operating results because they are quantifiable and regularly obtained anyway. Many organizations reward their top-level managers in particular on the basis of quarterly or annual profitability. This can have the obvious dysfunctional consequence of causing managers to be very short-sighted in their behavior and to ignore strategic objectives important to the long-term profitability of the organization. A similarly grievous error can be the tendency to depend on completely subjective performance appraisals for the allocation of pay rewards. Considerable evidence exists to show that these performance appraisals are often biased and invalid and instead of contributing to positive motivation and a good work climate that improves superior–subordinate relationships they lead to just the opposite.[3] These are just two of the most common errors that can develop in the administration of performance reward systems. Other common errors include the giving of too small rewards, failure to clearly explain systems, and poor administrative practices.

In summary, the decision of whether to relate pay to performance is a crucial one in any organization. The error of automatically assuming that they should be related can be a serious one. Admittedly, the advantages of doing it effectively are significant and can greatly contribute to the organizational effectiveness. What is often overlooked is that doing it poorly can have more negative consequences than positive ones. Specifically, if performance is difficult to measure and/or rewards are difficult to distribute based on performance, the effect of the pay-for-performance system can be the motivation of counterproductive behaviors, lawsuits charging discrimination, and the creation of a climate of mistrust, low credibility, and managerial incompetence. On the other hand, total abandonment of a merit pay system means that the organization gives up a potentially important motivator of performance and, as a result, may condemn itself to a reduced level of performance. The ideal, of course, is to create conditions where pay can be effectively related to performance and as a result have it be an important contributor to the effectiveness of the organization.

Market Position

The reward structure of an organization influences behavior partially as a function of how the amount of rewards given compare to what other organizations give. Organizations frequently have well-developed policies about how their pay levels should compare with the pay levels in other companies. For example, some companies (e.g., IBM) feel it is important to be a leading payer and they consciously set their pay rates at a level that is higher than that of any of the companies they compete with. Other companies are much less concerned about being in the leadership position with respect to pay and as a result are content to focus their pay levels at or below the market for the people they hire. This structural issue in the design of pay systems is a critical one because it can strongly influence the kind of people that are attracted and retained by an organization as well as influence the turnover rate and the selection ratio. Simply stated, those organizations that adopt a more aggressive stance with respect to the marketplace end up attracting and retaining more individuals. From a business point of view this may pay off for them, particularly if turnover is a costly factor in the organization and if

---

[3] Chapter 6 discusses the merits of alternative appraisal methods. See also Latham and Wexley (1981).

a key part of the business strategy demands attracting and retaining highly talented individuals.

On the other hand, if many of the jobs in the organizations are low-skilled and people are readily available in the labor market to do them, then a corporate strategy of high pay may not pay off. It can increase labor costs and produce a minimum number of benefits. Of course, organizations do not have to be high payers for all the jobs. Indeed, some organizations identify certain key skills that they need and adopt the stance of being a high payer for them and an average or below average payer for other skills. This has some obvious business advantages in terms of allowing organizations to attract the critical skills that it needs to succeed and at the same time to control costs.

Although it is not often recognized, the kind of market position that a company adopts with respect to its reward systems can also have a noticeable impact on organization climate. For example, a policy that calls for above market pay can contribute to the feeling in the organization that it is an elite organization, that people must be competent to be there, and that they are indeed fortunate to be there. A policy that splits certain skill groups into a high pay position leaving the rest of the organization at a lower pay level can, on the other hand, contribute to a spirit of elite groups within the organization and cause some divisive social pressures.

Finally, it is interesting to note that some organizations try to be above average in noncash compensation as a way of competing for the talent they need. They talk in terms of producing an above-average quality of work life and stress not only hygiene factors but interesting and challenging work. This stance potentially can be a very effective one, because it puts organizations in the position of attracting people who value these things and could give them a competitive edge at least with these people.

In summary, the kind of market position that an organization has with respect to its total reward package is crucial in determining the behavior of the members as well as the climate of the organization. It needs to be carefully related to the general business strategy of the organization and, in particular, to the kind of human resources that it calls for as well as to the organization climate.

Internal–External Pay Comparison-Oriented

Organizations differ in the degree to which they strive toward internal equity in their pay and reward systems. Those organizations where internal equity is highly valued work very hard to see that individuals doing similar work will be paid the same even though they are in very different parts of the country, and in different businesses. Some corporations (e.g., IBM) set the national pay structure for their organization based on the highest pay that a job receives anywhere in the country. Those organizations that do not stress internal equity typically focus on the labor market as the key determinant of what somebody should be paid and although this does not necessarily produce different pay for people doing the same job, it may. For example, the same job in different industries, electronics and auto, for example, may be paid quite differently.

There are a number of advantages and disadvantages to the strategy of focusing on internal pay comparisons and paying all people in similar jobs the same regardless of where they are in the organization. It can make the transfer of people from one location to another easier since there won't be any pay differences. In addition, it can produce an organizational climate of homogeneity and the feeling that all work for the same company and all are treated well or fairly. It also can reduce or eliminate the tendency of people to want to move to a higher paying division or location and the tendency for rivalry and dissatisfaction to develop within the organization because of poor internal pay comparisons.

On the other hand, a focus on internal equity can be very expensive, particularly if the organization is diversified and as usually happens, pay rates across the corporation get set at the highest level that the market demands anywhere in the corporation (Salschneider, 1981). The disadvantage of this is obvious. It causes organizations to pay a lot more money than is necessary in order to attract and retain good people. Indeed, in some situations it can get so severe that organizations become noncompetitive in certain businesses and industries and find that they have to limit themselves to those businesses where their pay structures make their labor costs competitive. Labor costs that are too high have, for example, often made it difficult for auto and oil and gas companies to compete in new business reas.

In summary, the difference between focusing on external equity and internal equity is a crucial one in the design of pay systems. It can determine the cost structure as well as the climate and behavior of organizations. The general rule is that highly diversified companies find themselves pulled more strongly toward an external market orientation, whereas organizations that are single industry or single technology-based typically find themselves more comfortable with an internal equity emphasis.

Centralized–Decentralized Reward Strategy

Closely related to the issue of internal versus external equity is the issue of a centralized versus decentralized reward system strategy. Those organizations that adopt a centralized strategy typically assign to corporate staff groups the responsibility for seeing that such things as pay practices are similar through-out the organization. They typically develop standard pay grades and pay ranges, standardized job evaluation systems, and, perhaps, standardized promotion systems. In decentralized organizations, policy and practice in the area of pay and promotion and other important reward areas is left to local option.

Sometimes the corporations have broad guidelines or principles that they wish to stand for but the day-to-day administration and design of the system is left up to the local entity.

The advantages of a centralized structure rest primarily on the expertise that can be accumulated at the central level and the degree of homogeneity produced in the organization. This homogeneity can lead to a clear image of the corporate climate, feelings of internal equity, and the belief that the organization stands for something. It also eases the job of communicating and understanding what is going on in different parts of the organization. The decentralized strategy allows for local innovation and, of course, closely fitting the practices to the particular business.

Just as is true with many other of the critical choices, there is no right choice between a centralized and decentralized approach to reward system design and administration. Overall, the decentralized system tends to make the most sense when the organization is involved in businesses that face different markets and perhaps are at different points in their maturity.[4] It allows those unique practices to surface that can give a competitive advantage to one part of the business but may prove to be a real hindrance or handicap to another. For example, such perquisites as cars are often standard operating procedure in one business, whereas they are not in another. Similarly, extensive bonuses may be needed to attract one group of people (e.g., oil exploration engineers), whereas it makes little sense in attracting other groups (e.g., research scientists). Overall, then, an organization needs to carefully look at its mix of businesses and the degree it wants to stand for a certain set of principles or policies across all its operating divisions and then decide whether a centralized or decentralized reward strategy is likely to be most effective.

Degree of Hierarchy

Closely related to the issue of job-based versus competence-based pay is the strategic decision concerning the hierarchical nature of the reward systems in an organization. Often no formal decision is ever made to have a relatively hierarchical or relatively egalitarian approach to rewards in an organization. An hierarchical approach simply happens because it is so consistent with the general way organizations are run. Hierarchical systems usually pay people greater amounts of money as they move higher up the organization ladder, and give people greater perquisites and symbols of office as they move up. The effect of this approach is to strongly reinforce the traditional hierarchical power relationships in the organization and to create a climate of different status and power levels. In steeply hierarchical reward systems the reward

---

[4]Greiner (1972) discusses the implications of organizational life cycles. See also Galbraith and Nathanson (1978).

system may have more levels in it than the formal organization chart and, as a result, create additional status differences in the organization.

The alternative to a hierarchical system is one in which differences in rewards and perquisites that are based only on hierarchical level are dramatically downplayed. For example, in those large corporations (e.g., Digital Equipment Corporation) that adopt an egalitarian stance to rewards, such things as private parking spaces, executive restrooms, and special entrances are eliminated. People from all levels in the organization eat, work, and travel together. Further, individuals can be relatively highly paid by working their way up a technical ladder and do not have to go on to a management ladder in order to gain high levels of pay. This less hierarchical approach to pay and other rewards produces a quite different climate in an organization than does the hierarchical one. It tends to encourage decision-making by expertise rather than by hierarchical position and it draws fewer status differences in the organization.

As with all reward system strategic choices there is no right or wrong answer as to how hierarchical a system should be. In general, a steeply hierarchical system makes the most sense when an organization needs relatively rigid bureaucratic behavior, strong top-down authority, and a strong motivation for people to move up the organizational hierarchy. A more egalitarian approach fits with a more participative management style, and the desire to retain technical specialists and experts in nonmanagement roles or lower-level management roles. It is not surprising, therefore, that many of the organizations that have emphasized egalitarian perquisites are in high technology and knowledge-based industries.

Reward Mix

The kind of rewards that organizations give to individuals can vary widely. The money, for example, that is given can come in many forms varying all the way from stock through medical insurance. Organizations can choose to reward people almost exclusively with cash, downplaying fringe benefits, perquisites, and status symbols. The major advantage of paying in cash is that the value of cash in the eyes of the recipient is universally high. When the cash is translated into fringe benefits, perquisites, and other trappings of office it may lose its value for some people and as a result be a poor investment (Nealy, 1963). On the other hand, certain benefits can best be obtained through mass purchase and, therefore, many individuals want the organization to provide them. In addition, certain status symbols or perquisites may be valued by some individuals beyond their actual dollar cost to the organization and thus represent good buys. Finally, as mentioned earlier, there often are some climate and organizational structure reasons for paying people in the form of perquisites and status symbols.

One interesting development in the area of compensation is the flexible or cafeteria-style benefit program. Here individuals are allowed to make up their own reward package so that it is sure to fit their needs and desires. The theory is that this will lead to organizations getting the best value for their money because they will give people only those things that they desire. It also has the advantage of treating individuals as mature adults rather than as dependent people who need their welfare looked after in a structured way. At the moment this approach has been tried in only a few organizations. The results so far have been favorable, thus there is reason to believe that others may be adopting it in the near future because it can offer a strategic cost–benefit advantage in attracting and retaining certain types of employees.

Overall, the choice of what form of rewards to give individuals needs to be driven by a clear feeling of what type of climate the organization wishes to have. For example, the idea of a flexible compensation package is highly congruent with a participative open organization climate that treats individuals as mature adults and wants to attract talented mature people. An approach that emphasizes rewards may, on the other hand, appeal to people who are very status-oriented, who value position power, and who need a high level of visible reinforcement for their position. This would seem to fit best in a relatively bureaucratic organization that relies on position power and authority in order to carry out its actions.

PROCESS ISSUES AND REWARD ADMINISTRATION

A number of process issues with respect to reward systems design and administration could be discussed here. In some respects process issues come up more often than do structure and content issues because organizations are constantly having to make reward system management, implementation, and communication decisions, whereas structures tend to be relatively firmly fixed in place. However, rather than discussing specific process issues here, the focus is on broad process themes that can be used to characterize the way reward systems are designed and administered.

Communication Policy

Organizations differ widely in how much information they communicate about their reward systems. At one extreme some organizations are extremely secretive, particularly in the area of pay. They forbid people from talking about their individual rewards, give minimal information to individuals about how rewards are decided upon and allocated, and have no publically disseminated policies about such things as market position, the approach to gathering market data, and potential increases and rewards for individuals. At the other extreme, some organizations are so open that everyone's pay is a matter of public record as is the overall organization pay philosophy. [Many new high involvement plants operate this way (Walton, 1980).] In addition, all promotions are subject to open job postings and in some instances peer groups discuss the eligibility of people for promotion.

The difference between an open and closed communication policy in the area of rewards is enormous. Like all the other choices that must be made in structuring a reward system, there is no clear right or wrong approach. Rather it is a matter of picking a position on the continuum from open to secret that is supportive of the overall climate and types of behavior that are needed for organizational effectiveness. An open system tends to encourage people to ask questions, share data, and ultimately be involved in decisions. A secret system tends to put people in a more dependent position to keep power concentrated at the top and to allow an organization to keep its options open with respect to commitments to individuals. Some negative side effects of secret systems are the existence of considerable distortion about the actual rewards that people get and creation of a low trust environment in which people have trouble understanding the relationship between pay and performance. Thus a structurally sound pay system may end up being rather ineffective because it is misperceived if strong policies are kept in place.

Open systems put considerable pressure on organizations to do an effective job of administering rewards. Thus if policies such as merit pay, which are difficult to defend, are to be implemented, then considerable time and effort need to be invested in pay administration. If they are done poorly, strong pressures usually develop to eliminate the policies and pay everyone the same.[5] Ironically, therefore, if an organization wants to spend little time administrating rewards but still wants to use merit pay, secrecy may be the best policy, although secrecy, in turn, may limit the effectiveness of the merit pay plan.

Decision-Making Practices

Closely related to the issue of communication is the issue of decision-making. Open communication makes possible the involvement of a wide range of people in the decision-making process concerning compensation. Further, if individuals are to be actively involved in decisions concerning reward systems, they need to have information about policy and actual practice.

In discussing the type of decision-making processes that are used in organizations with respect to reward systems, it is important to distinguish between decisions concerning the design of reward systems and decisions concerning the ongoing administration of reward systems. It is possible to have different decision-making styles with respect to each of these two types of decisions. Traditionally, of course, organizations have made both design and ongoing administration decisions in a top-down manner.

Systems typically have been designed by top management with the aid of

[5]See Chapter 13 and the discussion of Hewlett-Packard's corporate culture in Chapter 14.

staff support and administered by strict reliance on the chain of command. The assumption has been that this provides the proper checks and balances in the system and in addition locates decision-making where the expertise rests. In many cases this is a valid assumption and certainly fits well with an organizational management style that emphasizes hierarchy, bureaucracy, and control through the use of extrinsic rewards. It does not fit, however, with an organization that believes in more open communication, higher levels of involvement on the part of people, and control through individual commitment to policies. It also does not fit when expertise is broadly spread throughout the organization. This is often true in organizations that rely heavily on knowledge workers or that spend a great deal of effort training their people to become expert in technical functions.

There have been some reports in the research literature of organizations experimenting with having employees involved in the design of pay systems. For example, employees have been involved in designing their own bonus system in some instances and the results have been generally favorable. When employees are involved it seems to lead them to raising important issues and providing expertise not normally available to the designers of the system. And perhaps more important, once the system is designed the acceptance level of it and the understanding of it tends to be very high. This often leads to a rapid start-up of the system and to a commitment to see it survive long-term. In other cases systems have been designed by line managers rather than by staff support people because of the feeling that they are the ones that need to support it, maintain it, and be committed to it. In the absence of significant design input from line people it often is unrealistic to expect them to have the same level of commitment to the pay system as the staff people have.

There also has been some experimentation with having peer groups and low-level supervisory people handle the day-to-day decision-making about who should receive pay increases and how jobs should be evaluated and placed in pay structures. The most visible examples of this are in the new participative plants that use skill-based pay (Walton, 1980). In these, typically, the work group reviews the performance of the individual and decides whether he or she has acquired the new skills. Interestingly, what evidence there is suggests that this has gone very well. In many respects this is not surprising since the peers often have the best information about performance and thus are in a good position to make a performance assessment. The problem in traditional organizations is that they lack the motivation to give valid feedback and to respond responsibly, thus their expertise is of no use. In more participative open systems this motivational problem seems to be less severe and, as a result, involvement in decision-making seems to be more effective. There also have been isolated instances of executives assessing each other on a peer group reward system and practices (e.g., in Graphic Controls Corporation). Again, there is evidence that this can work effectively when combined with a history of open and effective communication. Deciding on rewards is clearly not an easy task for groups to do and thus should be taken on only when there is comfort with the confrontation skills of the group and trust in their ability to talk openly and directly about each other's performance.

Overall, there is evidence that some participative approaches to reward system design and administration can be effective. The key seems to be articulating the practices in the area of reward systems with the general management style of the organization. In more participative settings there is good reason to believe that participative approaches to reward systems can be effective because of their congruence with the overall style and because the skills and norms to make them effective are already in place. In more traditional organizations the typical top-down approach to reward systems design administration probably remains the best. From a strategic point of view, the decision then about how much participation and reward system design and administration must rest upon whether a participative high involvement type organization is best in order to accomplish the strategic objectives of the business. If so, then participation in pay decisions and reward system decisions should be considered.

REWARD SYSTEM CONGRUENCE

So far each reward system design feature has been treated as an independent factor. This was done for exposition of the concepts but it fails to emphasize the importance of overall reward system congruence. Reward system design features are not stand-alone items. There is considerable evidence that they affect each other and, as such, need to be supportive of the same types of behavior, reflect the same overall managerial philosophy, and be generated by the same business strategy.

Table 9.2 illustrates one effort to define congruent sets of reward system practices. Here the effort is to show how two different management philosophies call for two very different reward system practices. The two management philosophies portrayed here are a traditional bureaucratic management style and a participative employee involvement strategy. As can be seen from the table, every reward system practice needs to be different in these two cases. The reward system practices that go with traditional bureacratic models tend to be more secretive, more top-down, and oriented toward producing regularity in behavior. The participative practices encourage self-development, openness, employee involvement in reward system allocation decisions, and, ultimately, more innovation and commitment to the organization.

The importance of congruence is not limited to just the reward system in an organization. The reward system needs to fit the other features of the organization in order that total human resource management system congruence exists. This means that the reward system needs to fit such things as the way jobs are designed, the leadership style of the supervisors, and the

TABLE 9.2.   Appropriate Reward System Practices.

	Traditional or Theory X	Participative or Theory Y
Reward System		
Fringe benefits	Vary according to organization level	Cafeteria—same for all levels
Promotion	All decisions made by top management	Open posting for all jobs; peer group involvement in decision process
Status symbols	A great many, carefully allocated on the basis of job position	Few present, low emphasis on organization level
Pay		
Type of system	Hourly and salary	All salary
Base rate	Based on job performed; high enough to attract job applicants	Based on skills; high enough to provide security and attract applicants
Incentive plan	Piece rate	Group and organization-wide bonus, lump sum increase
Communication policy	Very restricted distribution of information	Individual rates, salary survey data, all other information made public
Decision-making locus	Top management	Close to location of person whose pay is being set

types of career tracks available in the organization, to mention just a few. Unless this kind of fit exists, the organization will be replete with conflicts and, to a degree, the reward system practices will potentially be canceled out by the practices in other areas. To mention just one example, an organization can have a very well-developed performance appraisal system, but in the absence of well-designed jobs and effective supervisory behavior it will be ineffective. Performance appraisal demands interpersonally competent supervisory behavior and jobs that allow for good performance measure.

CONCLUSION

Overall, the design of an effective reward system demands not only a close articulation between the business strategy of an organization and the reward system, but also a clear fit between the reward system and the other design features of the organization. The implication of this for-reward system design is that not only is there no one right set of practices for reward systems, it is also impossible to design an effective reward system in the absence of knowing how other design features of the organization are arrayed. This suggests that the key strategic decisions about the reward system need to be made in an interactive fashion in which tentative reward system design decisions are driven by the business strategy and then are tested against how other features of the organization are being designed. The key, of course, is to ultimately come up with an integrated human resource management strategy that is consistent in the way it encourages people to behave, that attracts the kind of people that can support the business strategy, and that encourages them to behave appropriately.

CHAPTER

10

REWARD SYSTEMS: PRACTICAL CONSIDERATIONS

A Case Study of General Motors Corporation

Andrew R. McGill

The philosophically appealing theory of rewards and compensation presented in Chapter 9 is complex and difficult to put into operation. The goals, constraints, and competing agendas—to name just three factors—of large organizations all contribute to the manner in which clean, uncomplicated theory is often implemented improperly and unsuccessfully.

One reason is that the challenges outlined in Chapter 9 often require major organizational changes before they can be successfully implemented. And such changes take time. Political change, a common precursor to structural change, comes slowly and, at least in established complex organizations, often only after organizational difficulty, such as sharply reduced profits or the inability to internally generate new ideas to keep up with a competitive world. And that political change, even when it does come, often confronts a hostile internal culture accustomed to doing things in traditional ways.

These concepts are critical to a clear understanding of the difference between theorizing about reward systems and actually changing reward systems. In most American corporations, for instance, changing reward systems also means altering a deeply rooted focus on short-term payoffs and successes. Changing from such an historic orientation to one driving long-term performance and goals requires changing the basic values within an organizational culture. Critical to such a change is the requirement that an organization's constituents—inside and out—accept, or at least understand, these new values.

REWARDING STRATEGIC RECOVERY: AT GENERAL MOTORS

As the decade of the 1980s began, time was something General Motors Corporation had in short supply. As one of the world's largest industrial corporations, GM was a textbook success. But its sales, profits, and stock prices led to an overemphasis on 10-day sales figures and quarterly profits, at the expense of long-term adaptability. GM was the increasingly inefficient battleship trying to maneuver with the svelte industrial fleets of Japan and Germany. That slowness to adapt combined with a cartel-squeezed surge in oil prices to put GM out of synch with its market. As demand for smaller cars soared, foreign manufacturers increased their U.S. market share to better than 25%.

GM needed to retrench and rebuild while retaining its highly skilled specialists and professionals, personnel in demand throughout the business world. This chapter focuses on the role that GM's reward systems played in its recovery.

First, some generic comments about reward systems are warranted. Foremost is the need for consistency and fairness. Historically, across the United States both factors were frequently missing from compensation programs, especially at levels distant from the top of the organizational chart.

In the good times—when profits were acceptable to high—finding the money to support an executive compensation system at all managerial levels was not a problem for the committed corporation. But when times were tough—as they were in the early 1980s, especially in the American basic manufacturing industries—different organizations resorted to different strategies.

This is the crux of the problem. Organizations treat approaches to compensation differently, depending on whether times are good or bad. Yet employees respond to compensation systems most effectively when the systems are similar and have continuity over time. This is the impasse between Lawler's theory and real world practices.

Many organizations may commit themselves to a strategically wise compensation system during good times, only to make that system one of the first victims when bad times return. This was made clear in the fall of 1982, when *Fortune*[1] magazine devoted its cover and a substantial portion of the magazine to detailing the real-life cutbacks that managers and executives were experiencing.

"Cutting back on pay and people is bound to cause some grief," the story said. The article went on to quote John M. Rosenfeld, a partner in Hay Associates, a consulting firm specializing in personnel matters, as saying: "You can't say, 'We just had a bad quarter, guys, so we're going to cut your pay.' "

Such behavior, the article suggested, causes younger managers to think about seeking employment elsewhere.

One consultant quoted by *Fortune*, Peter T. Chingos of Peat Marwick Mitchell & Co., a Big Eight accounting firm, suggested a clear list of priorities for companies that must make reductions in cyclical downturns:

1. Start with a freeze on hiring, which saves money without hurting employees.
2. Move next to cutting administrative costs by reducing travel, downgrading first-class tickets to coach, reducing long distance calls, eliminating seminars and sabbaticals.
3. Fire nonperformers.
4. Encourage early retirements.
5. Freeze or cut salaries, but this is "absolutely the last thing to do."

At General Motors, during 1982, auto sales had taken their deepest skid since the Great Depression. Making matters worse, the U.S. auto industry was in the midst of a major transition. General Motors alone was spending $40 billion on retooling.

Japanese automakers had risen from an annoying gnat in the U.S. auto market to a dominant competitor, posting huge sales gains at times when the sales of U.S. manufacturers were declining to 50-year lows. The Japanese had the benefit of more experience—and, ironically, a shorter pipeline to the U.S. market—with small cars, which had captured an increasing share of the market after a flurry of oil embargoes and gasoline price surges during the late 1970s and early 1980s.

Even worse than the sales gains, though, was the growing popular perception in the United States that the quality of Japanese-made cars far surpassed their U.S.-made competitors. Whether true or not, poll upon poll confirmed that most Americans believed it. And that belief was becoming a common, though far from a majority, view within America's largest automobile manufacturing corporations, including General Motors.

That heretical, but nonetheless growing belief was fueled partly by reality and partly by the fact that managers who had previously accepted or had

[1] Main, J. "Hard Times Catch Up With Executives." *Fortune*, September 20, 1982, 50–54.

been coopted toward the corporate value system were becoming increasingly critical as their bonuses quit coming in.

The traditional reward system in the automobile industry kept base salaries at relatively modest levels, considering the size and power of the industry. Middle and upper managers looked to bonuses (which frequently exceeded annual salaries two and threefold during the 1960–1970 heydays) for much of their total compensation. Bonuses were based on corporate and individual unit performance. The system worked fine as long as corporate profits stayed high.

The problem came when profits plumetted. Numerous middle and upper managers who had long warned of the impending problems posed by foreign competition and the trend toward smaller cars (warnings that had fallen on deaf ears in the high corporate offices) were forced to suffer total compensation declines of 40–60% when their worst fears materialized. These managers were penalized for decisions not their own.

Fundamental to the conceptual design of reward systems is the notion that you should only reward someone for something they can personally control. This was not the case at GM, where, middle and upper managers received the preponderance of their compensation in bonuses, although they could not control the total corporate performance on which their bonuses were predicated.

Instead, these managers suffered dramatically reduced paychecks at a time of high inflation, which caused some marketable GM managers to reevaluate their positions. In many cases this resulted in a loss of valued personnel.

At a time when rapid change and adaptation was essential to America's premier industrial corporation, GM could not afford to lose its most able bright managers. It would have been far simpler if GM had in place a rewards sytem such as Lawler would install which would have kept the total compensation of middle and upper managers at or above that of their professional peer group in other companies. But at GM, political realities argued against such a system which could have led to subordinates earning more money than their superiors, destroying a decades-old compensation hierarchy every bit as rigid as GM's organizational one.

The GM-UAW Profit-Sharing Plan

To cope with the problem, GM changed not the compensation philosophy, but the amounts with which it was put into operation. Its revised Executive Bonus Plan aimed

> to provide reward for performance and incentive for future endeavor to employees who contribute to the success of the enterprise by their invention, ability, industry, loyalty, or exceptional service. . . .[2]

[2]General Motors Notice of Annual Meeting of Stockholders and Proxy Statement, April 16, 1982, General Motors Corporation.

Revisions to the bonus plan had been two years in the making and they would provide a strong impetus to executives who had come to expect year-end awards for their performance.

The new plan proposed that 8% of GM's net annual earnings exceeding $1 billion be placed in a reserve for executive bonuses. The proposal would have lowered by $270 million per year the amount of profit necessary to activate the GM executive bonus plan. Also important under the proposed change, the bonus plan would have lowered from five to three years the amount of time over which a bonus was paid, and it would have increased from $5,000 to $10,000 the minimum amount of an annual bonus. Under the new plan, if GM had net earnings of $3 billion, the amount of money in the Executive Bonus Pool would be raised from $140 million to $174 million and that amount would be distributed among the 5000 GM employees eligible under the bonus program. What GM was doing was creating a larger pool of bonus funds from which it could pay larger bonuses to more executives. It was a significant strategic shift in the way GM distributed rewards, a shift that matched a basic change in GM's strategy.

Mired in a recession and confronted by increasing Japanese auto sales, GM executives decided that their problem was fundamental and acute. Simply put, the corporation had not been innovative or creative for years and executives felt that if the organization were to prosper, this must change. Such change could only come from the very executives the sweetened bonus was intended to attract and retain.

This is precisely what Chapter 9 suggests. According to Figure 9.1, once the strategic plan is developed, the organization needs to

> focus on the kind of human resources, climate, and behavior that are needed to make it effective. The next step is to design reward systems that will motivate the right kind of performance, attract the right kind of people, and create a supportive climate and structure.

Lawler advises that, "The reward system needs to fit the other feature of the organization in order that total human resource management system congruence exists." Hence, if GM wanted to signal a strategic shift to its workers, Lawler would say this was one way to do it, although far from the ideal way suggested earlier.

As such, the reward system must match the career tracks that are planned for promising young executives within the organization. Lawler in Chapter 9 suggests that a majority of organizations wait too long to do this and allow their reward systems to be a lagging, rather than a leading, part of the strategic picture. GM executives noted, as did Lawler, that among white-collar executives especially, bonus plans are generally higher on an incentive scale than are pay raises, stock options, or other forms of deferred compensation.

The situation was especially critical to GM because it had not paid a bonus to executives in either 1980 or 1981 and the previous half-decade had seen bonuses sharply reduced from the days of a booming U.S. auto industry.

So critical was the problem, according to *The Detroit News*, that GM was having difficulty recruiting the best students from the nation's best business and engineering schools. Even worse, *The News* said, some top managers—and many promising younger employees—were leaving GM in unprecedented numbers.[3] Fed up with small or nonexistent bonuses in a nonglamorous industry, with the long and chancy climb to the top no longer cushioned by a guaranteed job, these executives were voting no confidence, as one put it, "with their feet."

One popular belief was that a flurry of such departures, led by some of the few under age 40 stars on GM's super secret high potential list, provoked the company to announce its new plan even as the ink dried on GM's new concessions contract with the UAW. In fact, the new plan had been years in the works and its timing was not haphazard, rushed, or particularly geared to current events. Its timing was merely a function of when GM had to reevaluate its plan under the corporate by-laws (every five years), how the change had to be announced (in the proxy statement), and when that proxy statement had to be issued to provide sufficient lead time prior to the annual meeting.

But even though the change had been long planned and its timing fixed within a very narrow window, it had the powerful effect of gaining the immediate attention of two important GM constituencies. To exceptional insiders possibly on the verge of departing GM, it signaled a major change in the reward system. But to a second group of constituents, the United Auto Workers union members who had just made large contract concessions, the GM announcement was tantamount to an act of war.

Almost immediately the UAW vowed to fight the plan. The union said its members had just made financial concessions, only to have GM give more money to its executives. UAW Vice President Owen Bieber (now president of the union) said he was "shocked and angered" at the GM announcement, which violated "the spirit of the agreement that we just recently negotiated." Then-UAW President Douglas A. Fraser was more to the point: "The UAW finds these proposals to be an absolute outrage, particularly at a time when GM workers have just agreed to substantial sacrifices to help the company withstand the terribly depressed conditions facing the auto industry." It fell to William P. MacKinnon, GM's Vice President, Personnel Administration and Staff Development, to explain what GM was doing and why. "The modifications to the bonus plan are designed to assure that General Motors will continue to attract and retain the executive talent necessary to run the business over the next several years," MacKinnon said.

> The changes also reflect the significant capital expenditures which GM will undertake over the next several years to ensure that the automobile business remains competitive and to ensure the continued job security of all the employees.

[3]"GM–UAW Profit-Sharing Plan." *The Detroit News,* March 24, 1982, 8A.

In fact, GM executives were only implementing a plan that had been proposed months before by the Bonus and Salary Committee, comprised of outside members of the GM Board of Directors. That board committee said:

> . . . there must be an enlarged emphasis on long-term performance to better assure the future success of the corporation in an increasingly competitive world-wide market. Thus, while the stock option plan will continue to be related to the price of General Motors' stock, a new plan based on longer term corporate performance would motivate executives to achieve specific objectives, such as increased sales and earnings, which require a period of years to accomplish.

The Bonus and Salary Committee further said, " . . . the committee views the bonus plan coupled with the stock option plan as motivating executives to continue the most comprehensive vehicle downsizing program in our history at a time when earnings and market conditions remain depressed . . . "

So it was that the plan was well conceived, even if poorly timed, coming so close to the UAW'S concession contract with GM. In the end (six days after the plan was proposed in the GM proxy statement) GM backed off its plan to liberalize bonuses for its top executives in the face of heavy criticism. The GM decision came after a day-long meeting between Chairperson Roger B. Smith and officials of the UAW.

In a letter to Fraser, Smith concluded:

> In the spirit of cooperation with the UAW, the General Motors management will offer to forego for the period of the UAW agreement (April 12, 1982 to September 14, 1984) the possible increases in incentive compensation which could result from the modifications to the bonus plan.

Smith further promised that any bonuses paid during the period would not be "in excess of the amount that would have generated under the present formula."

It may seem that what happened to the GM bonus plan was inevitable given its timing.[4] But corporate insiders, according to *The Detroit News,* believe that even though the plan was temporarily rescinded, GM successfully signaled its important managers and up-and-coming executives that it intends to reward them well if they stay at GM.[5] Hence, as one insider put it, "Our people get the benefit of our intentions in the short run—and they'll get our money in the long run."

Workers at lower levels within GM hope they will do as well in the long term. For, in the course of negotiations between GM and the UAW in 1982 the company agreed to a profit-sharing plan for blue-collar workers not already covered by profit-sharing.

[4]Loomis, Carol J. "The Madness of Executive Compensation." *Fortune,* July 12, 1982, 42–52.

[5]"GM: A Portrait," *The Detroit News,* a reprint of a copyrighted series published between September 26, 1982 and October 3, 1982, in and by *The Detroit News.*

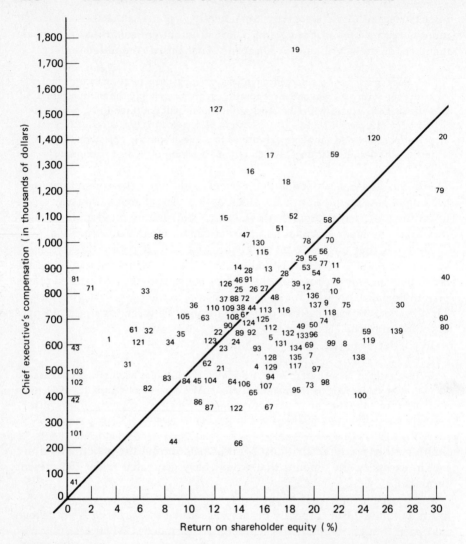

FIGURE 10.1.   Return on equity versus chief executive's compensation for 139 of the nations's corporations in 1981. 1. RCA; 2. Honeywell; 3. Signal Companies; 4. Greyhound; 5. Procter & Gamble; 6. Sperry; 7. 3M; 8. Raytheon; 9. R. J. Reynolds; 10. Pepsico; 11. Litton; 12. General Electric; 13. Westinghouse; 14. Gulf & Western; 15. ITT; 16. United Technologies; 17. Rockwell; 18. Tenneco; 19. W. R. Grace; 20. LTV; 21. Dow Chemical; 22. Celanese; 23. American Cynamid; 24. PPG; 25. Union Carbide; 26. Hercules; 27. Monsanto; 28. Dupont; 29. Allied Corp.; 30. NL Industries; 31. Inland Steel; 32. National Steel; 33. R. J. Reynolds; 34. Bethlehem Steel; 35. Kaiser Aluminum; 36. Alcoa; 37. Republic Steel; 38. Armco Steel; 39. U.S. Steel; 40. Northwest Industries; 41. Charter Co.; 42. Cities Service; 43. Coastal Petroleum; 44. Amerada Hess; 45. Ashland Oil; 46. Gulf; 47. Union Pacific; 48. Philips Petroleum; 49. Marathon; 50. Getty Oil; 51. Mobil; 52. Texaco; 53. Standard Oil of Indiana; 54. Alantic Richfield; 55. Shell; 56. Standard Oil of California; 57. Sun Oil; 58. Exxon; 59. Union Oil; 60. Standard Oil of Ohio; 61. Burroughs; 62. NCR; 63. Control Data; 64. Digital Equipment; 65. Pitney Bowes; 66. Data General; 67. Wang; 68. Xerox; 69. Storage Technology; 70. IBM; 71. Warner Lambert; 72. Pfizer; 73. Upjohn; 74. Eli Lilly; 75.

Under the plan, workers would receive for the first time a share of the profits in times of big earnings. In GM's record 1983, which produced total profits of $3.75 billion, GM's U.S. workers received an average of $640 under the new bonus plan.

Such a plan could become a critical link in a new effort at worker–company cooperation. And that is certainly the avowed intention of GM officials. But some critics are skeptical—an inevitability of the decades of adversarial and mistrusting relationships between management and union.

A few critics have suggested that because the specifics of the profit-sharing plan provide for shared benefits only on profits made in the United States, the agreement could end up giving little or nothing to GM workers who had made wage concessions. Instead, the critics suggest, GM could increasingly take its profits overseas to ensure that they do not have to be shared by GM workers in the United States. And such an approach could have a bottom-line strategic appeal to GM. Consider, for example, that Japanese automobile manufactures were still boasting a $1500–2000 per car cost advantage over U.S. manufacturers at the end of 1983.

The cynical scenario goes like this: When automobile sales rise, GM will have the option of increasing production in the United States. If increases in production and sales causes GM to surpass the $3 billion pretax profit hurdle, activating the blue-collar profit-sharing plans, GM could instead simply buy or manufacture those cars outside the country, say, in Japan. By taking the bulk of the profits on those cars (including the $1500–2000 per car cost advantage endemic to the Japanese) overseas, GM would effectively exempt those funds from being shared under the profit-sharing agreement with U.S. workers. They would, instead, become clean, clear profits.

GM officials suggest such a scenario is far afield from the corporation's real goal—to become more of a partner with the UAW and its members. Assuming GM's best intentions on both its new executive and blue-collar compensation programs, they both serve to emphasize the long-term outlook in an organization that has historically been faulted for short-sightedness.

Abbott Laboratories; 76. Merck; 77. Bristol Meyers; 78. Johnson and Johnson; 79. American Home Products; 80. Smithkline; 81. A&P; 82. Woolworth; 83. Carter Hawley Hale; 84. K-Mart; 85. Sears Roebuck; 86. Safeway; 87. ARA Services; 88. Allied Stores; 89. May Stores; 90. Federated Department Stores; 91. J. C. Penney; 92. Dayton Hudson; 93. Southland Corp.; 94. Kroger; 95. Supermarkets General; 96. Jewel; 97. Lucky Stores; 98. Winn-Dixie; 99. Albertsons; 100. American Stores; 101. Federated National Mortgage Assn.; 102. Great Western Financial; 103. H. F. Ahmanson; 104. Bank of America; 105. First Chicago; 106. Travelers; 107. First Interstate; 108. Chemical Bank; 109. Aetna; 110. Manufacturers Hanover; 111. Citicorp; 112. Bankers Trust; 113. Chase Manhattan; 114. J. P. Morgan; 115. Continental Illinois; 116. Merrill Lynch; 117. Loews; 118. American Express; 119. INA; 120. First Boston; 121. United Brands; 122. Campbell Soup; 123. Borden; 124. Beatrice Foods; 125. Ralston Purina; 126. Dart & Kraft; 127. Norton Simon; 128. Pillsbury; 129. General Foods; 130. Esmark; 131. Archer-Daniles-Midland; 132. H.J. Heinz; 133. CDC International; 134. Quaker Oats; 135. Carnation; 136. General Mills; 137. Nabisco; 138. A.E. Staley; 139. Kelloggs.

The benefit of the longer term is that it places employees who control the manufacturing process first-hand on the assembly line and executives who make the important strategic decisions on a more stable and less traumatic compensation structure. This has long been the case among chief executive officers, as Figure 10.1 shows. The graph plots return on equity on the x-axis and total chief executive compensation on the y-axis for 139 of the nation's largest corporations for 1981. A regression analysis indicates that CEOs received a compensation premium over and above that attributable to short-term performances as measured by return on equity figures. Such an award underscores the importance of a future based, long-term approach. This is the same emphasis rooted in the new reward systems at GM.

CONCLUSION

This chapter has attempted to merge some of the theory of compensation and rewards with some of the reality—especially cyclical economic times and business operating conditions—to underscore the real-world constraints that affect the implementation of any theoretical plan.

Since GM executives could not, politically, accept a separate high-salary, high-bonus structure for others, it ended up rewarding some people for results beyond their personal control. Many of these people were the ones who left the corporation when bonuses stopped, forcing GM to try to make other changes in its reward system. In the end, what the GM case shows is how difficult it is to implement good theory, even with good intentions.

As for the future, the GM example shows how one organization may be able to move through the methodical process of changing from a short- to long-term focus, and how it can bring its workers, at all levels, along, adapting their political and cultural systems along the way. In the end this is the best way to bring about lasting, effective changes.

CHAPTER

11

HUMAN RESOURCE DEVELOPMENT AND ORGANIZATIONAL EFFECTIVENESS

Douglas T. Hall

If strategic human resource management is rare in contemporary work organizations, then the strategic *development* of human resources is virtually non-existent. In most organizations, employee development has an extremely short time horizon, involves minimal corporate resources, and has little impact on the organization. Therefore, much of this chapter deals with "What should be" rather than "what is" in human resource development.

WHAT IS (AND IS NOT) STRATEGIC DEVELOPMENT

Strategic human resource development is *the identification of needed skills and active management of employee learning for the long-range future in relation to explicit corporate and business strategies.* Let us examine each of the component parts of this definition in turn.

159

The last part of the sentence is the most critical—and the element of strategic development which is most often missing: the linkage of development needs and activities to an explicit organizational mission and strategy. Many organizations invest considerable resources in training and development but never really examine how training and development can most effectively promote organizational objectives, or how development activities should be altered in the light of business plans. Even rarer is a recognition that business plans should be altered because of the portfolio of expected future employee capabilities. On the contrary, most organizations view training and development as either a "necessary evil," or "nice to do," or even somewhat of an "employee benefit."[1]

A second way in which development fails to be done strategically in many organizations is that the time span is often too short. The focus is frequently on skill requirements in new or present assignments rather than on requirements for positions 5 or 10 years into the future. In short, training and development (T&D) activities may be characterized as "big T and little D" in many organizations (i.e., much training and little development.)

Third, there is often an inadequate amount of energy devoted to *identification* of future skill needs compared to the *growth* of those skills. Training and development seems to entail more action ("Let's develop a new three-day seminar") than thought and diagnosis. To be strategic about development means to analyze future business opportunities and plans and to think deductively about the future employee skills that will be necessary to implement these plans. In many organizations, however, development consists solely of a set of formal classroom educational experiences. To get us started, let us consider just exactly what development is.

Development

Development is a process of enhancing an individual's present and future effectiveness. In the present case, we are viewing effectiveness in the context of the employee's career. And by career we mean, "the individually perceived sequence of attitudes and behaviors associated with work-related experiences over the space of the person's life"(Hall, 1976). Thus development in the career entails changing both perceptions and behaviors (or skills).

---

[1] This confusion over the meaning and purpose of employee development can work against the objectives of the organization. Consider tuition reimbursement programs as a case in point. Many organizations routinely reimburse employees for tuition on courses that are work-related (e.g., MBA courses) as a matter of corporate policy. Such reimbursement is costly but is often not associated with corporate developmental plans or a career development plan for the person. The person, however, sees university coursework as a part of his or her development. Then when the person completes a degree, such as the MBA, he or she expects the organization to treat them differently, perhaps with a new assignment. But in the view of the organization, the person is no different. The problem comes from two different meanings attached to tuition reimbursement: the employee sees it as career development; the organization sees it as an employee benefit.

More specifically, the targets of development are the four *outcomes* that measure career effectiveness: performance, attitudes, identity, and adaptability. These outcomes can be broken down by time-frame and locus of concern, as shown in the following:

| | Locus of Concern | |
Time-Frame	Task	Self
Short term	Performance	Attitudes
Long term	Adaptability	Identity

Performance and attitudes focus on the short term: attainment of present work goals and present feelings about the career, such as involvement, commitment, and conflict. Adaptability is the extent to which the person is preparing to meet *future* career demands. Identity is a measure of the congruence of integration of the person's self-perceptions over time (i.e., a measure of how the person sees the parts of the career fitting together or "making sense").

Any activity that enhances one or more of these four career outcomes constitutes development. Training, coaching, increased effort, and self-improvement to increase job performance are development. Socialization, job experiences, counseling, peer interactions, and other activities that alter or clarify career attitudes are development. Job assignments, education, and other learning that broadens the person's skills and abilities enhances adaptability and thus also development. And, finally, self-examination, self-assessment, feedback, counseling, and other activities that clarify and focus self-identity are also development. Too often, however, organizations define development as working only on the top left-hand corner on short-term, task-related skills. Too seldom are attitudes, adaptability, and identity the focus of plans for development.

In addition to considering the four career outcomes as *goals* of developmental activities, we can also examine various *strategies* for attaining these goals. In their review of organizational training and development processes, Wexley and Latham propose certain basic developmental strategies that organizations use. The first strategy is *cognitive*, and is conceived with altering thoughts and ideas. The second is *behavioral*, entailing the attempt to change behavior directly. And the third is *environmental* and consists of interventions aimed at altering the immediate work environment of the individual.

If we combine the career goals and these three basic strategies, we obtain a matrix of possible combinations of developmental strategies aimed at particular career outcomes, as shown in Table 11.1.[2] (Since the performance category is so important, it has been subdivided into technical, interpersonal, and conceptual skills.) The specific activities listed are not meant to be ex-

---

[2] The matrix of Figure 11.1 was inspired by Wexley and Latham (1981); however the goals here are significantly different.

TABLE 11.1. Goals

Performance			Attitudes	Adaptability	Identity
Technical	Interpersonal	Conceptual			
Cognitive Strategy					
Basic knowledge in specialty entry	Self improvement books and reading Films Inspirational lectures and speeches	University seminar in basic discipline University functional courses Sabbatical Industry boards	Orientation training Retraining programs Company career information Sabbatical	University retraining programs Career planning seminar Company career information Sabbatical	Self-assessment Seminar for personal interests University retraining programs
Behavioral Strategy					
On-the-job training Apprenticeship	Role playing Apprenticeship Behavior modeling Assessment centers	Role playing	Socialization Phased retirement Flex-time Flex-place	Outplacement Career counseling Early retirement Flex-time Flex-place	Assessment centers Outplacement Career counseling Phased retirement
Environmental Strategy					
Job challenge Job feedback Job autonomy Technical ladder Peer interaction	Team O.D. Matrix management Project teams Task force	Matrix management Project teams Task force Employee exchange programs	Matrix management Project teams Job challenge Technical ladder Internal consulting Employee exchange	Job rotation Temporary assignments Job variety Downward move Employee exchange programs	Job challenge Job autonomy Technical ladder Internal consulting Downward move

haustive, and some cells may represent somewhat incompatible combinations (e.g., cognitive approaches to developing interpersonal skills). Furthermore, several activities are found in more than one cell, as a given activity can produce multiple outcomes.

Although we do not comment on each cell of the figure, some comments on the three broad strategies are in order. First, it appears that excessive reliance in the past has been placed upon cognitive approaches, especially formal, in-class seminars. Although these activities might be useful for aiding performance (especially technical and conceptual), they do little for adaptability, attitudes, and identity. The more potent interventions for attitudes, adaptability, and identity are strategies aimed at behavior and the work environment. Furthermore, of the three strategies, this writer's opinion is that the environment-based activities are the most potent in producing changes in important skills, attitudes, self-conceptions, and ability to change; cognitive interventions may be the *least* potent. Unfortunately, environmental changes are the most difficult to create and cognitive activities the easiest, which is why so much "development" takes place in classroom settings.

To help explain why certain activities were placed where they were in Table 11.1, the cognitive activities all are basically forms of communication of information (either one-way or two-way), where the strategy is to alter the person's knowledge of ways of thinking. The distinction between behavioral and environmental strategies is a bit more subtle. Behavioral approaches attempt to change the employee's behavior within a particular environmental setting (e.g., behavior modeling or role-playing); the person is (hopefully) changing behavior but the environment is unchanged. In environmental approaches either the person is moved into a different environment (e.g., job rotation) or the target of change is the environment rather than the person directly (e.g., team building).

The Context of Strategic Development

Since the work environment represents such a rich source of untapped opportunities for development, this section focuses on environmental strategies in more detail. First, however, let us consider the basic "trigger" or motivating force for development within the individual.

The basic process by which the development of new skills and attitudes occurs can be shown by the *psychological success cycle.*[3] In this growth process the person works toward a challenging goal and achieves it through independent effort; with feedback, realizes that he or she has performed at a high level, receives intrinsic (satisfaction) and extrinsic (pay, recognition, promotion, etc.) rewards, and becomes more involved in and motivated for future goal-related activity. This helps us understand the familiar finding that: "Success breeds success." The psychological success cycle is illustrated in Figure 11.1.

[3] See the discussion of the staffing implications of the organization structure in Chapter 4.

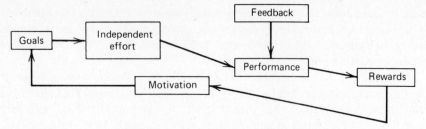

FIGURE 11.1.   The psychological success cycle.

Factors Affecting Development

What *external factors* of the organizational environment affect the success cycle? At the strategic level, there are at least three factors. Personnel policies provide the broad guidelines that direct all human resource activities. Unfortunately, many organizations do not have formal policies related to people, even though clear personnel policies formulated and practiced by top management are the most important element in developing human resources.[4]

Promotion from Within

The most critical policy for development is a clear organizational commitment to the development of internal candidates for job openings. Such a policy drives development, if only for the simple reason that there must be a pool of developed employees available to step into higher-level positions if those positions are to be filled from within. Also, the knowledge that the organization will replace from within provides employees with motivation to develop themselves to be prepared for a promotional opportunity. On the other hand, nothing discourages an employee as strongly as feeling qualified but being passed over in favor of an external candidate.

The key factor is that the promotion-from-within policy be strong, clear, and *practiced*. In many cases such a policy is espoused but not widely implemented. The result is that frequently a manager feels forced to "go outside" because no one internal is sufficiently qualified. In fact, a qualified insider is frequently available, but the assessment system was inadequate to identify that person. Someone inside could also have had the potential but not the proper training or experience. If the policy were truly operative, the necessary assessment and developmental activities would have been in place.

Companies with promotion-from-within policies tend to hire younger people with lower levels of education than do companies that recruit externally for middle and upper-level positions. In part, this is true by definition, since

---

[4]Kanter (1977) discusses the importance of opportunities in organizations.

promoting from within means *not* hiring more senior people. However, this policy also may lead to *not* hiring people with graduate (e.g., MBA) degrees, as these firms prefer to "grow their own" talent. Thus the policy of promotion from within drives more systematic employee development. This policy also leads to more committed and loyal employees as a result of long organizational socialization and the development of a rich network of social relationships in the organization.

Employment Security

Many organizations with promotion-from-within policies also have a policy of employment security. This is a commitment to provide continuing employment for all employees who have been with the organization more than a specified number of years (e.g., 2 years at Procter & Gamble, 10 in many heavy equipment manufacturing companies). This policy does not mean employees will not be fired for poor performance or for disciplinary infractions, but that they will be protected from layoffs due to economic downturns.

Perhaps one of the best-known employment security policies is that practiced by IBM. For over 40 years, no IBM employee has lost pay due to a lack of work. This policy started in the depression of the 1930s, when top management decided that skilled employees would be crucial to future corporate growth and effectiveness. So, even though the company was suffering through one of the worst economies in business history, it invested in a stockpile of human talent. Later, when the new Social Security Administration needed enormous quantities of business equipment, IBM was the only company with the human capability to meet this demand.

Such a policy forces the organization to plan carefully and to link its business plans with its human resource plans. For example, the hiring of a new employee takes on a much more serious significance when one considers that one is, in effect, granting lifetime tenure to the person. This could mean 40 years' worth of income, or a commitment of almost a million dollars, assuming an annual salary of $25,000. On this basis the organization will want to plan carefully about how to develop and deploy that resource, and will be less likely to let that person become obsolete or deadwood.

As an illustration of the strategic use of an employment security policy, consider the case of a large automobile equipment manufacturing company. The chairman (and CEO) of the company was an interested follower of Japanese management practices and was convinced that the commitment of certain Japanese firms to employee lifetime employment forced them to develop and manage people effectively. He appointed a task force comprised of three plant managers, the comptroller, the employee relations manager, and the author (as an outside consultant) to study the experiences of the company and to make a recommendation.

The task force's conclusion was that the most important benefit of employment security was the incentive (indeed, the demand) it created for managers to treat employees as assets and investments who are to be carefully managed and developed. Because hiring was often more controlled and limited in employment-security firms, managers saw employees as very *scarce* resources who had to be recycled (trained, developed) when necessary, as they could not be discarded.

Another conclusion was that the more subject an organization was to fluctuations in the business, the more financially risky an employment security policy was. If the financial swings are extreme, it may be less expensive to lay off people and subsequently rehire them when business improves. Companies with the strongest employment security policies tend to be those which are relatively unaffected by the business cycle, such as Texas Instruments and Johnson's Wax.

However, most organizations underestimate the full costs of large-scale firing and hiring, including administrative costs, unemployment payments, lowered morale, recruiting expenses, training, and lowered performance for new hires. One company (Weyerhauser) costed out the effects of cutting personnel costs through layoffs and through attrition and found the latter to be less expensive. Thus the costs of an employment security policy may not be as great as the managers might imagine.

Cross-Functional Movement

Although many companies have traditionally developed people up through one department, function, or operating unit, there is a new trend toward greater cross-functional movement. Experiences in different parts of an organization force the person to develop a wider range of skills, a wider network of relationships, and more of a company-wide perspective. As an executive from Union Carbide described their change to greater use of cross-division transfers,

> We were a holding company until the 1950s, and you could count on your fingers the number of people who moved from division to division. You grow up in a division, and you get about four miles tall but not very broad. . . . Everybody has sneered at lateral transfers. Now, they can point to us. I feel this gives me a chance to see the whole business. [*Business Week,* July 14, 1975]

Cross-functional movement is not as straightforward as these comments might indicate, however. First of all, such movement produces generalists rather than specialists. It may be necessary, however, to produce specialists in technical areas, so that the amount of within and between-function movement would have to be planned carefully in relation to future staffing requirements.[5]

---

[5] See Chapter 4 for a further discussion of the relationship between structure and staffing.

Another possibility is a mixed model of specialists–generalists. In this system a person might spend a period of time, say, five years, developing as a specialist within a particular function. Then, after that time, the person would be rotated through different functions and become more of a generalist. In this way the person's needs for broadening and preparation for general management could be met while the organization's needs for specialists could also be satisfied. (A hybrid form of this system is the second specialty model in which the person spends, say, five years in one specialty and then rotates to a second specialty, where he or she remains.)

Policies about movement, then, have potent effects on what kinds of skills are developed. In many organizations, mobility is either random or born of tradition rather than from a strategic plan for developing certain types of businesses and people.

Minimum and Maximum Incumbency Times

Whether it is a cross-functional move or a within-function change, nothing creates learning opportunities as effectively as a new job assignment. In many organizations, however, there are no policies governing how long a person should remain in a particular position. There is a tendency for mobility to be greatest in the early career years and then to level off in midcareer, so that the person enters a career plateau. In one study conducted by the author in a chemical company, it was not unusual to find people who had been in the same job for 10, 15, or 20 years. And, as one person understated it: "After 20 years in this same job, things get to be a little bit repetitious."

In their research on R&D scientists and engineers, Pelz and Andrews[6] found an optimal time-in-position of years. In other occupations this time might vary with the amount of on-the-job learning and experience required for effective performance. For example, a right-of-way negotiator for a gas pipe-line company, whose inclusion of an apparently insignificant contingency in a contract might save the company millions of dollars, indicated in a recent seminar that it may take well over five years to reach peak effectiveness in this position.

A company policy that no person should be in a given position more than a certain number of years (which might vary by position) would be a way to force management to assess the skills and placement needs of each employee. If an employee were difficult to move anywhere else because of narrow skills, this would force retraining, and movement to a new assignment would produce on-the-job development.

In practice, a minimax incumbency policy could be enacted by specifying that no person with less than the minimum time in position could be moved without the consent of, say, the division manager or the president. And,

---

[6] Chapter 13 discusses the systematic integration of the different systems through the human resource cycle and the corporate culture.

regarding the maximum, the policy could state that whenever an employee reaches the maximum number of years in position, the personnel record system will "flag" that employee's case and trigger an assignment review conducted by the human resource department, the boss, and the employee. It could be that the person might remain in the present position, but not without good reason.

Successor Training Before Promotion

Another corporate policy that promotes development by managers of their subordinates is a requirement that no manager will be considered a candidate for promotion until he or she has demonstrated that one of their subordinates is ready for promotion. It may not be necessary that the employee be developed specifically for the boss' position, but the organization does need people who have developed the capability of assuming increased responsibility somewhere in the organization. Managers are often reluctant to develop subordinates because there seems to be little incentive to do so. Linking the manager's career development with the subordinate's provides a powerful inducement in this direction.

Understaffing

Some organizations are systematically understaffed, perhaps by 10 to 20%. In addition to producing a more efficient operation, understaffing also stretches or challenges employees and develops a wide range of skills because they are called on to perform a broad set of tasks. If staffing and hiring are tight, it also induces the manager to devote more attention to the "care and feeding" of his or her people.

Of course, a risk of understaffing is that with a tight internal labor market a manager might tend to hoard talent and prevent people from moving cross-functionally. Development in-place might be achieved at the expense of development through movement. In this case, understaffing should be combined with a strong commitment to internal employee mobility and a human resource system that will assure managers that for each good employee they give up they will receive a good person in exchange from somewhere else in the organization.

Other Development Policies

Other corporate policies to affect employee development can also be developed. For example, one important policy issue regards how low in the organization a professional or management trainee starts. In some organizations the policy is for all trainees to start at the operating level so they can truly understand the business (e.g., Procter & Gamble brand management trainees all start off with a sales territory). In other cases the person starts off with managerial or professional responsibilities to provide greater initial job challenge (e.g., in the Bell System).

Other relevant policies affecting development would include the relative amount and timing of corporate versus field experience, the amount of geographic relocation, policies affecting spouse employment and spouse relocation assistance, and the expected rate of advancement ("fast track" versus "low burn.") All of these, as well as the policies discussed earlier, have profound effects on employee development. Often, however, such policies are operative but are not stated explicitly. The more aware and the more clear the organization is about development policies, the more effective control it can exercise over employee growth.

Structure's Effect on Development

The organization's structure has profound effects on employee development. Again, like policy, structure is rarely considered as a strategic variable to be manipulated in order to affect development. The structure of the organization represents the array of future opportunities available to the employee.[7] There are distinct ways in which structure can be employed for strategic development. First, strategic plans for the ways employees will be moved through various positions and between various units (divisions, companies, departments) can be developed. For example, at Sears it was possible to construct job progressions, based upon job evaluation points that could produce various types of career paths (fast growth, slow growth, functional specialization, general management orientations).[8] Few organizations take advantage of their corporate structure for strategic development. They usually fill positions based solely on organizational requirements, rather than also considering individual development issues.

The second way structure can be employed for strategic development is more extreme: the structure can be modified to provide different development outcomes. Perhaps the most common way structure is modified for this purpose is when additional grade (and pay levels) are added to a particular job area to provide additional incentives and opportunities for upward mobility. One example would be the position of associate partner that was added to the structure of a public accounting firm to provide advancement opportunities during what was seen by junior accountants as the long wait before they were considered for promotion to partner. Another way additional levels are often added is when the organization is developing the *dual ladder* concept,

---

[7] The breakdown is based on Reypert (1981).

[8] Kimberly et al., (1980) present various theoretical approaches to explain the lifecycles of organizations. Hall (1976) also discusses the career development implications of the organizational lifecycle.

which provides dual advancement paths, one into the management ranks and one into higher grades of professional responsibility. Often in dual ladders, the technical side is seen reaching a plateau faster than the managerial side, which has led many organizations recently to add higher grade levels to the technical side. This dual ladder concept was originally developed in research and development organizations, where the technical side included engineering and scientific job categories. Now the concept is being applied to a wide range of professional specialist positions, such as finance specialists in banks, information specialists in computer companies, and a range of staff specialists in other business organizations.

Strategic Use of Development to Influence Structure

Not only does structure affect development, but the relationship can work in the other causal direction as well: development can affect structure. Specific patterns of development can serve as *substitutes for structure*. For example, if an organization has a decentralized structure with few formalized communication and integrative mechanisms, a strong policy of promotion from within and cross-functional mobility can, through employee socialization, "program in" an organization-wide perspective, integration of corporate goals, and smooth communication based on trust and shared values and background. These promotion-from-within and mobility policies have been found to be effective integrative devices in organizations as diverse as the U.S. Forest Service and the Roman Catholic Church (Hall and Schneider, 1973).

Edstrom and Galbraith (1977) show in detail how organizational transfers are, in effect, part of an organization's verbal information system. They summarize this process as follows:

> Briefly, we believe that transfer changes managerial behavior; and that, collectively, changes in behavior change organization structure. More specifically, we hypothesize that transfer influences verbal contact with colleagues in other units and therefore amounts to designing the organization's verbal information system. The result is believed to be greater local control in the presence of interdependence.

Thus if structure is an attempt to provide rational control over organizational activities, the strategic development (i.e., socialization) of individuals is an alternative to structure for achieving the same objective.

Strategic Use of Other Human Resource Activities

One of the most powerful ways to facilitate employee development is to develop human resource systems for the achievement of other objectives, with the full knowledge that improved development will be an important spin-off benefit. The fact is that human resource functions tend to be interdependent, and these interdependencies can be employed strategically.

The two human resource functions that probably have the strongest impact on development are *performance appraisal* and *succession planning.* Each of these topics is considered in detail elsewhere in this volume but, in fact, they cannot be separated from the development process.

Let us consider rewards first.

A well-functioning performance appraisal system drives development. When employees receive clear feedback on their performance, when rewards are tied to performance, and when performance expectations are stated in clear behavioral or goal-related terms, the employee's second question (after asking, "How did I perform?") will be, "How can I perform better?" Learning to perform better requires the sharpening and acquisition of knowledge and skills—in short, development. Therefore, if a new performance appraisal and reward system is put in place, the natural next step would be a system for long-term performance improvement and skill development. In many organizations the performance appraisal form has a section that covers development (strengths, weaknesses, and a plan for development).

Strategically, then, one of the best ways for an organization to stimulate development would be to start with the performance appraisal system, either creating one, if there is none, or improving it if one currently exists. This will impress managers and employees with the need for performance improvement and will lead to a natural felt need for planned development. Another implication of this performance–development link is that if there is not currently an effective performance and reward system, the organization should *not* initiate a development system until the performance appraisal system is in place. It makes no sense to work on future performance if present performance is not being well managed.

Succession planning is another human resource activity which leads naturally to a felt need for planned corporate-wide development activities. A typical human resource forecasting model, from the Ontario Ministry of Transportation and Communication, is shown in Figure 11.2. In forecasting and succession planning, future demands, based on strategic business plans, are compared to sources of people. To assess "sources," there is a review of incumbents and identification of back-up, as well as expected losses from retirements, transfers out of the function, and resignations. These factors result in an equation of supply and demand that indicates any personnel imbalance which may exist. If a shortage exists, strategies such as redeployment (transfer out), stockpiling of surplus people, attrition, outplacement, and accelerated retirement might be considered. Many of these strategies, especially redeployment to different functional areas or operating units and outplacement, require a considerable developmental component. Thus an effective forecasting and succession planning system necessarily leads to strategic developments as well.

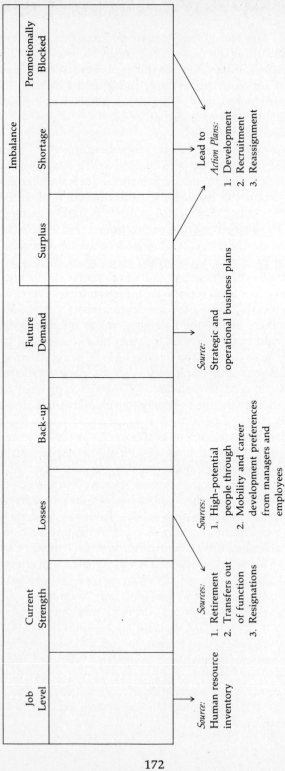

FIGURE 11.2. A representative human resource forecasting model. Adapted from Reypert, L. J. *Human Resouce Planning*, 1981, 4, 151–156.

Why bother attacking development indirectly, as a spinoff of other systems such as rewards and succession? Again, the issue is a strategic one: managers, especially middle managers who are primarily the implementers of any management system, are more concerned about activities that help them attain their business objectives (activities such as performance improvement and succession planning) than they are in individual employee development per se. Therefore, it may be difficult to motivate managers to work on employee development because the rewards for them may be questionable, but it is far clearer to them how they will benefit from performance improvement and succession planning. In short, to the manager, organizational needs are more pressing than individual employee concerns, and the manager often sees development as only a concern of the employee. The more development can be linked to the achievement of business objectives, the more development will take place.

DEVELOPMENT ACROSS THE ORGANIZATIONAL LIFE CYCLE

It is becoming clear that organizations and individuals have developmental lifecycles with each stage having distinctive needs and concerns (see Figure 11.3). Basically, both people and organizations are human systems with biological-type growth and decay curves: birth, growth, maturity, and decline. In a new and growing organization, personal development happens almost naturally because corporate growth provides such a wide range of opportunities for the individual. The risk, though, is that the person will be drawn into areas of organizational priority that are not of the greatest interest or of long-term benefit to him or her. During organizational maturity and decline, opportunities become more limited, and greater planning is required if individual growth is to continue.

INDIVIDUAL   **ORGANIZATION**

	Birth	Growth	Maturity	Decline
Exploration, Entry	x			
Establishment Advancement		x		
Maintenance			x	
Disengagement				x

FIGURE 11.3.   Individual and organizational life stages.

A diagram shows combinations of personal and organizational life stages to be congruent: young, fast-growing employees gravitate towards young, fast-growing organizations. Mature, stable organizations tend to have older, mature employees.

One promising avenue for strategic development, however, would be the encouragement of *intentional misfits.* In other words, assuming a "go-go" manager (in the establishment and advancement stage of the manager's career) would fit naturally in a growing organization, a counter-intuitive development strategy might be to put that person in a mature organization to develop budget-management and administrative skill. Or perhaps the manager might be put in a declining organization to develop planning, conflict-management, cost-reducing, and people-management abilities, all of which would be severely tested in such an environment.

Similarly, a steady-state-oriented administrator (in a maintenance career stage) might be placed in a fast-growth unit to revitalize the administrator's skills and attitudes. And a person near the end of a career (in the disengagement stage) might be highly effective as a mentor for people in new or growing organizations by passing on all that was learned earlier in the person's career about how to succeed in new, growing systems.

Strategic misfitting can also be a means of promoting organization development as well. A mature manager in a fast-growth environment can add needed stability and organization. On the other hand, a rapidly moving manager can revitalize a mature, "middle-aged" organization.

One risk of strategic misfitting is that the impact of the manager may be so great that it alters the course of the organization's development. A familiar example would be the young, aggressive manager who is put into a declining organization to help it die gracefully, only to develop new products and markets, putting it back into a growth stage. Such an outcome could be welcomed at the corporate level, or it could be a problem if that business simply did not fit with the firm's overall business plans. Implication: corporate expectations to the misfitted manager must be extremely clear. And rewards would most likely have to be uncoupled from the performance of the business unit as well (i.e., the manager assigned to wind down a business could not be put on a bonus plan tied to the projects of that business).

Along with clear expectations, great care must be exercised to communicate clearly the reasons why the manager is being placed in an intentionally imperfect fit. If this were not done, the manager, employing traditional means of evaluating the move, might misinterpret the organization's future plans for him or her. To illustrate, in a large commercial bank, an aggressive, advancing loan officer with a bright future was put in charge of the controller's division, traditionally seen as a nonmainstream area in the bank, and definitely *not* a career-enhancing place to be assigned. However, the officer was assigned there to shake up the division, to make it more responsive to the lending areas, and to stimulate creativity and productivity in the development of new information systems. Unfortunately, though, the officer was not adequately (or convincingly) informed of the reasons for placement there and of the fact that this was, in fact, a highly important and visible assignment. So for the first two months in the job, the officer moped around the bank, worrying about what top management was trying to say—time that should have been spent initiating major organizational changes. Implication: when misfitting people, tell them extra clearly why they are being put there, *especially* if it is "good news."

DEVELOPMENT ACROSS THE INDIVIDUAL LIFECYCLE

It is also important to establish a strategy for development as a function of the individual's career stage, independent of the organization's life stage. During the first, or exploration, stage the person is in need of information about self and about career opportunities. A new employee or an established employee who wants to change functions would most likely be at the exploratory stage. This information can be provided through counseling, internships and practice, informational interviews with people in the areas aspired to, self-directed career planning, learning or retraining programs, and support for exploratory behavior.

For the person becoming established and advancing in a particular area, challenging initial job assignments are probably the most important single career influence. Supervision that provides *autonomy, support,* and *high expectations* is also career-enhancing. Training for supervisors in job design, career coaching, and mentoring skills is also extremely useful, as is career planning.

In midcareer, when the person is in a maintenance mode, developmental strategies are just beginning to be identified. A recent study by the author has identified the following approaches. *Periodic job rotation* (lateral and perhaps even downward moves) provide great stimulation. *Cross-functional moves* are an especially good type of rotation to facilitate midcareer learning. *Job redesign* is an important way to develop midcareer employees in place. *Recognition and rewards for performance* is often the major deficiency reported by established employees. *Participative management* is an important way of utilizing the knowledge and experience of mature employees and especially important for professionals. *Information about corporate career opportunities* is another significant deficiency area, as most employees and managers become so highly involved in their own area that they know little about opportunities for movement in other parts of the organization. *Higher level technical or professional positions* or enhancement of the technical side of the dual ladder for advancements is an important motivator, as we said earlier. *Consulting or trouble-shooting assignments* inside the organization are another way to attack both important organizational needs and employee development simultaneously. In a similar vein, *temporary assignments* in a different function or division have the same limited time span as an internal consulting assignment, although the person would not be in such a visible "expert" role.

Some of the more popular remedies for a midcareer plateau, such as geographic relocation, university programs, and sabbaticals are not popular with employees and are not necessarily seen as effective by management. They seem to make good press but not necessarily good practice for human resource development. *Outplacement* and *early retirement* are seen as effective by management but are not highly popular with employees.

For later career employees, *phased transition* programs can be effective. Such programs give the person a gradual opportunity to move into another career activity or into retirement. One option here is flexible, part-time work as a buffer between full-time employment and the end of employment with that particular organization. Another phased model is one where the amount of vacation time increases near the end of the career, to help the person learn to manage and structure increasingly larger segments of personal time.

Preretirement life planning workshops can also be of great assistance in planning the move out of the organization. These should cover both the financial, emotional, and task activities involved in moving into a new lifestyle. Family involvement is an important feature of any transition planning activity. All the factors that ease entry into the organization (e.g., realistic previews, exploration opportunities, challenge, autonomy, emotional support) become equally critical during the exit process.

Top Management Involvement in Development

Perhaps the most important factor in ensuring that development is done strategically is the participation of top management in the process. Because top management is the strategic level of the organization, and because top management represents the strategic business planners of the organization, they should also be the human resource planners. Top management should plan and execute employee development activities.

Development should not be the responsibility of the human resource function. Personnel should act as a third party and assist and/or monitor the development process, but actual development decisions and strategies should be the responsibility of top management. The active involvement of management in development at organizations as diverse as Citicorp (Sakland, 1976), Southern New England Telephone Company (Hall and Hall, 1976), the Province of Ontario (Reypert, 1981), and the Arizona Public Service (Wellington, 1981) is cited as critical to the success of development in each. When the president and chairman of an organization meet monthly or biannually to review succession plans, back-ups, and developmental plans, planned strategic development is actually accomplished.

MANAGERIAL AND OPERATIONAL LEVEL DEVELOPMENT ISSUES

The key to strategic development is activities and policies at the strategic level of the organization, and that is where most of our attention is devoted in this paper. However, if supportive systems and practices are not in place at lower levels, strategic plans will not be executed.

At the managerial level, the critical factors are training for manager and rewards for developing subordinates. To effect development, the manager must see a personal payoff. Including development as part of a manager's job objectives and making development of subordinates a prerequisite for promotion are two important ways of providing rewards. Managers need skill training in job design, career coaching, succession planning, assessment of potential, and feedback to be more effective developers of talent.

Interunit cooperative arrangements are also necessary to facilitate movement throughout the corporation. Since managers are understandably wary of accepting unknown transferees, career brokers or internal placement managers are often necessary. A good way to give power to these internal brokers is to make these the same people who manage the corporate management training program. In this way the broker can say to the reluctant receiving manager: "You say you want some of our good trainees this year? You can have them *if* you accept some transfers from other departments as well."

Strategic development is at its weakest at the managerial level in many organizations. Often there is a strong commitment to development as the strategic level, coupled with specific programs and systems to aid individual employees at the operational level (e.g., career planning workshop, job posting systems). But there is often no attempt to "cascade down" the top-level strategy in the form of objectives for development so that managers are encouraged (or required) to develop their own strategies for implementing these organization-wide objectives. *The problem here is that strategy is often seen as the exclusive domain of the senior levels of the organization, so that middle managers are not held accountable for strategic planning for their level.* Then, in turn, the managers do not hold their operational-level subordinates responsible for planning strategy at their level.

Richard Vancil describes how this downward cascading of strategy can integrate the planning of all levels in the organization:

A personalized strategy is feasible in a complex organization if the statement of strategy is drafted carefully. As discussed earlier, the superior manager devises his strategy and expresses it in the form of constraints on the scope of the activities of his subordinates. However, he should take care to leave them some discretion as to how they will operate within these constraints. Each subordinate manager will then accept (or challenge) those constraints, devise 'his' strategy within them, and in turn express his strategy to his subordinates in the form of constraints on their activities. The resulting series of progressively detailed statements of strategy are personalized in the sense that each manager can see his imprint on his part of the series. Furthermore, they are integrated throughout the organization as a whole because each statement is consistent with the constraints imposed by higher authority.

Two of the several advantages of personalized strategies deserve mention here. First, encouraging each manager to use his imagination to devise the best strategy he can, increases the vitality and creativity of the organization. No one man, not even the president, can identify all the opportunities that exist; and a framework of progressive constraints that elicits personalized strategies, multiplies the sources of initiative in the organization. Second, as personalized strategy engenders a personal commitment. [*Sloan Management Review,* Winter 1976]

With this process of top-down communication about strategy (where the strategy at the higher level becomes the set of objectives to be achieved for the lower level), many of the reasons why managers resist developing subordinates would vanish. Let us just consider a few of the reasons managers give for not spending time on subordinate development.

1. *"There are no rewards for developing subordinates. In fact, we are punished for it, since when we develop people, they are often rotated out to another department."* This cascading policy-process becomes a nice way of linking the manager's development strategy to helping achieve the boss's objectives. In this way the boss is paying attention to development and is more likely to recognize the subordinate manager's performance in this area.

2. *"There is no time to develop our people."* There's a role-modeling effect here, as well. If top-level people spend a lot of time on strategic development, managers will find time for it.

3. *"Top management doesn't care about my career. Why should I care about my subordinates' careers?"* Again, if the top level is doing its own strategic planning for development, a prime target group for their activities will be people at the managerial level. This reasoning can then be reversed: "If my superiors are concerned about my development, it's only fair that I should attend to my subordinates' development."

4. *"My career advancement has slowed down. Why should I be expected to help my subordinate advance if I can't?"* First, with strategic development, this makes advancement opportunities more rational, more based on performance and potential at *all* levels, and thus helps managers continue advancing. Second, even if a given manager does not advance further, development is now part of his or her expected performance and will affect other rewards, such as pay and recognition.

5. *"I don't have sufficient company career information and skills in feedback and coaching to help subordinates."* This moves us on to the operational level. If developmental strategy is being communicated and implemented logically up and down the organization, one predictable result will be the need for operational career development information and training programs for managers.

At the operational level, specific employee development activities are necessary. These include career development seminars and workshops, assessment centers to identify potential, career monitoring and coaching, challenging assignments, and all the other activities discussed earlier in relation to different career stages. Perhaps the most critical factor at the operational level is specific programs and systems to permit organization-wide development policies and practices. Activities such as the Bell System's Initial Management Development Program (IMDP) give formality and visibility to the development effort.

Human resource information systems, often computerized, are extremely useful in identifying high-priority development needs and in matching job assignments and candidates. The role of personnel is probably greatest at the operational level in developing and managing development programs and systems.

A problem with an organization's engaging in developmental activities without taking a strategic approach is that it may start with a general, vague expression of commitment from the top, which gets too quickly translated into very concrete operational activities. For instance, in one U.S. auto company a massive program to train most of their first-line supervisors (a sizable group) in career-counseling skills was initiated and guided by a three-word directive from the executive committee in the course of discussion of affirmative action and career development: "Let's do something."

In another organization, a major insurance company, a key vice president, the head of the property and casualty division, by far the largest division in the company, initiated an effort to improve employee development and managerial succession planning. Responsibility for developing and implementing a division-wide program was immediately delegated to an entry-level training specialist. This person did a nearly miraculous job of developing the commitment of management levels between the specialist and the initiating vice president, a process which would have been unnecessary if the initiator had taken a strategic approach; then the staff person could have used the most energy as intended, on the design and delivery of the development program.

Figure 11.1 presented a detailed list of operational developmental activities. Some of the more promising approaches are summarized in the following.

1. *Job Movement.*   Job rotation should continue throughout a person's career. It should not be used only for younger employees on the way up. Lateral moves, cross-functional moves, and moves to operating companies can all be useful. However, geographical movement seems neither desired nor necessary. Other types of mobility, such as temporary assignments, trouble-shooting or consulting assignments, task forces, or project teams, can be useful alternatives to permanent moves. One possible approach would be to have an automatic "trigger" after the employee has been in a position for a certain period of time (say, five years). At this point there would be automatic review of the employee's assignment, a career-counseling session, and a possible job change. The strategic development plan would be of great value in these reviews.

2. *A Professional Placement Function.*   One way to promote more systematic strategic movement would be with a specific function in personnel whose responsibility is professional placement. The person charged with this function would ideally be a well-respected individual who knows various parts of the corporation well and is able to act as a broker for placing employees internally and for freeing up employees to be moved. Outplacement could be another part of this person's responsibility.

3. *Career Counseling and Exploration.*   Participants indicated they would be

more open to various kinds of job moves if they were part of a formal career plan and were career enhancing. Encouragement is needed for employees to do more exploration of career lternatives.

4. *Increased Company Career Opportunity Information.*   The most important career development need for many employees is better information about career opportunities in other parts of the organization. Various methods of communicating this information could be effective: employee career manuals, seminars and workshops with personnel specialists and executives familiar with the total corporation, chances to have informational interviews in other parts of the organization, job posting, and position descriptions from other areas, and so on.

5. *Improving Career Feedback.*   We have already discussed the need for more information about career opportunities elsewhere in the organization. In addition, more individual feedback to the employee regarding his or her own career is needed. This feedback could be part of a career-counseling discussion with the immediate supervisor and should provide frank, realistic information about the person's career prospects, strengths, weaknesses, and steps needed to increase career mobility.

6. *Reviewing Policies About Outside Work.*   Some organizations are finding that motivation of professionals is enhanced if they have an occasional opportunity to do consulting and other types of work on their own time for other organizations. Obviously, this must be done carefully, with concern for possible conflicts of interest and other potential problems. However, it can be a valuable way of providing more variety in work, more recognition, more external visibility, and more opportunity to explore second-career options. Some companies let professionals do outside consulting on their vacation time, whereas others let employees use unpaid leaves of absence.

7. *Enhancing a Linear Career.*   Many professionals often feel very fulfilled with their present specialist role as their life's work. However, they also often feel that the company no longer values a person who chooses to devote his or her career to a professional specialty (as opposed to supervision or management). A task force of committed professionals and managers might be able to brainstorm useful changes in this direction.

8. *Slower Early-Career Advancement; Enrichment of Lower-Level Jobs.*   Part of the problem of a career plateau is the direct result of a company's use of rapid early promotion as a means of developing and retaining young professionals. However, what the young professional needs most is *challenge.* However, the most challenging jobs are often those at higher grade levels. Some organizations have been successful at enriching entry-level and other lower-level jobs as a means of satisfying the growth needs of younger employees, so that fast promotions are less necessary. This is best done in the context of a general strategy for employee development. Many Japanese firms use this approach with some success.

CONCLUSION

A logical starting point in career development is the establishment of a strategic plan for personnel development. This would involve starting with the business and the projected personnel budget and identifying a long-range strategy for moving and developing staff in the appropriate directions. This would be a joint management–personnel process. The *collaborative process* of planning this development strategy would be a critical element. A *cascading process,* involving all levels in the organization, is recommended.

The strategic pursuit of development is one of the least developed areas of human resource management. In fact, where development is practiced most strategically, it is done as part of line management's job and is rarely even identifiable as a human resource activity. Development is properly invisible in this way—a human resource task of managing the enterprise, rather than a part of the human resource department. In working on development strategically, policy-makers have a mix of factors that affect development: job assignments, educational activities, formal training, reward systems for managers, succession planning systems, organization structure, and the like. Strategic development is a logical way to work backwards from business plans to human resource development plans, and to work down from organization-wide objectives to the actual delivery of developmental activities. By thus linking development business needs and linking level to level, clear developmental priorities can be established and the organization can avoid the all too common situation where, in its zeal to do everything it, in fact, accomplishes nothing. Focused, goal-centered development is an integral part of any effective strategic human resource management process.

12

STRATEGIC APPRAISAL AND DEVELOPMENT AT GENERAL ELECTRIC COMPANY

Stewart D. Friedman
with Theodore P. LeVino

The General Electric Company gives the development of executive talent strategic attention. In this diverse company, one that is generally acknowledged to be among the world leaders in management philosophy and practice, the Executive Management Staff (EMS) is responsible for overseeing the process of developing top echelon managers for the whole organization. This

This chapter is based on conversations with Ted LeVino, Senior Vice President, Executive Management Staff (EMS) at GE. Mr. LeVino gave graciously of his time and energy in making comprehensive contributions regarding the history and current workings of EMS. In addition he provided extensive editorial comments on earlier versions of this chapter. His participation in EMS' early stages of growth, and his current leadership role in it, are witnessed in this chapter. In sharing his experience and insight he offers a substantial and deeply appreciated addition to the field of human resource management.

involves early identification of individuals with top management potential and provides them with experiences that will enhance their growth and their breadth of knowledge. The EMS organization has matured into a well-respected, highly valued asset in the corporation. This chapter traces the evolution of EMS and of the executive development process at GE. Key principles guiding GE's practice of strategic executive development are identified.

HISTORY OF EMS

In the late 1960s, Fred Borch, then President and Chief Executive Officer, initiated the Corporate Management Manpower Development Staff (later to be called EMS) for two reasons. It was about to restructure the company, creating a number of general manager openings, and was not satisfied with the quality or quantity of managers that were coming up through the ranks. There had to be additional and better ways to develop the people who were going to run the company's businesses. Jack Parker, who headed the Aerospace and Defense Group, had a talent scout whose primary responsibility was to find the "good ones" and to see that they moved along. Fred Borch saw value in this and suggested that each of his Group Executives consider this approach. Ted LeVino, now Senior Vice President of the Executive Management Staff, was assigned to one of these talent scout positions. Initially, they reported directly to the line executive. Then these five talent scouts were pulled together in Corporate Staff under Roy Johnson, Ted LeVino's predecessor, and the individual credited with establishing the GE system. But the early stages as a centralized staff were not easy; allegiances to the line had already been established. Still, the shift to a direct corporate link proved to be very useful. Fred Borch wanted this to be the reporting relationship so that the search for and development of executive talent would occur on a corporation-wide basis, not just within components.

The second reason for creating EMS had to do with the way Corporate Employee Relations Operation (CERO) had evolved. Under Lem Boulware, CERO had been rooted in adversarial interaction with the national unions. Negotiation of union contracts was its main focus and hourly employee issues were the dominant concern of Employee Relations managers in the field. There was far less emphasis by CERO on the needs of managers and professionals.

Thus EMS started because (1) the task of developing general managers was not being done as well as needed to meet the company's growth objectives, and (2) the attention to Employee Relations was heavily weighted toward the hourly population. Gradually, Roy Johnson brought all exempt employees and professional relations, managerial education, recruiting medical staff, and exempt compensation under the aegis of EMS. However, this complexity spread EMS's resources too thinly. When Fred Borch reorganized

GE into Strategic Business Units (SBU), the corporate staff was altered as well. EMS was chartered solely with the development and appointment of the top people in the company. Responsibility for the overall professional employee population went back to CERO.

There are 29 salary levels of exempt employee rank at GE, reflecting various levels of responsibility. The line was drawn at level 15, which is the cutoff for eligibility for incentive compensation, or bonuses. Those above this point are the primary concern of EMS. CERO has the prime responsibility for the development of generic systems and practices which transcend both parts of the exempt population, such as employee benefit programs.

Today Ted LeVino's organization oversees approximately 5000 people. The other 395,000 GE employees are the concern of CERO. When Ted LeVino took over EMS in 1976 he was given responsibility for the executive man-power operation, organization planning, and executive compensation. (The title Executive "Manpower" Staff was later changed to Executive Manage-ment Staff out of concern for the former's sexist connotations.) This function is the home of the Executive Management Consultants (EMC), the talent scouts who work primarily with the seven line sector executives (see Figure 12.1) to find and develop the top managers at GE.

The EMC are also involved in top level compensation issues and coordinate organizational studies.

EMS, in addition to the EMC, also contains the Organization Planning and Executive Compensation functions. These three functions interlock, sometimes to tailor jobs to meet individual and company needs. In GE's management development philosophy, it is occasionally necessary to disregard otherwise sound compensation practice and/or to change organizational struc-ture to achieve developmental results. For this to occur, each of the three functions—Executive Management, Organization Planning, and Executive Compensation—have to be under the direction of EMS. Figures 12.1 and 12.2 show the current EMS organization and how it fits into GE's corporate struc-ture.

The top 600 employees at GE receive very close attention from EMS. The remaining 4400 at level 15 and above are also reviewed, but not in the same detail. They do receive detailed and thorough review in operations where EMS counterparts and line management follow similar procedures.

CONSEQUENCES OF THE FAILURE TO DEVELOP MANAGERS

To understand why those who run GE take executive development so seri-ously, let us examine the results of inadequate development of people. If the corporation is not viewed as a place where managers have the chance to realize their legitimate ambitions because top management is continually re-cruited from the outside, the better performers may leave the organization. As a result, the quality of managerial talent suffers over time. If high potential

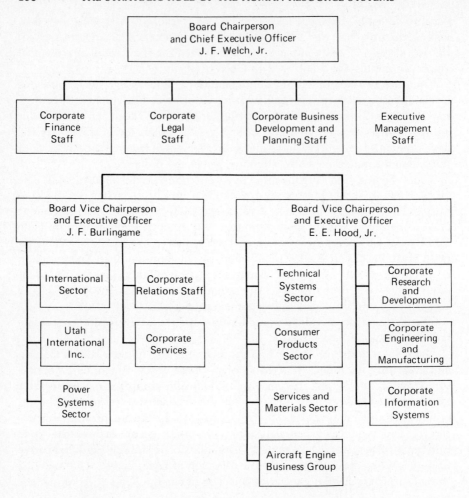

FIGURE 12.1.   General Electric Company's Organization Structure.

people leave, then the company *has* to recruit from outside. This is costly not only because replacement costs are high, but also because there is a loss of motivation, continuity, and stability in the managerial ranks. A break in continuity can deter competitive performance. The top echelon needs to have intimate familiarity with the company in order to run it well and that familiarity comes only from experience.

The motivational forces for individual executives to develop their people are clear at GE. Jack Welch (the current Chairman) sees the task of ensuring the development of managerial excellence in the company as *his most important responsibility.* This is demonstrated by the staff support and time allotted for organization and staffing reviews, by the key position Ted LeVino holds on

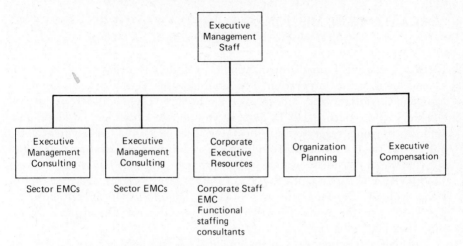

FIGURE 12.2. General Electric Company's Executive Management Staff.

Jack Welch's staff, and by Jack Welch's way of life: "Jack eats, sleeps, and lives the people equation," notes one senior executive. Indeed, despite the need to cut back other corporate staff, EMS was urged to add people in 1980. The Chairman models for the company the importance of executive development.

Individuals are held accountable for the care and feeding of their managerial talent. Certainly not everyone is evaluated primarily on how they grow people, but people performance is factored in with financial performance when bonuses are determined. Since EMS includes Executive Compensation, Ted LeVino can influence incentive decisions. Although it is more difficult to assess performance in the area of employee development than it is to measure business results, organizations should make an effort to identify managers who excel in developing their organization's human resources. For instance, depth of managerial talent can be assessed by looking at the quality of the backups listed in the Organization and Staffing Plans (discussed later). Another way is to see how well prepared one of an executive's key managers is when moved to another component. Similarly, if a segment of an executive's organization is handed over to another in a restructuring move, the reaction of the new executive to the incoming staff says something about the previous boss. Another indicator is to see where talented people want to work and from which components they want to escape. Finally, EMS staff plays a significant role in identifying and recommending managerial talent for open positions. They provide an independent evaluation of people gained through observation in staff meetings, business reviews, and through a multitude of data-gathering techniques. In this fashion, the quality of management development and the existence or absence of talented managers within a component can be carefully assessed.

ORGANIZATION, MISSION, AND PHILOSOPHY OF EMS AND ITS RELATIONSHIP TO EMPLOYEE RELATIONS

EMS is a relatively small organization. It parallels the first three layers of management in the corporation. Ted Levino is Jack Welch's executive management consultant and reports directly to him; Dave Orselet and Larry Buckley, who report to Ted LeVino, serve the Vice Chairmen, Ed Hood and John Burlingame, respectively. And there is an executive management consultant for the corporate staff functions, Ray Stumberger, who also manages the functional placement system at the corporate level. He too reports to Ted LeVino. An EMC is assigned to each of the sector executives, and they report either to Dave Orselet or to Larry Buckley. The other two direct reports to Ted LeVino are the heads of Executive Compensation and Organization Planning (See Figure 12.2).

The EMCs' independence of the line at the sector level is a critical feature of GE's system. The sector executives prefer this reporting relationship because independent status gives them (1) access to the entire pool of available talent across the corporation, and (2) an objective viewpoint. There is no perceived gain in having a solid line relationship with the EMC for a Sector Executive.

Below the Sector tier, the individuals who work with general managers on human resource planning are called Organization and Staffing (O&S) Managers. They report directly to the line, or indirectly to the line by way of the Employee Relations Managers in operations. Thus below the sector executive level, the O&S manager's position can be within Relations (as the Employee Relations "field" staff function is called) or parallel and equal to Relations. The particular arrangement depends on the size of the component's exempt workforce and on the capability and interests of the Relations Manager in that component. The O&S manager in operations, no matter whom he or she reports to, usually has responsibility for the entire professional population either directly, or by providing overall direction.

At the corporate level, the distinction between what is CERO's or EMS' responsibility is based, as previously mentioned, on a salary level cut. Since this line is somewhat arbitrary, there are occasions when both organizations have to confer on what course will be recommended to top management for approval (for example, exempt salary structure change, leave of absence policy, appointment of key employee relations managers in the field, etc.).

The difference in reporting relationship—CERO to a Vice Chairman and EMS to the Chairman—reflects the difference in missions and frequency of needed contact, not the scope of influence or size of the two organizations. But the implied power EMS has because of its mission and reporting relationship requires diplomacy and tact in dealing with CERO and the field Relations staff.

In sum, there are several reasons in favor of maintaining a clear distinction between EMS and CERO:

1.   The target populations are fundamentally different. EMS has expertise in dealing with general management level personnel concerns. CERO and the field Relations staff, on the other hand, are responsible for the more operational level human resource systems.

2.   Executives are considered to be corporate property. EMS must have the political strength of the Corporate Executive Office (CEO, comprising the Chairperson and the two Vice Chairpersons) to overcome provincial interest (i.e., of the sectors or of any business unit) to ensure broad-based development.

3.   The combination in EMS of executive management, organization planning, and compensation allows top executives easy access to staff help on interrelated issues that are of frequent concern to them.

Given this organization structure, EMS can pursue its *mission*:

To ensure that the best available talent is considered for each job and that each opening is considered for its developmental potential.

To see that there is a reasonable yet selective flow of managers across the corporation.

To ensure that the top organization structure is consonant with long-term company objectives and strategy and enhances top executives' development.

To provide a competitive compensation program to attract, retain, and motivate key employees.

The basic management philosophy driving the GE system of executive development can be described in 10 main points. They are presented in Table 12.1.

To successfully enact this mission and philosophy, there are three significant sets of activities in which EMS engages. These are the slate system, organization and staffing reviews, and accomplishment analyses. These are examined in the following.[1]

The Slate System

At GE, an executive with an opening in the top 600 positions must get a candidate slate from EMS and select from it. This slate is the basis for corporate control over the quality of staffing and executive development. The slate system gives the Chairman and Vice Chairmen, who must approve the slates, direct input on key staffing decisions so that the best company candidates will be considered and so that jobs can be used developmentally.

[1] The portrayal of these activities was aided by D.C. Rikert's case history, *General Electric Company: The Executive Manpower Operation*, Boston, MA: Harvard Business School Case Services, Harvard Business School, 1980.

TABLE 12.1. Ten Points of General Electric's Executive Development Philosopy.

1. Assuring development of managerial excellence in the company is the chief executive's most important responsibility.
2. Managers at all layers must be similarly responsible and must "own" the development system(s).
3. Promotion from within—for its motivational value—will be the rule, not the exception.
4. A key step in planning the development of managers is the manpower review process.
5. Managerial abilities are learned primarily by managing. Other activities are valuable adjuncts.
6. Control of the selection process is essential in order to use openings developmentally.
7. The company can tolerate and needs a wide variety of managerial styles, traits, abilities, etc.
8. Several different managerial streams and development planning systems are needed to accomodate the company's size, diversity, and decentralization.
9. Occasionally, it may be necessary to distort otherwise sound compensation practice and/or to change organizational structure to achieve developmental results.
10. Staff people must add value in these processes but their roles are secondary to the managerial roles.

When a position in the top 600 opens, the EMC for that Sector develops "specs" (specifications) for that opening from knowledge of the job and inputs from the hiring manager and perhaps higher-level management as well. He or she then shares these data with the other EMCs when they meet to discuss candidates. Each EMC presents potential candidates, if they feel their Sectors have any. The slate is constructed by the EMC, then, based on knowledge of: (1) the job specs, (2) who would best contribute to it, and (3) who would most benefit from the experience. Approval for the slate is then obtained through channels from the Corporate Executive Office. This varies with the level of the position. The Chairman and Vice Chairman, for example, must approve all slates at the officer level. Below that, but still in the top 600, all three see the slate and may comment on it, but the cognizant member of the Corporate Executive Office has slate approval authority. Below these 600 positions, the general rule is "one-over-one"; the hiring executive's boss must approve the candidate slate.

Once the EMS slate is approved, it is taken to the person to whom the position reports. The hiring executive interviews the available candidates and chooses one. Candidates are available if: (1) they would like the job, and (2) they have been in their current job long enough to have made a substantial contribution in it for generally, at least two years. Sometimes, however, a candidate is "fair game" after one-and-a-half years, or in rare cases, even one year. Usually there are from two to five names on the slate.

The key to successful slate development is agreeing on a common view of the job specs. This is not an easy task. Often the job requires a complex array of skills and background. Or the demands of the role may be known to change over time. It may be a new and unique position with a set of unknown qualities inherent in it. Even if it seems straightforward, the first and most critical responsibility of the EMC is to get an explicit agreement from everyone on what the job is going to require.

A problem can surface when the hiring executive has someone in mind for the position. The executive might push for the name to be on the slate without first objectively considering the requirements of the position. The EMC has to try to get the specs considered first, then talk about whether the person the hiring executive has in mind is right for the job. The hiring executive and his or her boss have to agree on the job specs. If it turns out that the person in mind does not meet the specs, the EMC can argue that the person is not the best qualified candidate. If the hiring executive persists, he or she must be prepared to defend the choice; the CEO can veto it. Or, the CEO can add a name to the slate. In either case, it is the responsibility of the EMC to provide the most comprehensive data available on who can do the job well and develop in it. Once the information has been imparted, the slate approval decision belongs to the Corporate Executive Office and the selection decision to the hiring executive.

The interview process allows the hiring executive to make a choice from the slate. It also raises the expectations of the interviewees. In preparing a slate, then, one consideration is the danger of exposing candidates to being bridesmaids. This can be demoralizing, and it is especially risky if the hiring executive is not seriously considering all alternatives. In most cases this is not an obstacle. The role of the EMC is seen as one who is knowledgeable across the company. Most hiring executives are eager to tap into that information base; they tend to be very open to suggestions. Furthermore, the process is viewed as equitable since all qualified candidates can vie for a position. Although there is still an urge to be selfish, to hold on to high potentials, most executives see that cross-fertilization serves the needs of the company. This is most noticeable at the Sector level and above, where the company-wide perspective is seen more clearly.

Organization and Staffing Reviews

Another key element in the GE executive development process is the executive organization and staffing (O&S) review by the Corporate Executive Office, which occurs in late Spring with a follow-up session in late Fall. This is a concentrated look at the executive talent in the company.

The O&S reviews serve many purposes.

Many decisions are made about organization structure and the people needed to fill organization needs.

Evaluations of specific managers lead to plans to develop or to place them. Top management interest in executive development is demonstrated.

Top management is better informed of the depth of talent; an inventory of talent is based on the reviews.

Attention to O&S issues is stimulated throughout the company.

The process begins with the department level manager sitting down for a face-to-face review with each of his or her subordinates of their Evaluation and Development Summary. For the subordinate, this contains career interest, self-evaluation, and development actions and plans. For the manager, this includes an evaluation of performance and qualifications, as well as development and career recommendations. Two other formal documents are required of the manager. First is the Individual Promotability Forecast in which each subordinate is rated on the following scale:

1. High potential—can move to next higher organization layer with potential to move at least another organization layer.
2. Promotable—to the next higher organization layer.
3. Advanceable—to a higher position within current organization layer.
4. More time needed—before designation as promotable or advanceable.
5. Not advanceable—but has satisfactory performance.
6. Unsatisfactory performance.

Optimal timing for the next move is also indicated.

The other document required of the manager is his or her Organization and Staffing Plans. Basically, this is a succession plan for the manager and his or her staff. It helps identify people, but it does not serve too well as a succession plan. For example, if a position opens six months after the review session, the job and the available people may be different than indicated on the plan. It does give EMS and others a clue as to how individuals are perceived in a manager's organization, and it gives them an opportunity to explore these perceptions.

The results of these three processes are presented to the manager's superior in the O&S review meeting. In addition, the data are input to the component and/or EMS inventory where it adds to the knowledge base for EMCs and O&S Managers to use in identifying future candidates. At the review, the manager is called on to amplify his or her stance on the promotability and development of subordinates. An EMC or an O&S manager is there either to advocate or to test the views of both superior and manager. When the reviews in the echelon are completed, the next level undergoes the same process. In May, each of the sector executives and senior corporate staff officers meets with the Corporate Executive Office for the O&S review. Attending these sessions are the Sector Executive and assigned EMC, both Vice Chairpersons, Dave Orselet or Larry Buckley from EMS, and Jack Welch and Ted LeVino. These sessions take place over the course of a week, approximately a half-day is allotted for each sector and one to two hours for each Corporate Staff Component. A week elapses, then Ted LeVino presents a wrap-up session in which the results of the reviews are summarized.

The rate of mobility across sectors is discussed in the wrap-up. This might lead to discussions about changes in organization structure. For example, if the flow of talent has been excessive in one year, one way to slow it down is to resist changes in structure that induce turnover. A related issue raised by the review process is the tradeoff between executive continuity and executive development through change. The average tenure in a position is three years. Approximately 20% change each year. Thus in five years all positions turn over, theoretically. There is a period of learning in a new job that may cost the business but will presumably pay off when the individual begins to contribute. The period of contribution should outweigh the period of learning for the sake of that particular business unit. But occasionally a change may be indicated before the individual has "paid back" to the business what he or she gained in the learning phase. Here then is the tradeoff: The needs of the business unit, the individual, and the company as a whole are not always congruent; for the business unit there is contribution to business health and financial performance, for the individual there is career progress by way of challenging experiences, and for the company there is the need to grow managers with broad scope. In a company as diverse as GE, there is a great risk in developing top echelon executives strictly in vertical fashion. On the other hand, in order to maintain a competitive edge there must be continuity of management within components. Balancing these sometimes opposing forces is an important part of the review and wrap-up discussions. The Chairman gives a report of the wrap-up session to the Management Development and Compensation Committee of the Board in June. It is updated and presented to the full board in November.

For each Sector and Staff component, approximately 10–15 issues and their resolution are identified in May. The appropriate Corporate Executive Office member sends a letter to each executive delineating these issues. In the Fall, a follow-up session is held. The full-blown review process is *not* repeated, but follow-up and any new issues are discussed. The Fall sessions are a very recent addition to the process; they began in 1981. The process gets better and better as the quality of managerial attention improves.

The change in attitude by the participants in O&S reviews over the last 10 years or so has been dramatic. Initially, there was a great deal of defensiveness; issues were not brought out in the open; resolution of dilemma occurred behind closed doors. Perfunctory attention was given to the review, both as a concept and in practice and it was seen as another drain on an executive's scarcest resource, time. The required paperwork was excessive, and managers felt that the sessions were too often a place for punishing those not perceived as doing their job in the human resource area. But refinement of the process with each successive Chairman has changed this. Now people look forward to the reviews as a forum for the resolution of real issues. Constructive work gets done; views are put on the table and disagreements are openly discussed. Whereas, in the past, ownership of the review process belonged to the EMS with the CEO's backing, it now belongs to the line executives. Its value is acknowledged.

One of the keys to the success of the O&S reviews is that there are no great surprises brought to light, yet there is plenty of spontaneous interaction. The O&S review session is a place to iron out differences; it's all right to disagree there. But the name of the game is: "Avoid sandbagging the manager." For the EMC, this means informing the manager in advance if there are known points of disagreement. The review is a good place to test ideas to see how the Corporate Executive Office feels about a specific issue. For example, if a manager has a subordinate he or she wants promoted, but the CEO is known to feel differently about the subordinate's progress, the review process allows for a give-and-take discussion on the question of promotability. Finding out sooner rather than later gives the subordinate an opportunity to re-evaluate his or her position, and perhaps to pursue another course of action.

Accomplishment Analysis

EMS gets to know about people in a number of different ways. The EMC visits operations and sees people work in their environment. The EMC is on the sector executive's staff and participates in staff meetings, major business reviews, plant tours, trade shows, and so on. And he or she develops still more information during O&S reviews, for the annual appraisal form (i.e., Evaluation and Development Summary), from informal discussions, and from the accomplishment analysis. Thus the EMC develops a credible database which the sector executive recognizes as valid.

The accomplishment analysis is the most concentrated data-gathering technique available to EMS. Usually, this occurs well into an individual's career. An EMC will interview the person for three to four hours. They will talk about what the person has done in the past few jobs, as well as what was not done that should have been. The EMC will also hold a two to three-hour meeting with the focal person's current boss. And, phone calls will be made to a handful of his or her former associates. Prior subordinates too may be contacted for their views on how the individual manages. The entire process—including the writing of a summary—takes about a full week of the EMC's time. The written report documents the EMC's conclusions about the individual: achievements, management style, possible development plans, realism of career goals, and the like. This report is then presented to the individual and his or her manager for review. If the EMC has any fact wrong, the report is changed. If the individual or the manager disagrees with a conclusion made by the EMC, the report may be annotated to show their disagreement.

The accomplishment analysis becomes part of the EMS file on the manager. Every attempt is made to separate this process from promotion decisions. This is done to downplay any potential or perceived EMS role as "kingmaker." That is, if an accomplishment analysis were completed and the next week the individual was given a promotion, or worse, a demotion, there is an association made between the decision and the analysis. This kind of association colors the data collection effort, weakening it by introducing a bias against openness and candor. Thus accomplishment analyses are ideally held somewhere in the middle of one's tenure in a job.

By the end of an analysis and all the other data gathering, the EMC knows the focal person as well as anyone at GE does. Hence, the EMC can represent that person in discussions about development moves and promotion decisions in the future. The EMC knows what that person has achieved and probably can and cannot do. And the process itself has developmental value. First, to be selected for such attention connotes interest in the person from "upstairs." Second, it provides the most comprehensive feedback he or she is ever likely to get. But, it is difficult work, and sometimes contentious. The EMC has to talk straight regarding one's strengths *and* weaknesses; it is the manager's responsibility to relate clearly how the individual is perceived. When the view is a poor one, and the person thinks otherwise, there is conflict. Here, the tact and discretion that EMS has built its reputation on is called into play.

The Executive Manpower Consultant

In order to carry out GE's executive development philosophy and its attendant activities—slate system formulation and implementation, O&S reviews, and accomplishment analyses—a very special kind of staff is required. The executive manpower consultant (EMC) operates in a complex and politically sensitive environment; a high level of professionalism is needed in the role.[2] The basic criteria for successful operation as an EMC in a GE component are: (1) high personal integrity, (2) knowing the culture, and (3) being able to assess people and their fit with the culture.

How is an EMC trained and developed? Typically, they grow from the company's Relations function into an O&S manager position in operations. The O&S managers are the feeder stock for EMS. Their training comes from experience in the field where one does many of the same things an EMC does, but in a smaller segment of the company and with a different set of relationships. The O&S managers report to the line directly. Thus there is less detachment structured in the role and much less of a company-wide

[2] The description of this role was supported by D. Rikert's case.

view. But the career ladder leads to EMS, which is more independent of the line. For the O&S managers, then, the balance between service to the line and service to the corporation has to be maintained: The manner is which this is handled provides data for those interested in selecting an O&S manager for a position in EMS.

If identified for such advancement, the O&S manager may be encouraged to take advanced courses in interviewing skills, conflict resolution, and other related areas. More important, he or she may be given the chance to work in EMS as a kind of apprentice, perhaps with Don Kane in Organization Planning. There they can work on a study commissioned internally by one of the Sectors or corporate staffs, or by the Corporate Executive Office. For example, a study might investigate the utility of maintaining a certain set of positions in the company, such as a layer of management. While working on a study, the prospective EMC gets experience and visibility in the corporate offices. EMS has a chance to evaluate, at close range, the individual's judgment, relationships with people, conceptual ability, and courage. The stages of an EMC's development are analogous to those for a general manger. They play in successively higher leagues; the risks, and the payoffs, are greater along the way.

THE LINE BETWEEN APPRAISAL AND DEVELOPMENT

Throughout this discussion the focus has been on strategic development without explicit referral to performance appraisal. Clearly appraisal plays a role in the developmental process (Tichy et al., 1982). In this section the ever-problematic subject of appraisal is examined in terms of GE's practices and how they affect the development of the company's top executives.

A great deal of time and energy has been spent at GE trying to improve the appraisal system. Internal research indicates there is a fairly low level of satisfaction with performance appraisals but a high level of felt need for appraisals to continue on a regular basis. Underlying the difficulty is an inherent cultural bias throughout our society against direct expression of negative evaluations. Punches are pulled; assessments of growth potential are done imperfectly. Nonetheless, there is an awareness at GE of the need to bolster the appraisal system and its connection to development, even if there is a long way to go.[3]

In the performance appraisal process, a boss and his or her subordinate will more likely talk about the mechanics of how to increase market share rather than about how an individual's perceived deficiencies might be im-

[3] Although the system is less than perfect, GE's appraisal efforts have been in the vanguard of change for many years. See, for example, H.H. Myer, E. Kay, and J.R.P. French, Jr., "Split Roles in Performance Appraisals," *Harvard Business Review,* January–February, 1965, 21–29; a classic action research project conducted at GE that showed the importance of distinguishing between appraisal for determining rewards and appraisal for discussing developmental needs and plans.

proved. The Evaluation and Development Summary, however, a document *not* linked to compensation decisions, clearly lays out the subordinate's developmental needs based on his or her career interests and the strengths on which growth experiences can build. Discussion of how best to meet the needs will ensue if both parties have given this serious attention. The subordinate's initiative plays a large role in determining the extent to which such consideration is given. One has to be proactive, ambitious, and self-confident to maximally utilize this part of the developmental system.

A clear link does exist, then, between assessment (if not formal performance appraisal) and development, at least on paper. However, the Evaluation and Development Summary is not always taken seriously. But this is not the only means by which development actions are chosen. The O&S review sessions feed recommendations for appropriate growth experiences. The accomplishment analysis, too, is a process that has powerful implications for next career steps and for specific training needs. Finally, there are the informal appraisal sessions that take place continuously that are frequently associated with suggestions for development. An individual can have such counseling or "career discussions" with his or her boss, peers, boss's boss, or with someone from EMS. When one approaches EMS, however, there is a risk: You will hear the perceived truth. Again, the truth is sometimes subtly delivered, but the aim at EMS is to be honest and direct. Unfortunately, this can lead to unwanted turnover. For example, an individual may have a very high career ambition whereas the consensus company view is for a lower ultimate trajectory. When the individual is confronted with this discrepancy, he or she may leave, or, re-evaluate his or her own goals. In either case, it can be an uncomfortable situation. For this reason there seems to be a self-selection bias that favors the best and the brightest when it comes to paying a call on EMS. Those who are not faring so well tend to stay away, to avoid confronting reality, and to readjust their sights. EMS also sees a fair number of people who, suspecting their boss may be pulling punches, just want to get it "straight."

GE encounters the same difficulties with appraisal as do other companies, but the role of EMS as truth-teller is unique. Also distinctive to GE is the extent to which data are collected on and from individuals about their interests and needs. Chase, for instance, has an excellent executive development program, but its data collection is not as comprehensive. IBM collects reams of data, but not much from the individual under review. Finally, Exxon's system is similar to that of GE's although documentation is not as extensive at Exxon. A major difference between GE and Exxon is that at Exxon the path to the top is well known; their major product is oil. Since GE is so diverse, an executive can climb the ladder of success in many different ways. Hence, the developmental steps required are eclectic and not clear-cut. This is one reason why the collection of valid data from the individual on performance achievements and career goals is so critical at GE: Choosing the right developmental plan varies for each person and there are many potential paths to career fulfillment. Working one out with an individual is a creative task that has no hard and fast rules.

An example of how elusive this can be was the unsuccessful attempt to match types of executives, based on evaluations of their performance, to the nine cells of the GE strategic business matrix.[4] The problem was that most people are multifaceted; labels proved to be unrealistic. Some individuals have dealt simultaneously with all the types of businesses that can be delineated in a portfolio.

Attempts were made to match types of individuals to types of businesses, but presumed "mistakes" were working where so-called "harvesters" were failing to "milk the cows." Although a match should be made, it must be based on job specifications and individual strengths and interests, each of which varies from case to case. In stable organizations it is easier to match according to types. But with a continuously changing product mix and growth cycles, a multiplicity of markets, and the complex internal environment of GE, typing is not useful. The match of people to strategy is not made according to business strategy at GE; in fact, almost the reverse is true. Jack Welch has said: *"Strategy follows people; the right person leads to the right strategy."* Knowing well who your people are, their capabilities and their ambitions, in essence, good appraisal and assessment, leads to staffing decisions that will benefit the corporation and the individual.

FROM BORCH TO JONES TO WELCH

The last decade has seen EMS, and the development of people overall at GE, achieve increased importance. The Chairman's posture *vis-à-vis* people is by far the most critical determinant of whether executive development receives quality attention throughout the company. Fred Borch initiated EMS; Reginald Jones, Jack Welch's predecessor, widely regarded as the senior statesman of U.S. executives in the 1970s, expanded and built on it; Jack Welch has taken it further still by, increasing the frequency of reviews.

The top executives must have the long-term interests of GE in mind. Whereas at first there was great resistance to corporate control of the flow of managerial talent, most executives now recognize that a long-term business perspective means a long-term view of people too. Concern with strategic development is illustrated by Reginald Jones, who after only two years in his position as Chairman, and with seven more to go, commissioned EMS to do a study to investigate alternative plans for his succession. Roy Johnson and Don Kane played the key roles in this study which eventually led to the selection of Jack Welch and his two Vice Chairmen.

There were seven candidates up for three jobs. The four not selected ultimately moved to other companies. Reginald Jones asked for Ted LeVino's input on the three candidates to succeed him, and the data supplied came

---

[4] See C. Hofer and D. Schendel (1978) for a description of this matrix.

from accomplishment analyses, observations of behavior in various contexts, discussions with associates past and present, and other sources noted previously. A great deal of Reginald Jones' and Ted Levino's time went into this selection process. The Management Development and Compensation Committee of the Board, and the full board too, spent long periods of time on this issue; for in the hands of the successor lay the future of the Company. (See Figure 12.3 for a description of Reginald Jones' unique method for adding to the database for this crucial decision.)

One of the distinctive characteristics of Jack Welch, aside from his youthful enthusiasm, is his knack for assessing talented people and knowing how to develop them. Jack Welch has a high tolerance for experimentation, even failure, as long as an effort for excellence is made. Thus he can choose managers for positions that will stretch and develop them with the expectation that a business loss might ensue. Whereas in the past failure was "pretty final," according to one executive, Jack Welch will encourage greater risk-taking with people in the interests of pursuing business opportunities and speedier development.

The method used by Reginald Jones to collect information about who was best suited to succeed him as Chairman of GE illustrates one reason why Jones was seen as the most respected chief executive officer in the country.[5] When he retired, his two Vice Chairmen did, too. Three people, then, had to be chosen to fill these slots. There were seven good candidates. The question: "How to choose the best team of three, and then, the overall leader?"

Jones used a series of "airplane interviews" to gather the necessary data to inform his decision. Unannounced, a confidential session was held between him and each of the seven candidates. He posed the following dilemma: "You and I are in an airplane; it goes down, and neither of us survive. Who should be the next CEO?" This "really catches them cold," says Jones. Its amazing what is learned about the chemistry of the group when each one talks about the others for a few hours. Similar conversations were held with other senior officers about to retire, those "with whom I could talk openly" because they held no personal stake. And the Senior Vice President of Executive Management, "who was intimately familiar with all these people," provided input. All this was shared with the Management Development and Compensation Committee of the Board (MDCC).

Three months later another conversation was held with each candidate. But this time they were prepared; notified in advance, they arrived with "sheafs and sheafs of notes." This time however, "I don't make it but you do," Jones told them. "Now who do you pick? And who else should be in the Corporate Executive Office?" Again the results of those discussions were shared with the MDCC of the Board, then with the full board. The top three were chosen with this data contributing significantly to the decision. Then, after 14 months with those 3 attending all board meetings and working with the Corporate Executive Office, the number one man was chosen, Jack Welch. Specific criteria Jones used include: (1) choosing someone unlike himself, and (2) looking at the future environment demands his successor would face.

The originality of Reginald Jones's approach lies in the innovative method of collecting information, the outright consideration of the "chemistry" among the leadership team, and the great deal of time and energy devoted to the process of management succession.

FIGURE 12.3.   Reginald Jones on the choice of his successor: the airplane interview technique.

[5] Jones' explication of this series of events took place at the Advanced Management Program at the Harvard Business School, 15 April 1982, and was recorded on a videotape entitled, "Management Succession," Boston, MA: Harvard Business School, 1982.

The new Chairman has set as a goal for all GE businesses to be number one or two in market share. This represents a shift in business strategy from Reginald Jones' position of slow, steady growth while maintaining a respectably high rate of profitability. Jack Welch wants entrepreneurs, "world class competitors" (Landro, 1982). This implies a change in the culture of GE. In order to develop this new breed of GE manager the pace in the fast track is being picked up at a significant rate. The key is earlier identification and testing of high potentials. For EMS, this means digging lower into the organization, not waiting until the best come into view at the higher levels of management. Once identified, these leaders of tomorrow have to be given assignments with large amounts of responsibility. No longer can there be hesitation in delegating to high potentials. Jack Welch's tolerance for mistakes is a necessary ingredient in making this development strategy work. The sooner one can try and err in managing a $150 million business, the sooner he or she can advance to a billion-dollar one. GE sees this as a practical way to respond to the need for growth.

There are two apparently conflicting messages emanating from Jack Welch. One is: "The manager owns his or her business." Following Fred Borch and Reginald Jones, Jack Welch continues to stress decentralization. He sees "ownership" as not only a pragmatic necessity but as an effective motivator for excellent performance. The second message is: "We share responsibility for people selection." Executives are forced to balance the staffing needs of their own business with those of the company. Ownership applies to most but not all things. The slate system ensures corporate control of the use of promotions for developmental purposes. Thus it would appear that in the future maintaining an equilibrium between decentralized business with centralized top level staffing may be an increasingly troublesome issue.

EMS IN THE FUTURE

As of this writing, a study commissioned by Ted LeVino is underway to take a close look at the whole managerial development process in GE. Such basic questions as "How well is the system working?" "What changes are needed to produce more and better general managers? and "How are the system and EMS perceived and what should be done differently?" are being addressed. It is hoped that the results of the study will lead to action that will improve the system. Some of the critical dilemmas faced by those responsible for executive development at GE are noted in the following.

1.   Will the powerful forces of decentralization and ownership, and the need for business excellence in very diverse produce and service markets, allow GE to continue its "one company" executive development system, and if so, what adjustments in that system will be required? If not, what will replace it?

2. The problem of utilizing those who fail will become more and more difficult as greater risks are taken to speed up the development process. Higher risks mean not only bigger payoffs (i.e., "world class competitors"), they mean greater penalties too.

3. Whether the recruiting efforts of the late 1960s and early 1970s were as successful as before is an issue that affects the flow up the pipeline. It may be that the supply of talent began to dwindle in the '60s. This fact, combined with a greater need for executive talent yields a gap. Closing this gap will require more direction from the top. But again, this conflicts with the strategy of decentralization.

4. The O&S managers are tied in directly to the line. Standards of EMS, however, are different than those held by much of the line. Further refinements in the role of the O&S manager in terms of his or her actions to benefit the company or a particular business unit are necessary.

5. GE is growing by acquisition much more than in the past. This has a great effect on the company's culture. How to manage the assimilation of new sets of managers, those developed in other organizational cultures, is a great challenge to the overall development and staffing system.

6. EMS is responsible for 5000 people with special emphasis on the top 600. The need to dig lower is clear. A larger EMS organizatiion to identify people and to respond to their developmental needs may not be the answer. Growth for EMS is inconsistent with decentralization philosophy. How to achieve the needed system gain is an unresolved issue.

13

CORPORATE CULTURE AND COMPETITIVE STRATEGY

Charles J. Fombrun

In recent years, it has become particularly fashionable to discuss the dynamics of behavior in organizations in terms borrowed from anthropology. Thus a corporation's past history is studied because its symbols, stories, and myths are thought to provide clues to its present "corporate culture." The concept of a corporate culture received full play in the Deal and Kennedy (1982) book of that name, and Peters and Waterman (1982) have articulated it in terms of the symbolic role of the chief executive officer in asserting and systematically encouraging adherence to a "dominant value" in well-managed firms.

The purpose of this chapter is to discuss the nature of a corporate culture in terms of the systems that are designed to support it. A concept of effectiveness is introduced as a way of addressing the notion of an "appropriate" culture for the society, industry, and strategic orientation of the organization. Although it is true that cultures cannot be designed, the point we make is that the various control systems of the organization can work to shape through reinforcement and feedback the desired attitudes and behaviors that are consistent with a particular strategic direction. The culture of the organization can, therefore, be defined as the emergent pattern of beliefs, behaviors, and interaction that uniquely characterize the organization as it operates within an industrial and a societal context.

LEVELS OF CULTURE

As we attempt to articulate the elements of an organization's culture, it is important to recognize the external context in which it emerges. Understanding the nature of culture at various levels of analysis is crucial if we are to properly position the concept of a corporate culture as a unique and worthwhile level of analysis. From a systems perspective three levels can be distinguished from the start:

The societal level
The industry level
The corporate level

We discuss these in turn. As we point out, there are some built-in contradictions and tensions between these levels that may help explain the difficulties inherent in the notion of *managing* a corporate culture.

Societal Culture

Anthropologists have successfully demonstrated the importance of culture in understanding behavior in different societies. They point to the unity between what people do and the meaning they attach to objects, activities, and events. For them, the proper level of analysis for analyzing individual behavior is the societal level, and the focus is an institutional matrix of structures and processes that attaches meanings to events for the members of the culture.

In this fashion a societal level contrast between Japan and the United States, for instance, opposes the two cultures in terms of their institutional frameworks and the values they support. Numerous authors have described the collective orientation of Japanese society, its historical origins in the *bushido* code of loyalty of the samurai warrior, and the perpetuation of the feudal system through the loosely coupled group structure of firms linked through their origins in the *zaibatsu* trading companies, formally broken up by antitrust legislation, but institutionalized as a decision-making structure nonetheless. Contrast that to the individual ethos of American culture, its institutionalization of bargaining relations within organizations and of negotiation among pluralistic interests at the national level.

In each case, a cultural context instills a value orientation that is reinforced through the educational system, the social system (manifested for instance in the male-dominated society of Japan and its use of women as a part-time slack labor pool, versus the search for equal opportunity in America), and the economic system (state planning and protectionism in Japan, versus *laissez-faire* in the United States).

From this perspective, then, a corporate culture must necessarily be at least *minimally* consistent with the societal culture from which it is derived. Societal exposure and heritage foster a labor force with a given value orientation, beliefs, and expectations about work and the work environment that are the raw material of corporate cultures.

Industry Culture

Little research has been done on the nature of an industry culture. However, much descriptive insight is provided by the discussions of industry executives and industry case studies. Thus it is well documented that the motion picture industry has norms and values that differ markedly from those of the banking industry. The advertising and public relations industry is rather closer in this respect to the motion picture industry. Similarly, the textile industry is frequently said to be somewhat "different" from, say, the automobile industry, the farm-products industry, or the telecommunications industry in terms of norms, career patterns, and the individuals attracted to it.

From this perspective, then, it is possible to describe a dominant value orientation for the industry, which an institutional structure at the industry level probably supports. The critical implications of industry culture would seem to be the kinds of norms that develop around secrecy, political stance, dress, lifestyle, and "the way we do business" in the industry. Anthropologists would suggest that this has a great deal to do with the nature of the work, or the product with which the industry is dealing (Geertz, 1973). Thus the fact that banks are buying and selling money means they must engage the trust of depositors and shy away from risk, all of which spells conservatism in lifestyle, dress, and politics. On the other hand, the motion picture industry in dealing in glamour must foster eccentricity, stimulate fantasy, and encourage liberalism. Similarly, in high technology industries, rapid technological change encourages values, myths, and norms that foster creativity and innovation. This generally means "closeness." Thus the inbred nature of California's Silicon Valley is described in an anecdote as "a change in firm without even having to change car pools."

These points suggest that, in addition to societal culture, the specific industry a firm operates in is an important context for understanding corporate culture. Critical dimensions will involve the following.

1. *The Nature of the Product.* This includes consumer goods, producer goods, public image, social function; can product be "stolen" or improved by competition (need for secrecy).

2. *Stage in Industry Lifecycle.* The early stage is characterized by uncertain function, low familiarity of product for consumer, uneven quality control, and later stages by declining importance of advertising and sophisticated customer demand.

3. *Technology.* This includes the kinds of skills required, pace of change, and nature of dominant work activities.

4. *Institutional Structure.* This includes the number of competitors, industry concentration, trade associations, and stakeholders.

These dimensions are interdependent. Together with the societal culture they are embedded in, they describe a more immediate cultural context from which the single organization derives its own unique corporate culture.

Organizational Culture

In the last few years we have witnessed a proliferation of articles in the popular press on the importance of corporate culture. A faddish wave of interest in so-called "Japanese management techniques" has provoked a plethora of seminars, conferences, and books on quality control circles, productivity management, and a resurgence of interest in operations management as well as personnel management techniques. William Ouchi's *Theory Z,* a forerunner of numerous others, suggests that American companies could design hybrid cultures in their corporations to emulate Japanese organizations. He and others suggest that many have already done so, citing Hewlett-Packard, Texas Instruments, 3M, and Intel, among others. Ouchi (1980), Pascale and Athos (1981), Deal and Kennedy (1982), and Peters and Waterman (1982) all address specific elements of corporate culture, and suggest that excellence (presumably high performance) results from the internal coherence and consistency of their corporate cultures. In stressing the internal dimensions of culture they fail to address the linkage between a single corporate culture and the external context of the organization—especially its *competitive* context. The point we stress is that firms who aspire to adopt a Hewlett-Packard or an IBM culture must first consider its appropriateness in the context of their business. For corporate culture to be a useful construct, it would be valuable to specify its relationship to both industry culture and societal culture, in addition to an analysis of its internal consistency as an institutional system of management.

Although a complex array of internal dimensions affects the corporate culture, the following would seem to be among the most critical:

1. *Size of Firms.*   Large organizations have the discretionary resources and the power *vis-à-vis* other firms in the industry to create "deviant" cultures.
2. *Stage in Product Lifecycle.*   Firms in the early stages of their lifecycle require a different corporate culture to support their entrepreneurial activities; firms in later stages need a culture that drives cost control and efficiency.
3. *Strategy of Growth.*   In specifying the value orientation of the firm, the corporate culture should support the strategic growth plans of the firm.
4. *Control Systems.*   A corporate culture depends in part on the systems the organization has created to control its activities, including the formal structure, financial systems, and the human resources systems.

In important respects, the emergent corporate culture—if it is to be effective at supporting excellence in the management of the organization—should strive for coherence in terms of these dimensions, in addition to consistency with

TABLE 13.1. Departmental Organization, Culture, and Human Resource Systems.

Type of Organization	Dominant Value	Recruitment	Appraisal	Reward	Development
Manufacturing/production	Cost control	Machine/manual skills	Hourly rate Quantified based on supervision	Monetary Individualized	On-the-job training Career path through production and finance
Marketing/service	Sales	Interpersonal skills	MBO Output-based Based on client feedback	Monetary Symbolic	On-the-job training Interpersonal skills Career path through marketing
Research/development	Innovation	Creativity Technical skills	Peer evaluation Subjective and qualitative	Group-based recognition	Informal activity Conferences/courses Career path through technical areas

the industry and societal level dimensions previously discussed. The rest of the chapter discusses the contingent relationships presented in Table 13.1 in greater detail.

CORPORATE CULTURE, STRATEGY, AND STRUCTURE

Given the wide variety of organizations in modern society, it will be useful to distinguish from the start between different organizational forms. Following Alfred Chandler, it is possible to contrast these forms:

1. *Single Function (or Departmental) Organization.* A single activity dominates the organization, such as marketing, manufacturing, or research.

2. *Multifunction (or Functional) Organization.* The vertically integrated sequential activities of the classical structure ranging across the development, manufacturing, and marketing functions servicing a single product.

3. *Multidivisional (or Conglomerate) Organization.* The broadly diversified organization with multiple products, operating in multiple markets.

As Chandler's historical account suggests, firms in American industry began as single plant operations growing through horizontal expansion to capture large market shares. The second stage of growth was dominated by vertical integration into activities that ensured the firm's supply of inputs and the markets for its outputs, hence the birth of the functional firm.

More recently, Chandler has argued, expansion has taken the form of diversification into related and unrelated products and markets, encouraging the birth of the conglomerate organization with a portfolio of products.[1] These three stages of evolution are diagrammed in Figure 13.1. Consistent with each strategic stage, we argue, a dominant value orientation could be said to characterize the corporate culture. They are discussed as follows.

Single Plant Culture

Characteristic of start-up businesses engaged in a single activity, the corporate culture of the single plant organization tends to be unsophisticated in that it is typically dominated by a charismatic entrepreneurial founder who controls the behavior of his or her small staff largely through direct supervision. Richard Edwards describes this as a "simple control" structure, an embryonic culture with few institutionalized rules.[2]

---

[1] Chandler (1962) describes the evolution of a sample of large firms (e.g., General Motors, Dupont) from their beginnings as small plants into large diversified conglommerates.

[2] Edwards (1979) interprets the evolution of American industry as sequential adaptation of organizations to changing circumstances. As technology developed and as markets opened up, organizations were faced with more complex control needs. The evolution from simple to technical to bureaucratic control was towards an increasingly sophisticated control of workers in organized activity.

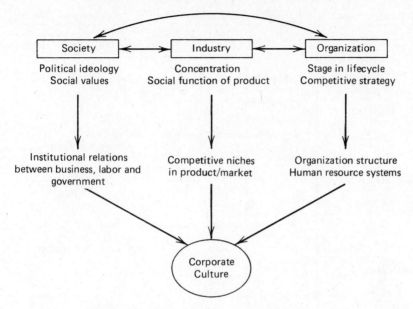

FIGURE 13-1   Society, Industry, and Corporate Culture.

This kind of corporate culture seems characteristic of the numerous small organizations on the periphery of modern industry. It dominates retail trade and agriculture, and accounts for a large part of the construction industry as well as many consulting firms, legal partnerships, and advertising agencies.

Departmental Culture

As the small-scale activity of the initial plant grows through market expansion, the culture of the organization tends to champion cost-efficient techniques for production that maximize competitiveness. A larger scale of operations decreases the average costs of production, thereby opening up demand. With growth in output comes growth in labor input, the need for delegation through structure, and the beginnings of systematic personnel management techniques.

For each type of departmental organization, the central value orientation will, of course, vary. In manufacturing, for instance, mechanization and technical control of the workforce tend to prevail. Pay systems and appraisal systems are piece-rate, and the necessary skills are simple, indeed. In a marketing organization, on the other hand, the sales function probably dominates, with pay and appraisal based on quantitative measurement. Figure 13.2 attempts to specify the different cultures and human resource systems consistent with the three principal departmental organizations. The unity of the corporate culture as a whole depends on the systematic support of the dominant value orientation across the four human resource systems of the departmental organization.

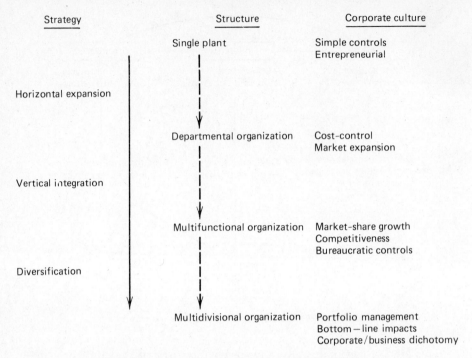

Strategy	Structure	Corporate culture
	Single plant	Simple controls Entrepreneurial
Horizontal expansion		
	Departmental organization	Cost-control Market expansion
Vertical integration		
	Multifunctional organization	Market-share growth Competitiveness Bureaucratic controls
Diversification		
	Multidivisional organization	Portfolio management Bottom—line impacts Corporate/business dichotomy

FIGURE 13–2   Strategy, Structure, and Corporate Culture.

Product Organization Culture

As the departmental organization grows through vertical integration both backwards into sources of supply and forward into its markets, the functional organization emerges. As a concatenation of departmental organizations under a single administrative umbrella, the functional organization's culture is a mixture of the departmental cultures that preceded it. Whether innovation, cost control, or sales dominates the culture of the functional form largely depends on the growth strategy the combined form pursues. Typically, this will manifest itself in terms of a dominant orientation at the business level, with the continued existence of subcultures within the original departments. Since at this stage, a variety of competitors is likely to have entered the industry, the concern for competitiveness can drive the business to pursue a growth strategy predicated on either (1) substantive or process innovation in the production of the firm's output, and hence a unique market niche of quality or function, or through (2) cost efficiency and the ability to minimize output price and hence increase market share. Each of these competitive strategies would then have to be supported through the appropriate business-level human resource systems described in Figure 13.2.

The creation of a business hierarchy above the departmental structures provides the context from which a business culture emerges. Thus the career paths and promotion opportunities could emphasize departmental specialization and the business culture is then dominated by a single function (e.g., the oil companies are culturally controlled at the business level by geological engineers). On the other hand, broad-based rotations through all the functions would emphasize generalism, and a "negotiated" business culture emerges (e.g., Texas Instruments, where functionalism is not emphasized and the ability to negotiate between functions is highly prized). The political configuration of the functional business organization and its early bureaucratic controls favoring cultural specialism or cultural generalism sets the stage for the emergence of the multidivisional organization and represents the underlayer of the corporate level culture.

Multidivisional Culture

Born of diversification in products and markets, the multidivisional organization creates a corporate administrative structure to manage the multiple businesses of the organization. Following Richard Rumelt's classification, these diversified conglomerates can be described on a continuum ranging from: (1) single or related products conglomerates, to (2) diversified or unrelated products conglomerates, or holding companies.

Holding companies tend to have undeveloped corporate level cultures and the organization as a whole is dominated by business level cultures. The corporate umbrella acts as a tool for allocating financial capital, and the human resource systems are not integrated across businesses.

Single product or related products conglomerates systematize the human resource systems of the different businesses to promote a corporate culture that binds the related businesses into a whole. Most of the examples of strong corporate cultures cited in the popular press describe dominant product or related products conglomerates such as IBM, Exxon, At&T, Proctor & Gamble, and Intel. At the other extreme are such weak corporate firms as Gulf and Western, Transamerica, and Honeywell where business subcultures dominate.

The recent failure of Exxon Enterprises is frequently cited as an example of a strong business culture (the "Exxon Way") dominated by traditional oil production, and unable to accommodate the deviant activities of a set of small single-function organizations committed to entrepreneurial values. It addresses the tension between business cultures in a conglomerated form.

Similarly, Hewlett-Packard's significant increase in computer sales is moving the organization from a single business configuration to a multidivisional organization. The dilution of its original business culture is a serious concern as it struggles with the concurrent loss of charismatic identification in the paternalistic culture designed by its founders who retired in 1978.

Figure 13.3 diagrams the critical dimensions of corporate culture at each of the three levels of a large conglomerate form. As the figure suggests, two kinds of cultural tension are symptomatic of organizations as they struggle to integrate their operations under ever-larger administrative umbrellas. The business-level culture partially reflects the strategic decision of the organization to be dominated by a single function or to work to balance the business through systematic job rotations, an integration across functions.

The second cultural tension is the dilemma faced by diversified corporate firms struggling to cement the different businesses and promote a unitary corporate culture, versus those that take the shape of holding companies dominated by business-level cultures. Taken jointly, these two sets of cultural tension represent the two managerial challenges born of the strategic control of the human resources dimension of the organization. They are probably the most undermanaged side of the modern corporation.

Figure 13.4 diagrams the functional/business cultural tension as a dilemma in the emergent configuration of the business organization and its attempt to specify dominant values. In Table 13.1 the life cycle concept is used to define the dominant value orientation of each business in a corporate portfolio and the human resource systems consistent with it. The business/corporate cultural tension the organization confronts involves the appropriate degree of systems differentiation between businesses, and their integration through a corporate culture.

Although these cultural tensions are central to the management task, they only address the internal consistency of the organization's systems, strategy, and structure. As was pointed out early in this chapter, the corporate culture of the organization is also a function of the industrial and societal context in which the organization is immersed. The next section develops some of the dimensions of these contexts and their relationship to corporate culture.

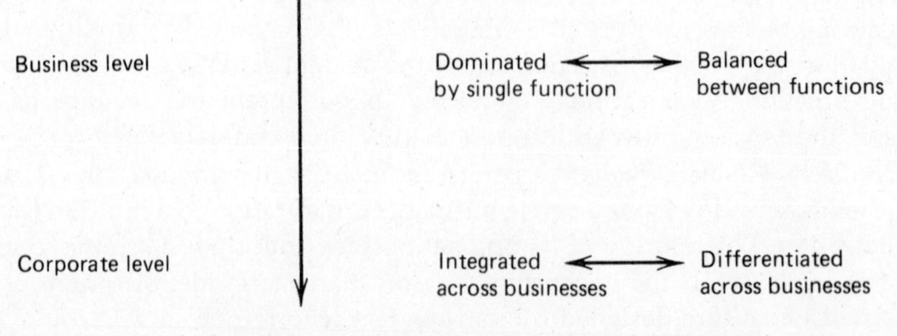

Critical Dimension of Culture

Functional level	Type of product activity engaged in (e.g., marketing, manufacturing, research)
Business level	Dominated ⟷ Balanced by single function between functions
Corporate level	Integrated ⟷ Differentiated across businesses across businesses

FIGURE 13–3 The Dimensions of Corporate Culture.

Business life cycle

	Start-up Businesses	Growth Businesses	Mature Businesses	Declining Businesses
Selection/placement	Recruitment for new activities Recruit entrepreneurial style	Recruit for future business	Lateral moves and advancement for enhancing efficiency	Transfers to different businesses Outplacement Early retirement
Appraisal	Appraise milestones linked to plans for the business, flexible	Linked to growth criteria, e.g., market share, volume unit cost reduction	Evaluate efficiency and profit margin performance Linked to market share increase	Evaluate cost savings
Rewards	Salary plus equity position	Salary plus bonus for growth targets, plus equity for key people	Incentive plan linked to efficiency and high profit margins	Incentive plan linked to cost savings
Development	Minimum until a critical mass of people in business — then job related	Job skills/ interpersonal skills	Emphasis on job training Good supervisory and management development programs	Career planning and support services for transferring people
Dominant value	Entrepreneurship	Sales	Competitiveness	Cost-control

Corporate culture integrates businesses

Support of distinct business cultures

FIGURE 13.4. Business/corporate cultural tension [Source: Adapted from C. Fombrun and N. Tichy, "Strategic Planning and Human Resource Management: At Rainbow's End." In R. Lamb (Ed.) *Competitive Strategic Management*, Englewood Cliffs, NJ: Prentice-Hall, forthcoming].

SOCIETY, INDUSTRY, AND CORPORATE CULTURE

Cultural Schizophrenia

Much of our previous discussion has made an implicit assumption about effectiveness that it is well to bring out. Namely, it has been assumed that an "appropriate culture"—the notion of an emergent configuration of values, norms, and behaviors that supports the strategy of the organization—will promote organizational effectiveness.

Such an assumption, of course, is rooted in an evolutionary logic through which firms suffering from cultural schizophrenia are thought to be non-competitive in the marketplace and driven out of business, whereas those cultural forms that support the organization's strategy and structure survive.[3] Given the wide range of cultural forms, it is possible to suggest that, at any single point in time, a specific firm in an industry occupies a segmented domain in the marketplace that minimizes all direct competition. Thus organizational cultures dominated by a concern with price, quality, service, and market segmentation can be interpreted as strategies for reducing competition within an industry. Each competitive strategy forces a value overlay on the internal organization that if reinforced through the human resources systems, orients the corporate culture in a different direction. Taken this way, it helps us understand the coexistence within a single industry of firms with widely divergent corporate cultures. Presumably, these firms have evolved their distinct cultures in the implementation of a specific competitive strategy. Thus IBM's strong corporate culture is a reflection of its service orientation, a value institutionalized in the corporation early on by Thomas Watson. It is a corporate culture that is undoubtedly deviant from that of its principal competitors.

Cultural Myopia

Deviance within an industry is not without its costs, however. It reduces the alternatives open to the organization by encouraging "cultural myopia," a form of tunnel vision that may inhibit organizational adaptation to abrupt environmental changes. Perhaps the automobile, steel, and rubber industries' lack of responsiveness to early signals of foreign competition and new technology reflect an entrenched outlook that emphasized their strength, power, wisdom, and a sense of invulnerability. As the automobile industry changed from a national to a global context, its deviance was a weakness.

It is probably true that deviant corporate cultures require internal labor markets. Promotion tends to be from within and few senior slots are filled by individuals drawn from the external labor market. The culture and human

---

[3] Aldrich (1979) summarizes much of the research on ecological adaptation of organizations to their environments. These evolutionary arguments help us understand how environmental pressures for competitiveness affect organizational forms.

resource systems, therefore, foster loyalty to the organization, average tenure tends to be high, and significant rewards accrue with seniority. Although this is undoubtedly a source of strength and continuity for the organization, it is also costly in terms of administrative burden, training, and socialization expenses.

For the rest of the industry, the deviant organization is frequently a training ground. Former employees are viewed as prestigious individuals to hire by the other (frequently smaller) firms who place them in priviledged positions of leadership. This is the case in the oil industry (Exxon), consumer goods marketing (Proctor & Gamble), banking (Citicorp, Chase Manhattan), electric goods (GE, Westinghouse), and electronics (Texas Instruments). Wage rates are, therefore, bid upwards by the rest of the industry and compensation is competitive (and sometimes lower) in the deviant (but desirable) organizations, though fringe benefits will likely as not overcome any cash discrepancies.

Finally, cross-cultural comparisons of organizations have long suggested the symbiotic relationship between organizations and the society in which they are embedded. Organizations, it is said, mirror the values and ideologies of the society to which they belong. Viewed as subcultures, they are institutions whose task it is to perpetuate the ideological bent of the society, and to maintain the legitimacy of that society's beliefs and values for its members. Viewed in this light, Japan's collectivism, West Germany's codetermination, Sweden's employee ownership, Israel's kibbutzim, and America's collective bargaining are structural manifestations (translated into corporate cultures) that reflect a broader institutional arrangement between business, labor, and government designed to support a particular social ideology. In this respect, then, America's pluralistic, conflictual model of political democracy stands in stark contrast to Japan's cooperative, cooptive model of joint business, labor, and government national planning. As it also does with codetermination and the collective ownership of equity capital.

The ability of a single firm to design a corporate culture is surely constrained by that societal context. Many experiments have been conducted that attempt to create corporate cultures around employee ownership, and collaborative decision-making. Where they have succeeded, they have largely depended on the charismatic leadership of a spiritual founder (for instance the Donnelly Mirror Company's adaptation of a modified Scanlon plan). Of the many experiments, if so few have succeeded, perhaps it is for lack of institutional support from the wider society.

CONCLUSION

Figure 13.1 diagrammed the interrelationship between the different levels of culture and some of the critical dimensions of each in terms of their impact on corporate culture. As Figure 13.1 suggests, corporate culture is the outcome of an interplay between a host of variables at each of the three principal levels of analysis: society, industry, and organization. Managing corporate culture is, therefore, an awesome task. It calls for a constant reassessment of the external context as well as the internal systems of the organization. Understanding the parameters of a corporate culture, however, will better enable an organization to chart feasible growth strategies based on the constraints of the existing culture and suggest considerations that facilitate their implementation. As organizations come to increasingly operate in multiple industries and multiple societies, they are more than ever before challenged to cope with the inertia born of cultural myopia and cultural schizophrenia.

CHAPTER

14

HEWLETT-PACKARD: SHAPING THE CORPORATE CULTURE

Stanley Harris

Corporate culture is in danger of being the latest in a series of faddish management panaceas designed to improve organizational effectiveness. A point often missed by advocates of a strong corporate culture is that it must also be strong in its relationships to, and support of, other components of the organization. As Chapter 13 stresses, of primary importance is the alignment of an organization's culture with its business strategy.

An organization's culture determines much of the way that "things get done" (Phillips and Kennedy, 1980). It encompasses the company's values, goals, and dominant ideologies. Although hard to grasp explicitly, an organization's culture can be expressed through its myths, heroes, stories, jargon, rites, and rituals. For example, International Business Machines (IBM) has the motto "IBM means service" which serves as a banner for its service-oriented culture. Within IBM, there is also the story of former CEO, Tom Watson, Jr. who personally answered a number of customer complaints during his tenure. Another story told at IBM concerns the firing of a leading salesman for overselling a customer. It is obvious that the slogan and both of these stories carry a "customer service" cultural theme. An oil refinery with which the author has worked also provides a good example of using jargon, myths, heroes, and the like to gain an insight into culture. In this particular refinery, safety is a big concern. There are hand-drawn cartoons stuck up in very conspicuous places satirizing some individual's breach of safe action. Laughing at the person serves as both a sanction and a relief from fear. Stories concerning major accidents abound. Units with good safety records are recognized. People who have saved the lives of others are talked of as heroes. One could go on but the point is obvious: a concern for safety is indeed a part of the culture of this refinery.

The relationship between an organization's culture and its strategy can be considered reciprocal—the strategy of an organization can be used to reinforce cultural norms, whereas certain cultural forms promote certain strategies. Problems and internal tensions emerge when the ideas, behaviors, and values stressed in an organization's strategy clash with those embodied in the organization's culture. Such a clash is exemplified by the attempt of Sears, Roebuck to become more like a department store and thereby reach a larger clientele. Although the market was there, the appropriate culture was not. Sears had employees who did not know how to run a department store. Another example is provided by AT&T which is currently struggling with altering its service-oriented culture to one more suitable for its new competitive stance. AT&T employees have never had to be involved in a fight for market share, particularly not a fight with the likes of IBM, and points to the importance of having an appropriate culture for driving the strategy of an organization.

Successful companies have learned to use various management tools to consciously guide and shape their company's culture to fit their strategy. One of the tools used to accomplish this shaping is the reinforcing of certain ideas, values, and behaviors and discouraging others by means of four human resource management (HRM) activities: selection and placement, appraisal, rewards, and training and development. It is with this role of HRM activities this chapter is concerned.

Hewlett-Packard (HP) provides an important culture/HRM case example because it has recognized the role that HRM plays in shaping and reinforcing a company's culture. HP has been cited several times for its overall business success, as well as the effectiveness of its strategy and culture in providing a guide for its functioning. Pascale and Athos (1981) describe HP as a company that fully utilizes and effectively integrates each of the "Seven Ss"—strategy, structure, systems, staff, skills, style, and superordinate goals. Ouchi (1980) refers to HP as a "Type Z" company with one of the most mature and consistent corporate philosophy statements around. In their book, *Corporate Cultures* (1982), Deal and Kennedy make several references to HP's strong corporate culture and Peters and Waterman (1982) include HP in their list of excellent companies. This case extends this literature by highlighting HP's

HRM activities and the role they play in shaping and reinforcing its culture to complement the HP strategy. The remainder of this chapter provides an overview of HP's strategies, cultural themes, and HRM practices followed by a discussion of the new cultural challenge faced by HP.

BUSINESS BACKGROUND

HP was started in 1939 in Dave Packard's Palo Alto, California garage around the new type of audio oscillator built by Bill Hewlett. Following the success of this, their first product, HP began introducing other test instruments based on the same general design. By the early 1950s they were introducing around two dozen new products yearly. This growth continued and by the mid-1970s, HP sales were nearing the $1 billion mark, they offered 3,300 products, the workforce numbered 29,000, and they had diversified into such products as computers, calculators, medical equipment, chemical analysis equipment, and solid-state components. This growth has continued (particularly around the new thrust into computers) behind the leadership of John Young, President and CEO since 1977, and at the end of fiscal 1982, sales were $4.25 billion with a net income of $383 million and over 52,000 employees worldwide.

HP STRATEGIC OBJECTIVES

One of the strengths of the HP approach to aligning its culture and strategy is that the importance of the relationship between the two is articulated and, therefore, salient to HP employees. One way that HP accomplishes this articulation is by employee-wide distribution of its "Statement of Corporate Objectives."

In 1957, Hewlett and Packard put the values that guided their managing of the company into writing. Since that time, this statement of objectives has been only slightly modified to reflect business and social environmental changes. These objectives reflect the HP culture (the "HP way"), serve to guide the continuance of the HP way, and also serve as the basis for HP's strategic focus. The "statement of corporate objectives" including its opening letter (as they appeared in 1977) is shown in the Appendix beginning on page 229. The purpose of this section is to outline the strategies and cultural themes implied by each objective and, therefore, provide a backdrop against which to examine HP's HRM activities.

Much of HP's attitude toward strategy, culture, and HRM is expressed in the opening letter to the objectives (see Appendix). In the opening letter, Hewlett and Packard indicate a desire to have the corporate objectives they present "reflect the organization's basic character and personality"—its culture. Also, three basic organizational requirements needed to meet the objectives are presented. All three of these requirements deal with human resource issues. In essence, this letter represents a recognition of the need for, and a commitment to, the management of HP's human resources, as well as recognition of the role HRM plays in shaping a company's culture.

The first requirement deals with selection and placement of individuals based on their appropriateness for the job (with particular emphasis on creativity) and the continuing development of those individuals. The second requirement also deals directly with selection and placement. Hewlett and Packard stress the need to select managers who have the ability to engender enthusiasm, particularly enthusiasm for the HP way. Finally, the need for cooperation between organizational levels is emphasized. One way to accomplish this cooperation (in addition to the decentralized organization employed by HP) is by reinforcing common objectives through HRM.

The opening letter begins to specify the role of HRM in reinforcing the HP way. Now we examine the objectives for a clearer definition of what is meant by the HP way. Each of the objectives must be considered in the context of the remaining six. They are not meant to stand alone. For example, the "profit objective" (see Appendix) could more appropriately be considered a "constrained profit objective." It does not stress a maximization of profit in its own right but, rather, discusses its role in light of the overall objective statement. This interdependency is also the case for the strategy and cultural forms implied by each objective.

Figure 14.1 presents a summary of the major strategies and cultural themes implied by each objective. The circles or partial circles appearing in Figure 14.1 are an attempt to indicate the importance placed on each cultural theme by the strategies associated with each objective. The strategies that HP employs are straightforward and require no indepth explanation. The discussion that follows, therefore, focuses on the major cultural themes presented in the Appendix (1) customer orientation, (2) workmanship, (3) familial atmosphere, (4) employee importance, (5) intraorganizational cooperation, (6) entrepreneurial spirit, (7) management style, (8) HP pride, (9) social neighbor attitude, and (10) profit.

Customer Orientation

A culture that states that the customer is crucial for HP's strategy. Product development, manufacturing, and service are all geared toward the customer. Therefore, individuals within HP must value the customer, listen to what he or she says, and be responsive to his or her desires. This theme, given HP's strategic focus, determines much of HP's success in the marketplace.

Workmanship

Workmanship as part of its culture is something every organization desires. It involves productivity and efficiency but not at the expense of quality. Only by providing high quality products at reasonable prices can HP maintain or

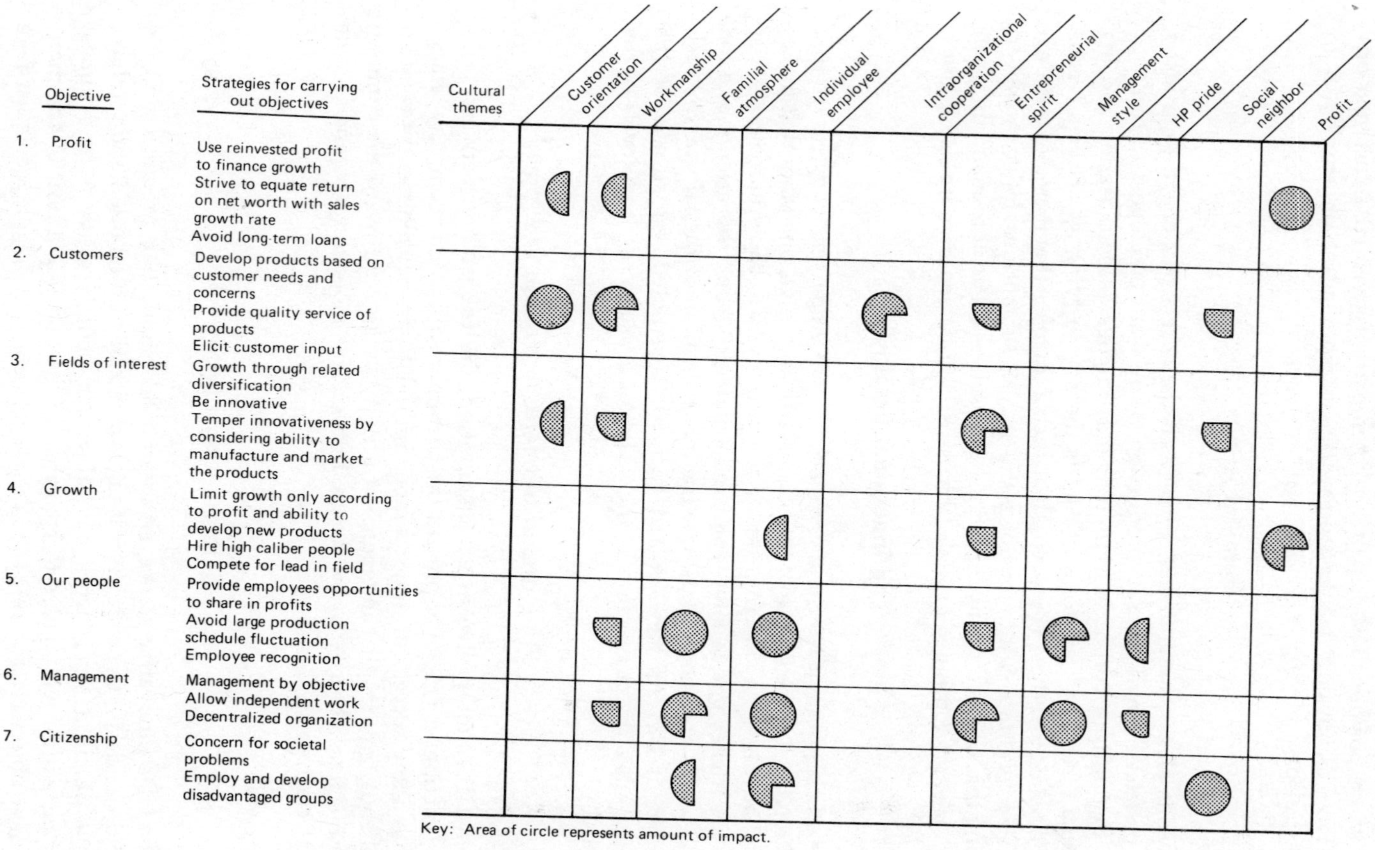

FIGURE 14.1. Major Strategies and Cultural Themes at Hewlett Packard.

Key: Area of circle represents amount of impact.

improve its position. This is particularly important given HP's customer orientation. HP not only wants good workmanship, it wants its employees to want it also.

Familial Atmosphere

HP wants all of its employees to feel as if they are a part of HP—not just a part of sales or marketing or production. They want employees to feel as if they belong to a corporate "family." This implies decentralization and individual "freedom": a strong culture is the key to tying all of this diversification back together. The strength of such a theme is that it creates a strong, cohesive corporate culture out of many smaller subcultures. HP is, however, finding this small company, "family," atmosphere difficult to maintain given their size and continued growth (this issue is discussed in more detail later).

The Individual Employee

HP explicitly recognizes the importance of each employee. They realize that the individual is the source of the enthusiasm, initiative, and labor that makes HP what it is. One way to promote this activity is to show individuals that they are trusted and to allow some independence. All of this attention to the individual is designed to facilitate the internalization of the HP way by each member of HP. As Hewlett and Packard have noted, the success of the company is a direct function of the activities of *individuals* at all levels of the hierarchy.

Interorganizational Cooperation

Given HP's highly diversified organization, the cooperation between units and functions is crucial to present the customer with a "one company" image and to allow successful internal integration. HP stresses independence at all levels but requires that independent activity be geared toward the common HP objectives, thereby laying the groundwork for cooperation behind a single set of clear goals.

Entrepreneurial Spirit

Given HP's innovative stance, creativity is essential. It also requires that the employees desire to be creative. It takes a special cultural orientation to have people put in a *creative* work day. However, being creative is moot unless coupled with a willingness to contribute. One puzzling aspect of the management objective (Figure 14.7) is the statement that "employees must take sufficient interest in their work to want to . . . stick their necks out when they have something to contribute." If HP wants a culture marked by creativity and participation, basic entrepreneurial behaviors, it must prevent these activities from being associated with sticking one's neck out.

Management Style

A key to much of the success of the HP way is management. Management must engender the trust in the employee, must stress the importance of the customer, and must promote enthusiasm. This requires the dissolution of the barriers between management and the rest of the organization.

HP Pride

To create the atmosphere necessary for HP's desired culture to survive, the employees must be proud to be a part of HP. They have to feel they play an important role in something important. The customer has to have faith in a company driven by pride. The workmanship must be of a standard of which one can be proud. In a nutshell, the employee must be proud of the HP way.

Social Neighbor

HP's customers, families, workers, and resources all come from the larger community and society. Therefore, HP has a commitment to this community and society. This cultural component is closely related to issues of pride and the individual and the customer.

Profit

A concern for profit plays an important role in HP's culture since much of HP strategy hinges on making profit. The strength of this theme lies in the fact that it is not the only one considered important by HP.

None of these cultural themes can stand alone. One strength of HP's objectives is that they reflect an attempt to define both global strategy and desired culture in a single unified document. The existence of this culture does not, however, just happen. In the section that follows, the role of HRM systems in weaving HP's culture are examined.

HEWLETT-PACKARD'S HRM SYSTEMS

As is relected in the statement of objectives, the human resources of HP are considered very important. A recent industry article calls HP the model company in Silicon Valley in personnel management (Murray, 1981). Intel, Tandem, and Rolm all acknowledge the fact that they have, to some extent, modeled their personnel systems after HP's. In this section, we examine HP's

HRM systems (specifically: selection and placement, appraisal, rewards, and training and development) and investigate the role they play in shaping and reinforcing the culture of HP. Before reviewing these specific HRM practices, however, it is useful to focus on the style of management at HP.

Management Style

HP has an open-door management policy and advocates MBWA—"management by walking around." MBWA involves unscheduled, friendly, casual, and spur-of-the-moment walking around and chatting with employees by the management. There is also an implicit invitation to the employee to feel free to repay the visit. HP has also done other things to help dissolve any management–employee barriers. The lack of management perks has already been mentioned. In addition, the office layout for management is open. The office of the CEO, Mr. Young, itself is a free-standing cubicle without an abundance of space. HP makes its management decisions with its human resources in mind. In fact, it recently placed a manager with a personnel management background in an upper-level R&D management position because the needs of the unit were human resource-related rather than line-oriented.

HP also uses its management to promote the desired familial and enthusiastic atmosphere. HP throws regular beer parties for all employees to encourage their getting to know one another. Profit results are often announced to all employees. These are just two more examples of HP's attempt to destroy barriers to management–employee relations.

Selection and Placement

Given the scarcity of engineers, it has become common practice of many of the Silicon Valley companies to offer bonuses to their company engineers for luring engineers away from other companies. This practice is disdained by HP which prefers to have its primary entry at the bottom. HP does not believe in using placement tests. Each year, HP sends out approximately 700 engineers and managers in small recruiting teams to colleges and universities across the nation. These teams interview the available candidates and select those they feel are best suited for HP. This method of selection promotes the HP way since people are selected for entry by people with whom they must work and who have already become a part of the HP culture. This creates a situation in which a prime determinant of organizational entry is based on a person's fit with the culture. The approach also allows the applicant to get a sense of the culture he or she may have an opportunity to join so that a conscious decision can be made as to whether it would be comfortable for them.

As selection concerns equal employment, *Black Enterprise* (1982) has designated HP as one of the "10 best places to work." Of approximately 47,000 domestic employees, 18.2% are minority with 9.7% of approximately 6700 managers and supervisors being minorities.

At managerial levels below the functional level, the talent identification and placement system is informal. However, managers at the functional level and above are reviewed quarterly by a corporate operations council. In both procedures performance and ability to perform are weighed against the HP objectives, with particular attention given to technical, leadership, and administrative skills. This ensures that future leaders will be "HP people" and thus the culture becomes, in a sense, self-perpetuating.

Also in an attempt to promote the HP way, it is common practice to move large groups of people into newly formed divisions to form a cohesive nucleus. This prevents the scattering of HP-way proponents and reduces the risk that the new environment and unit mission and an influx of new people will jeopardize the HP culture.

Peters and Waterman (1982) tell the story of a new HP development engineer working at a small calculator and electronics store so as to get "some first-hand experience in the users' response to the HP product line" (p. xix). Here is a case where individuals are placed in situations for the expressed purpose of instilling the HP culture (customer orientation) in employees.

Appraisal

HP employees have flexibility in setting personal objectives that they feel are compatible with the "statement of objectives" (the objectives they set must, however, receive supervisory approval). All performance appraisal is made against the individual's objectives and, ultimately, the broader HP objectives. This serves to foster employee actions consistent with the company's philosophy as embodied in the objectives. It helps create an atmosphere conducive to individual initiative and creativity, and communicates HP's trust and appreciation of the individual.

HP also does much of its appraisal (and subsequent rewarding) at the group level. This promotes the overriding HP way even across very diverse functional units. For example, to avoid problems of competition between sales teams, HP makes responsibilities clear and emphasizes functional as opposed to product responsibility.

Rewards

The rewards HP gives its employees come in many different forms. As for quantity, HP's salaries and benefits are considered generous. HP is also highly concerned with providing an egalitarian reward system. There is an ongoing attempt to make their worldwide pay and benefit practices uniform. Employee benefits the world over are reviewed annually by the executive committee to ensure consistency with the HP way. All salary administration practices are wide open. There are also minimal management perks. This approach reinforces a culture that reflects more of a "we," family attitude than an "us and them" attitude.

HP makes extensive use of group rewards. It is concerned with sharing its profits with those responsible for the company's performance—the employees. HP has one worldwide profit-sharing program for all employees which is equivalent to 12% profit before tax (PBT) divided in proportion to the employee's base pay. Furthermore, this bonus is not considered as pay or benefit in surveys; it is viewed as extra. Secondly, 80% of HP employees participate in a stock purchase plan (up to 10%) of salary, with HP adding one-third to the employee deduction). These practices also help instill the "common objective" idea within the culture: People are working for the benefit of the company as well as themselves. It also reinforces the goal of good workmanship and communicates the importance placed on employees.

Job security is another benefit provided by HP. HP maintains a remarkable turnover rate of less than 10% annually. How is this accomplished? First, employees don't lose their jobs because of management error. Layoffs are avoided by: (1) maintaining 7% overtime in normal times, (2) employing a 10% cut in pay and work across the board in extreme circumstances, (3) avoiding major contracts, (4) avoiding government business (this trend has been changing recently), and (5) maintaining a 15% direct labor subcontract buffer. These build a strong culture because they engender trust and reflect the organization's concern for its employees.

Training and Development

As for personal development of its employees, HP does such a good job that it is considered a feeder company from which others can draw well-developed managerial talent (Ouchi, 1980). HP's structure allows managers to run their divisions and units fairly independently. Therefore, each unit serves as a training ground for even greater responsibility. Here again, HP reinforces the idea that the company is on the employees' side—"one for all, all for one."

It should be clear from this description that at HP the HRM systems are major forces in shaping and reinforcing the cultural themes listed in Figure 14.1. Although the pieces fit together so well at HP, this strength may prove to be HP's Achilles heel. The business strategies needed for HP's success in the future may require cultural change.

HP'S NEW CHALLENGE

In late 1977 John Young succeeded Hewlett as CEO and President of HP. Young had been personally groomed and prepared for this position by both Hewlett and Packard. As planned, HP was becoming a company run by an internally developed management team. This new team's mission, however, was a difficult one: compete in the computer industry.

HP had been making its move into computers slowly. Hewlett and Packard pursued this market because they were determined to provide the company with a "second sturdy leg" to complement the test instrument "leg" before retiring (*Financial World*, 1979). When Young took over, he accepted a great deal of responsibility as well as a rough road. First, he had to face the competitive computer market in which many companies had been severely beaten about the head and shoulders. Secondly, he had to fill the shoes of a very influential founder and leader. This last point is particularly important when one recognized the influence that Hewlett and Packard, as founders, have had on the culture of HP.

As of 1982, HP remains the largest manufacturer of test instruments and, in addition, has become third ranked in the small computer world market behind IBM and DEC. More important, however, is the fact that for the first time HP's computer sales were higher than their test instrument sales; Mr. Young appears to have HP standing on two sturdy legs. It also appears, however, that because of the diverse nature of these two legs, HP may find itself tripping over its own feet.

It seems as if the structure and culture that was appropriate for HP's test instrument side may not be appropriate and may even be dysfunctional for its computer business. The $2 billion instrument "leg" faces little competition and has sharply defined market segments, such is not the case for the computer "leg."

One crucial problem lies in a lack of coordination between divisions and marketing groups. The decentralized structure and management style that HP used so successfully to promote entrepreneurial, innovative, and creative activity on the test instruments side has led to overlapping products, "reinventions of the wheel," inappropriate and incomplete marketing, and slow development on the computer side. HP has made a practice of giving the small divisions control over both the design and manufacture of its own products but gives sales responsibility to independent marketing groups. In the past this structure has been able to keep the motivational small business atmosphere alive even in the face of extraordinary growth. Unfortunately for HP, this approach does not appear to work in the computer arena which requires much greater sharing of resources and integration of activities.

Another major problem that HP must face is that they are an "engineering-driven company confronting a marketing-driven world." One computer analyst even states "they don't have a good understanding of how this market works." HP has stressed profitability instead of market share. The one time where this strategy was inadvertently reversed, the outcome was troublesome. During a period of high growth following the 1970 downturn in the aerospace and computer business, HP adopted a widely used tactic designed to achieve market share. Specifically, they began pricing new products based on anticipated manufacturing costs once the product had matured and economies of scale had been achieved. In using this tactic, however, HP began to run into difficulties. HP's inventories and accounts receivable increased substantially, products were put into production before they were fully developed, prices were set too low for an adequate return on investment, and there was a staggering influx of new employees that had to be trained and absorbed. This tactic also created a need for short-term borrowings and, when coupled with the other problems, led to a short-term debt of $118 million by the end of 1973. One can see how HP would be reluctant even now to stress market share. *Business Week* (1982) has emphasized, however, that given the nature of today's computer market, HP may be forced to seek a large market share in order to ensure long-term profitability and perhaps survival.

HRM Implications

It is obvious that for HP to protect and promote the development of its computer side, it must deal with strategic, structural, cultural, and HRM issues. It seems that certain strategic changes are already (even if only implicitly) occurring. For instance, Young is promoting the concept of program management: a form of centralization of decision-making, coordination, and direction in an attempt to integrate the divergent sections of the computer side.

Such strategic changes cannot occur without having some sort of impact on the present culture. The move toward centralization, has created a cultural–strategic clash with the entrepreneurial component of the culture. A partial result of this clash has been an increased exodus of HP managers and engineers who are starting new companies or attaching themselves to smaller companies. Interestingly, in most cases the companies started or joined have the HP dynamic of decentralization and entrepreneurial spirit—cultural dynamics that are becoming eroded in HP.

The question that faces HP is how to be successful in computers while at the same time promoting the entrepreneurial spirit and familial atmosphere that Young, Hewlett, and Packard feel is important to motivate professionals. Since Hewlett and Packard (Chairman of the Executive Committee and Board Chairman respectively) insist on the current organizational structure, it will be hard to change. Therefore, the question remains how can the culture and HRM be used to help alleviate the strain that HP faces? As *Business Week* (1982) so elegantly observes: "If HP can solve this conflict, it will have written another chapter for the managerial textbooks."

SUMMARY AND CONCLUSIONS

This HP case provides a useful example of the dynamics of the alignment of a company's strategy and culture. Also impressive is the way in which HP consciously employed HRM systems to build, shape, and reinforce a culture necessary to drive its strategy. For HP, the question remains as to whether it can alter its culture (that to a great extent has been designed to be self-perpetuating) enough to have it fit with the new strategic directions in which HP appears to be heading.

What lessons does this HP case provide that can be used in other organizational settings? There seem to be several.

1. A characteristic of high performing companies is good strategy and cultural alignment.
2. HRM activities, by reinforcing certain ideas, norms, and behaviors and by discouraging others, can be used to shape and reinforce a certain type of culture.
3. When its strategies change, an organization must also alter its culture.
4. Cultures have the property of being, to some extent, self-perpetuating and, therefore, hard to change.

Appendix

STATEMENT OF CORPORATE OBJECTIVES

The achievements of an organization are the result of the combined efforts of each individual in the organization working toward common objectives. These objectives should be realistic, should be clearly understood by everyone in the organization, and should reflect the organization's basic character and personality.

If the organization is to fulfill its objectives, it should strive to meet certain other fundamental requirements:

First, the most capable people available should be selected for each assignment within the organization. Moreover, these people should have the opportunity—through continuing programs of training and education—to upgrade their skills and capabilities. This is especially important in a technical business where the rate of progress is rapid. Techniques that are good today will be outdated in the future, and people throughout the organization should continually be looking for new and better ways to do their work.

Second, enthusiasm should exist at all levels. People in important management positions should not only be enthusiastic themselves, they should be selected for their ability to engender enthusiasm among their associates. There can be no place, especially among the people charged with management responsibility, for half-hearted interest or half-hearted effort.

Third, even though an organization is made up of people fully meeting the first two requirements, all levels should work in unison toward common objectives and avoid working at cross-purposes if the ultimate in efficiency and achievement is to be obtained.

It has been our policy at Hewlett-Packard not to have a tight military-type organization, but rather, to have overall objectives which are clearly stated and agreed to, and to give people the freedom to work toward those goals in ways they determine best for their own areas of responsibility.

Our Hewlett-Packard objectives were initially published in 1957. Since then they have been modified from time to time, reflecting the changing nature of our business and social environment. This booklet represents the latest updating of our objectives. We hope you find them informative and useful.

David Packard
Chairman of the Board
William Hewlett
President and Chief Executive Officer

THE PROFIT OBJECTIVE

To achieve sufficient profit to finance our company growth and to provide the resources we need to achieve our other corporate objectives.

In our economic system, the profit we generate from our operations is the ultimate source of the funds we need to prosper and grow. It is the one absolutely essential measure of our corporate performance over the long term. Only if we continue to meet our profit objective can we achieve our other corporate objectives.

Our long-standing policy has been to reinvest most of our profits and to depend on this reinvestment, plus funds from employee stock purchases and other cash flow items, to finance our growth. This can be achieved if our return on net worth is roughly equal to our sales growth rate. We must strive to reach this goal every year without limiting our efforts to attain our other objectives.

Profits vary from year to year, reflecting changing economic conditions and varying demands for our products. Our needs for capital also vary, and we depend on short-term bank loans to meet those needs when profits or other cash sources are inadequate. However, loans are costly and must be repaid; thus, our objective is to rely on reinvested profits as our main source of capital.

Meeting our profit objective requires that we design and develop each and every product so that it is considered a good value by our customers, yet is priced to include an adequate profit. Maintaining this competitiveness in the marketplace also requires that we perform our manufacturing, marketing, and administrative functions as economically as possible.

Profit is not something that can be put off until tomorrow; it must be achieved today. It means that myriad jobs be done correctly and efficiently. The day-to-day performance of each individual adds to—or subtracts from—our profit. Profit is the responsibility of all.

THE CUSTOMER OBJECTIVE

To provide products and services of the greatest possible value to our customers, thereby gaining and holding their respect and loyalty.

The success and prosperity of our company will be assured only if we offer our customers superior products that fill real needs and provide lasting value, and that are supported by a wide variety of useful services, both before and after sale.

Our responsibility to the customer begins with product development. Products must be designed to provide superior performance and long, trouble-free service. Once in production, these products must be manufactured at a reasonable cost and with superior workmanship.

A prime objective of our marketing departments is to see that the finished product is backed by prompt, efficient service. Moreover, good communication should be maintained with the customer and among various HP sales teams.

Because of our broad and growing line of products, very often several sales teams will be working with a single customer. Each of these teams has a high degree of technical knowledge

230

and sales skill. There must be considerable cooperation among teams to assure that the products recommended best fulfill the customer's overall, long-term needs.

HP customers must feel that they are dealing with one company with common policies and services, and that our company is genuinely interested in arriving at proper, effective solutions to their problems. Confusion and competition among sales teams must be avoided by a clear assignment of sales responsibilities, plus sound judgement by HP sales people in understanding customer needs and HP.

THE FIELDS OF INTEREST OBJECTIVE

To enter new fields only when the ideas we have, together with our technical, manufacturing, and marketing skills, assure that we can make a needed and profitable contribution to the field.

The original Hewlett-Packard products were electronic measuring instruments. Today our product line has expanded to include instruments for chemical and biomedical measurement and analysis, computers to automate measurement and to process the data, as well as electronic calculators and complete computer systems. Thus our growth has led to a continuing expansion of our fields of interest. To a large extent, diversification has come from applying our resources and skills to fields technically related to our traditional ones.

The key to HP's prospective involvement in new fields is *contribution*. This means providing customers with something new and needed, not just another brand of something they can already buy. To meet this objective we must continually generate new ideas for better kinds of products. It is essential that before final decision is made to enter a new field, full consideration be given to the associated problems of manufacturing and marketing these products.

THE GROWTH OBJECTIVE

To let our growth be limited only by our profits and our ability to develop and produce technical products that satisfy real customer needs.

How large should a company become? Some people feel that when it has reached a certain size there is no point in letting it grow further. Others feels that bigness is an objective in itself. We do not believe that large size is important for its own sake; however, for at least two basic reasons, continuous growth is essential for us to achieve our other objectives.

In the first place, we serve a rapidly growing and expanding segment of our technological society. To remain static would be to lose ground. We cannot maintain a position of strength and leadership in our field without growth.

In the second place, growth is important in order to attract and hold high caliber people. These individuals will align their future only with a company that offers them considerable opportunity for personal progress. Opportunities are greater and more challenging in a growing company.

THE OUR PEOPLE OBJECTIVE

To help HP people share in the company's success, which they make possible; to provide job security based on their performance; to recognize their individual achievements; and to ensure the personal satisfaction that comes from a sense of accomplishment in their work.

We are proud of the people we have in our organization, their performance, and their attitude toward their jobs and toward the company. The company has been built around the individual, the personal dignity of each, and the recognition of personal achievements.

We feel that general policies and the attitude of managers toward their people are more important than specific details of the personnel program. Personnel relations will be good only if people have faith in the motives and integrity of their supervisors and of the company. Personnel relations will be poor if they do not.

The opportunity to share in the success of the company is evidenced by our above-average wage and salary level, our profit-sharing and stock purchase plans, and by other company benefits.

The objective of job security is illustrated by our policy of avoiding large ups and downs in our production schedules, which would require hiring people for short periods of time and laying them off later. We are interested that each employee carry a full load and be eager to remain with and grow with the company. This does not mean we are committed to an absolute tenure status, nor do we recognize seniority except where other factors are reasonably comparable.

In a growing company there are apt to be more opportunities for advancement than there are qualified people to fill them. This is true at Hewlett-Packard; opportunities are plentiful and it is up to the individual, through personal growth and development, to take advantage of them.

We want people to enjoy their work at HP, and to be proud of their accomplishments. This means we must make sure that each person receives the recognition he or she needs and deserves. In the final analysis, people at all levels determine the character and strength of our company.

THE MANAGEMENT OBJECTIVE

To foster initiative and creativity by allowing the individual great freedom of action in attaining well-defined objectives.

In discussing HP operating policies, we often refer to the concept of "management by objective." By this we mean that insofar as possible each individual at each level in the organization should make his or her own plans to achieve company objectives and goals. After receiving supervisory approval, each individual should be given a wide degree of freedom to work within the limitations imposed by these plans, and by our general corporate policies. Finally, each person's performance should be judged on the basis of how well these individually established goals have been achieved.

The successful practice of "management by objective" is a two-way street. Management must be sure that each individual understands the immediate objectives, as well as corporate goals and policies. Thus a primary HP management responsibility is communication and mutual understanding. Conversely, employees must take sufficient interest in their work to want to plan it, to propose new solutions to old problems, to stick their necks out when they have something to contribute. "Management by objective," as opposed to management by directive, offers opportunity for individual freedom and contribution; it also imposes an obligation for everyone to exercise initiative and enthusiasm.

In this atmosphere it is particularly important that the strength of the whole company is kept in mind and that cooperation between individuals and between operating units is vital to our profitable growth.

It is important for everyone to realize there are some policies which must be established and strictly maintained on a corporate-wide basis. We welcome recommendations on these corporate-wide policies from all levels but we expect adherence to them at all times.

THE CITIZENSHIP OBJECTIVE

To honor our obligations to society by being an economic, intellectual, and social asset to each nation and each community in which we operate.

All of us should strive to improve the environment in which we live. As a corporation operating in many different communities throughout the world, we must assure ourselves that each of these communities is better for our presence. This means building plants and offices that are attractive and in harmony with the community; it means solving instead of contributing to the problems of traffic and pollution; it means contributing both money and time to community projects.

Each community has its particular set of social problems. Our company must help solve these problems. As a major step in this direction, we must strive to provide worthwhile employment opportunities for people of widely different backgrounds. Among other things, this requires positive action to seek out and employ members of disadvantaged groups; and to encourage and guide their progress toward full participation at all position levels.

As citizens of their community, there is much that HP people can and should do to improve it—either working as individuals or through such groups as churches, schools, civic, or charitable organizations. At a national level, it is essential that the company be a good corporate citizen of each country in which it operates. Moreover, our employees, as individuals, should be encouraged to contribute their support to the solution of national problems.

The betterment of our society is not a job to be left to a few; it is a responsibility to be shared by all.

CHAPTER

15

THE HUMAN RESOURCE MANAGEMENT AUDIT

Charles J. Fombrun
Mary Anne Devanna
Noel M. Tichy

Each of the preceding chapters of Part II has stressed the potential contribution to strategic management of a carefully crafted selection, appraisal, reward, and development system (the components of a systematically supported corporate culture, as it were). However, none have directly addressed the pragmatic query of the manager: How does an organization implement strategic human resource management?

The purpose of this chapter is to discuss the overlapping dimensions of strategy formulation and implementation through the Human Resource Management Audit (HRMA). The HRMA is a databased approach to organizational change that involves personnel drawn from both a lateral slice through the staff and line functions and a diagonal slice within each of these functions.

The audit itself revolves around five frameworks, all of which are discussed at length in Chapter 3. These frameworks form the backbone of the data-collection effort which is central to the HRMA.

THE PROCESS OF CHANGE: THE HUMAN RESOURCE
MANAGEMENT AUDIT

Following Richard Beckhard, any improvement process or change effort can be broken into three distinct phases: (1) advancing a diagnosis of the present state, (2) preparing a clear statement of the desired future state, and (3) developing a strategy for managing the transition from the present to the desired state.

In order to get good data about the current state, to successfully define the desired state, and to effectively guide the transition towards the desired state, the HRMA assumes that broad-based participation of the different levels and groups affected by the change effort is required.The following individuals should, therefore, be involved in any reorientation of the human resource management function.

1. *Senior Management.*   Their active support is required to (1) provide the necessary human, financial, and informational resources, and (2) obtain the symbolic effect of their commitment on lower-level line management.

2. *Line Management.*   Any attempt to redesign the role of the human resource management function requires the line's participation since most of the activities of selection, appraisal, reward, and development are prerogatives of the line organization.

3. *Human Resource Staff.*   A successful change effort will influence the jobs and activities of the personnel in the function. Their active cooperation is obviously required.

These three groups are the individuals principally concerned with the three organizational components of strategy structure and systems discussed in Chapter 3: senior executives develop strategy, line management controls the structure, and the human resource staff runs the human resource systems. At the same time, the involvement of these groups addresses the three implementation concerns: the technical, political, and cultural implications of the change will manifest themselves in the involvement (or lack thereof) of these groups.

The HRMA assumes that all organizations have a range of human resource service needs. The audit, therefore, takes an overall organizational perspective, focusing on the human resource function as an organization delivering services to an internal marketplace of client users. Figure 15.1 indicates the relationships that guide the data-collection effort.

The human resources organization (represented by the circle in the lower portion of Figure 15.1) is embedded in the corporation. It interacts with client groups and is affected by the corporation's business strategy as well as the world outside the corporation. The core of the framework is represented by the items labeled (*a*) through (*f*), each of which represents a key organiza-

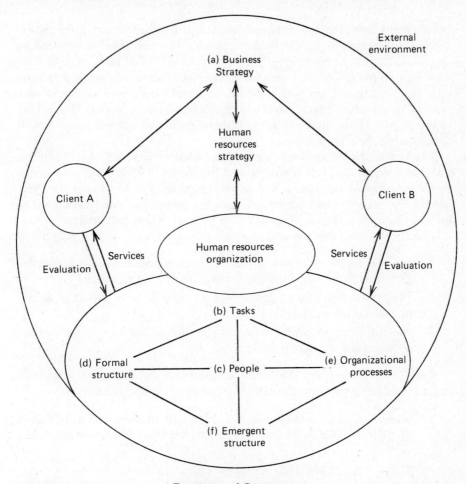

External environment

(a) Business Strategy

Human resources strategy

Client A

Client B

Services

Services

Evaluation

Evaluation

Human resources organization

(b) Tasks

(d) Formal structure

(c) People

(e) Organizational processes

(f) Emergent structure

Description of Components

(a) Business mission/strategy. This includes the organization's reason for being, its basic approach to carrying out its mission, its strategy, and its criteria for effectiveness.

(b) Tasks. This refers to technology by which the organization's work is accomplished.

(c) People. This includes the characteristics of the members of the organization, their background, motivational patterns, managerial style, and so forth.

(d) Prescribed structure. This refers to the organization's explicitly designed social structure. It includes the organization of subunits, communication and authority networks, and structural mechanisms for integrating the organization.

(e) Organizational processes. These are the mechanisms (for example, communication, decision making, conflict management, control, and reward) that enable the formal organization to carry out the dynamics of work.

(f) Emergent structure. This includes the structures and processes that, while not planned or formally prescribed, inevitably emerge in the organization.

FIGURE 15.1. The human resources management audit.

tional component. These components are defined at the bottom of the figure. Using these components, the human resource function itself is depicted as an organization in its own right. To do the tasks that must be done (selection, training, compensation, etc.), people are hired and placed in a formal structure; they make decisions, get into conflicts, and build their own emergent networks. As a result of their activities a distinct package of services is provided to the clients. These clients, in turn, evaluate them and provide a mechanism for assessing their performance.

The key to the organization's effective functioning is not to be found in the characteristics of each component of the model in Figure 15.1, but in *how well they fit together as a system.* The more compatible, or the better the "fit" among the people, tasks, structures, and processes, the more effective the human resource organization is likely to be in servicing its clients.

The HRMA uses this framework to try to answer such questions as these.

1. Are the mission and strategy of the human resource organization designed to match the business strategy of the organization?

2. Does the design of the human resource organization enhance its ability to accomplish its strategy?

3. Are the kinds of people who run the human resource function good choices for the ongoing tasks?

Table 15.1 summarizes the kinds of questions and data-gathering techniques used in conducting the HRMA. The primary sources of data are:

1. *Interviews with Senior Management.*   Focus on strategy and a definition of the current state of the organization and the desired future state.

TABLE 15.1.   Diagnostic Plan of HRMA.

Information Sought	Primary Method of Data Collection
Business environment	Senior management interviews
	Line management questionnaires
Business strategy	Senior management interviews
Business formal structure	Documents
Human resource strategy	Senior management interviews
	Line management interviews
	HR staff questionnaires
Characteristics of HR staff	Documents
	HR staff questionnaires
	Line management evaluations
HR formal structure	Documents
	HR staff questionnaire
HR emergent structure	Sociometric questionnaire
Performance of HR function	Senior management interviews
	Line management questionnaires
	Line management interviews

2. *Interviews and Questionnaires with Line Management.* Focus on their interactions with the HR function, their human resource problems, and the role they envision for the HR organization.

3. *In-Depth Questionnaires from the Human Resource Staff.* Diagnose the jobs, activities, conflicts, and internal strengths and weaknesses of the function.

4. *Archival Information and Documents.* Describe job histories, past evaluations, formal structures, and general background on the organization as a whole and the HR function in particular.

Figure 15.2 presents some of the specific questions that might be asked of interviewers to diagnose the degree of integration of the human resource systems in the HR cycle around a dominant value of performance. The questions would also help fill out the matrix of ongoing HR activities of Figure 3.3 in Chapter 3 for any specific organization.

Conducting the HRMA

An HRMA is a major organizational intervention. It raises expectations that something will be done in response to its findings. Therefore, careful consideration should be given to the organization's responsiveness to change. In particular, the following issues should be addressed.

1. *Focus of Audit.* What unit is to be analyzed? In large corporations, the focus of the audit can be the total corporate personnel/human resource management function, or it can be the divisional or subsidiary level. Whatever the focus, the audit's boundaries must be specified from the start.

2. *Resources.* What resources are available for conducting the audit? Staff time as well as money are key resources that must be available. In addition, line management's involvement should be given particular consideration. Pressures for change could well result from an HRMA. If the audit is likely to uncover areas requiring major policy changes but senior line management is not ready or willing to address these issues, it might be appropriate to delay or abort the audit. Line management's commitment, understanding, and involvement with the HRMA is essential if it is to be of real value to the organization.

3. *Diagnostic Plan.* The audit should begin with the development of a diagnostic work plan that specifically takes into account the *data* to be collected, the *methods* to be used in data collection, the *individuals* who will do the data collection, and the *individuals* responsible for analyzing the data.

4. *Managing the HRMA.* There are alternative methods for managing, overseeing, and carrying out an HRMA. The basic methods are (1) having an external consultant manage it, (2) having internal staff and an external consultant manage it jointly, and (3) having line management join internal staff and an external consultant in managing it.

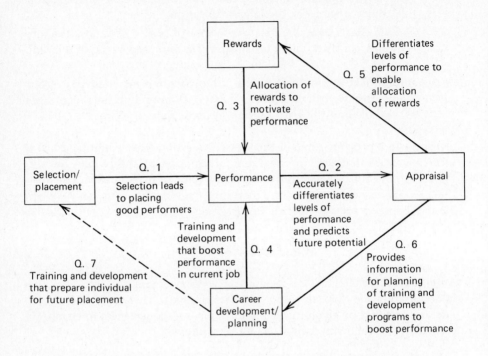

Q.1. How effective is the selection process in ensuring that people are placed in appropriate positons? Explain.

Q.2. How effective is the appraisal process in accurately assessing performance? Explain.

Q.3. How effective are rewards (financial and nonfinancial) in driving performance? Explain.

Q.4. How effective are the training, development, and career planning activities in driving performance? Explain.

Q.5. How effective is the appraisal process in differentiating performance levels for justifying reward allocation decisions? Explain.

Q.6. How effective is the appraisal process in identifying developmental needs of individuals to guide training, development, and career planning? Explain.

Q.7. How effective are the training, development, and career planning activities in preparing people for selection and placement into new positions in the organization? Explain.

Q.8. Overall, how effectively are the five components integrated and mutually supportive? Explain.

FIGURE 15.2.   To what extent are the components of the human resource system integrated at the operational (managerial, strategic) level to provide effective services?

Each method has advantages and disadvantages. The external consultant format is both simplest and fastest to carry out. Potentially, however, it has the least impact because it is likely to generate the most defensiveness and may cause key staff members to dismiss the findings. The use of an external consultant with an internal staff is moderately simple to manage and can be conducted quickly. It has some of the same weaknesses as the outside consultant format—that is, line management may not feel a proprietary interest in either the process or the results. The three-party format has the advantage of committing all parties to the process and the results. Although it has the greatest potential for bringing about needed change, it calls for the most complex organization and management and can easily run into problems. Managing the process effectively is probably the single most important requirement of the HRMA because it will determine the audit's future impact on the organization.

THE DYNAMICS OF STRATEGIC CHANGE

Based on the data developed by the HRMA, a detailed diagnosis of the current staff–line interface can be developed. Through feedback meetings and follow-up sessions with appropriate diagonal and lateral slices of the organization (the transition teams), a desired future state can be formulated. It is through careful and systematic cooperation with these transition teams that the implementation of the change plan will take place. Three interrelated sets of processes will have to be carefully monitored: the technical, political, and cultural dynamics of the organization. Technical change would require using rational problem-solving tools to come up with analytically sound blueprints for change and engineering model fits for the organization. Because the political area is based on conflict, change there must rely on such tactics as bargaining, manipulation, and confrontation. Change in the cultural area calls for an examination of norms and values, using such group-based methods as action research, data feedback, and team building.

Technical Changes. The human resource organization will probably have to review its mission and strategy to see whether they fit the complexity of its environment. In addition, the mission and strategy must be clearly communicated, understood, and adhered to by all key parties.

Political Changes. The technical changes will trigger a set of political issues. First, the proposed changes have political implications for the human resource organization's relationship with line managers. By moving into the strategic arena, human resource staff must also bargain with senior management about the amount of influence each group will have on decisions that were previously the sole prerogative of senior managers. In addition, the human resource organization's budget may have to be increased. Within the human resource organization, technical changes could mean that some people's power bases are increased, whereas others' are decreased. More experienced staff members who may be more operationally focused may find themselves in less powerful positions, whereas newer staff members with more generalized training may gain power. New roles that emerge as a result of the organizational structure (e.g., human resource generalist in a functionally structured department) may create new power bases. The change process will need to handle the inevitable political conflict created by the technical changes.

Cultural Changes. The technical and political changes in the organization will trigger changes in the cultural area. New norms will emerge that tend to reinforce and place a higher value on orientation that focuses on managerial and strategic responses. The process will have to deal with the transition to a new culture with, most likely, the emergence of conflicting subcultures.

Pragmatic Steps for Implementation

The following steps are proposed as guidelines to help in designing a strategic human resource management function in the organization.

Step 1: Set Priorities

The first task is for the human resource function to clarify its own priorities based on the audit's findings. Then, on the basis of a technical, political, and cultural assessment of the corporation, it should determine whether it was a good time to launch a major change activity. If the decision to go ahead is made, the group would have to set its priorities for change and develop a technical, political, and cultural set of strategies for managing the transition.

Step 2: Get a Mandate From Senior Management

The next step entails getting a new mandate from senior management concerning the human resource department's role in the organization. If senior management refuses to support the proposed move into managerial and strategic activities, it would be politically destructive for the department to make a major change in this direction. The audit could be used as a means of bringing the problem to senior management's attention. The data feedback could give them a handle on the problem.

Step 3: Get Staff Commitment and Development

Once the scope of senior management's mandate is set, the total human resource staff would have to be brought on board. The audit would have to be thoroughly reviewed with them, and the management strategy shared and understood. At this stage, a combination educational and problem-solving process would be useful. The staff could use the audit review as a means of buying into the change strategy and of becoming educated about operational, managerial, and strategic issues. The human resource staff should then become involved in developing ways to manage the transition, for example, setting up task forces to focus on different aspects of the changes that have to be addressed. These task forces could be organized according to the components of the model of Figure 15.1.

Step 4: Set Strategy for Working With Clients and Users

Groundwork must be laid with clients and users who would have to deal with any changes in the human resource organization's operation. One approach might be to provide them with summary feedback from the study, showing them what the audit found and how the human resource department plans to improve its operation and upgrade its service. It would be best for the staff to work out political issues involving clients as they arise. The change process could extend over several years and any changes in power would occur gradually. It will be important, however, to monitor clients over a period of time by readministering the portions of the audit that collected data from them, and generating ongoing market research information and performance data on the effectiveness of the function.

Step 5: Set up a Development Plan for the Organization

To help the human resource department staff during the transition, the development plan should probably follow the sequence presented here.

Mission/Strategy.   Change here should be based largely on needs created by the external environment, a complex changing market, and a changing regulatory and economic environment. A strategic decision-making process should be put into place to accomplish the following:

1. Tie into the business strategic plan by providing the organization's strategic decision-makers with useful, quantitative data on current and future human resource needs.
2. Have a strong marketing orientation to the multiple client and user groups in the organization. This will require development of ongoing market-scanning mechanisms.
3. Involve key human resources staff at many levels of the strategic decision-making process so they understand and are committed to the human resources strategy.

Tasks.   These follow from the mission and strategy. Once they are developed, the matrix of human resource activities can be used to list critical tasks for each function at the strategic managerial and operational levels. Then an assessment of what is needed to successfully carry out each task in terms of people, organization design, processes, and emergent networks can be made.

Formal Structure.   The critical concern here must be to design a structure that integrates and coordinates organizational resources to accomplish the priority tasks. The design is not automatically plugged in; it must be incrementally developed and the organization must be helped to move toward it. Thus an ongoing organization design process needs to be developed for the transition. The change might start with task forces assigned to certain tasks, then the task forces might become teams, and finally, they might be placed into permanent matrix structures to manage the tasks. It is conceivable that higher-level human resource managers' jobs could include operational and managerial tasks as well as strategic tasks.

It is also important to use the same motivational assumptions when constructing individual components of the human resource function and integrating operational-level tasks. Too often, the motivational assumptions behind the design of such components as the compensation system, the development system, and the selection system are inconsistent or even mutually exclusive.

People.   The shift in the human resource function to more managerial and strategic-level tasks calls for a shift in the orientation of human resource managers. The points of view of both the general business manager and the technical specialist are needed. Although MBA graduates have not traditionally been hired as human resource staff members, they are one group that combines both the business and human resource points of view and, as such, could be a valuable source of new managers.

Processes.   The two key processes that need major attention are reward and control. As the tasks and the organization design shift, these two processes must be brought into line so that they reinforce the change. The audit data that were collected should help the organization match the rewards the staff values with the rewards the organization can afford. Control systems that monitor tasks at all three levels should also be developed.

Emergent Networks.   These are best fostered by using the reward system to encourage human resource staff to informally address managerial and strategic concerns. Also, transfer and promotion procedures can be used to weave together emergent networks that foster the development of the human resources department.

REORGANIZING THE PERSONNEL FUNCTION

The success of the reorientation of the organization towards the strategic management of human resources largely depends on overcoming the following factors.

1. *History.*   The human resource systems have traditionally been administered through the personnel function and thereby suffer from perceptions of inefficiency, inaccuracy, and irrelevance, as a result of which the function and its activities have been largely relegated to the periphery of organizational concerns.
2. *Structure.*   Partly for the historical reasons just raised, the function is often structurally isolated from the planning activities of the organization. This makes dialogue between them difficult and any significant

degree of influence virtually impossible since the function is not "on the scene."

3. *Staffing.*   Accustomed to operational servicing and powerlessness, the personnel function has tended to attract few "superstars." Human resource activities are typically administered by competent specialists largely unfamiliar with either planning jargon or quantitative analysis, with backgrounds in psychology, education, and counseling. The lack of common experience, education, and orientation is undoubtedly a stumbling block in integrating the human resource system into mainstream strategic planning.

4. *Resources.*   Effective involvement in a reciprocal relationship with the planning side of the organization requires discretionary control over the allocation of a significant pool of resources for hiring and training, human resource staff, as well as the development of programs and projects uniquely designed to support the strategic thrust of the organization. Personnel functions have traditionally faced circumscribed budgets and lack the quantitative ability to show a bottom-line ROI on its activities. This is especially important at the business level.

Figure 15.3 presents a brief sketch of the kinds of structures, staff, and resources required to operate the human resource function at each level of the organization. The size of the corporate staff will depend largely on the degree to which the organizational culture supports an integrated set of sys-

	Corporate Level	Business Level	Functional Level
Structure	Direct report to CEO Equal level with planning group Member of planning group Sets business level guidelines for design of systems	Direct contact with division management Dialogue with planning group Sets policy for field service groups Constant internal interaction among subareas	Field offices for on-site service delivery Implement programs designed at business level Refer unusual cases to business staff
Staffing	Generalists with rotations across businesses and functions Ability to speak in business language	Some business training for promotion Rotation across subareas (e.g., compensation and recruitment)	Specialists in subareas Part of field rotation
Resources	Vary with degree of integration across businesses	Discretionary funds to initiate programs Allocations to field staff	Budgets set through business plan

FIGURE 15.3.   The human resource function.

tems across businesses. Nonetheless, to be effective, the function should be staffed with highly visible executives reporting to the CEO on a par with other functional groups, and with enough of a broad business background to have an effective dialogue with them.

At the business level, the function must be responsive to business trends and concerns, and is responsible for designing the basic systems to support the business strategy within the corporate guidelines. As such it should be staffed with individuals conversant with the activities of the business.

Finally, onsite field offices (in large organizations) are responsible for service delivery according to the policies designed at the business level (themselves consistent with corporate-level guidelines). As entry-level human resource positions, they largely require the expertise of specialists in the traditional areas of industrial relations. Through field rotations across subdisciplines, they come to qualify for business-level involvement, and with rotations and managerial training may qualify for corporate positions. A key responsibility of field staff at the functional level will be the identification of systemic contradictions between the systems as they are implemented to support cross-functional programs born of the strategic business plan.

SUMMARY AND CONCLUSIONS

This chapter has suggested a process for moving the human resource management function from one dominated by operational level concerns toward one that supports and improves organizational activities at the managerial and strategic levels.

Three sets of linkages must be established as follows:

Strategic Link

On the business side, the key issues involve deciding what business the organization is in, choosing objectives and reviewing them, identifying major priorities, specifying major programs, and developing policies to achieve goals. On the human resource side, the key issue is determining the kind of people needed to run the business in the long term, choosing the specific policies and programs for the long-term development of human resources for the future, and fostering the appropriate social and cultural context within which the objectives are likely to succeed.

The strategic link calls for dialogue between the business concerns and the human resource concerns. This dialogue is reflected in the establishment of boundaries around the human resource context for strategic planning (e.g., what kind of human resources will the organization need over the long term?). In addition, the strategic link involves a dialogue about the tradeoffs between human, financial, informational, space, and other resources as reflected in the organization's different strategic commitments.

Managerial Link

The business side of the process begins with the strategic plan as the guiding framework. The major focus is on resource acquisition to carry out the strategic plan as well as the development of procedures for measuring and monitoring performance. The focus is on the human resource system for acquiring, appraising, rewarding, and developing human resources to achieve the strategic goals.

The managerial link involves dialogue around such issues as: Do we promote from within or hire from outside to develop the human resources needed in the medium term? How do we meet the needs of the internal markets for human resources services? What are the strategies for each of the subfunctions of human resources?

Operational Link

At the operational level, the business side is concerned with the execution of day-to-day tasks—producing the organization's products. On the human resource side, the concern is ensuring that the people come to work, perform, get evaluated, rewarded, and that they have the job skills they need or are trained in acquiring them.

Guidelines for Moving to Strategic Human Resource Management

In order to forge these strategic, managerial, and operational linkages, a number of guidelines can be suggested. Before beginning the change process, however, an HRMA should be conducted to provide databased support for the change efforts. Using these data as an energizing medium, the following recommendations can be formulated.

The Internal Organization of the Human Resources Function

The first area of focus is on how to properly organize, staff, and manage the human resource function. This involves the following steps.

1.   Identify the portfolio of human resource tasks at the strategic, managerial, and operational level for each human resource element.

2.   Reorganize the human resource function to reflect the operational, managerial, and strategic needs of the business. The *operational level* is best served by a traditional functional personnel department where there are separate units carrying out recruitment, compensation, development, and so on. The *managerial level* must be organized to cut across the subfunctions identified at the operational level (recruitment, development, compensation, etc.) by using such design tools as liaison managers, teams, or, under limited conditions, a matrix organizational design. The *strategic level* activities require an elite senior human resource management (individual or team, depending on

the size of the organization) that is supported by strong managerial human resource service.

3.   The human resource staff must be trained in the more strategically focused organization. At the operational level, the function must be staffed with technically focused professional personnel. At the managerial level, individuals who possess a more general managerial orientation and background either through actual work experience or through an MBA degree, should be selected from the operational level. Finally, at the strategic level, staffing should be based on selecting human resource executives who have political skills, a broad business orientation, and a broad human resource management background. A proactive stance toward the strategic future of the organization is also required.

4.   The reward and control systems must be altered to support the strategic human resource function. The rewards and controls should reflect specific tasks at each of the three levels. Most personnel reward and control systems are geared toward operational level activities; these should be expanded to reward and control people in terms of the new strategic and managerial level activities.

Linking the Human Resource Function to the Line Organization

Major changes are also required to link the human resource function to the user organization. Most personnel functions are linked to the operational business activities. With the addition of new managerial and strategic activities, new linking mechanisms will be required.

1.   Provide the business with good human resource databases. These include environmental scanning of labor markets and social and economic issues that influence the long-term human resource context of the organization. In addition, data on the internal labor pool are required in both a present and a future context. Internal marketing data on the human resource needs of various user groups in the organization are especially helpful.

2.   Alter the senior management role when it comes to human resource management issues so that these concerns receive quality attention. The managers need to be committed to weighing human resource issues with the same level of attention as that of other functions such as finance, marketing, and production.

3.   The line organization must alter its incentive and control systems so that the overall human resource function is managed. It will also be necessary for the organization to have ways of measuring the overall performance of the human resource function at the strategic, managerial, and operational levels. This will entail ongoing audits of the human resource function to determine how well it is doing in providing services to its clients. Adjustments should also be made in budgeting for human resource services, as some of these activities will require new sources of corporate funding.

CHAPTER

16

STRATEGIC HUMAN RESOURCE MANAGEMENT AT HONEYWELL INC.

Steward D. Friedman
Noel M. Tichy
Dave O. Ulrich

This chapter presents an illustration of the design of a strategic human resource management (HRM) system: the case of Honeywell Inc., Aerospace and Defense Business (ADB). It is based on the frameworks and concepts described in the previous chapter. First, we present a synopsis of ADB's response to environmental pressures on its business, emphasizing the need for increased productivity and higher quality of work life (QWL). Second, we review the process of integrating ADB's strategic business plans and human resource management strategies. In particular, the process and content of the diagnostic phase of a collaborative endeavor between ADB management and a University of Michigan action research team are described. We then discuss the diagnostic implications for ADB's strategy for human resource management. Finally, the early phases in the implementation of a new, integrative strategic management process are delineated.

ADB's STRUCTURE AND OBJECTIVES

Honeywell's ADB was, until January 1983, the Aerospace and Defense Group (ADG), a somewhat smaller segment in terms of revenue and personnel than it is today. Since many of the efforts described in this chapter took place prior to the structural change, much of the descriptive data about ADB must necessarily refer to ADG. Aerospace and Defense after the restructuring remains substantially the same organization, albeit a larger one. Figures 16.1 and 16.2 show the current organization of ADB within the Honeywell corporation.

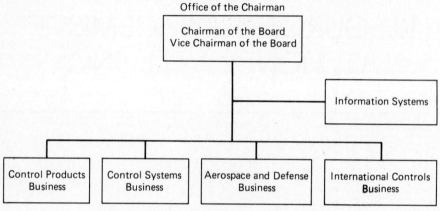

FIGURE 16.1. Honeywell corporate organization.

In the former structure, Aerospace and Defense was the largest group in Honeywell with 1982 revenues estimated to be $1.2 billion (out of $5.4 billion for all of Honeywell) and nearly one-quarter of Honeywell's 73,000 domestic employees. According to its brochure,[1]

> ADG's strength lies in an organization of divisions operations, and centers built along broad disciplinary lines. Experience within the group encompasses space and light systems; ordnance systems for land, sea, and air applications; electro-optical technologies and products; naval acoustic and commercial marine technologies and support; electronics production; training and weapon control equipment; tactical support.

Honeywell's 1981 Annual Report notes that

> government spending in the United States and abroad is the greatest influence on growth in aerospace and defense markets. The defense budget passed by the current administration will benefit Honeywell's business, with the major impact occurring in 1983 and beyond.

[1] *Brochure.* Aerospace and Defense Group, Honeywell Inc., no date.

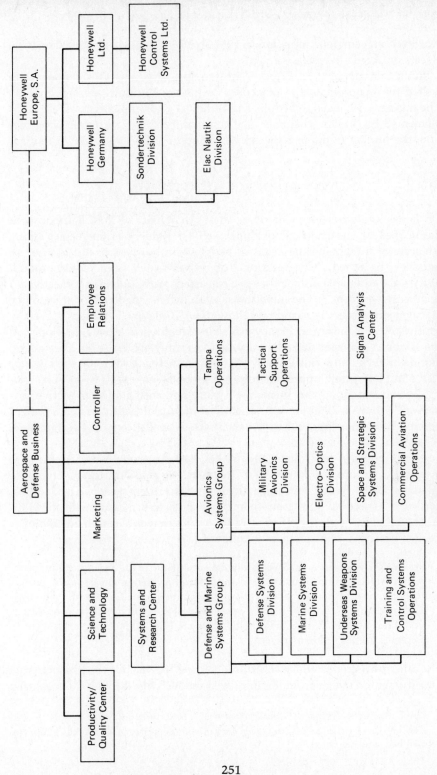

FIGURE 16.2. Aerospace and defense business organization.

However, an economic recession in 1981 and 1982 is likely to have damaging effects on ADB's business strength.

In the Summer of 1982, Warde Wheaton, Executive Vice President of ADB, posted the major goals and objectives of his organization (see Figure 16.3). The business, financial, schedule, and technical goals and objectives are complemented by human, customer, and community aims. In the following section, the human resource activities that support these targets are examined.

HUMAN RESOURCE ACTIVITIES IN ADB

Dr. James Renier, as Vice Chairman, shares the Office of the Chairman with Edson Spencer, the Chairman of Honeywell. Dr. Renier has long been a strong advocate of integrating the needs of people with business needs. In a recent interview he noted, "Organizational objectives—such as increased productivity—are attainable only if they are consistent with individual objectives—such as self-esteem."[2] The importance of an active, healthy human resource management system is recognized throughout Honeywell; perhaps especially so in ADB. For instance, Honeywell's first quality circle was developed at the Avionics Division (a subsidiary of the former ADG) in St. Petersburg, Florida in 1974. Now called Employee Teams, there are over 600 such groups active in Honeywell, approximately 400 in ADB.

The focal program and theme for a more humanistic and productive Honeywell culture is "People in the '80s." ADB's philosophy of management defined by senior line and staff executives is spelled out in its statement, "Our Way" (see Figure 16.4).

At the business level (in ADB) the key human resource staff working to promote a culture supportive of "Our Way" is the Director of Employee relations, Larry Smith. Although there are other staff groups that address particular aspects of the issue—namely, quality and management development—ER spearheads the effort in ADB. An internal publication on Employee Teams[3] describes this function as follows:

> *Employee Relations* personnel serve as internal consultants to the various operations within ADG. Efforts focus on four areas: Raise awareness on issues of productivity, quality, and a quality work life; facilitate information transfer among ADG operations; conduct practical research related to productivity, a quality work life, and team issues; and develop team and human resource management processes useful to line managers.

The other staff groups which contribute to the effort include the Productivity/ Quality Center, which promotes improved productivity through the organized

---

[2] See P. Pascarella, "Humanagement at Honeywell", *Industry Week*, July 1981, 33–36.

[3] *Employee Teams: People Committed to Quality and Excellence*. Aerospace and Defense Group, Honeywell Inc., no date.

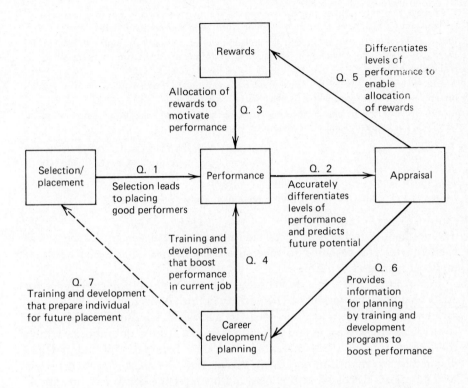

Rewards

Differentiates
levels of
performance to
Q. 5 enable
allocation
of rewards

Allocation of
rewards to
motivate
performance

Q. 3

Selection/
placement

Q. 1
Selection leads
to placing
good performers

Performance

Q. 2
Accurately
differentiates
levels of
performance
and predicts
future potential

Appraisal

Training and
development
that boost
performance
in current job

Q. 4

Q. 7
Training and development
that prepare individual
for future placement

Q. 6
Provides
information
for planning
by training and
development
programs to
boost performance

Career
development/
planning

BUSINESS: The mission of ADG is to provide quality components, subsystems, and
                 systems to enhance the strength and effectiveness of military capabilities
                 of the United States, our allies, and related commercial markets.

FINANCIAL: Growth: 13%/YEAR
                 Profit: 8.5% OPERATING PROFIT
                 Return: 18% ROI
                 Productivity (value added by ADG):   +2%/YEAR
                 Loss program: No major losers

SCHEDULE: All programs on or ahead of schedule.

TECHNICAL: All programs equal to or better than SPEC.
                 All work done right, the first time.
                 Consistent application of best available technology.

HUMAN: Positive climate: "Our way."
                 Employment stability and development opportunity.

CUSTOMERS: Effective and constructive relationships, with all customers.
                 Respect for work quality, by all customers.

COMMUNITY: Positive citizenship.

FIGURE 16.3.   ADG's major goals and objectives, July 1982.

OUR WAY

We believe that successful accomplishment of ADG's business goals and of our own personal goals requires a high level of awareness, involvement, and cooperation by all.

Our way of achieving this is through the advancement of mutual trust, high self-esteem, and team goal-setting, along with high standards of performance and a firm commitment to the highest quality of work.

A work environment which fosters openness, fulfillment, and the mutual utilization of everyone's unique talents and responsibilities is essential to reach our goals.

In this way, we will be able to meet our customer's needs and bring meaningful rewards to ourselves, our company, and our community.

HONEYWELL
AEROSPACE AND DEFENSE
GROUP 1982

FIGURE 16.4.   ADB's philosophy of management.

advancement of technology and systems, and the Management Development Center, which is designed to meet the training and educational needs of midlevel managers in ADB.

In November 1981, Warde Wheaton sponsored a two-day conference for ADG on quality of work life.[4] The primary objective was to "provide a greater awareness of people and their needs in managing a business."[5] Executives from each of the Divisions and Operations in ADG (the major subunits within the Group prior to 1983) presented what they had accomplished and had planned to accomplish in improving human resource management. A review of the projects discussed at this session illustrates the depth and breadth of the ground swell of support for the changing approach to management in ADB. Table 16.1 lists some of the programs under way in the organization at that time.[5]

In addition to the activities in ADB, the Corporate Employee Relations (ER) Office, headed by Fosten Boyle, Vice President, has been making substantial contributions to the human resource management initiative in ADB as well as throughout Honeywell. In late 1981, 18 strategic issues faced by Corporate ER were delineated.[6] High on this list were: "How to define and implement career development strategies/programs which meet individual and business needs," and "How to provide an employee organization structure and climate which assists in increasing productivity." For each of these issues

[4] W. F. Wheaton, Opening address to ADG's Quality of Worklife Conference, Minneapolis, MN, 10 November 1981.

[5] This list is adapted from an interoffice memo from R. M. Johnson, Management Development Center, to QWL Conference Participants, subject: "QWL Conference Summary Notes," 3 December 1981.

[6] "Corporate Employee Relations Strategic Issues." Honeywell Inc., internal document, 17 November 1981.

at least a half-dozen action steps were highlighted. These programs from Corporate ER complement the work of human resource staff throughout Honeywell. Within the Corporate ER Office, the two key positions responsible for carrying out the mandate for the broad-gauged effort at upgrading Honeywell's human resources are the Vice President of Human Resources, Dr. Arnold Kanarick, and his primary staff in this area, the Manager of Human Resource Development, Dr. David Dotlich. The corporate human resource staff has grown in recent years and its range of operations has broadened. The challenge is to tie together a large array of activities into a coherent well-aimed strategy. Foss Boyle said recently: "We are searching strategically," looking for ways to bring about long-term change.

One of the activities for moving towards strategic human resource management at Honeywell was a workshop that Dr. Renier held for his staff in September 1981 where Warde Wheaton met Noel Tichy, head of an action research team at the University of Michigan. Warde Wheaton expressed his desire to somehow integrate the large number of human resource activities already in place into his organization's strategic business plan. Warde Wheaton and the action research team perceived a potential transition process to integrate HRM and business planning. They began work to develop an action research program to help ADB manage its transition towards strategic human resource management.

INTEGRATING ADB's HRM TRANSITION: FIRST STEPS

Client Goals

First, the action research team worked to determine the goals of Warde Wheaton and Larry Smith (Project Manager for the transition process). Mr. Wheaton and Mr. Smith defined three primary purposes of working towards strategic human resource management:

1. Encourage synergy/integration of the array of human resource management activities at the Group and ADB level, with Larry Smith as Director of ADB ER coordinating the effort.
2. Encourage ER staff to begin to apply human resource management concepts to deal with internal and external pressures for change in the organization. The need was to know the underlying principles of strategic HRM and how to implement them within ADB.
3. Create a collaborative spirit between line and staff so that the line, which retains primary responsibility for implementing human resource management, could amplify effectiveness in this area.

After a series of preliminary meetings, which included the presentation of theoretical concepts to key line managers and ER staff, ADB contracted with

TABLE 16.1. Capsule Summary of Projects Discussed at November 1981 QWL Conference.

Unit[a]	Executive	Highlights of Presentation
Defense Systems Division (DSD)	Dick Boyle, Vice President and General Manager	Emphasized the objectives of his division's QWL process, dubbed "IT": "A way of managing and operating the organization that pays off in productivity, problem-solving, and motivation" Activities used to achieve these goals include: employee involvement, task teams, performance communication program (i.e., new appraisal system), award programs, improved communications systems, and upgraded professional development.
Underseas Operations	Clint Larson, Vice President	Focused on the "measurable benefits" (e.g., adjusted hours, learning curve, production rate) and the "intangible results" (e.g., cohesiveness, ownership, pride) of quality circles in his unit.
Ordnance Operations	Bob Mockenhaupt, Vice President	Highlighted the task teams working on various issues and reporting to a steering committee composed of Vice Presidents and Employee Relations.
Marine Systems Operations	Mike Bonsignore, Vice President	Spoke about the gainsharing program underway in his operation which appears to be bringing good results in its early stages.
Avionics Division (AvD)	Matt Sutton, Vice President and General Manager	Stated his objective as: "Quality of work life is key to productivity for the organization and the individual." Mentioned numerous programs underway in AvD, including behavior and climate changes (e.g., participative management series, teaming, Honeywell organization of women, black caucus) and individual growth programs.
Space and Strategic Systems	Stan Moeschl, Vice President	Stressed top management personal involvement to encourage change.

TABLE 16.1. (*Continued*)

Unit[a]	Executive	Highlights of Presentation
Military Avionics	Glenn Peters, Vice President	Pointed to such accomplishments as the start in worker participation teams in 1974 to now over 100 such groups in Military Avionics.
Group Operations	Bob Rynearson, Vice President and General Manager	Spoke of the philosophy of QWL as "determined by the success of the organization and the individual's ability for self-fulfillment."
Training and Control Systems Operation	Linc Hudson, Vice President and General Manager	Stressed the importance of the manager's role in leading such activities as flextime and flex-compensation, suggestion awards, and delegation of responsibility.
Electro-Optical (E-O) Operations	Bob Ziernicki, Director, Space E-O Systems	Focused on cultural factors which have prevented turnover and raised productivity in spite of rapid growth, which may have been unsettling. Visible evidence of caring, communications, and advancement opportunities have been critical support factors.
Tampa Operations	Sheldon Busansky, Vice President and General Manager	Emphasized QWL improvements such as a 50% reduction in grievances over the past two years.
Systems and Research Center	Roger Heinisch, Director	Reported on a variety of strategies (e.g., on-the-job career counseling, conflict facilitation, and award/recognition systems) to meet the objectives of quality decision making and ownership of goals by all.

[a] Units are based on the organization as it was in November 1981. The current structure is illustrated in Figure 16.2.

the action research team at the Institute for Social Research (ISR), The University of Michigan, to conduct a diagnosis of the human resource management system and to derive plans and activities to meet these purposes. In April 1982, Larry Smith presented the rationale and plan for this effort to the ADB executive committee, who agreed to the study. Given the support of top management the assessment process unfolded with data collection, analysis, feedback, and implementation of recommendations.

Data Collection

To conduct the diagnosis, a joint effort by the Michigan action research team and ADB was undertaken. Data were collected primarily with two methods (interview and questionnaire), each using a set of structured questions. In addition, archival records and observations supplemented the interview and survey data and were included in the findings. The design of the instruments was a collaborative effort to tailor and put into operation the theoretical concepts for the ADB culture. The questions asked in the questionnaire and interview reflect the concepts explicated in the previous chapter as applied to ADB. The topics and some of the specific questions are listed in the following. The interview topics were these:

1. *Organizational cycles.*   The predicted technical, political, and cultural changes for ADB were plotted and explained. Respondents were asked to "plot these three systems over time in terms of how dominant you feel each cycle will be at different times during the 1980s. A cycle peak indicates that there is a great deal of uncertainty in the system that requires managerial attention; a cycle valley indicates a period of low uncertainty, hence little need for managerial action."

2. *Managerial tools and organizational systems.*   Interviewees indicated amount of change required in each cell of Figure 16.5 for ADB's future success (1 = very little change required, 5 = great deal of change required).

3. *Description of strategic, managerial, and operational business activities.*   Respondents were asked for a brief overview of "business activities carried out by you and your management team. In getting this picture we would like to ask you to describe the activities of your unit in terms of three categories of business functions, namely, strategic, managerial, and operational functions."

4. *Ratings of the effectiveness of human resource activities at the operational level in the respondent's business unit.*   For this and subsequent questions, the human resource management functions were presented as a cycle of activities. Questions were asked about each of the seven links of the cycle and about the cycle overall. (See Figure 16.6 for specific questions asked about each link in the cycle at the operational level).

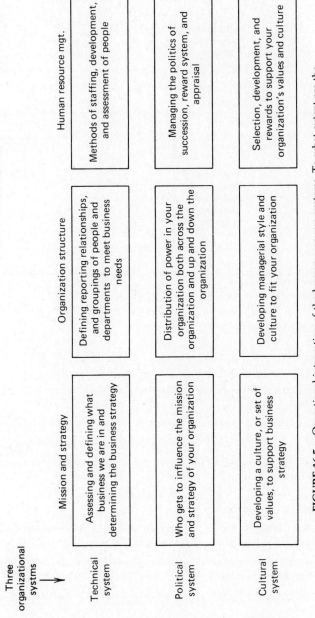

FIGURE 16.5. Operational integration of the human resource systems. To what extent are the components of the system integrated at the operational (managerial, strategic) level to provide effective services?

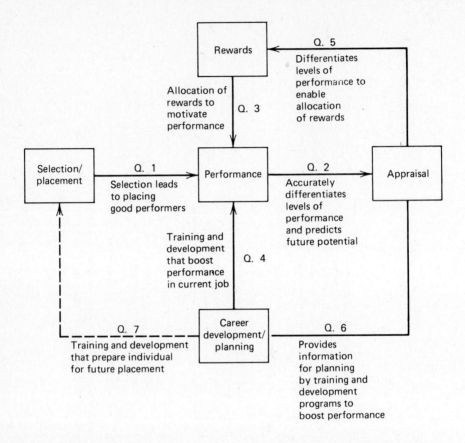

Q.1. How effective is the selection process in ensuring that people are placed in appropriate positions? Explain.*

Q.2. How effective is the appraisal process in accurately assessing performance? Explain.

Q.3. How effective are rewards (financial and nonfinancial) in driving performance? Explain.

Q.4. How effective are the training, development, and career planning activities in driving performance? Explain.

Q.5. How effective is the appraisal process differentiating performance levels for justifying reward allocation decisions? Explain.

Q.6. How effective is the appraisal process in identifying developmental needs of individuals to guide training, development, and career planning? Explain.

Q.7. How effective are the training, development, and career planning activities in preparing people for selection and placement into new positions in the organization? Explain.

Q.8. Overall, how effectively are the five components integrated and mutually supportive? Explain.

FIGURE 16.6. To what extent are the components of the human resource system integrated at the operational (managerial, strategic) level to provide effective services?

5. *The four human resource functions at the managerial level.*   Respondents were asked to rate the effectiveness of each of the functions on a 1 to 5 basis, as well as to indicate what services were provided at this level and by whom were they performed.

6. *The human resource cycle at the strategic level.*   At this level, the questions were concerned with how key people were selected, evaluated, rewarded, trained and developed for strategic activities.

7. *The organization and structure of ER.*   Included here were such questions as: What should be the role of the Employee Relations staff who work in your unit? What should the role of Corporate Employee Relations staff be? How would your ideal Employee Relations organization be staffed, that is, what kinds of people should be in personnel roles? and How do you feel human resource services shold be paid? (Totally allocated to business, totally corporate overhead, a mixture, fee for certain services depending on utilization, etc.).

8. *The effects of the cycle on the respondent's last career transition.*   For example, the respondent was asked to rate the extent to which "the appraisal of your work helped you to learn the (new) job."

Items on the survey questionnaire allowed for comparison of ADB's strategic business and human resource management systems with other large firms from whom similar data had been collected. The specific questions were tailored to suit ADB's culture and to respond to Mr. Wheaton's and Mr. Smith's goals. Questions were asked in the following areas.

1. *Constraints affecting ADB's performance.*   Respondents were asked to assess the extent to which the following act as constraints: shortage of managerial talent, lack of opportunities for personnel to grow and develop, government regulations, labor troubles, and others.

2. *Factors affecting ER's ability to carry out its responsibilities.*   The factors that were rated included: top ADB management, ADB middle management, image of ER in ADB, Honeywell Corporate ER, and organization structure of ADB.

3. *The extent to which certain practices are encouraged in ADB.*   For example, communication, risk-taking, participation in decision-making, delegation of authority.

4. *Forces influencing the direction of ER.*   Respondents were asked to indicate how influential each of the following is in directing ER: business executive of ADB, group general managers, manager of ER at the business level, professional staff of ER, clients of ER's services, Honeywell Corporate ER staff, historical precedent, and external factors (e.g., government regulation, economy, etc.).

5. *Performance ratings of ER and ADB, in the groups, in the divisions, and in the operations.*   These ratings were concerned with such issues as: caliber

of work produced or accomplished, reliability in carrying out commitments, ability to relate effectively and productively with other units, profit and cost sensitivity, overall evaluation of performance, and others.

6. *Technical competence of ER.*   Respondents were asked to assess the extent to which ER is outdated, current, or innovative in such areas as benefit plans, labor relations, EEO, affirmative action, manpower planning, selection and placement, education and development, data systems, and others.

7. *Human resource issues in strategy formulation and implementation.*   Interviewees were asked to assess the extent and effectiveness of formal business planning; the extent to which human resource data are available and the extent to which these data are used in strategy *formulation* (e.g., data such as external manpower studies, inventories of current managerial talent, of technical talent, and audits of human resources of companies considered for acquisition).

8. *The extent to which HRM activities are currently and should be engaged in.*   In particular, respondents addressed the need for strategic HRM activities.

9. *Factors affecting career decisions within ADB.*   Interviewees rated the importance in deciding on a career move of such things as "my future with the company required it," "salary," "autonomy," and others. Also, various factors were rated as to their importance in determining career progress during early, recent, and future career of the respondent. These factors included: working hard, being politically astute, knowing the right people, being lucky, doing a better job than my peers, planning my career carefully, good managerial skills, and others.

10. *Personal work attitudes.*   These included satisfaction with work, degree of involvement, orientation to the long-versus short-term view, feelings about taking risks, and others.

Interviews were conducted with 110 ADB managers. These individuals were selected for study by discussions between the ADB transition team and the Michigan research team. Respondents included three levels in the organization: Warde Wheaton and his direct reports (level 1); level 1s direct reports [Divisional and Operations Vice Presidents (Ops VPs) and Group staff]; level 2s direct reports (line and staff to the Divisional and Ops and VPs). Representatives from all aspects of ADB's top echelon (see Figure 16.2, then, served as the primary information source. Characteristics of participants in the study are detailed in Table 16.2. The interviews were conducted and surveys administered by the Michigan research team, Larry Smith, and his Manager of Human Resource Management, Dr. Mary Ann Donahue. Average time for the interviews was two hours. Comments were written and tape

TABLE 16.2.   Characteristics of Individuals Who Participated in the Study.

TOTAL NUMBER OF
PARTICIPANTS: 110

LEVEL IN THE ORGANIZATION OF PARTICIPANTS

Level 1 (Warde Wheaton and his direct reports)	7.2%
Level 2 (Level 1s direct reports)	28.2%
Level 3 (Level 2s direct reports)	61.8%

EDUCATION OF RESPONDENTS

No college degree	5.5%
Bachelor's degree	61.8%
Graduate degree	33.0%

DEPARTMENT OF RESPONDENT

Employee relations	13.6%
Nonemployee relations	86.4%

TENURE IN HONEYWELL (years)

01–10	22.7%
12–20	35.5%
21–28	25.5%
30–36	14.5%

AGE OF PARTICIPANT

31–40	18.2%
41–45	16.4%
46–50	30.0%
51–55	18.2%
56–65	15.5%

recorded. The questionnaire was left with the respondent to mail back to ISR for analysis. Anonymity was guaranteed. During the interview, respondents spoke with candor about positive and negative experiences within Honeywell. After each interview, interviewers made summary notes about the implicit ADB culture as characterized by the respondent.

Data Analysis

Two sets of data analyses were performed. Both sets involved collaboration with ADB and Michigan personnel. First, with the quantitative data (from the survey questions and from some interview questions), traditional quantitative analyses were performed; for example, reliability tests and descriptive statistics (i.e., mean, standard deviation, frequencies) were run. Efforts were made to prepare the most accurate presentation of the data for managers within ADB.

Second, with qualitative data (from interviews and observations), analyses were performed. First, content analyses were done on key interview questions (e.g., description of the role of ER). These analyses were done by independent raters to arrive at descriptive percentage scores for respondents to interview questions. Second, cultural themes were defined within ADB. All members of the project team worked independently to define the major cultural themes. Then the team met to exchange impressions. A modified nominal group technique was used to identify key cultural themes within ADB. Specifically, efforts were made to identify cultural themes about the "Honeywell ADB Way" and what it takes to succeed at Honeywell.

Disseminating Results

The findings of the study were reported in three waves, the third of which, at the time of this writing, is still occurring. The first wave was to Warde Wheaton and his direct reports (level 1). The main objective for this audience was to identify policy decisions for ADB based on the data. The second wave was to the Employee Relations Council (ER Council), comprised of all ER Directors for the Operations and led by Larry Smith. The ER Council viewed the findings in light of specific recommendations for ER's changing role in strategic change and human resource management. The third wave, to be completed in early 1983, will be to the Divisional and Operations VPs and their staff. To these groups, 12 in number, the data will point towards action implications for each particular unit.

The content of the report received by each audience (level 1, ER Council, Divisional and Operations VPs) varies slightly. Everyone sees responses aggregated for the total sample, for ER respondents only, and for level 1 only. However, the finer-tuned report that distinguishes the responses for each unit or location is reserved for the ER Council and for the Divisional and Operations VPs.

The feedback sessions are conducted jointly by the Michigan/ADB action research team. The report is *not* a freestanding document. It is meant to be reviewed by means of a discussion meeting, not to be distributed and read without discussion. Three main areas were highlighted in the 67-page report as most pressing for managerial attention:

First, *strategic concerns* were noted. There was some lack of consensus regarding the technical, political, and cultural directions of ADB in the future. Executives were aware of the need to address culture and human resource management for ADB to be successful in the coming years. The two human resource issues rated the highest (i.e., most constraining) were shortage of managerial talent and resistance on the part of managers to changes needed for growth.

The major strategic implications in the report were organized according to the technical, political, and cultural categories.

Strategy: Technical

Top-level ADB managers need agreement on the strategic direction of ADB. If the dominant view of moving from a component producer to a systems maker facing stiffer competition is correct, then this strategy needs to be discussed and understood more widely. In addition, top-level ADB managers have a mixed view of the decade in terms of the technical, political, and cultural challenges facing the organization; some common vision is important to develop.

Strategy: Political

Succession issues are going to become increasingly important as the middle of the decade evolves; ADB needs a better process for effectively managing succession politics. Reward systems need to be revamped to support strategic shifts in ADB.

Strategy: Cultural

The organization is not perceived to have a culture consistent with the "Our Way" statement; hence, a "culture strategy" is needed. Human resource management is seen as a major vehicle for reshaping the ADB culture.

Second, various aspects of the *human resource management cycle* (selection, appraisal, rewards, and training and development) were seen as points of concern. HRM functions were not viewed as very helpful in career transitions. Only selection was seen as effective in enhancing strategic performance. At the operational and strategic levels, selection is the only function consistently rated above moderately effective. Human resource data are more systematically available than it is used. Human resource data play a small role in strategic planning and implementation in ADB, yet many managers feel they should be more utilized for strategy formulation and implementation.

The strategic human resource implications from the diagnosis were as follows.

HRM: Technical

Improve human resource processes at all three levels—operational, managerial, and strategic. Alter strategic planning and implementation processes to include human resource aspects.

HRM: Political

Reward the line for effective utilization of human resource management to drive the business. Provide a legitimate role for human resources in the strategic planning process.

HRM: Cultural

Work toward shaping a culture that values good HRM. Work toward shaping a culture that views strategic planning as a multifunctional process.

Third, the report focused on the *role of the ER.* ER is currently looked to for operational services but should be looked to for more strategic services. There is little support now for making ER personnel more strategic. Also, ER is a service organization that needs to understand its marketplace (i.e., ADB personnel) and to be aware of its performance as perceived by clients. ER was seen as "current" in many of its activities, but not "innovative." Finally, there was little agreement as to how ER should be organized.

The recommendations from the study for the organization and development of ER included the following.

ER Function: Technical

The push for a new strategic mandate for ER needs to be translated into a coherent mission and strategy agreed to by both line and ER staff. ER professionals need to develop new skills and services to carry out a new mission.

ER Function: Political

In order to play a stratregic role, ER staff will need more power. Rewards will be required for both line and ER staff to engage in strategic human resource activities.

ER Function: Cultural

The "second class citizen" status regarding ER, imposed by both its own staff and by the line, will have to change. A culture that values HRM is required to support these changes.

IMPLEMENTATION OF NEW STRATEGIC MANAGEMENT PROCESS

The results of the assessment of strategic human resource management in ADB call for specific courses of action. The areas of change to be most immediately addressed are in (1) strategic planning, (2) human resource planning, (3) development of staff, and (4) upgrading ER services. They represent the next steps in fostering an organizational culture that is more in tune with the needs of its members, is more productive, and meets the goals outlined by Warde Wheaton and other senior ADB personnel.

Strategic Planning Changes

The study found evidence of a need to improve the business strategic planning process in ADB. Human resource considerations ought to be incorporated in the formulation of strategy and human resource activities should be viewed as means of business strategy implementation. In order to accomplish this it was recommended that ADB adopt an integrated strategic planning process.

Figure 16.6 proposed a set of core strategic planning questions that ADB managers would be asked to address as they work through their extensive annual strategic planning processes. The framework expands the traditional strategic planning task by focusing on political and cultural issues as well as by giving consideration to organization structure and human resource management. To facilitate this expansion, a revamping of the planning calendar will also be required. New management processes will be needed to support the new framework for strategic planning at ADB. Specifically, ADB ER should work with a Task Force on Strategic Planning, made up of one or two key line executives, the ADB strategic planner, the corporate strategic planner, and the corporate ER executive. In overseeing the transition towards strategic human resource management, the Task Force could tackle these issues: assess strengths and weaknesses of current strategic planning process, identify required changes in content and process of strategic planning, focus on the human resource role in strategic planning process, and review progress over time and make changes as indicated.

Human Resource Planning Changes

The key to change in this area is to build on the strength that already exists. Currently in place is a talent review process, a means of identifying employees with the greatest potential for growth. It should be expanded into a *Strategic Human Resource Review*. Currently, the Talent Review focuses only on the top 10%, and they are usually the easiest to manage! An effective talent review process ought to include all key positions and should make managers truly responsible for guiding the development of the company's people. The line organization should be influenced directly by the business strategy in creating plans for key positions and key people. The present review process, then, lacks two critical elements: an explicit link to business plans and a focus on the larger population of people, not just "high talent." The revised review process can add these two dimensions by having managers address the following issues, several times a year: (1) the organization of their business to support the strategic plan, and (2) their human resource needs, followed by detailed discussion of key positions, who currently fills them, their performance and their potential, and succession candidates and their performance and potential. A task force, similar to the one proposed for strategic planning, should be initiated and given the mandate of overseeing the evolution of strategic human resource planning.

Development of Staff

There is at present a lack of clarity concerning the role of ER within ADB. Yet some ADB executives recognize that the manner in which this role is shaped will determine, in large part, whether human resource management ever becomes strategic. At least these implications are clear: first, ER needs a direct link in the strategic planning process. Starting with ADB ER, and including ER managers throughout ADB, there must be a legitimate role in strategic planning for ER in the same way that it exists for financial staff. Second, ADB ER should have responsibility for ER professionals in ADB. That is, at the head of ER there ought to be the legitimate authority to manage and develop a cadre of competent professionals. Again, the analogy to the financial side of the organization is apparent. Traditionally, financial people have considerable control over the promotional moves in their part of the company. The "people" people should have the same power. Indeed, to allot this power to the human resource organization would be an indication that people and money are equally as important in running a business; a sign of a culture that is changing.

Developing ER and other personnel (i.e., strategic planners and line managers) in order to support change in the strategic planning and HRM processes will require a great deal of time and energy. ER professionals, especially, will feel greater demands to know more about the business, about strategic planning, and about the management of change. The first step will be a pair of strategic management workshop sessions. The objectives of the program will be to (1) introduce ER staff to strategic management concepts and methods; (2) initiate dialogue between ER staff, line, and planning staff on strategic human resource implications of business strategy; (3) provide ER staff and planning staff with concepts and methods of strategy implementation; (4) provide ER staff and planning staff with human resource planning concepts and methods; (5) provide ER staff, planning staff, and line managers with action plans for using the integrated strategic business and human resource management processes being developed by ADB.

In the first session, ER staff will spend two days hearing and learning about strategic planning frameworks. The session will include coverage of such topics as environmental assessment, market niches, competitive analysis, corporate portfolio analysis, financial analysis, and business strategy development. The second day will conclude with a presentation of the strategic management matrix (technical, political, and cultural framework) which will be used as the basis for the ADB integrated strategic planning process.

The second session will be conducted to assist line and staff in the implementation of the new planning process. This will include a review of current business strategic plans to identify human resource issues and implications and to begin to explore the answers to the strategic questions listed of Figure 16.6. In preparation for the second session, the ER staff will be given the assignment of meeting with the line along with the planners to review the answers to these questions and to prepare a list of discussion issues. ER staff will have approximately three weeks to carry out these tasks.

The second session will be attended by teams of ER and planning staff as well as by line general managers. The staff will attend for three days, whereas the line will attend for two days. The first day will be on concepts and the methods for meeting strategic objectives through organization design. On the second day, general managers will join the staff. The topic will be strategy and HRM. The day will be spent on the strategic level human resource staff role; how the human resource systems of selection, appraisal, rewards, and development can drive strategy; how human resource issues limit and constrain strategic alternatives; the role of HRM in strategy implementation. The third day will be devoted to action planning with general managers, ER staff, and planning staff developing plans for implementing the integrated strategic business and human resource management process for their unit.

The intended outcomes for the program are for an integrated planning process. ER and planning staff will have a common understanding of the strategic management process. General managers, ER, and planning staff will have joint action plans for implementing the strategic management process. Action plans will be presented and discussed with the line and implementation commitments will be made.

There will also be workshops held on the management of change. This program will be designed to provide concepts, skill development, and reinforcement for ER, planning staff, and the line as they work through the implementation process. The objectives of the sessions on change management will be to (1) introduce line, ER, and planning staff to concepts and techniques for managing strategic change; (2) continue the collaborative change effort by ER staff, planning staff, and the line in developing an integrated strategic human resource management process; (3) provide ER staff, planning staff, and the line with revised action plans.

Upgrading Employee Relations Services

In addition to the strategic ADB activities, each of the units within ADB will be developing their own strategy and plans for improving the human resource functions at the strategic, managerial, and operational levels. These will take place under the umbrella of the previously mentioned strategic planning changes.

SUMMARY

In this chapter we overviewed the activities currently underway in Honeywell's ADB and reported the process and content of an effort to integrate these activities and to stimulate further maturation of ADB's human resource management system. A diagnosis of this system was described and the strategic directions to be taken as a result of this assessment were presented.

In general, the goals outlined for the project are being realized. However, it will take more time to fully evaluate the impact of the strategic human resource management function as a whole. HRM is becoming more a part of the strategic management process in ADB. Activities done independently within operations are becoming more coordinated. Human resource functions (selection, appraisal, rewards, and development) are being reassessed and restructured to promote a more strategic focus. Finally, more collaboration is being achieved between line and ER staff in working to fulfill these goals.

Without being definitive, the strategic reorientation of the human resource management function seems to be succeeding. Some of the following reasons stand out as important.

1. Reorientation is supported from the top. Warde Wheaton and James Renier have been aware of the project and supportive from the beginning. They encourage and support the ADB ER Director (Larry Smith) to work towards strategic HRM. They are receptive to action plans that evolve from the project and encourage these action plans throughout the organization.

2. The project involves many levels of both line and staff. In addition to working with level 1 management (Warde Wheaton and his direct reports), many levels of the organization are involved. The Employee Relations Council are involved in coordinating data collection and feedback to their unit. Line managers are involved in interviews and in working with data as they relate to their unit. Policies for ADB will, as the transition continues, be fitted for the particular needs of each Group, Division, and Operation.

3. The project has a sound basis in theory. The concepts set forth in the previous chapter formed the theoretical springboard for the intervention. They were understood from the beginning by all key players. Data collection and action plans derived from these concepts.

4. A variety of data sources was tapped. The diverse and comprehensive sampling of opinions contributed to a sound understanding of the organization and its needs.

5. Policy recommendations were politically realistic and meshed with the culture of ADB. They evolved from continual interaction between the outside researchers and ADB staff.

All of these considerations, in our opinion, are transferable to other sites. They suggest that if strategic human resource management is to be effected, it must be concerned with changing the management process as well as the substance of strategic planning.

PART

III

STRATEGIC ISSUES IN HUMAN RESOURCES MANAGEMENT

Part III of the book presents ample evidence of the wide variety of contexts in which human resources must be managed. The challenge to both the practitioner and the researcher is to understand the unique problems that must be addressed in organizations with strategic agendas that require human resource policies to support innovation as well as organizations whose needs focus on managing human resources in a declining context. The generic functions covered in Part II remain the same: people must be selected, appraised, rewarded, and developed so that these organizations will prosper but the processes differ widely depending upon the circumstances. To add to the complexity of the task, many large organizations are faced with the need to manage multiple scenarios simultaneously in different parts of the organization; and, more and more frequently, conflicting demands are being made of managers if they wish to survive. For example, much of smokestack America is attempting to survive through the introduction of sophisticated technology aimed at reducing costs while operating in mature or declining markets. These and related issues are explored in Part III.

In Chapter 17, Peter Lorange and Declan Murphy report the results of a study focused on examining the extent to which effective strategy implementation requires consistency between the firm's overall strategy and the personal aspirations of its management. Lorange and Murphy's findings point to the relatively primitive state of human resource practices in the companies studied. Although the study is exploratory, it raises interesting issues that warrant further investigation. More than a third of the human resource executives and the strategic planners reported dissatisfaction with

271

the management incentive systems and the selection and promotion mechanisms used in their companies. They felt that these systems tended to thwart the implementation of corporate and business strategic plans rather than aid in their execution. These data provide an impetus to both researchers and practitioners to further investigate why some systems are perceived to support strategy and others to detract from it.

In Chapters 18 and 19 the authors examine the human resource implications of two of the dominant business strategies in the 1980s. Gilmore and Hirschhorn look at the problems endemic to managing in a declining context whereas Jay Galbraith focuses on the human resource policies and systems needed to support innovation in organizations. The juxtaposition of these articles provides us with an interesting contrast between the world of "high tech" and smokestack America. At the same time, they bring us to the realization that top-level management in many organizations is trying to juggle both of these balls. Many of the strategies involved with salvaging declining industries require innovative manufacturing processes, and organizations faced with maturing businesses often look to innovation for their future growth and well being. Thus managers often need to manage two cultures and businesses with different human resource requirements, and human resource managers need to be sensitive to the unique requirements of each situation.

In Chapter 20 John Fossum focuses on an aspect of human resource management that is central to the success of changing strategies in declining and mature businesses: how to deal with the historical realities that constrain the evolution of new relationships between management and labor needed to facilitate the survival of industries beset by competitive cost pressures. Ledford and Camman look at the quality of work life programs utilized in many companies as a possible solution to problems of declining productivity and in Chapter 22 a case history of the productivity and quality improvement effort at Westinghouse is discussed by Borucki and Childs.

Finally, Vladimir Pucik discusses the problems being faced by organizations that operate in global markets. The overlay of cultural differences and regulatory requirements on businesses that are frequently experiencing pressures from their technological and financial constraints provide significant challenges for human resource managers.

These seven chapters give us a view of the complexity facing human resource managers and they hint at an issue contributing to the challenge we face in the 1980s, the pace of change that makes adaptation an issue which the manager must constantly keep in mind. The speed with which today's solutions become the basis for tomorrow's problems is one of the factors that separates the past from the present for human resource managers. There is little reason to believe that the pace of the changes we are witnessing will abate in the near future. Indeed, all indications point to the need to manage a more diverse and challenging environment in the future. Some of the issues that concern us are as follows.

1.   The pace at which new research and information in the area of human resource management is being generated has increased dramatically, but the

dissemination of this knowledge remains painfully slow. We need to learn more about the structures and incentives needed to get valuable research into practitioners' hands more rapidly and we also need to find ways of transferring this information so that it can be more easily applied.

2.   Human resource systems need to recognize the opportunities and problems that accompany the proliferation of computer technology in organizations. The need to develop incentives to encourage the use of new technologies and the need to develop new managerial techniques to deal with the changes in methods of communication, information handling, data processing, and managerial decision-making will challenge human resource managers. Moreover, we will need to find new ways to thinking about managerial careers and organizational culture as the nature of jobs and organizational structure are influenced by these phenomena.

3.   Organizations will be faced with the need to rethink the way in which people are deployed, advanced, and rewarded as a result of the demographic changes they are confronting. There will be larger numbers of people from the "baby boom" generation, who currently occupy middle-management positions, vying for positions in top management. Most will not make it. At the same time, there will be a dearth of people available to fill entry-level positions as the "zero population growth" generation reaches the labor market in approximately five years.

Thus the future looks even more challenging than the past. It may well be that the organizations who learn to deal successfully with their human resource problems will dominate their industries in the next decade. As the chapters in this section suggest, those that fail to do so may not survive.

CHAPTER

17

BRINGING HUMAN RESOURCES INTO STRATEGIC PLANNING: SYSTEMS DESIGN CONSIDERATIONS

Peter Lorange
Declan Murphy

The human resource question is rapidly becoming a major issue in corporate strategic planning. In search of solutions for America's declining ability to compete internationally, corporations are now coming to view scarce management talent as a critical strategic resource that requires the same careful allocation customarily reserved for money and technology.

This new seriousness of purpose with regard to the human resource issue is, in itself, a significant step forward. There can be little doubt, however, that American business practices for linking human resource concerns into an overall strategic management system still require much refinement and improvement. As always, there is a lag between the initial perception of a problem and its solution.

This survey study sheds light on current corporate practices in strategic human resource management. It also serves as a vehicle for the identification and dissemination of some critical issues that practicing managers expect to confront in this area in the immediate future. It should be stressed, however, that this study is exploratory and that the conclusions presented are tentative in nature. An important objective for this pilot study is to generate insights leaking to the formulation of more precise, testable hypotheses to be explored in subsequent research.

STUDY DESIGN PREMISES AND METHODOLOGY

The general proposition that informed the logic of our study can be summarized as follows: in a rationally designed planning system, effective strategy implementation requires consistency between the firm's overall strategy and the personal aspirations of its management "stakeholders." In this case, the firm's executive assignment, promotion, and incentive systems should facilitate strategy formulation and implementation procedures.

A strategic planning system, it is often argued, should possess a hierarchical structure that reflects a "division of labor" in strategy formulation and implementation between three distinct levels of the firm—the portfolio or corporate level, the business family or divisional level, and the business or product/market element level.[1] At each of these three levels, management will confront different (though interrelated) sets of strategic variables. It is critical for successful strategy implementation that the firm's promotion and incentive systems assist rather than obstruct the fulfillment of these strategic agendas.

To measure this crucial consistency across the firm's three levels of strategy, we develop three sets of normative propositions regarding how human resource systems might effectively contribute to the strategizing process at each level.

At the business or product/market element level, the principal strategic challenge is to reach a specialized set of customers with the corporation's own products or services in competition with clearly identified rival firms. Hence the elaboration and implementation of competitive business strategies is the primary issue here. Our normative assumption at the business element level has been that human resources should be allocated so that the personal characteristics and skills of a manager fit the requirements of a given competitive strategy. Furthermore, incentives should reinforce the manager to pursue the prescribed strategy with genuine vigor.

To illustrate, mature, "cash cow" business and entrepreneurial ventures

---

[1] See Lorange (1980, pp. 16–28) for a more detailed discussion of the three levels of corporate planning. Chapter 9 discusses the relationship between two of these levels at greater length.

pose very different managerial challenges.[2] In the former case, competitive success depends upon highly efficent, cost-conscious management. A streamlined internal organization, for example, might significantly lower a cash cow's cost function and, thereby, provide it with critical competitive advantage. In the latter case, success in the competitive battle would probably hinge much more on the ability to adapt effectively to a rapidly changing environment. Certain managers will excell at cost-conscious, efficient management in a relatively stable environment, whereas others will find their true metier in an entrepreneurial setting where the external parameters are constantly shifting. From a human resources point of view, therefore, the critical problem is the attainment of an optimal match between competitive strategic needs and the skills and strengths of individual managers.

At the divisional or business family level where several products are grouped together, the key issue is the realization of synergistic efficiencies. For example, shared production facilities, sales force distribution, or research and development all become possible for a group of related products. In addition to these internal synergies, specific market conditions may also permit the realization of external synergies. Consider, for example, the case of a firm that produces stoves, refrigerators, and dishwashers. Rather than view their products as totally separate lines, the respective managers might be able to achieve synergistic efficiencies if they perceive "the kitchen" as a common focal point of their marketing efforts and coordinate their competitive strategies accordingly. An ability to capitalize on such synergies would result in significantly lower costs for the business family as a whole.

For the business family level, our normative assumption has been that human resource management should cultivate teamwork between managers of similar products to foster a spirit of cooperation that would facilitate the realization of any potential synergies. In this context it is crucial to motivate managers to look beyond their own narrow business element "kingdoms" to the broader challenges of the business family unit. To rectify any tendency toward parochialism among business element managers, we hypothesize that a policy of dynamic management reassignment within the same business family would be appropriate. Under this arrangement, business element managers could expect assignments in both the declining, mature business elements of the family and in the newly emerging ones as well. Such in-house experimentation, we feel, could provide an invaluable source of data for the eventual specialization of managers by the business types referred to previously.

At the corporate or portfolio level of the firm, the main task is the strategic success of the company as a whole. And success at this level depends to a large extent upon the development of a good fit between business families

---

[2]These applications are based on the growth share matrix popularized by the Boston Consulting Group. For further detail, see discussion in Chapter 4 on "staffing" for different types of businesses.

and their constituent business elements so that an overall balance exists within the company between strategic resource generation and expenditure. Obviously, for a company to survive and grow, it must generate more strategic resources that it uses over time. Moreover, there should be a reasonable economic and political risk exposure for the portfolio as a whole. Our normative assumption at this level of the firm concerns the desirability of perceiving general management talent as a strategic resource like financial resources and the consequent deployment of these managers within the corporation so that they can contribute effectively to the development of the optimal portfolio of businesses for the firm.

We also seek to measure perceptions of the consistency between strategy and human resource systems across the various staff *functions* that would be involved in the design and maintenance of various aspects of the systems within the firm. Specifically, we wish to ascertain whether planners and human resource executives view this issue in the same or in markedly different ways. Both groups, after all, are custodians of different, though presumably highly related aspects of the overall management system. Human resource managers, however, are generally directly responsible for the integration of human resource concerns into the firm's management system, whereas planners are generally "users" of this part of the system. Figure 17.1 gives an overview of the basic elements of a strategic management system as it applies to any one of the three strategic levels.

This system consists of a set of *discrete* direction-setting steps, typically repeated once per year, and often called "planning" and "budgeting." We also have a *continuous* control system which might lead to modifications of the initially set direction. This control system includes a process of giving incentives to employees based on their contribution to the various aspects of performance laid out during the direction-setting steps.

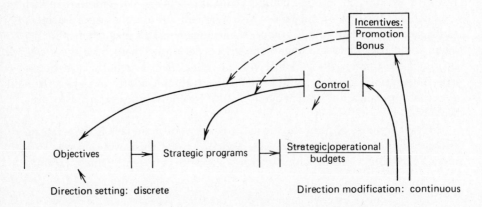

FIGURE 17.1. The strategic management style.

At least three different staff offices tend to have responsibility for maintaining different parts of this system, namely, the corporate planner, the controller, and the human resource officer. Often, however, these staff groups do not share a sufficient common understanding of the integrated nature of the system. By adopting a parochial view and protecting their part of the system, each contributes to a breakdown in the system's functioning. This is indicated by the heavy vertical lines in Figure 17.2.

The achievement of consistency between a firm's overall strategy and its human resource practices deserves special notice in this context. Hence we directed our research questions to those corporate level executives who are responsible for the design of the planning and human resource systems in their respective firms.[3]

We also attempted to discover whether the strategy/human resource system consistency vary across industry types. Accordingly, we included executives from the food, pharmaceutical, and electronic industries in our sample. We selected these three industries for the following reasons.

The long-term strategic self-renewal of a firm requires reinvestment of some of today's resources in the development of the future products or services the firm will supply. We use the term "reinvestment" here in its broader strategic sense, that is, reinvestment implies reallocation of technological knowhow and management resources in addition to funds. In the food industry development of new brands usually requires a comparatively modest investment and a comparatively short R&D horizon; moreover, the investment

[3]Ideally, we would have liked to study the perceptions of the users as well as the designers of these systems. Unfortunately, however, the need for a manageable scope forced us to restrict the size of our inquiry to the system designers alone.

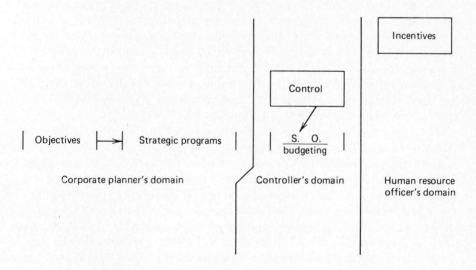

FIGURE 17.2.   Blockages in the strategic management system.

will generate relatively certain levels of quick returns. In high technology industries, by contrast, the investment commitments necessary for the development of new products are usually much greater, the R&D horizon much longer, and the returns less certain. These differences, we feel, would pose very different challenges to the establishment of consistency between a firm's overall strategy and its human resource management systems. Although long-range planning may be much more difficult in high technology industries, the vast multiplicity of products that certain food companies manage may create cognitive problems for the achievement and monitoring of this consistency. Within the high-tech group, we draw a distinction between the pharmaceutical industry, where the development of an overall strategy and new products requires a comparatively narrow set of scientific competencies, and the electronics industry, where the need to integrate and coordinate many highly disparate scientific and technical disciplines is a major issue for strategic management. We also feel that the highly abbreviated product lifecycle characteristic of the electronics industry could contribute to greater problems in linking the planning and human resource management processes than one would expect in the pharmaceutical industry.

To summarize, the focal point of this study is the measurement of consistency between strategy and human resource management systems in a sample of *Fortune* 500 firms. We approach this issue along certain distinct dimensions.

First, we wish to measure the achievement of this critical consistency at each of the three levels of strategy formulation and implementation within the firm: the business element level, the business family level, and the corporate level.

Second, we attempt to measure the perception of strategy/human resource management system consistency across the planning and human resource functions. Hence we contacted one corporate level planner and one corporate level human resource executive at each of 24 *Fortune* 500 firms.

Lastly, we wish to measure the variability of strategy/human resource management system consistency across industry types. We, therefore, divided our sample of 24 firms among eight food companies, eight electronics companies, and eight pharmaceutical companies.

There is one additional broad underlying issue that the study ultimately hopes to shed light on, namely, whether the presence of a consistently designed strategic management process and system will, in fact, be associated with corporate success. Significant research has been done documenting the impact of strategic forms on corporate success (Rumelt, 1974), industry structure's impact (Montgomery, 1982), and the association between the presence of formalized planning systems and corporate success (Thune and House, 1970; Grinyer and Bazzaz All three categories 1981): are thus likely to have an impact on corporate success. The third category of research however, has not focused on issues of perceived consistency and usefulness of the strategic management process among the process users. We attempt to shed light on this dimension through our preliminary study, our hypothesis being that consistency between internal systems and process should improve a corporation's performance.Of the 48 executives contacted, 34 responded: 18 human resource managers and 16 planners. Among the 34 respondents, 10 were from the food industry, 11 from the pharmaceutical industry, and 13 from the electronics industry. Of 34 respondents, 20 represented complete pairs from 10 firms; the remainder represented a single response from 14 different firms. We would interpret our comparatively high level of response as an indication of the strong interest among managers.

In what follows we provide a preliminary report on the results of our research and suggest some tentative hypotheses to explain our major findings. Our sample is small, and this means that our quantitative findings, in particular, should be interpreted with care. In analyzing the breakdown of the sample into industries and the set of complete pairs from responding firms, it is clear that the small sample size (10–12 units per industry) is confining. This study is exploratory and attempts to generalize are not warranted. The results are sufficiently provocative to bear reporting, however, and encourage further research.

HUMAN RESOURCE MANAGEMENT AT THE BUSINESS ELEMENT LEVEL

Executive Assignment Incentives and Performance Criteria Context of the Strategy Cycle of the Firm

To test the validity of our normative assumptions regarding strategic human resource management at the business element level of the firm, we drew up four qualitative questions.

Our first qualitative question sought to provide the executives in our sample with an opportunity to expand upon the problems their companies currently face in the deployment of managerial talent and the design of managerial incentives at the business unit level. A vast majority of the respondents felt that our normative assumption—the need to develop a good fit between a manager's personal talents and behavioral propensities and the lifecycle requirements of the given competitive strategy—was, in fact, the key issue in management assignment. As one food industry executive remarked, "The worst possible pitfall at the business element is to mismatch a cash cow manager with a newly emerging business. It's the quickest way to kill off both." At the same time, most respondents were also aware that many problems can arise in the pursuit of the optimal match. "We view the product manager's job as a testing or winnowing-out period," stated another food executive.

Managers either make it at this level or they leave our firm. This leads to horrible inefficiencies. The Peter Principle takes its toll on our operations, for

> many managers who fail in this position do so at the expense of their product's profitability. Yet we remain committed to this training ground.

The statement suggests that in this firm the product manager system may constitute a "strategic filter," that is, a feature of the organizational structure that obstructs the development and implementation of appropriate strategic direction at one of the three levels of strategy. More systematic selection procedures for business element managers would seem imperative for this firm.

Then, too, other respondents were quick to point out that the attainment of an optimal match between manager and business element does not automatically guarantee good long-term results. In the words of another food executive,

> We find it difficult to keep good cash cow managers interested in cash cows. While this is less of a problem with Europeans, Americans often regard cash cow assignments as tantamount to relegation to the back room. The tragedy is that executives who are best suited to cash cow management often feel this way.

With regard to the design of effective incentive systems for business element managers, we detected a sense of intense frustration among a sizable minority of respondents. Many executives felt irritated that despite long years of effort, truly effective, rational incentive systems remained elusive. One pharmaceutical executive was quite blunt about it: "We should get rid of all incentive plans at this company." Others in the electronics industry reechoed this sentiment. One stated, "I long for the days when the promise of promotion was our only incentive." This executive would undoubtedly agree with Sir Henry Taylor's observation: "The hope, and not the fact, of advancement is the spur to industry" (Taylor, 1957). Similar frustration is evident in the food industry. In the words of one executive,

> I argue that the right individual will pursue the necessary strategic direction with or without an incentive scheme. Most good managers are hard driving, success-oriented people, and I feel that if the right manager is chosen for the job, he will do it well even in the absence of a formal incentive compensation system.

Two problems surface repeatedly in this discussion of incentive schemes. First, many respondents felt that the larger aggregates such as the business family or sector can tangibly affect the performance of a business element manager, and that it is often difficult for a business element manager to achieve a sense of personal contribution. Hence the intended good effects of an incentive scheme are often diluted. As an electronics executive put it:

New business element managers often complain that their unit's performance is not measured solely on the basis of factors that are under their control. Later they come to understand that there is simply not very much that is under the exclusive control of the lower level manager.

Second, some respondents felt that the determination of suitable performance measures for incentive awards is a continuing problem. A food executive, for example, commented:

> We are a marketing company and we want to encourage our business element managers to improve their marketing performance. But how does one measure improved marketing performance for incentive award purposes? Certainly sales is not an adequate measure here.

These problems notwithstanding, most respondents in our sample saw utility in incentive compensation systems and were continually looking for ways to improve them.

Our second qualitative question focused on the extent to which the companies in our sample attempted to identify appropriate types of management talent for cash cow versus newly emerging businesses. We have already noted that many respondents view this problem as the critical issue in the deployment of management resources at the business element level. About 80% of our sample stated that they made some attempt to identify management talent along these lines. Most stated, however, that they did so in an informal way as part of an annual performance appraisal. As one food company executive put it: "We don't try to identify 'cash cow skills' as such. We review past performance assessments and then build a composite portrait of the manager in which the identification of these skills will figure."

The companies that were not currently attempting to identify managers in this way usually offered one or two explanations for not doing so. One group claimed that they were not yet sufficiently advanced in the implementation of their planning systems to undertake this kind of management segmentation. One food industry executive was quite candid on this point: "We're not smart enough yet." Another group made up largely of pharmaceutical companies simply rejected this approach because they found the cash cow versus entrepreneurial distinction irrelevant to their businesses. As one executive commented: "We don't really have cash cows. We're in only one line of business: the development of ethical pharmaceutical products. This business is oriented toward research and development, and we expect levels of growth from all our businesses."

Our third qualitative question sought to ascertain the extent to which these companies attempted to tailor-make their incentive schemes according to the relative maturity of the businesses in which a manager was involved. About 50% of the companies in our sample said that they attempted to do some tailor-making of incentives. Many stressed, however, that their incentives were tailor-made less to the lifecycle position of the business than to the macroeconomic conditions anticipated for the coming year or to the job or position that a manager held. One electronics executive commented: "We need managers at the business element level who can manage through an adverse economic cycle. After all, even growth businesses have down periods."

The same sense of frustration that emerged in response to our first question regarding the delineation of incentives for business element managers surfaced once more on the issue of incentive tailor-making. A food industry executive, for example, commented: "We don't tailor-make incentives at all. This is a big problem and we have no solution. Frankly, I don't know of a single tailor-making system that works well. Managers rarely understand them." Furthermore, some executives saw a danger in excessively formalizing incentives. In this context, one electronics manager commented:

> We don't tailor-make incentives formally. If you have an intuitive approach that works well, why bureaucratize it? On the other hand, there is a danger that if the managers who run such an intuitive approach leave the firm, the whole system will disintegrate.

Our last qualitative question at the business element level addressed the issue of managerial performance criteria. About half of our sample stated that they recognize open quantitative criteria alone at this level. Roughly 20% said that their firms employed qualitative criteria and the remaining 30% utilized a combination of the two. As expected, many executives who claimed their firms used quantitative criteria exclusively at this level cautioned that qualitative criteria took on more importance at the general manager level where such nonquantifiable issues as training and motivating successors become rucial.

Some firms had experienced difficulties with a perceived arbitrariness in the assessment of qualitative performance criteria at the business element level; most felt, however, that they were able to control these problems through the use of peer group reviews.[4]

A most intriguing result emerged in response to a question concerning the perceived need and ability to combine long and short-term criteria in assessing a business element manager's performance. Fully 90% of the sample felt that they were not doing it adequately. One pharmaceutical executive summarized the problem quite forcefully: "We're totally derelict here. We don't tie in success on the long-range plan to the business plan. The links are bad. Our rapid turnover at this level further complicates the measurement of a manager's long-term success." An electronics executive complained, "Short-term thinking is a habit. We're stumped here and looking for an answer." Some

---

[4]See Chapter 6 for a discussion of appraisal dimensions for strategic planning.

executives stated that their firms found it difficult to graft long-term considerations onto their MBO systems. These systems, they claimed, were fixated on the short term and, thereby, contributed to the problem. In contrast, a small but vocal minority of executives asserted that the purported failure of American business to deal adequately with long-term considerations was a false issue. As a pharmaceutical executive noted:

> The long term is not a real issue for American industry. We may appear short-term-oriented compared to the Japanese but not compared to the rest of the world. The Japanese commitment to lifetime employment makes their preoccupation with the long-term comprehensible, but we operate under different ground rules here.

SATISFACTION WITH HUMAN RESOURCE SYSTEMS AT THE BUSINESS ELEMENT LEVEL

Our two quantitative questions asked our respondents to rate their degree of satisfaction with their firms' overall policies for management assignment and incentive delineation at the business element level. The distributions of the answers can be found in Tables 17.1 and 17.2.

With regard to management assignments, a majority said that they felt their firms were doing an above-average job. With respect to incentive design, an slightly higher majority voiced a comparable level of satisfaction.

However, when the sample was analyzed to measure perceptual differences between planners and human resource executives (see Table 17.1), some differences emerged. Fewer planners expressed above-average satisfaction with the allocation of managerial talent at the business element level than seemed to be the case for the human resource executives. With respect to incentive delineation for this level of the firm (see Table 17.2), a much smaller fraction of the planners expressed above-average satisfaction with these systems, whereas more of human resource executives echoed these opinions. We would speculate that, for reasons of proximity, planners might be more sensitive to the critical importance of tailor-making to successful competitive strategy implementation and were, therefore, more demanding in this regard than their human resource counterparts. In fact, some human resource executives

TABLE 17.1. Perceptions of Management Selection Process at the Business Element Level.

	Low (Satisfaction)	High (Satisfaction)
Corporate planners	9	7
Human resource officers	7	11
Total	16	18

TABLE 17.2. **Perceptions of Incentive Schemes at the Business Element Level.**

	Low (Satisfaction)	High (Satisfaction)
Corporate planners	9	7
Human resource officers	4	12
Total	13	19

confessed that they were still insufficiently attuned to strategic issues at the business elements level. As one electronics executive put it:

> Traditionally, human resources had to provide very short-run, tangible services at this level. It has been a real problem for us to try to view human resource issues at this level from a strategic perspective. We've only been doing this here for two years.

When we examined the data for the business level across the three industry groups, we observed no significant differences regarding the degree of satisfaction with incentive compensation schemes. With regard to management assignments, however, a majority of the pharmaceutical and the food executives felt their firms were performing at an above-average level; a somewhat lower fraction of the electronics industry executives expressed a similar degree of satisfaction. Part of the reason for this lower level of satisfaction within the electronics group may lie in certain management assignment problems unique to this industry. As one electronics human resource executive pointed out:

> Many of our new business element managers come to these positions directly from the engineering side of the company. Technologists are rarely sensitized to human resource management issues and we have found that they must often be educated to these concerns.

The clear implication is that excellence in engineering does not automatically translate into excellence in management. Engineers may experience acculturation problems when placed in a management situation for the first time, and this pattern may cause problems that do not occur in the food or pharmaceutical industries where business element managers customarily rise up from lower-level management as opposed to engineering positions.

In summary, there appears to be a strong recognition of the desirability of tailor-making executive assignments and incentive compensation systems to the requirements of the competitive strategic tasks at the business element level. However, in many companies the management processes and systems required to achieve these tailor-making goals have not evolved; hence the high degree of frustration with these problems evident at many firms (Jennergren, 1980). The differing perceptions of the planners and human resource executives as to the seriousness of these problems is more troubling. It may indicate that human resource managers are too far removed from strategic problems to contribute effectively to the integration of human resource concerns into the planning process.[5] Such estrangement would imply deep linkage problems in the design and operation of the overall management system of the corporation.

HUMAN RESOURCE MANAGEMENT AT THE BUSINESS FAMILY LEVEL

At the business family level the critical concern is with the realization of the synergistic efficiencies that become available to groups of related products. Our normative assumption was that the organization would want to encourage attitudinal flexibility and cooperation among managers to facilitate the full exploitation of synergies. One way to develop this cooperative spirit would be to pursue a policy of dynamic management rotation within the same business family so that managers might appreciate the problems of both the cash cows and the newly emerging, high growth business elements.

Executive Rotation and the Realization of Synergies at the Business Family Level

Our principal qualitative question directed to the business family level sought to ascertain the extent to which companies routinely engaged in this dynamic intrafamily reassignment process. Approximately 50% of our sample stated that they perceived the usefulness of this technique and utilized it on a regular basis. However, an interesting pattern emerged among the high technology companies. High-tech executives argued that the scientific specialization of their products, even those grouped within the same families, had progressed to the point that there were now real diseconomies involved in rotating a manager out of a product he or she had learned well. One electronics executive, for example, stated:

> We used to rotate managers around within the same sector quite routinely. This policy is on the wane. Our businesses now require very specialized knowledge of products and markets and we now believe that too much turnover would lead to real inefficiencies.

Similarly, a pharmaceutical executive noted: "We don't do this much at all. The days of *a manager is a manager* are over. We like to keep them specialized." In the food industry, by contrast, where the products have a much less

---

[5] This lack of input by human resource staff is discussed at greater length in the corporate level section later in this chapter.

scientifically specialized character, the notion of a manager is a manager is still quite strong. As one food executive told us, "We need managers who can function in the 1980s. We need generalists, not specialists or technicians." Interestingly, when we asked an electronics executive who adhered to the specialist philosophy how his firm went about management development in the absence of intrasectoral rotation, he replied, "We keep them where they are and develop them progressively by increasing their responsibilities." Hence management development at this company looks to depth rather than breadth. This approach, however, raises another issue. If management cannot redeploy a strategic resource then, one can argue, that the resource has little or no strategic value.

Executive Satisfaction with In-Place Resource Systems at the Business Family Level

Our two quantitative questions asked the executives in our sample to rate their degree of satisfaction with management assignments and incentive compensation schemes at the business family level. Tables 17.3 and 17.4 give the distributions of the responses.

With regard to management assignments, a resounding majority of the respondents credited their firms with above-average performance in this area. This compares with a much weaker positive response pattern at the business element level (Table 17.1). One factor in particular, we feel, might have contributed to the substantially higher degree of satisfaction at the business family level: the existence of a track record for the evaluation of managers eligible for promotion. In this context, it is useful to contrast the business element and the business family. At the element level, a much more limited track record exists for assessing business executives who are candidates to manage the business element's competitive strategy. Typically, managers are promoted to this job from positions that have a much more limited span of control or a much more specialized functional responsibility. These deficiencies in the relevant track records may have made the tailor-making of assignments at the business element level more difficult. As an electronics executive remarked, "Within the business element, we have executives who are functional specialists; yet to *manage* a business element we need somebody

TABLE 17.3.   Perceptions of Management Selection Process at the Business Family Level.

	Low (Satisfaction)	High (Satisfaction)
Corporate planners	4	11
Human resource officers	5	14
Total	9	25

TABLE 17.4.   Perceptions of Incentive Schemes at the Business Family Level.

	Low (Satisfaction)	High (Satisfaction)
Corporate planners	8	7
Human resource officers	5	11
Total	13	18

who can establish a synergistic relationship between functions. How do you find somebody with that broad perspective?" In a similar vein, a pharmaceutical executive observed, "Selection criteria need much better definition at this level. Also, we need to match the criteria much more closely to the technical and behavioral competence required for positions at this level." At the business family level, however, corporations can consider the successes, failures, and experiences of the practicing business element managers who are vying for promotion. Here the track record is much more helpful, for there is at least a modicum of general management talent required for the successful management of the business element. It may, therefore, be possible to predict a future business family manager's performance with a greater degree of certainty. Although an "argument from silence" is always risky, we feel that the absence of any explicit executive complaints regarding track records or management selection criteria at the business family level may be a weak indicator that executive selection is less problematic here.

The difference in perception between planners and human resource executives that emerged at the business level with respect to management assignments lessens at the business family level. A strong majority of the planners expressed strong satisfaction with assignment practices at this level of the firm, and the human resource executives expressed similar opinions. Note that the planners and human resource executives seem to have even reversed roles slightly, with the planners now somewhat more pleased than the human resource managers. It may be that planners play a greater role in the management selection process at the middle level of the organization than they do at the lowest level. Accordingly, they feel more confident about the achievement of consistency between strategy and the management selection process at this level.

An especially interesting result surfaced when we analyzed the data along industry lines. Although the food and electronics industry executives registered similar levels of satisfaction with management assignment procedures at the business family level, pharmaceutical executives voiced similar sentiments. This result was surprising and defies easy explanation, but may reflect in part the well-defined, distinctive corporate culture that sets the pharmaceutical industry apart from the more diffuse electronics and foods industry.

With regard to incentive delineation at the business family level, (see Table 17.4) a majority of the executives surveyed expressed strong safisfaction with their firm's performance. Note the strong similarity between the distribution of the responses to this question at the business element and business family levels, comparing Tables 17.2 and 17.4. It is also worth noting the substantial difference in the degree of satisfaction when one compares incentive systems with management assignments at the business family level. The clear implication is that the sense of frustration with incentive compensation systems evident at the business element level remains unchanged at the business family level. As a food executive observed: "Our incentive system at this level is strictly geared to total corporate performance. It's a failure. Individual managers fail to see how they can influence a measure like this."

When we analyzed this data along functional lines, we found the same pattern evident at the business element level (Table 17.4). A substantial difference again surfaced between the perceptions of planners and human resource executives, with a fairly low share of the planners voicing strong satisfaction with incentive schemes at this level, whereas a higher share of the human resource managers seemed to feel the same way. Again, as at the business element level, it is the human resource executives who are much happier with incentive systems. Some planners were clearly worried that the incentive systems at this level were not pulling in the same direction as the strategy. As a pharmaceutical executive told us: "Our incentive systems at the business family level fail to facilitate achievement of strategic objectives. Indeed, they act as a barrier against it. They generate far too many turf fights over who should get the credit." Such a remark strongly suggests that another type of strategic filter has arisen here.

Replicating still another pattern from the business element level, no significant differences or noteworthy patterns surface when the response to this question is analyzed across industries.

HUMAN RESOURCE MANAGEMENT AT THE CORPORATE/ PORTFOLIO LEVEL

At this level of the firm, our normative assumption centers on the desirability of perceiving general management personnel as a scarce strategic resource that the firm must first cultivate and then deploy effectively to fulfill its overall portfolio objectives.

Executive Selection, Career Pathing, and Incentives at the Corporate/ Portfolio Level

The first qualitative question asked our respondents to elaborate upon the critical problems and challenges their firms faced in management selection and incentive design at this level of the organization. With regard to management selection, many executives stressed the lack of congruence between the skills needed to succeed as a business family manager and the skills required to succeed at general management (Levinson, 1980). As one electronics executive put it,

Success at the business family level is a poor predictor of success at the general management level. Many people who would make excellent general managers never get the chance because they fail at the business family level, and we lose sight of the fact that different skills are involved.

On this theme, a pharmaceutical executive noted, "A good general manager must be able to delegate and he must be able to make major decisions with insufficient data. A good business family manager can succeed without possessing either of these qualities."

Another big problem that complicates management selection procedures at this level is the lack of a corporate-wide perspective among the candidates for general manager positions. "Parochialism is a real danger," stressed one electronics executive. "Many of the candidates for these jobs have grown up in one line of business and have lost sight of the whole. They have no corporate viewpoint and often must develop it on the job and that's very inefficient."

A number of executives cited the problems involved in attempting to develop meaningful measurement techniques for calibrating incentive awards at this level. As one executive phrased it, "It's very hard to isolate the precise contribution of any one general manager to the portfolio development of the firm."

We also attempted to gauge the perceived desirability and utilization of flexible career paths as an important means for the development of general managers. Approximately 70 percent of the respondents claimed that their firms were successful in the creation and use of flexible career paths for this purpose. Among the 30 percent who felt otherwise, those from highly diversified conglomerates felt they confronted special problems in this regard. One executive at a major conglomerate commented:

We're terrible at flexible career pathing across businesses. There is an awful lot of parochialism in this corporation because we grew rapidly by acquisition and as a result we're a patchwork not a monolith. There is a lot of resistance here to reassignment around the company.

We also focused on the extent to which our respondents felt their firms had developed a sufficiently explicit plan for the development of a general management talent pool. The vast majority of the executives interviewed (over 95 percent) asserted that their companies had developed workable plans.

Finally, we tried to determine the degree to which the companies in our sample hired or fired at the corporate level in response to major shifts in the portfolio strategy of the firm. About 35 percent of our respondents claimed that their firms adhered to such a policy, whereas 65 percent said no. Among the latter, several executives expressed opposition to outside hires at this level because of their firm's strong commitment to promotion from within. Similarly, some executives claimed that their companies were too paternalistic to fire at this level.

Executive Satisfaction With In-Place Human Resource Systems at the Corporate/Portfolio Level

As for the two lower levels of the firm, our two quantitative questions for the portfolio level sought to measure the level of satisfaction with management selection procedures and incentive systems. Tables 17.5 and 17.6 present the distributions of responses.

With regard to management selection procedures at the corporate level, a large proportion of the sample expressed strong satisfaction with their firm's track records. This percentage represents a steep decline, however, from the response patterns for the same question at the business family level (see Table 17.3). Nevertheless, the distribution at the corporate level is notably higher than what we found at the business element level (Table 17.1). The transferability of skills between business family manager and general manager responsibilities may be a factor here.

A cross-functional analysis of the data at the corporate level reveals that the perceptions of planners and human resource executives regarding the effectiveness of management selection procedures have now come full circle. Recall that at the business element level, human resource executives had much more confidence in these procedures than the planners. At the business family level, the perceptual gap was greatly reduced and the planners were now slightly more satisfied with these systems than the human resource executives. At the corporate level a large gap in perceptions has opened up once again but it is the planners who are now much more highly satisfied with these selection procedures than the human resource executives.

This mirror-image reversal may derive from the relative sense of participation in management selection processes that each function feels. It is well known that in many large corporations human resource executives play little or no role in the selection of top management but quite a large role further down the ladder. An electronics planner, for example, stated, "Our human resource people play virtually no role in the selection of our top management team." By contrast, it is easy to see how the corporate planner, with concern for general management issues and environmental changes, might be asked to play a highly active role in the selection of new members of the top management team. At the same time, the planner could have little or no role to play at the business element level. The strong enthusiasm of most planners with respect to their firms' top management selection processes may also

TABLE 17.5.   Perception of Management Selection Process at Corporate Portfolio Level.

	Low (Satisfaction)	High (Satisfaction)
Corporate planners	3	13
Human resource officers	8	10
Total	11	23

TABLE 17.6. **Perceptions of Incentive Schemes at Corporate/Portfolio Level.**

	Low (Satisfaction)	High (Satisfaction)
Corporate planners	7	7
Human resource officers	4	12
Total	11	19

reflect the closer day-to-day interaction that planners have with top management in comparison with human resource executives.

Across industries, our analysis of the data reveals that although pharmaceutical executives and food executives are highly satisfied with management selection procedures at the corporate level, fewer of the electronics executives surveyed express similar enthusiasm. The need to manage and coordinate a broad variety of scientific competencies and the pressures of the severely truncated product lifecycle in the electronics industry may require a very special type of executive at the corporate level. Perhaps the respondents from this industry felt their management selection processes were slow to recognize this.

A majority of the respondents voiced strong satisfaction with incentive compensation systems at the corporate level of the firm (see Table 17.6). This figure resembles very closely the distributions that were recorded in response to the same question of the business element and business family levels of the firm (see Tables 17.2 and 17.4). We may, therefore, generalize that the problem of designing effective, rational incentive systems persists across all three levels of strategy in the firms in our sample.

Once again, the planners seem much less satisfied with these systems than their counterparts on the human resource side. Thus at all three levels of the firm the enthusiasm of the human resource executives for their in-place incentive schemes far outstrips that of the planners. In this case the planners may contribute little input to the design of these systems and may doubt the extent to which the critical consistency between strategy of human resource management systems has been achieved in this area.

Considering once more the industrial dimension, we note that in contrast to the business element and business family levels, pharmaceutical executives are somewhat more satisfied with incentive systems at the corporate level than their counterparts in food or electronics.

CAVEATS AND CONCLUSIONS

Caveats

Before we summarize our findings and conclusions, we would like to enter a plea that the reader interpret them with caution. Such caution is justified for the following reasons.

First, our sample of 34 respondents from the *Fortune* 500 is small when viewed from the perspective of classical statistical methodology and standard sampling procedure. Nevertheless, we felt that there was another consideration that justified publication of our findings—the quality of our data. The administration of our questionnaire over the telephone allowed for much more extensive interaction between questioners and interviewers than would have been possible in a research format that centered upon a blind mailing of questionnaires to 500 executives. In this regard, it is worth noting that a typical interview for this study lasted 60 minutes and, in some cases, ran to 90 minutes. Hence the primary tradeoff, as we see it, is between quality of data versus generalizability of results. Although we would not claim to have achieved the level of detail possible in a case study of one company, we would suggest that we have achieved more depth than would normally be possible in a mass survey.

Second, there may be certain biases in the response patterns. We have noted, for example, that human resource executives were generally much more satisfied with their firm's incentive schemes across all three levels of strategy. Typically, it is the human resource function, not the planning function, that is responsible for the design of these systems. Hence the consistently more favorable human resource response on incentive systems may reflect a defensive, "pride-of-authorship" reaction rather than an impartial critical assessment.

Third, we have not stratified our sample between highly successful and troubled companies. Success, however it is defined (sales levels, ROI, ROE, etc.), may create a more favorable impression of one's planning and human resource management systems than reality warrants. Conversely, poor performance might cause a frustrated respondent to be hypercritical.

These points should be kept in mind in evaluating the results of this study.

Conclusions

When one studies the pattern of responses to our questions regarding the degree of general satisfaction with management selection, promotion, and incentive processes across the three levels of strategy in the firm, the following results and conclusions emerge.

With regard to management selection and promotion, there is a modified "humpback" pattern to the responses. At the business element level (Table 17.1) a lower fraction of our respondents expressed strong satisfaction, a higher fraction at the business family level (Table 17.3), and again a lower fraction at the corporate/portfolio level (Table 17.5). Clearly, the business element level and, to a lesser extent, the corporate level are problem areas. In both cases the absence of sufficiently extensive and/or relevant track records on which to base promotions at these levels has adversely affected the achievement of strategy and human resource system consistency on this dimension. This is a serious problem, for, as we suggested early on, the strategic tasks across these three levels are closely interrelated, and the human resource systems must pull in the same direction across all three levels. Although progress has clearly been made at the business family level, these results indicate that the business element and corporate levels still need further refinement. A perceived inability to grapple successfully with the delineation of long and short-term managerial performance criteria at the business element level was also a major issue.

With regard to incentive compensation systems across levels, slightly more than a third of all respondents at each level were dissatisfied with their firm's performance. Furthermore, as our qualitative responses suggested, the frustration level with these sytems among this group was very high. Here, too, more patient experimentation will be necessary.

Analysis of our responses across functional lines raised some troubling issues. In the area of management selection processes a fascinating but disturbing pattern emerged. Planners' satisfaction with these systems progressively *increased* from the business element level up to the corporate level, whereas the satisfaction of human resource executives with these processes *declined* across the same levels. The bottom-up versus top-down orientation of human resource executives and planners, respectively, imply structural problems in the overall management systems of many firms (see Figure 17.3). There are *strategic human resources* tasks and problems at all three levels of strategy and logic would dictate that human resource executives should play a greater role than they apparently do at many firms in the selection of the top management team. Likewise, planners should take an interest in the management selection process at the business element level where successful competitive strategies are critical to the success of the overall strategic plan.

With respect to management incentive systems, planners were much more dissatisfied than the human resource executives with the in-place systems at each of the three levels of strategy. About half the planners clearly perceive a lack of consistency between strategy and incentives in their firms. Their disaffection may reflect their lack of input into the design of those systems. Certainly, a higher degree of consultation and interaction between the human resource and planning functions would be warranted here.

Finally, there is the question of industry differences within our sample. As concerns management selection processes, the electronics industry executives rated their firms' efforts significantly lower than their food or pharmaceutical counterparts at the business element and corporate/portfolio levels. In both cases, we have suggested that structural problems peculiar to the electronics industry may account for these results. At the business element level, the need to convert engineers into managers quickly may cause problems, whereas at the corporate level the need for rare abilities to coordinate a great multiplicity of scientific competencies and to cope with the frenetic pace of product change may pose special challenges. At the business family level, we observed a significantly higher degree of satisfaction with management selection processes in the pharmaceutical industry. This is a mysterious finding. We hypothesized that it may reflect the more closely knit corporate culture characteristic of this industry. With regard to incentive systems, we observed no significant differences across industries at the business element and business family levels, but a much higher degree of satisfaction among pharmaceutical executives at the corporate level. This result is also enigmatic, but the corporate culture issue may be a factor here as well.

One overall system design conclusion emerges with reasonable certainty from these results. Although firms have made progress in erecting rational, reinforcing planning and human resource systems, much improvement is still needed. In particular, the corporate level planners and human resource executives who are responsible for the design of these systems must interact and consult much more closely with regard to their respective tasks than they appear to do at many firms.

Our results have provided a look at state-of-the-art planning and human resource systems in *Fortune* 500 firms. Although much progress has been made in meshing these two critical systems, much still remains to be done.

CHAPTER

18

MANAGING HUMAN RESOURCES IN A DECLINING CONTEXT

Thomas N. Gilmore
Larry Hirschhorn

The problems of downsizing, layoffs, plant closings, and head count reductions are by no means new. Yet they are occurring with greater frequency and in ways that suggest they are not simply related to business cycles but may signal deeper shifts that will involve substantial restructuring.

In this chapter we address why the issues of managing decline have become so salient and identify some of the challenges for those in employee relations (ER) and human resource management (HRM) to help both organizations and individuals cope with the pain and uncertainty associated with downsizing.

Retrenchment and downsizing are used to indicate both planned and/or implemented actions that reduce the scope or level of activity of an organization (Hirschhorn et al., 1983). Typical actions would include layoffs, cost-cutting programs, reduction of capacity, and divestitures. Furthermore, the focus of this chapter is on the issue of downsizing when significant numbers of managers, professionals, and technical staff are involved. One of the most significant differences is that in the current environment it is frequently

white-collar personnel who are being laid off. Previously, white-collar reductions in force were confined to a specific industry (e.g., aerospace) that
was experiencing seasonel difficulties. During the mid 1970s recession, more
than three-fifths of the *Fortune* 500 implemented personnel cuts, with higher
level employees more likely to face permanent separation than blue-collar
workers (Kaufman, 1982, p. 2). Demand for professionals and managers has
stabilized or declined, whereas the entry of highly educated personnel into
the labor force has continued to grow. As companies adapt to the economic
challenges of the 1980s, white-collar layoffs will increase.

In the past companies adapted to reduced demand by laying off blue-
collar workers, most of whom expected periodic unemployment over their
careers. Moreover, the manager did not have to personally confront the laid-
off worker. Most often, the lay-off process was channeled through bureaucratic mechanisms, the pink slip, and union accords, and was organized
through impersonal mechanisms such as seniority. Therefore, the interpersonal dimension was not significant. Today, the interpersonal dimension has
become more salient because the decisions to cut are no longer organizationally distant from the victims of the reduction in force. The superior who
lays off managerial subordinates may often identify with that subordinate,
"There but for the grace of God go I," so that it is harder for the superior
to defend himself or herself against the natural feelings of sadness and guilt
when someone is terminated.

In addition, when top managers lay off technical and professional workers,
they must assess the impact of such a layoff on the remaining corps of
employees. There is good evidence that managerial and professional workers,
who feel they have been loyal to the company and its mission, feel shocked
and betrayed when their peers are laid off. Layoffs can thus create a climate
of mistrust and lead the remaining workers to either withhold initiative or
quit. Similarly, technical workers often identify with particular projects on
which they are working, for example, the development of a drug or an electronic product. If they are retained but shifted to another project as a result
of cutbacks, they may also quit. Thus as companies cut back managers,
professionals, and technicians, they create a new set of problems: how to
manage the "commitment" that remaining employees bring to the work of
the company.

WHY RETRENCHMENT?

The discussion of downsizing and decline is emerging not simply because
decline is a relatively new phenomenon as it affects white-collar workers,
but rather because the problems of underemployment and unemployment of
managers and professionals are converging with other processes that give the
managing of downsizing a new quality and color. The task is not simply to
develop mechanisms that ease the ebb and flow of educated personnel into
and out of organizations but also to see the restructuring and developmental

challenge within the presenting issue of white-collar reductions in force. The following processes are central here.

1. Shifts in the patterns of careers and the decreased opportunities for traditional vertical mobility.
2. The increased emphasis of white-collar productivity and the resulting scrutiny of professional work.
3. Retrenchment-driven shifts in patterns of supervision, control, and risk-taking that upset the culture and style of management.
4. Long-term reorganization of the economy.

Shifts in Career Patterns and Decline in Vertical Mobility

There is ample evidence that the architecture of managerial careers is changing. Twenty years ago managers were expected to be loyal to their companies and not to switch jobs simply because another company offered better opportunities. Job-hopping was frowned upon, and top managers believed that job-hoppers were unreliable. Today, in contrast, job-hopping is valued as a sign of flexibility, initiative, and entrepreneurship. An institutionalized executive labor market, in the form of headhunter firms, career-counseling services, and outplacement services, has emerged to structure and facilitate the process of job switching.

In addition, middle managers between the ages of 27 and 37 (born between 1945 and 1955) face an unfavorable labor market in which the supply of potential top managers far exceeds the demand for them. This cohort faces new problems in the management of personal careers. Some will have to adjust to a failed career. Others will have to find new opportunities in more entrepreneurial careers. Companies, in turn, must learn to manage the commitment of managers and others in a promotion-poor hierachy. This cohort-specific decline in career opportunities, combined with a job culture that devalues loyalty, creates a more complex climate for managing people. Commitment becomes a scarce commodity, and managers must learn to create the conditions of work and career that facilitate the emergence of commitment. Companies facing the new interpersonal motivational dynamics of downsizing in a professional culture confront these dynamics just when the historic underpinnings that support the making of commitments by individuals to companies are giving way. This convergence of retrenchment with the changing architecture of careers complicates the process of managing retrenchment itself.

The Emphasis on White-Collar Productivity

These career pressures are emerging with the reorganization of white-collar work. As companies invest in office equipment, the productivity of decision-making becomes central to the profitability of company operations. For the first time each company must examine the activity patterns of its managers to determine if the disposition of managerial time (e.g., on the phone, in meetings, in memo preparation, in sales discussions, etc.) maximizes the use of its potential "intellectual" capital. In the past, managers felt relatively autonomous within their work domains, deploying their time and resources as they best saw fit. Increasingly, top management will scrutinize the manager's activities and operations, not only with respect to performance but also with respect to "inputs," that is, the allocation of resources, human and material, within departments and divisions. This may reshape historic management cultures. Managers may feel that they are being treated as "factors of production" just when, ironically, an increasing number of workers are going on salary, being offered lifetime employment, and being organized into teams in which output, not input, measurement becomes the central method for monitoring activity. The measurement of managerial productivity will, in turn, converge with retrenchment management as superiors look for systematic and impersonal criteria with which to evaluate and assess who should stay and who should go.

Shifts in Traditional Culture and Style of Management

Retrenchment, particularly when it raises basic mission issues, can often distort traditional patterns of supervision and control. For example, a company may support a culture in which managers at the bottom propose initiatives and managers at the top approve or disapprove. But under conditions of retrenchment the managers at the bottom may feel paralyzed. They may feel that they need leadership and clarification of priorities from the top, whereas the top may feel impatient with the bottom when the bottom fails to propose options. This vicious cycle of expectation can create a stalemate in which neither top nor bottom makes a decision until the top, anticipating a crisis, makes a unilateral decision. The bottom then feels betrayed because they were not consulted. In turn, the top feels angry that the bottom feels betrayed, since the bottom could not "take the ball and run with it" when they were given the chance. Thus under the conditions of retrenchment, when basic mission questions emerge, the historic culture of management may prove ineffective and, indeed, may distort the traditional relationship between leader and follower which had produced effective decisions in the past.

Long-Term Reorganization of the Economy

Finally, we believe that the skill of managing decline is becoming more important as the "mission redefinition" and market turbulence problems replace "business cycle" problems as the major determinants of market dynamics and structure. In the past decline was caused by normal and expected economic processes that periodically created excess supply in the market for goods and services. Thus declines could be interpreted as temporary, overhead could be carried through the downturn, and variable costs could be reduced by laying off blue-collar workers. In contrast, under conditions of turbulence, decline is the outcome of a long-term and pervasive process of market reorganization in which historic boundaries among products, services, and consumers break down. For example, communications–computer technologies are reorganizing the markets of many industries. Newspapers, television stations, movie houses, and telephone companies now find that they are in each other's backyards. Past sales and production strategies do not suffice, and as companies adjust, many have to cut back certain activities without a clear understanding of how they can adjust to their new situation. In this setting retrenchment takes place in a climate of chronic uncertainty, and many managers feel that the first wave of cutbacks may be followed by others until the new organization of markets become clear.

EFFECTS OF DOWNSIZING ON HUMAN RESOURCE MANAGEMENT

Each of these trends constitutes a new challenge to human resource managers. Together they pose a particularly difficult problem that will significantly reshape the HRM function and, in particular, its relationship with line management. The skills go beyond managing transitions to "change management towards uncertain future states" (Nadler, 1982).

In any organization there are often latent tensions, like geological fault lines, that become visible under conditions of stress and tension. In addition to the customary differences between any staff and line function, there are several major differences in perspective that often are present in any specific transaction between a line department and HRM (See Table 18.1). The differences are task-related, and the process of resolving these tensions can lead to higher quality decisions.

These tensions grow when the organization experiences the pressure to

TABLE 18.1.   Line–HRM Tensions.

Line	HRM
Quick processing	Quality, thoroughness of decisions, processing takes time
Needs exceptions and flexibility	Exceptions create precedents, rules should be followed. HRM wants "answers that stick"
People are different, units are different. The compnay should follow a policy of *differentiation* in personnel matters	The company has a philosophy of employee relations, HRM systems are part of the control framework for integrating diverse settings. The company must follow a policy of *integration* in personnel matters

cut as a crisis. The time and slack that are necessary to translate the differences into higher quality decisions are often absent. Most organizations develop their plans for cuts over much shorter time periods than they would plan comparable increases in the labor force. The line's desire for speed and flexibility increases. The threats to the survival of the entire enterprise make line managers less concerned about long-run precedents. On the HRM side, often the problem of downsizing is new, at least in terms of the scale and level of managers involved. HRM may not have the procedures and systems in place for managing the reduction in force at an operational level, let alone contributing to the business strategy that would inform the cuts.

Furthermore, the initial response to a crisis on the part of top management is often to centralize all decision-making in a dominant coalition that, in many cases, does not include HRM. Therefore, the perspectives that they bring are underadvocated. A recent study of 30 companies' experience in reductions in force revealed many problems with the short-term perspective. For example, early retirement plans failed to consider the long-term effects on those remaining who felt trapped under relatively young senior managers, the decrease in natural retirement over the coming years, and the loss of critical skills and knowledge that resulted in increased training costs (Flynn and Niven, 1982).

The time pressures force HRM to work creatively when their past competence has been managing the personnel systems. In a recent study of users' (line departments) evaluation of 10 dimensions of an ER's performance, ER rated higher on reliability, work quality, and job knowledge than on ability to generate ideas and ability to plan (Ruane, 1982). These latter two skills quickly become critical in a downsizing situation, yet are quickly developed.

Under conditions of scarcity, HRM faces a double shift. First, the relative mix of support functions (e.g., training, organizational development) and control functions (pay systems, headcount control transfer policies) changes in the direction of more control and less support. Second, within both of these components of HRM the methods or procedures must be changed.

In good times HRM support functions include generic training, usually delivered offsite in a pleasant setting. The training may be integrated with the career ladder such that people must cycle through certain programs prior to promotions, but the content is generic management skills varied by level. The programs are loosely coupled to the business strategy.

In hard times the slack within which this approach to development can occur is reduced. The work must be less training-oriented and more focused on organizational development. The work becomes more closely linked to the strategic plan, developing teams, or particular job skills to meet present organizational challenges rather than part of individuals' career ladders. The work is onsite, case-based, and clinical rather than generic. The challenge, in the words of an internal organizational development consultant, is "to build a bicycle while also riding it." The stages of design and implementation come together, requiring a developmental action learning perspective rather than the pilot test, debug, disseminate model.

For example, an office product firm developed a business plan that shifted from separate sales forces for different products to an integrated sales strategy. The effective retraining of the sales forces is essential to the strategy's success and must be developed and delivered with extremely tight deadlines.

The control-support tension is particularly salient in the appraisal process under conditions of retrenchment. In times of growth and expansion of career lines, a well-done appraisal can be seen as support. Under conditions of cutback, it becomes part of the control system and can be used to determine who goes and who stays. This will inevitably change the meaning of the appraisal for both appraiser and appraised, and may require additional training for the appraisers to be effective under new conditions. Second, it can be a source of tension between line and ER because line conducts the appraisal under ER's supervision. In one company line managers were under survival pressures to move a product from small-scale lab production to commercial production. They fell behind in appraisals and the ER manager, not wanting to add to their burdens, did not press for the completion of the appraisals. However, the president felt that, given the survival pressures and the real possibility of cutbacks, everyone should know their performance appraisal on a timely basis and sharply criticized the ER manager for the delay. These triangular dynamics between levels and across the ER–line relationship are particularly likely under the stress of cutbacks. The control processes no longer are viewed as harnessing the resources within the company in a goal-oriented fashion, but as taking on the additional function of determining who will stay and who will go.

Under conditions of scarcity, HRM's resource management task shifts from distributing or allocating resources (e.g., training slots, consultants, bonuses) to generating new resources by reconceptualizing tasks and rewards. For example, many organizations have replaced central resources on HRM staffs with a network of people in local sites each of whom has different skills, and through a peer consulting process the organization can replace a specialized resource that previously was centralized.

New Approaches to Control

The control aspects of HRM also shift under cutback conditions. ER often has taken on responsibilities during the building and implementing of systems that must be delegated to the line departments with HRM in a overseeing role. The procedures for making exceptions will require attention since downsizing often produces one-of-a-kind special cases with much greater frequency than do growth or business as usual conditions.

Control systems are often looked at in terms of their flexibility ranging from inflexible prescriptions to directional controls that allow considerable flexibility (Michael, 1979). By adding to this dimension of flexibility a dimension that captures clarity of philosophy, we can create a framework that helps examine the developmental shifts that retrenchment drives in HRM and the role that philosophy can play. Table 18.2 suggests four different positions that the interaction of flexibility and philosophy create.

TABLE 18.2.   Positions Created by the Interaction of Philosophy and Flexibility.

Degree of Flexibility	Articulation of philosophy	
	Low	High
High	Laissez-faire	Developmental
Low	Bureaucratic	Paternalistic

CLARITY OF PHILOSOPHY

Most HRMs, prior to the onset of retrenchment, can be located in the lower left quadrant in which a body of specific procedures and policies has been built up over time, often with little explicit articulation of a human resource philosophy. Rules as a mode of organizing have been described by Galbraith (1973, p. 10) as decisions in advance. They are appropriate only when the conditions under which they will be applied can be readily anticipated. Downsizing creates genuine uncertainty that makes responding by rules dysfunctional. Hierarchy, another mode of coordination, is costly in terms of the delay of information moving up and the overload imposed on the top of an organization during downsizing. Yet many organizations respond to the crisis of retrenchment by both centralizing and tightening up.

There is some suggestive evidence in the literature on natural disasters that the normal tendency to tighten control during fiscal stress may be counterproductive. A finding in the natural disasters literature (Rubin, 1983) is that authority and hierarchies become less controlling and release a process of cross-class and group cooperation with many multiple centers of leadership who only over time become loosely organized into a temporary organization that may contain the seeds of an emergent new structure. A trial-by-fire process identifies who can cope and adapt. By analogy, in organizations it might be beneficial to encourage the emergence of multiple leadership at different levels who take responsibility for special tasks, who may not be in the existing chain of command but who act within an overall sense of direction that the top articulates, and who become organized outside the normal organization structure.

A move from the bureaucratic quadrant towards the laissez-faire quadrant can come about due to the intense pressure from line management for flexibility to enable them to cope with novel problems that downsizing might generate; for example, special retention bonuses for a particular class of employees who are essential to keeping a plant running during a final year of operation. If there is no compensatory development of an HR philosophy that integrates the flexible decisions at a higher level, then a "let's-make-a-deal" culture develops that can fragment and divide an organization.

A move in the direction of articulating a philosophy without any increase in flexibility will deny the organization the benefits of local problem-solving around the novel problems. Flynn and Niven (1982) find that companies that put forth non-negotiable separation packages miss many opportunities to develop novel options (part-time employment, unpaid leave, job sharing, sabbaticals, start-up assistance with new businesses) that might cost the company much less, achieve the same results, and satisfy the employees more. Under the turbulence and uncertainty that is associated with downsizing, HRM will be more adaptive to the degree it is in or can move towards the high/high quadrant (developmental). The necessary increase in flexibility must be compensated for by an increase in control through a shared, articulated philosophy. As exceptions get processed, they are integrated within an overall philosophy that gives coherence to the decisions and prevents fragmentation.

An example might clarify how the exceptions and philosophy might interact. Many companies have standing policies about transfers. These policies were often developed during an overall climate of growth and when a transfer was associated with positive movement up a career ladder. Under conditions of retrenchment, moves become necessary under very different conditions. Consolidation may lead to transfers in which the move is not an advancement and also may contain significant risks of future layoff, especially if the unit in question poses a rear turnaround challenge. Here the employee is being asked to take a risk in making the move, yet the existing policies do not offer any way of compensating for that additional risk. The result may be increased difficulty in getting talented managers to take challenging assignments.

A thoughtful discussion among senior managers and HRM professionals about the pricing of risk and the costs and benefits of different approaches (e.g., in the beginning, during some shift, after termination) could lead to a coherent philosophy in this area that would allow greater flexibility to fit the decisions to the business needs without the twin risks of rigidity on the one hand, or fragmentation and divisiveness on the other. The development of a philosophy of HRM that is not mere platitudes and offers actual guidance to difficult decisions is hard even in the best of times. The added pressure of downsizing often squeezes out such discussions just when they may be most necessary. Obviously, the more an HRM unit has moved to develop a philosophy prior to experiencing the crisis of downsizing, the better prepared they will be to cope with the attendant uncertainties of retrenchment.

If we simplify the choice facing an HRM unit as moving in the developmental direction or in a bureaucratic dimension, we can look at the costs and benefits of these two approaches as shown in Table 18.3.

As Table 18.3 suggests, the cost of the bureaucratic approach may inhibit the process of negotiation towards a new order and lock the organization into past routines and procedures. This would be particularly true when a bunker mentality develops at the top with few involved in the major decisions. Outsiders have time on their hands, unable to help; insiders are increasingly overloaded and cut off from new information as the situation unfolds. How-

TABLE 18.3.   Alternate HRM Approaches.

Philosophy	Cost	Benefits
Developmental	Excessively leader-dependent fragmentation if philosophy is not clear, shared, or too abstract	Promotes team work, more lateral problem-solving, encourages local innovation
Bureaucratic	Bureaucratic, undermines negotiation and development, little innovation	Holds system together, establishes climate of fairness in time of stress, creates certainty of procedures

ever, as Table 18.3 suggests, the developmental approach is not without its own risks.

We have looked at how downsizing brings to the fore latent tensions in the HRM–line relationship and alters both the mix and nature of HRM's dual focus on control and support. We have suggested two alternative lines of development in the role of HRM in responding to downsizing. We now turn to HRM's role in the overall process. First, we look at the pre-cut time period and the role of HRM in the formulation of the cutback strategy. Then we look at the administration of the reduction in force. Finally, we examine the challenges to HRM in taking a lead role in maintaining or rebuilding commitment and productivity in the period following retrenchment.

ROLE OF HRM IN FORMULATION OF THE OVERALL PLAN

HRM's role in the formulation of a downsizing plan can range from simply implementing the decision of senior management to being a full partner in the development of the plan and proposing some of the major options. The arguments for HRM's high involvement include their central role in effecting the reductions in force and the fact that most of the major post-cut issues have significant human resource management aspects (e.g., revised salary structure because of job redefinitions, developing new career ladders and reward systems, performance appraisal processes and their future link to both rewards and potential further cuts). The earlier that HRM can be involved, the more effectively they can perform their role in the overall downsizing process.

If an HRM unit is on a developmental path towards playing a strategic role before the downsizing begins, the crisis of a cutback can be an opportunity to increase their influence (Devanna et al., 1981). Organizational power theorists (Crozier, 1973, p. 26) have noted that different functions are powerful insofar as their unit controls significant relevant uncertainties. Under downsizing many of the relevant uncertainties can be viewed as human resource issues, and if the unit can take the lead in shaping some of these issues, proposing options, and assessing consequences of alternatives, it can become a major player in the development of a strategic response.

One key role that HRM can play is advocating a major rethinking of the strategic plan at the first signs of a possible need for substantial cutbacks. Senior management often defers confronting the limits of the current implicit or explicit strategic plan; they begin with expense controls, job freezes, and elimination of frills, thereby hedging on the need for deeper cuts. This has a number of negative consequences for both human resource and line management.

First, hedging undermines the leaders by sending a signal that they will not or cannot take risks. If the signs of trouble in the business are readily evident throughout the organization—inventory build up, reduced sales, industry-wide rumors, and so on—subordinates begin to wonder if the leaders are really in touch with the problem. The effects of a business crisis on morale, productivity, and performance will be heightened if people do not feel that someone is in charge. What top management views as keeping options open is experienced by the middle and bottom as vascillation. The difference in perspective of senior management and unit managers is significant. To the top, thinking through a portfolio of options, for example, about plant consolidation, a number of alternative futures are desirable; to the staff associated with each of these units, it is not some portfolio of options but their jobs that are at stake in the decision.

The most difficult task for HRM is to implement cuts in the absence of a newly validated strategic plan. In one case, an organization did not adequately address the strategic plan and yet had to make cuts based on instructions from a higher level for cost reductions. The first response was to control expenses and implement a small cut. Those laid off were fairly treated. Those remaining felt positively about the cuts, feeling that the organization was now leaner, that it had pared down on some low performers and was now ready to meet the business challenges. Only six months later, the organization was faced with a deeper cut and a plant consolidation—still in the absence of a meaningful product strategy that would have enabled the cuts in manufacturing to be meaningfully linked to changes in marketing and engineering. This cut was devastating to morale. People could not see legitimate differences between themselves and those laid off. Instead of feeling chosen, those remaining feared future cuts with little clarity about the criteria for severance. Engineers who were retained but whose projects had been eliminated left voluntarily in high numbers after the cut. The mistrust between middle and top management grew significantly.

We can contrast the preceding process with a similar organization, one that underwent a very deep cut (almost 50%) that was driven by a clear vision of what the organization needed to do to survive. In this instance, however, the aftermath was much less troubled; people got over the shock and were absorbed in the real work that needed to get done.

The lesson we draw from these cases and others we have studied is that the initial pressure to cut should be used as a trigger to rethink and further develop the strategic plan, rather than take some short-term steps to buy time; these short-term steps often have a counterproductive effect in that they reduce the pressure to confront the overall plan. If small cuts are being contemplated, it can clarify everyone's thinking if top management imagines a contingency of much deeper cuts and examines their probable pattern prior to taking small cuts. Then, at least, the initial response is taken in the context of where the organization might have to go if the threats become greater. Flynn and Niven (1982) found that only 2 of 30 companies had effectively linked cuts with a clear corporate strategy.

One of the reasons that HRM needs to take an advocacy role for such work is that people's natural optimism and desire to put unpleasant matters behind them causes serious problems in the future. Yet the central anxiety in a post-cut period is whether another cut may come in the near future. The one deep cut, guided by a strategic plan, appears to make the post-cut anxiety focus more clearly on survival of the overall enterprise, and the presence of the plan gives some outline of what might be the next areas for reduction if the plan fails. A series of cuts without a plan keeps the anxiety focused on personal survival with no sense of where the next cuts would come.

An executive, in reflecting on his own experience in guiding an organization through a period of significant downsizing, spoke of the need "to know the anatomy." This knowledge of anatomy differentiates the butcher from the surgeon. But the anatomy of a business organization can only be judged relative to a business plan. When cuts are guided by a credible business plan, people (both those retained and those let go) sense a rationale, in contrast to a process that suggests that the cuts are informed more by the priorities of the person in charge (e.g., personal likes and dislikes, loyalties) than by the priorities of the organization.

Another cost of hedging at the first signs of distress is that the company makes no clear statements as regards its future which are essential for individuals to clarify their own futures. One executive who had lived through two deep cuts, the first without a product plan, the second with a well-developed plan, commented, "At least our plan is clear enough that people can decide if it's for them or not. Some have said, Great! When do we get started? Others that this was not what they wanted and, therefore, they will begin looking elsewhere." A company offered a voluntary severance program to aid in the reductions in force that they were trying to achieve. Two weeks after the closing of the voluntary offer, the senior management announced a geographical shift in the headquarters. In this situation the company is asking people to think about their own futures either in or out of the company, but, in not announcing the move during the sign-up period for the voluntary severance, they have not clarified likely organizational futures within which people can then make their own assessment.

If HRM can encourage sufficient disclosure and discussion of the issues, the discussion of individual futures can be linked fruitfully to the collective futures (Hirschhorn et al., 1983).

In addition to helping to develop the overall strategic plan, HRM can play a lead role in putting before the senior management some creative responses to the pressures for downsizing. Because of the newness of downsizing as a business problem, we lack the body of well-developed knowledge on alternatives. Later we list some of the ideas that are currently being used and the issues that they pose for HRM.

Many large companies use a period of voluntary severance during which people are offered the chance to leave the organization and get certain benefits for doing so. Some of the central issues for HRM are whether this policy should apply to all categories of employees, and within categories to all grades. They argue that if high performers feel they are being denied what to them may be a benefit (e.g., leaving to start their own company), they may be less motivated if they stay. Those favoring application to only low preformers suggest that the company may risk the loss of too many key people. A technical issue within the voluntary method is also the accurate forecasting of who will respond. This clearly varies by age cohorts, but many companies will have little experience, and any models will need to be sensitive to external factors of alternative employment and internal policies of how aggressively low performers who are at risk in a subsequent involuntary phase are counseled. After the voluntary process, the organizational demographics may have been significantly transformed in ways that create both new opportunities and problems for HRM. Legal issues are critical in voluntary reductions in force, particularly with regard to age discrimination (Taylor, 1983).

Divestment of various units may be another consideration of the discussions and a subcategory of this approach is the possibility of employee buyouts. These are still relatively rare and difficult to accomplish under the time and resource pressures. They are often fantasized by units that are being divested. Insofar as HRM staff becomes knowledgeable about such processes they can be more useful both to the units themselves as well as to top management.

Rank Xerox (*Business Week*, August 30, 1982, p. 46) actually helped middle managers in personnel, purchasing, and pensions to leave to become outside consultants. Rank Xerox bought back a percentage of their time at almost their current salary, resulting in significant savings in the benefits and pensions. They are linked into the company by a computer network. These were roles that contained slack that the company now externalizes and the consultant can sell elsewhere.

Job-sharing and leaves of absence may be applicable. Some companies contract out employees to others, especially if the reasons for the downsizing are local rather than global within the particular industry.

In the absence of a well-developed mission and business strategy that can drive the cuts, HRM must work with a people-driven strategy to retain the most flexible and high quality people who stand the best chance of being able to cope with the uncertain future and to respond as new challenges become clearer. These two approaches are briefly highlighted in Table 18.4.

TABLE 18.4.   Strategies for Downsizing.

People-Driven	Mission-Driven
Assess people	Business strategy
Flexibility	Key tasks
Skill	Level of effort
Compatibility	Organization designs
Performance under pressure	Assess people's performance
Career ambitions	and skills and fit to jobs
Risks	Readjust where misfits
Who will keep us honest	
Where in lifecycle	
Establish contingencies and ranges	
Develop structure that can flexibly	
meet alternative futures	

MANAGING REDUCTIONS IN FORCE

The previously stressed inportance of HRM's involvement in the formulation of the overall plan makes administration of the plan easier. In managing the downsizing, HRM must steer a course between overidentification with the process and not having a sufficient role. In this section we touch on a number of important areas for HRM's successful performance during the layoff process.

The role of work in our society is so closely identified with an individual's identity and role in the wider society that the process of eliminating jobs is frequently compared to death and murder. Executives have been described as collaborators in Nazi prisons camps selecting those who will live and those who will die (Gilmore, 1983). An HRM staff member who was developing the list of employees who would be fired was referred to as "Dr. Death." An HRM staff member who was supporting an executive during a layoff process was called "the handle of the ax."

The pain and anxiety stirred up by reductions in force can lead to people or roles becoming overly identified with the cuts, as if to contain the bad parts in a few roles so others could be more favorably regarded. HRM is at risk of being labeled as the agent of the cuts. On the other hand, it is just as dysfunctional for HRM to be viewed in a caring, support role, labeling the line executives as the devils in the drama.

If HRM has participated in the overall planning of the reductions, then communicating joint ownership of these difficult choices is made easier. The line–staff role in this process must be carefully managed. In general, most of the hard tasks of communicating the overall news and the particular news to particular individuals must be kept in the line relationship with HRM in an active support role. This is particularly true with regard to the role of middle management.

Usually, middle managers are not party to the strategic decisions that lead to the layoffs, but they carry the dual burden of having made the evaluative judgments that are used and conveying the news to those laid off. If senior management and HRM do not fully support middle management, the middle managers are likely to deal with their discomfort by siding with the employees and attacking senior management. HRM can play a vital role in providing support for middle managers. In one case, HRM sponsored half-day seminars for all middle managers with outplacement specialists to be briefed on the psychology of termination, the legal issues, and procedures that would be followed. These were followed up by senior management giving a full briefing of the strategic rationale and a script of what was being done, why, what resources were available for those leaving, and the like. HRM then developed a list of all the questions they could anticipate from those being terminated with sample responses. By deliberately trying to prepare managers for the worst case, they provided a floor to their anxiety. At this session, middle managers developed some additional questions and the list was revised. HRM helped managers practice needed skills and suggested backup resources to which they could make referrals.

During the reductions in force, HRM plays a vital role in helping those who have been laid off. Often HRM negotiates on behalf of those laid off to get a package of benefits that will signal those laid off, as well as those remaining, that the situation was handled well. Small details such as calculating severance in half-year intervals versus a year can help. Honoring educational commitments if the cuts have been made in midsemester, and carrying health care coverage with individual options to extend by paying the premiums on one's own can take care of a major worry of the unemployed.

The details of the notification process are also important. In one organization, a common letter from the president to all employees that gave the overall rationale for the cuts ended with an insensitive closing paragraph about working together in the future that only applied to those being retained. A well-designed informing process lets everyone know their fate relatively quickly. One manufacturing site handled the situation with a plantwide overview of the situation: those who were being terminated were informed by their boss in the next half-hour, followed by group meetings to go over benefits and outplacement procedures. Each employee was given the afternoon off; they were all transferred to nearby hotel and received initial outplacement services.

HRM often takes on aggressive outplacement functions. One company worked so actively to place their people after a shutdown (developing a résumé book, telephoning contacts in the industry) that local employment services were angry at the lost business. HRM often plays an ongoing counseling role and helps former employees prepare resumés and send out letters. Usually HRM stays sufficiently in touch with those laid off to know and to tell those retained the rate at which those laid off find new work.

During the notification process, HEM must scan all the terminations for any situations that require special attention. Often there are a few employees who are experiencing particularly difficult circumstances in their nonwork worlds that may require some additional support during this difficult period.

In summary, a cut that is characterized by the following features appears to provide the best basis for putting the painful period of downsizing behind and looking to the future.

1. *Professionalism.* A reduction in force that is professionally carried out with attention to details has two effects. Those who are retained have a sense that should another round of cuts be needed, they will be competently handled. Second, it creates the sense of discipline and command during a highly uncertain time, an atmosphere of "someone is in charge." Thoughtful handling of the layoff process makes some of the larger strategic uncertainties more bearable.

2. *Cuts were made with a "knowledge of the anatomy."* When one's job is at stake there is obviously a tremendous bias in evaluating whether cuts were taken in the right place. Reasonable people can differ both on the extent to which and where cuts were taken. But it is remarkable how willing even those who have lost their jobs are to see cuts as necessary. A cut seems to have something analogous to the concept of "face validity"—it seems right to follow understandable contours of the organization. In one company, deep cuts (almost 50% across all levels) were taken by managers who were extremely knowledgeable about the business and the people. The process was not participative, and the cuts were made quickly. The organization was shocked but quickly rebounded because those remaining could see the logic of the decisions. The same management followed a similar process in a similar business that they had acquired but found that they had considerable difficulty during the post-cut period because they lacked the same level of knowledge to make the cuts that had legitimacy for those who were left. This then required further cuts and reorganizations that prolonged the period of crippling uncertainty and kept morale depressed.

3. *Full communication of the reasons underlying the cuts and the rationale for how they were taken.* The preceding process of assessing the quality of the surgery critically depends on employees being promptly informed of the reasons underlying the decisions. Furthermore, by communicating the criteria, the organization gives some signs to employees of how their behavior in the future might be linked to their survival. Without this understanding, people feel at risk of some random process.

4. *Thoughtful treatment of those who are laid off.* Survivors, immediately after the relief at not being let go, usually look ahead to the further uncertainties and their chances for being cut at some future date. If the severance package is generous, and if people have been supported during this painful time (outplacement, counseling, etc.), this sets a floor to the worry of those retained. At the worst they will receive some support. In one situation, those who were retained regarded the treatment of these cuts as so generous that there was a backlash: "Now that you have done so much for those who are leaving,

what are you going to do for us, who now face more work and terrific pressure to make a go of this business." This might suggest not becoming so completely preoccupied with those cut to the exclusion of giving support to those retained.

Rebuilding Morale and Productivity

A cut is not only painful for all involved, but it usually results from or implies some message from the wider environment that the product or services are not valued. If the cuts have been made by higher levels of management, the unit reads the action as a vote of no confidence. Therefore, one of the central issues facing a group after a cut concerns organizational self-image or pride. Often they have not only had a negative label ascribed to them from the outside, but if the process of decline has persisted for any length of time, the group itself may have internalized the negative image. "We're incompetent. We're unable to make the transition from R&D to production."

Therefore, the first task of a leader seeking to rebuild a group is to refuse to accept the negative identity and to increase the organization's indpendence, its belief that it can go it alone with no more subsidy or tolerance for missed deadlines and targets. This process has some of the characteristics of "weaning"—becoming more self-sufficient and creating hope (Trist, 1980).

This entire area of managing the turnaround process is relatively new with many more stories about success and failure than reliable information. A major role of HRM can be to build a knowledge base in this area and support the activities of the line leadership in rebuilding and motivation, productivity, and morale. Some initial ideas based on our interviews follow.

1. *Attend to the Physical Environment.* If self-esteem is an issue, the physical setting is a powerful lever. A deep cut has often left a workspace in chaos. People might have left in a hurry, clearing out their desks of personal belongings in an afternoon, leaving behind equipment and supplies. The survivors' workspaces may be scattered among those who have been let go. The sooner the physical setting can be cleaned up and consolidated, the quicker the group will take on a cohesive future-oriented identity rather than thinking of themselves as survivors, those who were left after the layoffs. Military films often illustrate this theme ("Bridge on the River Kwai," "Twelve O'Clock High").

2. *Get People Working.* The most powerful rebuilder of a group is meaningful work. Usually the pre-cut situation of an organization was overmanned. Overmanned settings often are characterized by low morale because individuals know (sometimes unconsciously) that they are being carried, that there is not enough real work to go around. If the cuts have been deep enough (and it's better to err on the side of too deep versus too shallow), then the organization may be in an undermanned situation in which there is more work to go around than people. This can be salutary. People feel needed,

critical (Barker and Gump, 1964, pp. 24–27). They are often called upon to play more roles than before. Those situations that require new skills offer the challenge of learning while still getting on with the job.

3. *Develop and Communicate an Overall Plan.* Organizations that have been able to develop a workable plan that either guided or redirected the post-cut resources appear healthier than those that are still being guided by a pre-cut plan or none at all. Under the pressures of deep reductions in force, those remaining are constantly making priority decisions aobut what tasks to leave undone, which to put off, and which to do. A plan that signals both priorities and optional tasks helps each person who is making these decisions correlate their actions so that the sum of the effort is channeled in a common direction.

4. *Place an Extraordinary Emphasis on Effective Communications.* Alexander Leighton (1945) in a chapter on leadership in a stress situation writes:

> When communities are suffering from adverse influences, imaginations are busy with conjured images of hopes and fears that pass for reality, systems of belief become more than ever recalcitrant to reasoning, and with the general breaks in social organization there is often extensive damage to the routes by which reliable information was formerly passed. . . . The whole situation was charged with inevitable uncertainty. However, this made it all the more important to make sure that those facts which were available were disseminated so that no *avoidable* uncertainties would be added to those which could not be helped . . . men cannot do good work when uninformed concerning its significance. Reports regarding morale in the armed forces stress time and time again the need of keeping men informed regarding what is happening to them and the meaning of what they are doing. T. E. Lawrence observed concerning his experiences in Arabia, "Morale, if built on knowledge, was broken by ignorance."

The environment of cutbacks can be isolating, making each individual think of his or her personal situation. Communications become critically important to rebuild and renew a sense of community by talking about what they share in common, the tasks ahead, by providing a forum for venting and surfacing of concerns.

5. *Acknowledge That Even Those Who Were Retained Have Gone Through and Still Face Rough Times.* The processes of working through a deep cut, in which work groups have been broken up, friends lost jobs, and people reassigned, takes time. Leaders who pursue an exclusively future orientation—"when the going gets tough, the tough get going"—may not provide outlets for people to make sense of what they have been through. If not vented, these issues may interfere with the future work. Furthermore, by excessive pressures to get on with the work, leaders may not hear some of the concerns that are keeping people from being productive. For example, in one organization that used a forced distribution system in its appraisal process which required that at least 5% of a group be in the bottom rating category, those retained who were in the next category worried whether they would be artificially down-

graded to fill the quota. If managers do not address these concerns, they are adding to the inherent uncertainty about the business future, additional uncertainties that could easily be clarified by adopting a policy on that matter.

6. *Let Go of Unnecessary Routine Tasks—Debureaucratize.*   One of the benefits of a crisis is that if often refocuses a group on what is really important. During a downsizing crisis, many routine procedures do not make sense. For example, one HRM manager found himself engaged in a time-consuming career assessment process for a group of managers who faced either layoffs or a future with another company if the unit could be divested. Some managers respond to crisis and uncertainty overload by adhering more rigorously to old habits. This is maladaptive. The organization should take more risks with regard to routine tasks. Experiment with not doing them and see if anyone notices. Many tasks simply fall away as no longer relevant.

7. *Take Advantage of Understanding.*   The research on undermanned settings (Barker and Gump, 1964) suggests that there are many positive features to a lean organizational setting. By creating jobs that require individuals to cover more areas and to broaden themselves, and by developing teams and networks to cover other tasks that might have formerly been managed through a hierarchy or by staff, people can find their new situation more challenging and exciting. Given the loss of vertical careers, expanded jobs and/or lateral career moves can often offer opportunities to develop their human capital that may increase their marketability both inside the company and equally important, outside the company. This type of reward may have to substitute for a traditional promotion and pay increase.

8. *Examine the Organizational Design to Ensure That It Promotes Greater Risk Taking and Supports an Entrepreneurial Culture.*   Often the pre-cut condition has been one of oversupervision and control. One manager described the pre-cut style in his organization as "hovering delegation" which now had to be replaced by authentic delegation of major tasks to lower levels in the organization. This requires greater risk taking. The use of teams and groups can be critical in giving people both emotional support and support for innovation. Marshall (1947) in his classic study of performance of infantry men, cites the critical role of small cohesive groups with natural leaders. The respect of one's peers becomes a powerful motivator for high performance, even at considerable personal risk. Teams personalize an employee's commitment to the task. Attention to leadership throughout the organization is important, not just at the senior levels. Leaders at the middle levels can manage the boundary between the wider organization and the work group, absorbing some of the uncertainty, and negotiating for the requisite level of support to keep the group productive and motivated (Kanter, 1982).

9. *Examine the Links Between Risk/Reward and Authority.*   In many survival situations the risks become distributed in dysfunctional ways relative to levels of authority and reward. People at the top, or sometimes staff in the control functions (law, HRM, comptroller), can be seen as getting high rewards while

taking relatively few risks if a particular unit does not succeed. Conversely, people in struggling units may view themselves as taking major risks while lacking the requisite authority or rewards. These issues may become particularly salient when some key managers are asked to move locations or to take new roles in units that are critical to the organization's survival. Barry Stein (1979) discovered in one case that good managers become so traumatized by the risks that they prefer assignment to safe settings instead of wanting to be placed in the units that need to be turned around. HRM may have to develop more flexible policies to price out risk than company practices about transfers allow.

CONCLUSION

The crisis of downsizing places HRM under considerable stress. The nature of the challenge can be better understood by looking at the interactions of time pressures and novelty as illustrated in the framework of Table 18.5.

In the pre-cutback situation most HRM units found themselves faced with many activities that were both low novelty and low time pressures (category I) that called for routine administration. As new problems emerged (e.g., the dual career family), staff would develop new policies and approaches but rarely within a crisis atmosphere (category III). Once developed, the administration of these new policies would once again become routine and loosely coupled with the line organization.

Under conditions of scarcity, HRM units face double pressures. There is relatively little novelty in some activities but extreme time pressures for accurate processing and calculations of records and personnel transactions. The costs of errors are high, particularly if individuals are making significant personal decisions based on information on their accumulated pension benefits and other details about a severance package. Therefore, one challenge is to increase service efficiency and reduce turnaround time for many routine tasks.

At the same time, the unit faces the need to innovate in many new areas under great time pressures (category IV). For example, few units have any previously developed model for predicting response to a voluntary severance package. Delivery of training may need to be reconceptualized as a result of budget cuts. Communication packages and strategies during a layoff may need to be developed; strategies for retaining key personnel, and remotivating

TABLE 18.5. Developmental Challenges for HRM.

High	III	IV
Time Pressure	I	II
Low	Low	High
	Novelty	

those remaining—require both speed and creativity. The second major challenge is to increase creativity under tight time pressures.

Together these challenges place an internal strain on the organization of HRM. The people who are good at innovating under pressure are often not the types who are best at zero defects and efficient administration. Rather than organizing functionally, some HRM units should create a cadre of generalist troubleshooters to handle innovation and centralize all routine functions.

In downsizing, HRM units face these challenges even as they lose people, resources, and specialized functions. Some specific developmental challenges we see for HRM units are the following.

1. *Redesign of Work and Team Development.* As downsizing goes beyond simply trimming, it will require redesign of the methods of organization. For example, eliminating staff units and layers of supervision will suggest building into groups some of the skill and support that were previously provided externally. Furthermore, help must be delivered to units with increased responsibilities as the work continues.

2. *Rationalization of Administrative System.* In undermanned settings, poorly designed control systems have a double cost in that they require line management time to comply with them and generate staff bureaucracies to process and react to what the line submits. HRM must become expert at nonbureaucratic controls (Michael, 1979).

3. *Integrating HRM Planning with Strategic Business Planning.* As cutbacks occur, HRM units and the line become more tightly coupled. Many of the consequences of headcount reduction will require new initiatives in HRM to resolve the new problems; career lines, new training content and delivery systems, compensation review, inventing new rewards. The overall business strategy may critically depend on retaining a core of key engineers or developing new competencies among the marketing staff.

4. *Developing Adequate Negotiating Skills.* Such skills are necessary to retain the integrity of control systems while applying them flexibly to meet some of the particular special cases that downsizing creates. The ability to look behind initial positions to the underlying interests is necessary to develop new options (Fisher and Ury, 1981).

5. *Designing the Internal Organization of HRM.* The function needs to be carefully designed to ensure that the tensions between support and control are internal to the unit and are worked out within it, not at the boundary with line units. This will prevent the line from hunting from the answer they want. Given that HRM are likely to be caught up in the cuts themselves, their own organization must be built on redundancy of functions—multiskill and new resources developed by networks among HRM people throughout the organization and between HRM and the line.

One of the major fears of human resources managers during the time of cutbacks is that the support functions of HRM will be cut deeply, leaving

only the control aspects. Just as the overall organization faces the challenge
to keep the work exciting, challenging, and developmental, HRM staff themselves wonder if they will not be cut back to operational control just as they
were beginning to move towards the strategic level (Devanna et al., 1981, pp.
51–67). We think that if HRM staff can find ways to respond creatively and
to move on some of the developmental challenges that downsizing presents
their function, they can, in turn, be a leading resource for the other divisions
of the company.

CHAPTER

19

HUMAN RESOURCE POLICIES FOR THE INNOVATING ORGANIZATION

Jay R. Galbraith

Innovation is currently sought by most organizations. Somewhere in their strategic plans they all discuss the importance of searching for new businesses, fostering new products, or new processes. But despite the fact that innovation is so revered, it remains very difficult to achieve. Why is something so desirable so elusive?

There are several reasons. First, innovation is *destructive*. It destroys investments in capital, careers, and installed bases of power. It is always interesting to see the "about face" of someone who urges innovation but finds one which renders a personal specialty obsolete. These cheerleaders quickly become Luddites.[1] Second, innovation is a *political process*. It is political in part

[1] The Luddites were a band of British workmen who joined in riots between 1811 and 1816 for the destruction of machinery under the belief that its introduction reduced wages and increased unemployment [after Ned Lud; Ed.].

because of its potential destructiveness, but also because new ideas raise issues of charters, territories, missions, and future direction. With the advent of microcomputers and user-friendly languages many innovations are discovered by users in manufacturing, engineering, or marketing. The innovation, if discovered, immediately raises territorial issues with the data-processing department. Therefore, almost every new idea runs counter to the established ways of doing business. The new and unproven ideas get killed very often by the Luddites and politicians. The third reason that innovation is so difficult is that it requires an innovative organization specifically designed to produce commercially successful ideas. Most of our organizations are operating organizations. They are designed to do something well for the millionth time. Organizations that efficiently produce the millionth product are not very good at doing something for the first time. That is the task of the innovating organization. Thus to be innovative a firm needs two organizations—one to operate the current business and one to innovate into new businesses. This chapter describes the structure of the innovative organization and the human resource policies and systems needed to support it. Again, most human resource policies are designed for the operating organization. Because the task of innovating is inherently different than operating, an innovating organization needs human resource policies that support innovation.

The innovating organization need not be an expensive, duplicate structure. For some organizations it may simply be an occasional effort wherein a half-dozen people are set up in a trailer in the parking lot. The point is that even in these temporary ventures there is structure, some key processes, special rewards, and a type of person that must be blended into an innovating organization. The next sections describe this structure and the key processes consistent with it. Then the human resource policies to fit this structure and process are discussed in greater detail. Before describing the innovating organization, a case example of an innovation is presented from which a number of lessons can be drawn.

THE INNOVATING PROCESS

This section presents a typical process by which innovations occur in organizations. The organization is a new venture that was started in the early 1970s. A group of engineers developed a new electronics product while working for a well-known innovative electronics firm. Because they were in a division that did not have the charter for this product, however, a political battle ensued and, as is frequently the case, the engineers left to form their own company. They successfully found venture capital and introduced their new product. Initial acceptance was good, and within several years they were growing rapidly and had become an industry leader.

However in the early 1970s, Intel invented the microprocessor. By the mid to late 1970s the Intel innovation began to spread through the electronics industries. Manufacturers of previously "dumb" products now had the capability to infuse "intelligence" into their product lines. A competitor who understood computers and software introduced just such a product into the new venture firm's market. It met with initial high acceptance. The president of the firm in point responded by hiring someone who knew something about microcomputers, some software people, and instructed the engineering department to respond.

The president spent most of his time raising capital to finance the venture's growth. Realizing one day that the engineers had not made much progress, he instructed them to get a product out. They did, but it was a half-hearted effort. The new product had a microcprocessor in it but was less than the second generation product that was needed.

The president then pursued international opportunities. He started up in Europe and Singapore, but there again he noticed that his main competitor was growing faster than his company was and had begun to steal market share. The competitor quickly became the industry leader. The president decided that he had better take charge of the product development effort.

Upon his return he found that the hardware and software groups were locked in a political battle in engineering. Each felt its "magic" was the more powerful. Since the lead engineer and cofounder had a hardware background, the hardware establishment prevailed. But they then clashed head-on with the marketing department who agreed with the software group. The result was a set of studies and presentations but no new product. The situation as it presents itself is that of a young, relatively small (1200 people) entrepreneurial firm that cannot innovate. The president wanted innovation and provided resources to produce it. That was not enough. Much more was needed.

The president became more involved. One day he received a call from his sales manager in the New England territory. The sales manager said, "I think you should come up here. A field service engineer has made some modifications to our product and programmed it in a way that my customers are asking us to do. We may have something here."

The president was impressed with what he saw. The engineer wanted to use the company's product to track his own inventory. He wrote to the company headquarters for programming instructions. The response from headquarters was that it was against company policy to send instructional materials to field engineers. Undaunted, the engineer bought a home computer and taught himself to program. He then modified the product in the field and programmed it to solve his problem. When the sales manager happened to see what was done, he recognized its significance and immediately called the president.

The field engineer accompanied the president back to headquarters. He presented his work to the engineers who had been working on the second generation product for so long. Their response was that the application was nice but idiosyncratic. They said that their planned product would be superior. Again, the hardware group prevailed. The field engineer was thanked and returned to his position.

Weeks later, the same sales manager called the president again. He said that the company would lose this talented guy if something wasn't done. Besides, he thought that the field engineer was right and not the engineering group. The president recalled that he had been impressed and that the field engineer had produced something more valuable than his entire engineering department had. He brought him back to headquarters and tried to find something for the field engineer to do while he decided what should be done. Within a few days, the president received a request from the European sales manager to assign the engineer to him.

The European sales manager was visiting headquarters for a period of training. During that time he heard of the field engineer, sought him out, and listened to his story. It turned out that the sales manager had a French bank that wanted the kind of application that the field engineer had created for himself. A successful application would be worth an order for several hundred machines. The president gave the go-ahead and sent the field engineer to work in Europe. The engineering department said it wouldn't work. Three months later, the field engineer successfully developed the application and the bank signed an order for several hundred machines.

When the field engineer returned, the president assigned him to a trusted marketing manager who was told to protect him and get a product out. The engineers were told to support the manager and reluctantly did so. They created some applications software and a printed circuit board which could easily be installed in all existing machines in the field. The addition of this board and the software temporarily saved the company and made its current product slightly superior to that of the competitor.

The president was elated. He congratulated the young field engineer and gave him a good position on the staff working on special assignments to develop software. Then he began encountering problems. The president tried to get personnel to give the engineer a special cash award. Personnel was reluctant. "After all," they said, "other people worked on the effort, too. It will set a precedent."

Then the finance department wanted to withhold $500 from the engineer's pay. He had received an advance of $1000 for his European trip but only turned in vouchers for $500 upon return.

The young engineer didn't help himself very much either. He was hard to get along with and refused to accept supervision from anyone except the European sales manager. The president, therefore, arranged to have him permanently transferred to Europe. The personnel department had prepared the necessary paperwork three times and three times the engineer had changed his mind about going at the last minute. Today the president is still wondering what to do with him.

In this not uncommon story we have a number of lessons we can use to construct the characteristics of an innovating organization. The next section takes these lessons and elaborates upon them in order to develop the structure and processes that constitute the innovating organization. The reward systems and people practices that make up the human resource policies of the innovating organization are then described.

THE INNOVATING ORGANIZATION

The innovating organization is no different from an operating organization in the make-up of its component parts. It consists of a task, structure, processes, reward systems, and people as shown in Figure 19.1.[2] Each component must fit with each other component and with the task. A basic premise of this chapter is that the task of the innovating organization is fundamentally different from that of the operating organization. The innovating task is more uncertain and risky, takes place over longer time horizons, assumes failure is good in the early stages, and so on. Therefore, the organization that performs that task should be different as well. A firm wishing to innovate needs both an operating organization and an innovating organization. But what is the innovating organization? The next sections describe the structure, processes, rewards, and staffing practices of the innovating organization.

The Structure of the Innovating Organization

The innovating organization has a structure of its own, and can be described in terms of several roles. These roles define one of the three structural dimensions of the innovating organization. Each dimension incorporates a lesson from the example presented in the preceding section.

[2]For a similar model of an organization, see Chapter 3. See also Galbraith (1977) and Nadler and Tushman (1977).

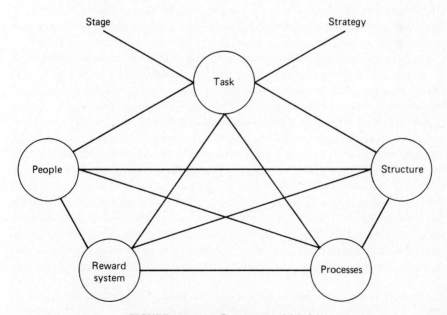

FIGURE 19.1 An Organizational Model

Roles

Like the result of all organized phenomena, innovation occurs from a combination of roles, whether the innovation occurs inside or outside a formal organization. Innovation is rarely an individual phenomenon.[3] There are three main roles in the commercialization of any new idea. The three roles are well illustrated in the case example.

Every innovation starts with an *idea generator* or idea champion. In the preceeding example the field engineer was the person who generated the new idea. This is the inventor, the entrepreneur, or risk taker on whom much of our research attention has been focused. The main conclusion of this research is that an idea champion is needed at each stage of an idea's development into an innovation. That is, at each stage, a dedicated, full-time individual whose success or failure depends on developing the idea is necessary for innovation. Very little more need be added here. It is the other roles—traditionally ignored—that will receive most of our attention.

The need for other roles begins because the idea generator is usually a low-level person who experiences a problem and develops a new response to it. The lesson here is that many ideas originate down where "the rubber meets the road." The lost status and authority level of the idea generator creates a need for the next role.

Every idea needs at least one *sponsor* to promote it. In order to carry an idea into implemetation, someone has to discover it and fund the increasingly disruptive and expensive development and testing efforts that shape it. Thus idea generators need to find sponsors for their ideas in order to perfect them. In our example, the New England sales manager, the European sales manager, and finally, the marketing manager sponsored the idea of the field engineer. Thus one of the functions of the sponsor is to lend his or her authority and resources to an idea to carry it down the road toward commercialization.

The other function of the sponsor is to recognize the business significance of an idea. In any organization there are hundreds of ideas being promoted at any one time. The sponsor must select among these ideas those that might become new business ideas. Thus it is best that sponsors be generalists. That is not always the case, as the case example illustrates.

Sponsors are usually middle managers who are distributed throughout the organization. They frequently work for both the operating and the innovating organization. Some of the sponsors run divisions or departments and it is their task to balance the operating and innovating needs of their business or function. Other sponsors work full-time for the innovating organization when the firm can afford the creation of venture groups, new product development departments, and the like. In the example, the sales managers spontaneously played the sponsor role. The third sponsor, the marketing manager, was formally designated. The point here is that by formally designating the role

---

[3] Throughout the chapter, the term "innovation" is used to mean either a substantive or process idea *that is brought to market.* This typically requires the coordinated involvement of two or more individuals [Ed.].

or recognizing it, finding it with money earmarked for innovation, creating innovating incentives, and developing and selecting sponsorship skills, the organization can improve its chances of successfully innovating. Little attention has been given to sponsors. They are fundamental for innovation to take place.

The third role illustrated in the case example is that of the *orchestrator*. The president played this role. An orchestrator is needed because new ideas are never neutral. In fact, truly innovative ideas are destructive. Innovation destroys investments in capital equipment and affects people's careers. The management of ideas is a political process.[4] The problem is that the political struggle is biased toward the establishment who have significant authority and control of resources. The orchestrator must be a power balancer if the new idea is to have a chance to get tested. The orchestrator's role involves protecting idea people, promoting the opportunity to try out new ideas, and backing them when proven effective. This person has to legitimize the whole process. The president did exactly that with the field engineer. Before he became involved, the hardware establishment prevailed.

Orchestrators play their role by using the processes and rewards described in the following sections. That is, one orchestrates by funding innovating activities and creating incentives for middle managers to sponsor innovating ideas. Orchestrators are the top managers of the organization. It is their task to design the innovating organization.

The typical operating role structure of a divisionalized firm is shown in Figure 19.2. The hierarchy consists of operating functions reporting to division general managers who, in turn, report to group executives. The group executives report to the chief executive (CEO). Some of these people play roles in both the operating and the innovating organization.

The role structure of the innovating organization is shown in Figure 19.3. The chief executive and a group executive function as orchestrators. Division managers are the sponsors who work in both the operating and the innovating organizations. In addition several "reservations" are created in which managers of R&D, corporate development, product development, market development, and new process technology function as full-time sponsors. These reservations allow the separation of innovating activity from the operating core. This separation is an organizing choice we label *differentiation*, and is described in the next section.

Differentiation

In the case example, the innovation was perfected at a remote site and was relatively advanced before it was ever discovered by management. It suggests that if one wants to stimulate new ideas, the odds are better if the early effort is differentiated from the operating organization in order to perfect and test

---

[4] The politics of innovation are well documented in such case studies as A. Pettigrew, *The Politics of Organizational Decision-Making.* London: Tavistock, 1973; see also Pfeffer and Salancik (1977).

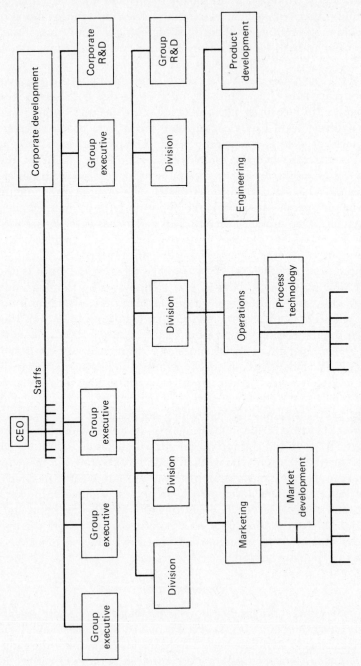

FIGURE 19.2 A Typical Organization Structure.

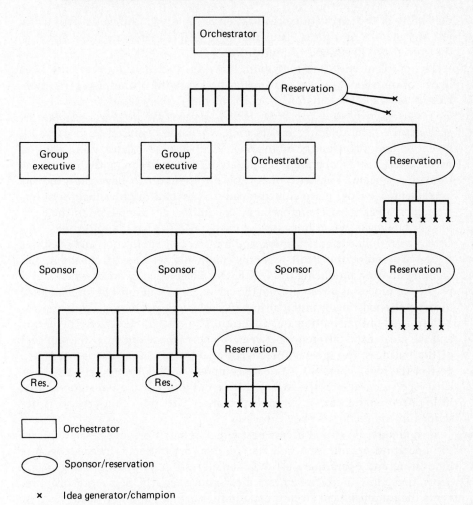

FIGURE 19.3 Human Resource Roles in the Structure.

"crazy" ideas. An effort is differentiated when it is separated physically, financially, and/or organizationally from the day-to-day activities likely to disrupt it. Had the field engineer worker worked within the engineering department or at company headquarters, his idea probably would have been snuffed out prematurely.

Another kind of differentiation is to free initial idea tests from staff controls designed for the operating organization. At one company, they used to make decisions on whether to buy a new oscilloscope in about 15 or 30 minutes with a shout across the room. After being acquired, that same decision would take 12–18 months because the purchase required a capital appropriation request. Controls based on operating logic and current business logic reduce the ability of the innovating organization to rapidly, cheaply, and frequently test and modify new ideas. Thus the more differentiated an initial effort is, the greater the likelihood of innovation.

The problem with differentiation, however, is that it decreases the likelihood of transferring a new proven idea back into the operating organization. Herein lies the differentiation/transfer dilemma. *The more differentiated an effort, the greater the likelihood of transferring the new idea into the operating organization for implementation.* The dilemma occurs only when the organization needs both invention and diffusion for innovation. That is, some organizations may not need transfer to an operating organization. When Exxon started up its information systems business, there was no intention to have the products implemented by the petroleum company. They had to grow their own operating organizations. Therefore, they maximized differentiation in the early phases. However, when Intel started on the 64K RAM, the effort was consistent with their current business, and transfer into fabrication and sales was critical. Therefore, the effort was only minimally separated from the implementing division producing the 16K RAM. The difficulty arises when a new product or process is different from the current ones, but must be implemented through the existing manufacturing and sales organizations. These organizations need both invention and diffusion. The greater the need for invention and the greater the difference between the new idea and the existing concept of the business, the greater the degree of differentiation that is needed to perfect the idea. The only way to accomplish both is to proceed stagewise. That is, differentiate in the early phases and then start the transition so that little differentiation exists at implementation. The transition process is described in the section on key processes.

In summary, invention occurs best when initial efforts are separated from the operating organization and its controls. Separation is needed because innovating and operating are fundamentally different and opposing logics. Separation allows both to be performed simultaneously. Separation also prevents the establishment from prematurely snuffing out a new idea. The less the dominant culture of the organization supports innovation, the greater is the need for separation.[5] Often this separation occurs naturally as in the example, or clandestinely, such as in "boot-legging." If a firm wants to foster innovation, then it can create reservations where innovating activity can occur as a matter of course. Let us now turn to the third and last structural dimension of the innovating organization.

Reservations

Reservations are organizational units (such as R&D) that are totally devoted to creating new ideas for future business. Their purpose is to reproduce the garagelike atmosphere of inventors where people can rapidly and frequently

---

[5]Chapter 9 discusses the impact of corporate culture on the organization. The importance of innovation in turbulent environments speaks to the design of an "overlay" on the human resource system and corporate culture of most organizations to foster innovation [Ed.].

test their ideas. Reservations are meant to be havens for "safe learning." When innovating, one wants to maximize early failure to promote learning. On reservations, separate from operations, this cheap, rapid screening can take place.

Reservations consist of people who work solely for the innovating organization. The reservation manager works full-time as a sponsor. Reservations permit differentiation to occur. They are also located both in the divisions and at corporate headquarters to permit various degrees of differentiation.

Reservations can be internal or external. Internal reservations are like research groups, product and process development labs, market development, new ventures, corporate development, and some staff groups. They are organizational homes where idea generators can contribute without becoming managers. This was one of the intentions of staff groups. However, staffs often assume control responsibilities or are narrow specialists who contribute to the current business idea. Because these groups can be expensive, outside reservations such as universities, consulting firms, and advertising agencies are often used to tap nonmanagerial idea generators.

Reservations can also be permanent or temporary. The reservations described such as R&D units are reasonably permanent entities. Others can be temporary. Members of the operating organization can be relieved of operating duties to develop a new program, a new process, or a new product. When developed they take the idea into operating organization and resume their operating responsibilities. But for a period of time they are differentiated from operations in varying degrees in order to innovate, fail, learn, and ultimately perfect a new idea.

Collectively, the roles of orchestrators, sponsors, and idea generators working with and on reservations constitute the structure of the innovating organization. Some of the people such as sponsors and orchestrators play roles in both organizations, whereas reservation managers and idea generators work only for the innovating organization. Virtually everyone in the organization can be an idea generator and all middle managers are potential sponsors. However, not all choose to play these roles. People vary considerably in their innovating skills. By recognizing these roles, developing people for them, giving them opportunity to use their skills through key processes, and rewarding innovating accomplishments, the organization can do considerably better than just allowing the spontaneous process to work as described in the example. Across this structure of the innovating organization are several key processes. These are described in the next section.

Key Processes in the Innovating Organization

In our case example, the idea generator and the first two sponsors found each other through happenstance. The odds of such match-ups can be significantly improved through the explicit design of processes to help sponsors and idea generators find each other. Processes of funding, idea getting, and idea blending are key ones for improving match-ups. In addition, transitions and program management are processes for taking ideas from reservations into operations. Each of these processes is described in the following.

Funding

One of the key processes to increase an organization's ability to innovate is an explicit funding process for the innovating organization. A leader in this field is Texas Instruments. TI budgets and allocates funds for operating and separate funds for innovating. In essence the orchestrators make the short run–long run tradeoff at this point. They then orchestrate by choosing where to allocate the innovating funds: to division sponsors or corporate reservations. The funding process is a key tool for orchestration.

A lesson from the case example was that it often takes multiple sponsors to launch a new idea. The field engineer's idea would never have been brought to management's attention without the New England sales manager. It would never have been tested in the market without the European sales manager. Multiple sponsors keep fragile ideas alive. If engineering had been the only sponsor for technical ideas, there would have been no innovation.

Some organizations purposely create a multiple sponsoring system and make it legitimate for an idea generator to go to any sponsor that has funding for new ideas. Multiple sponsors duplicate the market system of multiple bankers for entrepreneurs. At 3M, an idea generator can go to his or her division sponsor for funding. If refused, the idea generator can go to any other division sponsor or even to Corporate R&D. If the idea is outside the current businesses, the idea generator can go to the New Ventures group for support. By this point if the idea is rejected by all sponsors, it must not be a very good idea. However, the idea is kept alive and given several opportunities to be tested. The presence of multiple sponsors keep fragile, young ideas alive.

Idea Getting

The idea-getting process occurs in all organizations, as it did in the example. The premise of this section is that the odds of match-ups can be improved by organization design. First, the natural process can be improved by network building actions such as multidivision or multireservation careers, companywide seminars, and conferences. All these practices plus a common physical location facilitate matching at 3M.

The process is formalized at TI through an elaborate planning process called the OST System (Objectives, Strategies, and Tactics) which is an annual harvest of new ideas. Innovating funds are distributed to managers of Objectives (sponsors) who fund projects from idea generators which become tactical action programs. Ideas not funded go into a creative backlog to be tapped throughout the year. Whether formally, as at TI, or informally, as at 3M, there is a known system for matching ideas with sponsors.

Ideas are also obtained by aggressive sponsors. Sponsors sit at the crossroads of many ideas and often arrive at a better idea as a result. They then pursue an idea generator to champion it. Good sponsors know where the proven idea people are located and attract them to come and perfect an idea on their reservation. Sponsors will go inside or outside to pursue these idea people.

Finally, formal events can be scheduled for matching purposes. At 3M there is the annual fair at which idea generators can set up booths to be viewed by shopping sponsors. Exxon Enterprises held a "shake the tree event" at which idea people could throw out ideas to be pursued by attending sponsors. Any number of such events can be created. The point is that by devoting time to ideas and making innovation legitimate, the odds of having sponsors find new ideas are increased.

Idea Blending

An important lesson to be derived from our scenario is that it is no accident that a field engineer produced the new product idea. Why? Because the field engineer spends all day working on customer problems and also has knowledge of the technology. Within the mind of a single person, there is a blending of two vital elements of innovation: knowledge of a need and a means for satisfying that need. In addition, our field engineer had a personal need for which the technology could be designed. The premise being espoused here is that innovation is more likely to occur when knowledge of technologies and user requirements are combined in the minds of as few people as possible, with one person the optimal.

On other occasions it is often debated whether innovations are need-stimulated or means-stimulated. Do you start with the disease and look for a cure or start with a cure and find a disease for it? Research shows that two-thirds of the innovations are need-stimulated (Tushman and Moore, 1981). But this argument misses the point. As shown in Figure 19.4(a), the debate is over whether use or means drives the downstream efforts. This kind of thinking is linear and sequential. Instead, the model suggested here is shown in Figure 19.4(b). That is, for innovation to occur, knowledge of all key components must be simultaneously coupled, and the best way to maximize communication among the components is to have the communication occur intrapersonally. If not intrapersonally, then as few people as possible will effectively communicate interpersonally. The point is that initial innovative ideas occur when knowledge of the essential specialities is coupled in as few heads as possible. This coupling can occur intrapersonally by growing or selecting people. These practices are discussed in the people section.

There is a variety of processes that are employed to match knowledge of need and knowledge of means. At IBM, marketing staff are placed directly in the R&D labs where they interpret the market requirements documents. People are rotated through this unit and a network is created. Wang holds

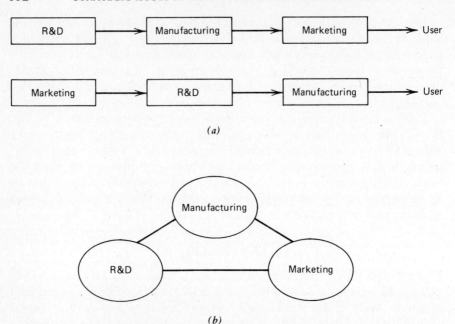

FIGURE 19.4   Nature of Functional Interdependence.

an annual users' conference at which customers and product designers interact over the use of Wang products. Lanier insists that all top managers, including R&D management, spend one day per month selling in the field. It is said that British scientists made remarkable progress on developing radar after actually flying missions with the RAF. In all these cases there is an explicit matching of the use and the user with knowledge of a technology to meet the use. Again, these processes are explicitly designed to get a user orientation among the idea generators and sponsors. They increase the likelihood that inventions will be innovations. The more complete a new idea or invention is at its inception, the better the likelihood of transfer into the operating organization and the communication of the innovation.

Transmitting

The most crucial process is the transition of an idea from a corporate reservation to an operating organization for implementation. This process occurs stagewise as in the case example. First, the idea was formulated in the field before management ever knew about it. Then it was tested with a customer, the French bank. And, finally, development and full-scale implementation was the third stage. In other cases several stages of testing and scale-up may occur. Transitions should be planned stagewise. At each stage the orchestrator has several choices that balance the need for further invention with the need for diffusion. The choices and stages of idea development are shown in Figure 19.5.

The choices facing the orchestrator at each stage are: Who will be the sponsor? Who will be the champion? What is the source of the staff for the effort? At what physical location will work be performed? Who will fund the effort? How much autonomy or how differentiated should the effort be? An idea must go through a transition from a reservation into an operating division in this stagewise manner. For example, at the initial stage of new idea formulation the sponsor could be the corporate ventures group with the champion working on the corporate reservation. The effort would be staffed with other corporate reservation types and funded by corporate. The activity would be fully separate and autonomous. If the results were positive, the next stage would be entered, but if the idea needed further development, some division people would be brought in to round out the needed specialties. If the data were still positive after the second stage, then the effort could be transferred physically to the division but the champion, sponsor, and funding would still be corporate. In this manner, by orchestrating through choice of sponsor, champion, staff, location, funding, and autonomy, the orchestrator balances the need for innovation and protection with the need for testing against reality and diffusion.

This is an all too brief outline of the transition process. Entire books have been written on the subject of technology transfer (Rogers and Rogers, 1976). The goal here is to highlight the stagewise nature of the process and the decisions to be made by the orchestrator at each stage. The process is crucial because it is the link between the two organizations. That is, in order to consistently innovate, the firm needs an operating organization, an innovating organization, and a process for the transition of ideas from one to the other.

Choice/Stage	I	II	. . . .Nth	Implementation
Sponsor	Corporate	Corporate		Division
Champion	Corporate	Corporate		Division
Staffing	Corporate	Corp.-Div.		Division
Location	Corporate	Corporate		Division
Funding	Corporate	Corporate		Division
Autonomy	Corporate	Complete		Minimal

FIGURE 19.5   Choices and Stages of Idea Development.

Program Management Process

Finally, equally critical to the innovating organization is the program management process of implementing new products and processes within a division. That is, the idea generator usually hands the innovation over to a product/project/program manager at the time of implementation, who follows it across the functional organization within the division. Although the systems and organizational processes for project management have been discussed elsewhere (Galbraith, 1977), the point is that a program management process is vital.

In summary, across the innovating structure run several key processes. These are the funding, idea getting, idea blending, transition, and program management processes. Many of these occur naturally in all organizations. The implicit hypothesis of this section is that the odds for successful innovation can be increased by the explicit design of these processes and the devotion of corporate resources to them.

HUMAN RESOURCE POLICIES

To complete the design of the innovating organization, the human resource policy areas of rewards, selection, and people development need to be addressed. In this section human resource policies for idea generators and sponsors are specifically addressed. In many cases these policies are different from the systems needed in the operating organization.

Reward System

The innovating organization, like the operating organization, needs an incentive system of its own to motivate innovating behavior. Since the task of innovating is different from the task of operating, the innovating organization needs a different reward system. The innovating task is riskier, more difficult, and takes place over longer time horizons. These factors usually require some adjustment to the reward system of the operating organization. The amount of adjustment depends on how innovative the operating organization is, and on the attractiveness of outside alternatives.

The functions of the reward system are threefold. First, the rewards are to attract and hold idea people in the company and in the reservations. As firms have different attraction and retention problems, they will vary in the reward systems they use. Second, the rewards should motivate the extra effort needed to innovate. After failing 19 times, something has to motivate the idea generator to make the twentieth attempt. And, finally, rewards should be given for successful performance. These rewards should accrue to idea generators primarily. However, the reward measurement system for the sponsors is equally important, and each is discussed in the next section.

Rewards for Idea Generators

The choice of reward system consists of encouraging internal motivation by providing opportunity to pursue one's ideas, promotion, recognition, and special compensation. People can be attracted and motivated intrinsically by simply giving them the opportunity and the autonomy to pursue their own ideas. Autonomy is provided by placing them in a reservation. Many idea people are internally driven as was the field engineer in the case example. As such, the provision of opportunity to an idea generator to come to a reservation, pursue his or her own ideas, and be guided and evaluated by reservation manager constitutes a minimal level of reward. If the minimal level attracts and motivates idea people, the innovating organization should go no further in creating a separate reward system.

Additional motivational leverage can be obtained if needed through promotion and recognition for innovating performance. The dual ladder is the best example where an individual contributor can be promoted and given increased salary without becoming a manager. At 3M a contributor can rise in the organization to an equivalent level of a group executive and not be a manager. The dual ladder has always existed in R&D but is now being extended to other functions as well. Other firms use special recognition for career performance. At IBM there is the IBM Fellows program in which a fellow is selected and can then work on projects of his or her own choosing for the next five years. At 3M there is the Carlton Award which is described as an internal Nobel prize. The promotion and recognition systems reward innovation and aid in building an innovating culture.

When greater motivation is needed and/or the organization wants to signal the importance of innovation, special compensation is used in addition to providing opportunity and recognition. Different systems have been used. They are discussed in order of increasing motivational impact and of increasing dysfunctional ripple effects.

Some companies reward successful idea generators with one-time case awards. For example, International Harvester's share of the combine market jumped from 12% to 17% due to the introduction of the axial flow combine. The scientist whose six patents contributed to the product development was given $10,000. If the product continues to succeed, he may be given another award. IBM uses the "Chairman's Outstanding Contribution Award." The current program manager on the 4300 series was given a $5000 award for her breakthrough in coding on her last assignment. These awards are post hoc and serve to reward rather than to attract and motivate.

Stronger motivation is achieved through programs that offer a "percentage of the take" to the idea generator and early team members. Toy and game companies give a royalty to inventors, internal and external, of toys and games that are introduced. Apple Computer claims to give employees a royalty for software programs they write and which will run on Apple equipment. A chemical company started a pool which was created by putting 4% of the first five years of earnings aside from a new business venture. The pool was to be distributed to the initial venture team. Other companies create pools from percentages (2–20%) of cost savings created by process innovations. In any case, a predetermined contract is created to motivate the idea generator and early joiners of the risky effort.

The most controversial effort to date are those attempts to duplicate free market rewards inside the firm. A few years ago, ITT bought a small company named Qume which made high-speed printers. The founder became a millionaire. He had to quit his initial organization to found the venture capital effort. If ITT can make an outsider a millionaire, why not give the same chance to entrepreneurial insiders? Many people agree with that premise but have not found the formula to implement the idea. One firm created some five-year milestones for a venture, the accomplishment of which would result in a cash reward of six million dollars to the idea generator. However, the business climate changed after two years and the idea generator, not surprisingly, tried to make the plan rather than adapt to the new, unforeseen reality. Another scheme is to give the idea generator and the initial team some phantom stock. That stock gets evaluated at sale time the same way any acquisition would be evaluated. This process duplicates the free market process and gives internal people the same venture capital opportunities and risks as they have on the outside.

Although the special compensation programs produce motivation, they also have dysfunctional consequences. Other people often contribute at later stages and feel like second-class citizens. Also, any program that discriminates among people produces perceptions of inequity and possible fall-out in the operating organization.[6] Care should be taken to manage the fall-out if the benefits are judged to outweigh the costs.

Rewards for Sponsors

Sponsors also need incentives. In the case example the sales people had an incentive to adopt a new product because they were being beaten in the market. Sponsors will not sponsor innovating ideas unless the sponsor has innovating incentives. The task of the orchestrator is to create and communicate those incentives.

Sponsor incentives take many forms. At 3M, division managers have a bonus goal that 25% of their revenue should come from products introduced in the last five years. When the percentage falls and the bonus is threatened, these sponsors become amazingly receptive to new product ideas. The transfer process becomes much easier as a result. Sales growth, percent revenue increase, number of new products, and so on are all bases for creating incentives for sponsors to adopt innovating ideas.

Another controversy occurs when the idea generators get phantom stock.

---

[6] For a detailed discussion of the research on equity in organizations, see J. S. Adams (1965).

Should the sponsors who supervise these idea people get some phantom stock, too? Some banks have created separate subsidiaries so that sponsors can get stock in the new venture. To the degree that sponsors contribute to idea development, they will need to be given the stock options as well.

Thus the innovating organization needs its own reward system for idea generators and sponsors. The firm should start with as simple a reward system as possible and move to more motivating, more complex, and possibly more upsetting rewards as attraction and motivation problems require.

Staffing the Innovating Organization

The last policy area of the innovating organization is that of staffing practices. The assumption is that some people are better at innovating than others and these other people are necessarily those who are good at operating. Therefore, the ability of the innovating organization to generate new business ideas can be increased by systematically developing and selecting those people who are better at innovating than others. But first the attributes must be identified. They are discussed in the following for the idea generators and the sponsors.

Attributes of Idea Generators

The field engineer in the case example is the quintessential inventor. He is not mainstream. He is hard to get along with and breaks company policy in order to perfect an idea. These people have strong egos which allow them to persist in swimming upstream. They generally are not the kind of people who get along well in an organization. However, if there are reservations, innovating funds, and dual ladders, these people can be attracted and retained.

The psychological attributes of successful entrepreneurs are those of *high need for achievement and risk taking.* But several other attributes are needed to translate that need into innovation. First, there is usually an irreverence towards the status quo. These people often come from outcast groups such as immigrants. They are less satisfied with the way things are and have less to lose with a change in the current business idea.

Another attribute is that of *previous programming in the industry.* Successful innovation requires indepth knowledge in the industry gained either through experience or formal education. Hence the innovator needs to obtain the knowledge of the industry, though not the "religion." Previous start-up experience is also associated with successful business ventures. Attracting people from incubator firms (high technology) and areas (Boston, Silicon Valley) can increase the odds of finding innovators.

The amount of organizational effort required to select these people varies with the ability to attract them to the organization in the first place. If idea people are attracted through reputation, then by funding reservations and employing idea-getting processes, idea people will select themselves and over time earn a reputation for idea generation. If the firm has no reputation for innovation, then idea people must be sought out or external reservations used for initial idea generation. One firm made extensive use of outside recruiting. A sponsor would develop an idea and then attend annual conferences of key specialties to determine who was best in the area, interview them, and then offer the ones with entrepreneurial interests the opportunity to develop the venture.

Another key attribute of successful business innovators is *varied experience.* This variety creates the coupling of knowledge of means and use in the mind of a single individual. It is the generalist not the specialist who creates an idea outside the current business idea. Specialists are inventors; generalists are innovators. These people can be selected or developed. One firm selects the best and the brightest from the ceramics engineering schools and places them in central engineering in order to learn the system. Then they are assigned to field engineering where they spend three to five years with clients and client problems. Then they return to central engineering product design. Only then do they get to design products for those same customers. The internal coupling can be created by role rotation. Some aerospace firms rotate engineers through manufacturing liaison roles.

Thus there are some known characteristics of idea generators. These people can be attracted or selected. By role rotation a varied experiential background can also be created. These people will be retained, however, only if there are reservations for them and sponsors to champion them.

Attributes of Sponsors and Reservation Managers

The people who manage the idea development process must also be attracted, developed, retained, and trained, as well as those who generate and test ideas. Again, some attributes and skills are better for managing ideas than others, and the innovating organization needs those who have learned the idea management skills. The attributes to be selected and developed are a management style for idea people, early experience in innovating, idea-generating capabilities, skills at putting together deals, and generalist business skills. A description of these attributes follows.

One of the key skills of the innovating organization is to manage and supervise the kind of person who is likely to be an idea generator and champion. In the last section these idea people were described as those who do not take to being supervised very well. This is certainly true. Idea generators and champions have a great deal of ownership of their ideas. They gain their satisfaction by having "done it their way." The intrinsic satisfaction comes from ownership and autonomy. However, idea people also need help, advice, and sounding boards. The successful sponsor learns how to manage these people the same way a producer or publisher learns to handle the egos of stars and writers. The style was best described by a successful sponsor:

"It's a lot like teaching your kids to ride a bike. You're there. You walk along behind. If the kid takes off he or she never knows that they could have been helped. If they stagger a little, you lend a helping hand, undetected, preferably. If they fall, you catch them. If they do something stupid, you take the bike away until they're ready."

This style is quite different than the hands-on, directive style of an operating organization. Of course, the best way to learn it is to have been personally managed that way and seen it practiced in an innovating organization. This reinforces the value of experience in an innovating organization.

More than the idea generators, the sponsors need to understand the logic of innovation and have experienced the management of innovation. As for any activity, the managers need to have an intuitive feel for the task and its nuances. Managers who are only experienced in operations will not have developed the managerial style, understanding, and intuitive feel that is necessary to manage innovations because the logic of operations is counterintuitive to the logic of innovations. This means that some of the idea generators and champions who have experienced innovation should become managers as well as individual contributors. The president in the example scenario was the inventor of the first generation product and, therefore, understood the long agonizing process of developing a business idea. Perhaps this is why it is rare to find an R&D unit that is managed by someone who did not come through the ranks of R&D.

The best idea sponsors and idea reservations managers are people who have experienced innovation early in their careers and are comfortable with it. They will have been exposed to risks, uncertainty, parallel experiments, repeated failures (which lead to learning), coupling as opposed to assembly-line thinking, long time-frames, and personal control systems based on people and ideas rather than numbers and budget variances. Other managers who have already developed their intuition and style in operations have difficulty in switching to the innovating organization late in their careers. These sponsor and reservation managers can then be developed or recruited from the outside.

Sponsors and reservation managers need to be idea generators themselves. Ideas tend to come from two sources. The first is at low levels of the organization where the problem gap is experienced. The idea generator who offers a solution is the one who experienced the problem and goes to a sponsor for testing and development. One problem with these ideas is that they are partial since they come from a specialist whose view can be parochial and local. But sponsors are at the crossroads of many partial ideas. They may get a larger vision of the emerging situation as a result. These idea sponsors can generate a business idea themselves or blend several partial ideas into a business idea. These sponsors and reservation managers at the crossroads of idea flows are an important second source of new ideas. Therefore, they should be selected and trained for idea generation.

Another skill the sponsors and, especially, reservation managers need is deal making and brokering. Once an idea has emerged, a reservation manager may have to argue for the release of key people, space, resources, charters, production time, or a customer contact. These deals all need to be made through persuasion. In that sense it is no different than project or product management roles. But people vary in their ability to cut a deal and bargain. Those who can should be selected. Those who have the other idea management skills can be trained in negotiating and bargaining.

And, finally, the sponsors and reservation managers need to be generalists with general business skills. Again, this skill is needed to recognize a business idea and to shape partial ideas into business ideas. They need to coach idea generators in specialties in which the idea generator is not schooled. Most successful research managers are those with business skills who can see the business significance in the good ideas that come from scientists.

In summary, the sponsors and reservation managers who manage the idea development process should also be recruited, selected, and developed. The skills that these people need relate to their style, experience, idea-generating ability, deal-making ability, and generalist business acumen. These skills can either be selected or developed. Since some of the attributes of successful idea generators and idea sponsors can be identified, the innovating organization should staff and develop according to these criteria. In so doing, the organization improves its odds at generating and developing new business ideas.

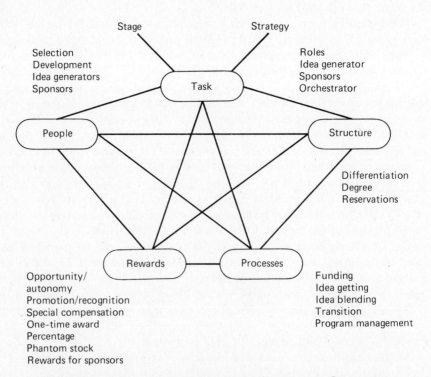

FIGURE 19.6 Human Resource Activities for the Innovating Organization.

CONCLUSION

The innovating organization that has just been described is one that recognizes and formalizes the roles, processes, rewards, and people practices that naturally lead to innovations. The point emphasized throughout is that by purposely designing these roles and processes, the organization is more likely to generate innovations. This purposely designed organization is needed to overcome the obstacles to innovation. Innovation is destructive to many established groups and will be resisted. Innovation is also contrary to current business operations and will be ignored. These obstacles and others are more likely to be overcome with an organization designed to innovate.

Managers have tried to overcome these obstacles by creating good policies but by themselves will not generate innovations. The message is that a consistent set of policies concerning structure, process, rewards, and people is needed. The characteristics of the innovating organization are illustrated in Figure 19.6. It is the combination of idea people, reservations for them, sponsors to supervise them, funding for ideas, and rewards for success that increase the odds in favor of innovation. Simply implementing one or two of these practices will result in failure and will teach people that such practices do not work. A consistent combination of these practices will ensure an innovating organization.

CHAPTER

20

STRATEGIC ISSUES
IN LABOR RELATIONS

John A. Fossum

Some might say that the introduction of unions to represent employees reduces the ability of management to design and implement strategy in human resource management. Much of the material in this chapter argues that strategy becomes more important for employers with unionized employees and that unions are only one of several constraints or competitive factors that employers might continually recognize when proposing goals and strategies for their organizations.

Employers with unions operate in a different manner than those whose employees are unorganized. These differences, in turn, may be likely to affect the performance of unionized organizations. Although employers generally expect that the effects of unions are negative, recent evidence reveals a far more mixed and complex relationship with both negative and positive outcomes for industries and employers who are heavily unionized. These effects are examined in detail in this chapter. For instance:

1. Many employers have adopted so-called "union-free" campaigns during the past 5–10 years. These campaigns rest on the basic assumption that the organization will be better off without unions. Alternative

methods for remaining union-free and their consequences are carefully examined also from a strategic perspective.

2. Evidence suggests that smaller plants are more vulnerable to organizing than larger ones. Some of the evidence regarding why individuals are willing to organize and the demographic characteristics within plants can help employers formulate strategies to deal with potential organizing campaigns.

3. Contract negotiations usually require a balancing of preferred collective bargaining outcomes with other organizational goals and a recognition of the bargaining power each party actually commands. The methods used successfully by employers to accomplish goals are also examined.

4. Contract administration injects the union into day-to-day human resource management. The manner in which the contract is implemented should give the employer some information on what appropriate future strategy should be. This chapter, therefore, suggests strategies for using information in labor negotiations.

All together, a rational calculation of an employee relations strategy is proposed, suggesting appropriate relationships and degrees of involvement between employers and unions. This chapter does not cover tactics used at the operational levels of labor–management relations, but focuses on the strategic aspects of industrial relations.

LABOR UNIONS IN THE UNITED STATES

Labor organizations in the United States are not like those of most other industrial nations. There is not labor or labor-dominated political party. There are few, if any, doctrinaire issues to which most or all labor organizations subscribe.

This does not mean that there is no continuity or historical purpose associated with organized labor in the United States. Recently, Maurice Neufeld, a labor historian in the Industrial and Labor Relations School at Cornell reflected on some of the issues that have prevailed in American labor since Andrew Jackson's time (Neufeld, 1982). The following are recurrent.

First, members of the working class, definable as those who actually produce tangible goods or provide services, have continually been concerned with the governance of the workplace. They do not concede that owners or managers have the right to establish all rules governing employment, and see themselves as stakeholders in the enterprise, and entitled to a role in decision-making.

Second, the working class has been continually concerned with inequality in the distribution of wealth in the United States. This does not mean that unions believe that all employees should receive the same income. It does mean that unions generally feel the differential between salaries earned by the working class and managers, or the share of the gains from production accruing to employees *vis-à-vis* owners, is inequitable.

These prevailing points of view must be recognized by management when planning strategy. The perceptions of owners, managers, other employee groups, and unionized employees are seldom the same. Each group has different needs and goals. There is little likelihood that unions can be convinced that management philosophies are appropriate, just as unions are unlikely to convince management of the legitimacy of their positions. However, some mechanisms within collective bargaining may help to improve both of their positions simultaneously.

Historically, industries that developed early or had rudimentary or reactionary methods for human resource management became the most heavily unionized. Among these were the mining, steel-making, auto-producing, and construction industries. As shown later, each of these ignored or were incapable of dealing with economic or noneconomic employment conditions of importance to workers.

The heavier industries such as steel and autos have not increased employment for several years. Durable goods manufacturing employment has not grown recently and is not expected to grow much in the future regardless of economic conditions. The only group with reasonably rapid growth in which union penetration has been increasing in the recent past is the public sector.

Occupations that have been heavily organized in the past include skilled trades, operatives, and miners. Clerical, professional, and service occupations have seldom been organized. These are the occupations with the most rapid growth rates in recent years.

These trends suggest that the labor movement is likely to change its organizing focus if it is to maintain or increase its size in the future. New issues and tactics are to be expected, and organizations concerned with formulating competitive strategy should be prepared to respond.

Member Desires for Union Bargaining Outcomes

A recent national survey of a cross-section of union members disclosed that grievance handling, fringe benefits, wages, and job security were the issues union members felt were most important in bargaining (Kochan, 1979). These same members felt that their unions were most successful in gaining wage increases, followed by effective grievance handling processes, fringe benefits, and job security.

It is important to note that both fringes and job security issues are of long-run concern to management from a cost standpoint. It is also interesting to note that of the four major bargaining issues, members were least likely to agree that their unions were effective in bringing about improvements in job security.

From a more recent bargaining outcome standpoint, it is clear that when faced with concession demands, union leaders and members have been willing to give up paid time-off and to make some work rule concessions in exchange for job security guarantees for presently employed members. The evidence is also clear that union members are unwilling to give up negotiated fringes such as pensions and insurance. Particularly in the case of fringes, union members might rightfully argue that the reduction of these rights would be giving up wages foregone in the past for the ability to exercise rights in times of future need; that these rights are really deferred compensation for effort previously expended.

Differences in Union and Nonunion Behavior

There is clear-cut evidence that the provisions of contracts in unionized organizations differ from personnel policies and compensation programs in nonunion firms (Foulkes, 1982). First, union members receive higher wage levels (an issue we explore in detail later in this chapter). Second, explicit attention is paid to handling grievances in a formal manner (over 99 percent of current contracts specify a formal procedure). Third, the portion of total compensation assigned to fringe benefits is significantly higher in unionized employment than in nonunion organizations.

The reason for these differences involves the joint determination of employment issues rather than the unilateral management decision made in nonunion organizations. In nonunion organizations, many compensation programs are designed to influence the behavior of the marginal worker (not marginal in terms of performance, but marginal in terms of firm membership). Compensation systems are frequently designed to attract new employees and to retain valued employees. Thus promotional structures within jobs are created allowing grade level differences that supervisors can use as promotional increase rewards. Great attention is paid to market pay rates, needed to attract new employees. But little attention is paid to the large majority of employees who are already with the organization, are unlikely to leave, and are average performers.

Nonmarginal employees usually make up a majority of the bargaining unit, and since the union is a political organization, it is not unusual that contract demands are skewed to benefit this group and away from the marginal employee that management is more interested in influencing. Since the contract must be ratified by a majority of employees, the demands that are proposed and the position the union fights for might be typified as a "median voter" approach (White, 1982). If the median voter prefers fringes to other economic outcomes, it is not unusual that compensation systems in union environments differ from those where the employer controls their design. It is also likely that across-the-board pay increases, which are frequently negotiated, follow from the fact that large numbers of employees are concentrated in the lower pay grades within the bargaining unit and their gain is relatively greater under this method of generating increases.

The Role of Dissatisfaction in Union Success

It is generally believed that higher wage levels, an opportunity to gain redress for grievances, and methods for improving job security positively influence job satisfaction. However, a set of recent studies has concluded that union members are not more satisfied than those who are not represented, and that when income is held constant, they may be slightly less satisfied (Freeman, 1978).

This apparent contradiction has recently been unraveled by Chris Berger and his colleagues in a study showing that satisfaction is only lower in areas in which unions concentrate their demands, particularly wages. They postulate that lower satisfaction is coupled with the job consciousness that unions emphasize. To fulfill their advocate roles and to remain faithful to the adversarial environment in which they were created, unions continually suggest to workers that their situations can be bettered, and they raise settlements in other organizations as examples of what can be won. As a result, employees can be expected to be dissatisfied with their present lot. Without dissatisfaction, the need for a union to represent their interests declines (Berger et al., 1982).

Promotional Opportunities in Unions

Several years ago researchers noted that urban workers were generally less likely to react positively to job enlargement and job enrichment than were rural workers. One of the explanations offered for this phenomenon was that urban workers had longer experiences with narrow, manufacturing types of jobs. Their jobs might simply be seen as instrumental for gaining important off-the-job outcomes. Therefore, changing the nature of the job would be unimportant to them because jobs were not a central part of their lives.

It was also suggested that the lowered importance of the job, per se, might stem from the realistic belief that significant advancements were not available through good performance on production jobs. Capable employees could perhaps aspire to a supervisor's job in the future, but little else. The union, on the other hand, offers opportunities to attain leadership positions and possible significant advancement through full-time union employment. For some employees, then, the union offers both on-the-job improvements and career opportunities.

There is little evidence that large numbers of employees have "union" or "supervisory" mentalities. Studies have shown that employees elected or appointed to steward positions in unions quickly become stronger union advocates. The opposite holds for bargaining unit members that are promoted into supervision. Interestingly, stewards and supervisors who subsequently return to the ranks become more like rank-and-file employees in their attitudes than those in the positions they previously held.

Union politics and leadership succession mean that labor organizations will emphasize dissatisfaction among employees and point out where unions can help to achieve important outcomes for employees. Working majorities must be assembled and maintained. In this regard, comparisons raised by members and the leadership stimulate issues around which majorities can coalesce for action and stability. Union leaders must be aware continually of the effect their actions will have on the formation and maintenance of the majority power base necessary to remain in office.

Implications for Union Strategy

Union culture, built since the 1800s, is based on the expectation of continual improvements of those employment issues important to the members. This means that the major goals of labor organizations probably relate to job security and economic gains for present members. Union culture also recognized the importance of organizing nonmanagerial employees at all levels of the organization. Class consciousness suggests that there are inherent divisions of interests between owners and managers and other employees.

In the political arena the creation and maintenance of a majority coalition is necessary. This means that unions are likely to pay attention to the "median voter." On the other hand, membership is necessary for a survival of the union, so significant minorities are likely to receive leadership attention. Craft ratification provisions in union industrial union constitutions recognize this problem.

From a technical standpoint, the strategy of unions is likely to concentrate on organizing employees into occupations that have previously had little representation, and to recognize and win concessions in areas that employees consider of prime importance, where employers are not willing to change voluntarily.

THE IMPACT OF UNIONIZATION OF ORGANIZATIONS

Organizations whose employees are represented by unions frequently have different human resource management systems and employee and employer outcomes than do unorganized employers. Most employers probably feel that they are worse off with a union, but the evidence suggests that this is not necessarily the case. They are, obviously, in different situations, but whether they are better or worse off depends on how one interprets the evidence. This section examines the effect of unions on employers and employee outcomes in staffing bargaining unit jobs, the operation of the internal labor market, the level and form of compensation, the productivity and profitability of the organization, and the bargaining relationship. Besides looking at differences between union and nonunion situations, the extent of unionization within organizations and industries is another important influence on the potential impact of labor unions.

External Staffing

The presence of a union has several effects on external staffing. First, the wages, benefits, work rules, and promotion and job security structure of a unionized organization may be more clearly known to applicants. Second, the wage level is generally higher than in comparison firms. Third, the promotion and job security system is usually (at least partially) based on seniority.

The effects of these features of unionized employment are generally positive for the employer who is filling bargaining unit vacancies. The evidence shows that unionized employers usually obtain a larger pool of applicants for job openings and can thus be more selective about new hires. Seniority systems generally lead to a larger proportion of younger applicants in the pool because relatively long periods of employment may be necessary for significant advancement and older applicants might not accrue the seniority necessary for consideration during their careers (Abowd and Farber, 1982). These two effects may mean that unionized employers can hire better prepared, younger employees, who will invest longer time periods with their employer.

Evidence also suggests that during periods of layoff, unionized employers are better able to recall employees from layoff than are nonunion employers. The employment rights that have accrued through seniority make laid-off employees reluctant to accept new jobs, and allow employers relatively low-cost warehousing of labor where the only additional costs for layoffs are larger future unemployment insurance premiums.

Internal Labor Markets

A number of recent studies, particularly those of Richard Freeman and James Medoff (1981), have examined differences in the behavior of employees in union and nonunion establishments as they relate to internal job changes and turnover. The studies all agree that turnover rates from unionized organizations are significantly lower than in nonunion establishments. They find further that the rate of internal job changes (transfers and promotions) is far higher in firms with unions. There are several ramifications for organizations in these differences which need some exploration.

Employee Preferences

It is unlikely that employers have favored the negotiation of job security and promotion clauses which use seniority as the primary criterion for decision-making. But a large proportion of contracts explicitly mentions seniority as a major factor in promotion decisions and the controlling factor in departmental layoffs. By their inclusion, it is clear that on this governance issue, employees prefer an unambiguous criterion and one that rewards tenure in the organization. The whole idea of seniority-based staffing decisions is squarely within the concept of job property rights.

Plant Demographics

Besides the evidence that unionized employees are less likely to turn over, we also know that older and more senior employees are less likely to leave. Most plants have a designed physical capacity that limits the number of employees in a given location. Even when capacity is added, the additions tend to be in chunks rather than in continual small increments. This means that the major staffing efforts take place within relatively concentrated time periods, such as when a shift is added or a plant opened. After the initial turnover has ocurred and a stable plant cadre has evolved, new additions to the workforce simply cover replacements for terminations, retirement, and the like.

With a fixed plant size this means that early hires are more likely to have good promotional opportunities and that the age composition of the workforce is likely to become more elderly over time. If the useful life of the plant and the worklife of the present workforce is roughly similar, this should not pose great problems for the majority of the work force or the employer. But if there is a discrepancy, then the furloughing of a senior workforce, or the severing of their eventual replacement may be difficult.

Specific and General Training

Human capital theorists distinguish between specific and general training. *Specific training* relates to those improvements in employees' capabilities that make them more valuable to their present employer. For example, a knowledge of rules and procedures within the plant would be classified as specific training. *General training* refers to employee capabilities that are of value to all employers who hire that occupation. For example, the knowledge and ability to operate a turret lathe is of roughly equivalent value to all employers who require this operation.

In unionized situations where seniority is the major criterion for promotion, employers make more investments in general training than where they are free to staff internally or externally using their own criteria. On the other hand, their investments in specific training must be lower since their turnover levels are lower.

Where employees are not competing with each other on knowledge and job skill bases, they may be more willing to train each other. Through the use of seniority systems, unions effectively remove jobs from competition just as pattern bargaining removes wages from competition.

Compensation Systems

The belief among employers that union wages are higher than nonunion wages is true. Earlier estimates summarized in H. Gregg Lewis's classic work suggested that the premium (holding occupations, industries, etc., constant) was on the order of 10%. More recent estimates by Dan Mitchell suggest the premium is closer to 15–20% and is independent of the extent of union organization in an industry. It is also clear that wage rates in labor-industries such as apparel, are lower for unionized workers than they are for nonunion workers in more capital-intensive industries. But within industries, the premium Mitchell found predominates (Mitchell, 1980).

Wages and Fringe Benefits

There are also differences between union and nonunion employers in their mix of wage and fringe benefit payments. In Richard Freeman's studies (1981), almost all unionized situations are found to have a higher rate of fringes. This may be reasonable given the greater attachment to firms of union workers, and is reflected in their preference for vesting benefits to provide income security and deferred compensation. It is also apparent recently that unionized employees have been less reluctant to give up hourly salary levels than they have been to concede economic fringe benefits.

Effects on Nonunion Employees

Within firms, negotiated wage increases influence compensation policies for nonunion employees. Typically, benefit types and levels bargained by unionized workers are soon passed on to white-collar employees. Further, to maintain differentials necessary to motivate an interest in promotions, compensation structures are frequently adjusted to maintain relative distances from union structures. Thus the extent of internal organization may not be an important variable when a union's influence on the overall compensation structure is examined. Evidence suggests there is an upper limit on labor's share of total revenue. In the heavily unionized sectors of industry, labor's share of total compensation has not increased recently, whereas the nonunion sector share (currently lower) continues to rise.

Predictability of Compensation Costs

Where unions have negotiated cost-of-living allowances (COLA), future compensation costs can only be estimated. In other situations, straight-time wages are clearly predictable over the life of the contract. Because of the relatively low turnover unionized employers face, during rapid increases in demand in the labor market the increase in compensation costs in unionized firms lags behind those in nonunionized organizations. On the other hand, during a downturn, wage rates (and total compensation costs, particularly if supplementary unemployment benefits are available) are likely to be resistant to a decline. In both events, labor costs are predictably higher for the unionized firm. In an expanding economy, costs may not rise as rapidly, allowing a unionized organization to capitalize on stable labor costs; in a declining economy, however, it may suffer losses if it is to be successful in bidding against a competitor.

Productivity and Profitability

If other things were equal, the wage penalty that unionized employers encounter would make them less productive and less profitable. A large number of studies, led by Richard Freeman, found that unionized employers are about 20 to 25% more productive than comparable nonunion employers. Coupling this with the 15–20% wage penalty they encounter, this means that there is an overall productivity benefit for the unionized firm.

These differences may stem from a number of factors. First, unionized employers become immediately motivated to look for ways to become more productive since they are at a disadvantage compared to the nonunion firm's wage costs. Second, if experience operates to increase learning and the capabilities of employees, the longer tenure of unionized workers would benefit the employer's productivity. Third, evidence shows that worker investments in human capital reflected in experience and education measures are higher in unionized as compared to nonunionized organizations. Fourth, if capital prices do not change when wages increase, the relative returns to capital improve and the employer may gradually reduce employment and replace it with machines and more modern plants. In jobs where significant capital improvements have not been possible in the past (e.g., clerical and white-collar occupations), unions are not found to produce productivity improvements. In fact, the data suggest that unionized white-collar employees are between 5 and 10% less productive than their nonunion counterparts.

Although there is evidence that productivity is higher, profitability does not appear to be greatly influenced. Rates of return to capital are lower in unionized organizations, perhaps reflecting the greater intensity of its use, and hence a lower marginal return to additional equipment.

VULNERABILITY TO UNION ORGANIZING

Union organizing campaigns may begin as the result of dissatisfied employees contacting national or other local unions for assistance in organizing, or of the national or local union's decision to conduct an organizing drive. New plants are seldom the focus of organizing campaigns because there are, as yet, no common issues around which a majority opinion might coalesce. Unstable organizations also make relatively poor candidates for organization because the turnover rates are so high that a working majority may never be formed for a substainable period. But in the vast majority of employment situations, the age of the facility and the stability of the workforce make most establishments potentially vulnerable to unionization.

Certain issues are more salient in organizing campaigns than others. Jeanne Brett (1980) found large differences between expressed employee dissatisfaction with particular issues and their subsequent reported votes in NLRB certification elections. Generally, job security and wage dissatisfaction were most likely to predict a prounion vote, whereas dissatisfaction with the type of work being done had relatively little influence on voting behavior.

Job Security and Job Property Rights

Most union organizing campaigns do not arise as the result of a carefully constructed strategy by a national union's organizing department. They tend, instead, to generate from within or around issues of mutual concern that employees see as unfair and/or threatening. The unfairness issues are associated with comparisons with other organizations or feelings that other classes of employees in the same organization are more favorably treated. The job security issue arises when employees believe that other issues in the organization are accorded more importance and/or the methods used to ration job opportunities are not those believed to be most appropriate by those seeking to organize.

The use of factors other than seniority, or the unilateral changing of customary criteria during periods of cutbacks can lead to union activity. Here the employer is quite likely to lose, because employees perceive that they cannot be worse off than they are now. Unionization is aimed at preserving what employees believe are job property rights. The probable future assault on "at will" employment reflects this view.

Employee Demographics

Evidence suggests that two employee characteristics are related to voting for unions in organizing campaigns. Women are generally reluctant to vote for representation and minorities are very likely to desire unionization. Both groups have generally been excluded from union leadership positions, but it is likely that minorities are more able to gain leadership positions at local levels than women. Age generally does not make a difference in voting behavior although the issues that different age groups find important have an influence on collective bargaining.

Locational and Plant Characteristics

Contrary to popular belief, employees in the South are no less likely to vote against unions in representation elections than in other parts of the country. Marc Sandver (1982), in an analysis of several years of NLRB election results finds that when plant size, industry, occupation, and internal plant demographics are held constant, no regional differences in election outcomes occur. In many of the newer Southern plants, opportunities for advancement are still relatively unknown to employees and comparisons with alternative employment within the area are still good. On the other hand, national comparisons unions might make with local situations for similar work may move Southern employees to demand representation.

When establishment characteristics are examined, it is clear that smaller units are more vulnerable to organization than those that are larger. The difficulty in identifying common issues and uniting coalitions for a union victory is greater in large units. Larger employers are also more sophisticated in combatting an organizing campaign.

Many of the establishment characteristics have subsequent impacts on the bargaining structure and outcomes of contract negotiations across organizations. These issues are explored in the next section.

CONTRACT NEGOTIATION

The outcomes for contract negotiations depend largely on the bargaining power of the two parties and how that power is put into operation in a particular negotiation. This section examines bargaining power, bargaining structure, and internal organization for bargaining as they relate to bargaining outcomes.

Bargaining Power

Neil Chamberlain and Donald Cullen (1971) have defined bargaining power for a party to collective bargaining as "my cost of disagreeing on your terms relative to my cost of agreeing on your terms. Thus an employer who may lose many customers if it is struck will be likely to agree to higher wage demands than does one who is the sole supplier of a product. Paradoxically, the sole supplier is also the least likely to be affected by the cost of a settlement because it can pass on the labor cost increase to its customers who have no acceptable substitute.

John Magenau and Dean Pruitt (1979) suggest that a bargainer would have high power if (1) agreement is less advantageous for the bargainer than it would be for the opponent, (2) more ways exist to satisfy the bargainer's needs than exist to satisfy the opponent, (3) more credible threats can be made by the bargainer than by the opponent, (4) maintenance of the bargaining relationship is more important to the opponent, and (5) the opponent is under heavier time pressure.

Within the framework, an example of condition 1 might be an organization with a large backlog of orders. The company might be more motivated to settle because large profits would be lost. Relatively little pressure might exist for the union, because it might reasonably believe that lost wages would be made up through overtime when the plant reopened. As an example of situation 2, a conglomerate organization or one that is struck in one of many plants producing a final product would have a distinct bargaining advantage. Situation 3 could involve beliefs about the likelihoods that threatened actions will be taken. This point underscores the impact that a previous strike may have value for future bargaining situations. In situation 4, unions would be expected to be more responsive because the bargaining process would be necessary to maintain the relationship. Finally, condition 5 relates to organizations dealing in perishable goods such as food producers and transportation companies (Christmas travel foregone due to strikes). Such companies are under greater pressure to settle.

Bargaining Structure

Bargaining structures have evolved to serve the separate and joint interests of labor and management. Each desires a structure that enhances its bargaining outcomes. Each also seeks a structure that will enable its particular goals to be accomplished. For the union, this means a structure that will allow it to meet its economic and membership goals, for management, a structure in which bargaining will have the least impact on its profits.

In the past, for both labor and management, this has meant the creation of bargaining units (quasi or actual) that included several employers and/or unions negotiating simultaneously. Pattern bargaining is a quasi multiple employer/union bargaining situation. For the union multiemployer bargaining has meant that all employers are covered by the same terms of an agreement, lessening internal divisiveness within the union by taking wages out of competition. Each employer may have less reason to replace labor with capital because each incurs the same hourly labor costs. Inasmuch as each employer simultaneously incurs a wage increase, these can be more easily passed on to the consumer.

Employers may also find multiemployer bargaining to their advantage in resisting union demands. Because the employers often constitute most of the relevant suppliers of a good or service in a particular market, the profits foregone from striking may not be lost, but merely postponed, as customers have no alternative purchase source.

These types of bargaining structures tend to break down where product markets are competitive. Two major situations where this breakdown has recently occurred are in basic industries producing durable goods and the contract construction industry. It is clear that producers of durable goods do not all have the same cost structure. Ages and sizes of plants affect productivity. In the past where these producers were not faced with substitutable products (e.g., aluminum and fiberglass for steel in auto production), or other sources not covered by their collective bargaining agreements (e.g., foreign producers), even inefficient producers could be profitable. In contract construction the inroads of open shop operations have restored competition to the market and reduced the craft unions' bargaining power.

Under the direction of Audrey Freedman (1979), the Conference Board conducted a survey of 668 American companies with at least some unionized employees. Most of the surveyed companies had multiplant operations and many had significant international operations.

The internal organization for bargaining in the surveyed companies tended to be rather centralized, even in situations where bargaining was done on a plant-by-plant basis.

BARGAINING OBJECTIVES

Many bargaining outcomes can be costed with a fair degree of accuracy, but a bargain made at a certain point may be difficult to rescind in the future, and the cost of the concession may be difficult to control. For example, health insurance benefits are usually specified in terms of coverage rather than a premium level that an employer will pay. The recent Chrysler negotiations made clear that employees are adamant in their refusal to give back health benefits they have previously negotiated. Even where the contribution is specified, the cost level may be difficult to determine. Because entitlements to pensions generally vest after a certain minimum level of service, estimates must be made of the proportion of employees for whom contributions are made that will ultimately accumulate pension rights. Costs are likely to escalate as a plant matures with accompanying low turnover among long service employees, even though benefit levels may not have been renegotiated.

Then the Conference Board examined considerations of organizations in setting economic targets, productivity or labor cost trends was ranked below such indicators as industry patterns, local labor market conditions, and expected company profits. Employers have a tendency to expect that comparability with other settlements of the level of local pay will be an important issue for unions.

Contract Administration

Problems in contract administration surface at all levels of management. But the primary tone is set during contract negotiations and the subsequent reactions of union and management practitioners to the contract terms. Freedman (1979) found company managements to feel generally that unions represented their employees well, tried to be cooperative with management, and generally operated in a nonhostile manner. Some differences did exist when employers emphasized union containment or avoidance as a major part of their labor relations strategy. Here existing unions were more likely to be seen as hostile.

TAKING A STRATEGIC STANCE TOWARD COLLECTIVE BARGAINING

If human resource management is to support organizational goals, then an analysis must be made of how various strategies will support their accomplishment. Just as marketing strategies identify markets and potential products, pricing and volume, human resource management must identify the needs of present and potential employees, their beliefs about how these needs should be secured, and how need accomplishment can be tied into organizational goal accomplishment.

It is unlikely that all employees at all levels of the organization care significantly about the goals of the organization. It is also unlikely that employees at all levels agree that similar methods should be used for determining employment outcomes. A variety of methods exists for their identification and achievement, and the choice of appropriate methods ought to be related to the accomplishment of the organization's overall goals.

Union Avoidance

It is fashionable for organizations to have "union avoidance" campaigns. Many of these are orchestrated from high levels in the organization and employee relations managers earn high marks from management in successfully resisting organizing attempts or in decertifying existing unions. There is a "macho, bias toward action" image involved in this approach, particularly when union avoidance is a goal, rather than a strategy of the organization. If it is a goal, then the battle is on ideological grounds rather than an attempt to improve the effectiveness of the organization.

Fred Foulkes has recently published an analysis of large companies that are either completely or substantially nonunion. He divides these companies into two categories: "philosophy-laden" and "doctrinaire." Philosophy-laden companies are not concerned with unions and do not have unions because they have implemented human resource management programs that provide employees with outcomes most often won by unions because employers believe that employees should have them. Doctrinaire companies provide these outcomes also, not because employees should have them, but because employees would unionize if they did not (Foulkes and Morgan, 1977).

If it is absolutely essential that interruptions in supply be avoided, and no substitute production facilities are available, then union avoidance may be an appropriate strategy. But it must be recognized that union avoidance is only possible if employment outcomes are in the type and magnitude that employees desire. If the union is seen as more instrumental for attaining these outcomes than the employer, then representation is likely. Further, a doctrinaire orientation will likely be identified by employees who may use the threat of organizing as a means for extracting gains from employers.

Contract Negotiations

Bargaining on new contracts is usually an event that takes place every two or three years. Thus it can be planned for and it influences greatly the operating conditions of the employer and the union for the next contract period.

Most often, employers view bargaining as a process to determine how much they lose and how much the unions gain; or, more recently, what concessions can be wrung from the union that will benefit the employer. However, a clearer examination of the goals of the union and the interests of union member workers, in general, should help the organization to concoct bargaining tactics to link gains for the employees with gains for the company. It is clear that job security, wages and benefits, and grievance procedures have been the three most important issues for organizing and bargaining.

Integrative bargaining might be used more often to tie the accomplishment of the goals of the employer with the achievement of union goals. For example, job security and retraining opportunities might be tied to modification of work rules and more modest wage increases. Integrative approaches can also more closely align the three major groups of organizational stakeholders and their goals. Consider, for example, the Scanlon Plan and its derivatives. For enhanced labor productivity, labor gains wage bonuses, profits for shareholders increase, and the basis for managerial profit-sharing improves. At Ford Motor in 1982, job security for presently employed workers was guaranteed in return for wage concessions.

Contract Administration

Joint problem-solving that addresses the goals of both parties and makes the union a legitimate partner in problem-solving can improve outcomes for both. Because the union is likely to need to create and resolve employee dissatisfaction to maintain its postion as the bargaining agent, a successful strategy must allow for apparent union victories on certain positions.

Managerial Decision-Making

Decision-making should take into account the variables recently explored by Freeman and others. Strategies toward unions should take into account issues such as the occupation of workers being considered, productivity differences, human capital differences, wage differences, the intended results of the operation of the organization's internal labor market, and profitability. A human resource management strategy ought to be one that best supports the goals of the organization. If the short-run ability to recruit qualified employees is the goal, evidence suggests unionized establishments will be more successful. On the other hand, if the employer wants to promote solely on the basis of ability, nonunion operations will be necessary to accomplish the goal; however, employees must perceive advancement as an important outcome and expect a reasonable chance of accomplishing promotions if performance is good. Employers should not waste a lot of effort to remain nonunion if they are not perceived as able to provide outcomes that employees desire. Plant age and workforce demographics should also influence employer staffing responses.

Unionization is frequently said to reflect poorly on the abilities of the management. It does not. The real abilities of management are reflected in their competitive record against other organizations in their industry.

CHAPTER
21

PRODUCTIVITY MANAGEMENT THROUGH QUALITY OF WORK LIFE PROGRAMS

Cortlandt Camman
Gerald E. Ledford, Jr.

Ten years ago Quality of Work Life (QWL) programs were virtually unknown in the United States. Today they represent a key element in the human resource management strategy of many major corporations. AT&T, General Motors, Ford, Westinghouse, Xerox, Honeywell, Bethlehem Steel, and Proctor & Gamble are just a few of the growing number of companies using this approach. About 1500 companies are using one version of QWL programs, the quality circle (*Business Week*, January 11, 1982). Moreover, QWL programs

Order of authorship is alphabetical. The authors of this chapter, together with Edward E. Lawler, III, and Stanley E. Seashore, are compiling a review study of eight union-management QWL projects conducted during the 1970's. The study, supported by the U.S. Department of Labor, will be published by Wiley as part of the Wiley-Interscience Series on Organizational Assessment and Change.

are no longer limited to isolated experiments in single plants. QWL is becoming not just a corporatewide strategy, but an industrywide strategy in autos, steel, and communications.

Our purpose in this chapter is to examine QWL programs as a human resource management strategy. We begin with a detailed answer to the question, "What is QWL and how is it related to other approaches to organizational change?" Then we examine some of the factors that account for the apparent trend toward greater use of QWL programs. Next we consider the issue of effectiveness of QWL programs and the major barriers to program success. Finally, we discuss an emerging set of issues that we believe will be vital for QWL programs in the future.

WHAT IS QUALITY OF WORK LIFE?

Varieties of QWL

The term Quality of Work Life has gained wide currency in recent years, but there is little consensus about the meaning of the term. There are at least three common uses of QWL. First, QWL refers to a *set of outcomes* for individual employees, including job satisfaction, opportunities for psychological growth, job security, good employee–supervisor relations, and low accident rates. This is perhaps the most common use of the term. QWL also refers to a *set of organizational practices* such as participative management, job enrichment, pay systems that reward good performance, employment guarantees, and safe working conditions. Finally, QWL often refers to a *type of organizational change* program. In this respect QWL programs may be viewed as a strategy of human resource management that employs QWL practices in order to improve QWL outcomes as well as to improve such organizational effectiveness measures as productivity and quality. In this chapter we are concerned primarily with QWL as a program of organizational change.

Figure 21.1 illustrates how the different meanings of QWL are related. The QWL program provides a framework for coordinating the introduction, maintenance, and improvement of QWL practices in order to produce improvements in QWL outcomes and organizational effectiveness. The program is usually composed of a variety of elements. It includes a set of objectives that the program is intended to accomplish, a set of principles and values that are to govern all QWL program activities, a strategy for implementing the program and a person or group responsible for overseeing and altering the strategy as required, and a set of resources that are dedicated to implementing the strategy within the organization.

Based on the objectives, principles, and strategies, the QWL program will introduce QWL practices into the organization as a means for accomplishing the objectives. The practices used in different QWL programs vary widely, but they include methods for solving problems such as quality circles and participative decision-making, methods for building cooperation among

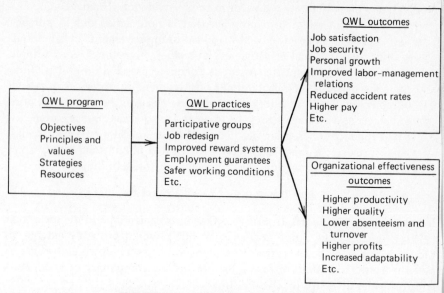

FIGURE 21.1.   Different meanings of QWL.

groups such as joint union–management QWL committees and cross-functional task forces, and methods for organizing work and altering working conditions such as job enrichment programs, the use of autonomous work groups, the introduction of flextime programs, and the development of worker–management safety committees. Other QWL practices involve methods for managing human resources such as the use of gain sharing plans, moving to an all-salaried workforce or to skill-based pay programs, the use of work group-based selection practices and realistic job previews, a priority placed on stability of employment in planning, and heavy investment in skill training—economic education and communication about organizational performance.

The introduction of QWL practices should, in turn, begin to transform the dynamics of the organization. If successful, the new practices will begin to provide employees with more opportunities to meet their needs and develop their capacities while at work, and will result in more effective problem-solving, more effective operations, and a more capable workforce within the organization. In organizations where the QWL program becomes the central element in the organization's human resources management strategy, the introduction and development of QWL practices can be a critical agent in transforming the organization's culture to embody and reinforce QWL principles and values.

If the pattern depicted in Figure 21.1 always presented organizational experience, there would not be so much confusion about the meaning of the term QWL. Unfortunately, QWL programs do not always lead to the adoption

of QWL practices. In many cases, for example, inadequate management support for QWL can result in a program that is not carried out in practice. Similarly, QWL practices do not always lead to improvements in QWL outcomes and organizational effectiveness outcomes. Sometimes, for example, new practices are implemented without adequate preparation and training, and the consequences are negative, not positive. Finally, some organizations try to implement QWL practices without being clear on the objectives, principles, values, and strategies they will use and, as a consequence, often discover that their QWL program has little coherence and less effect. In the last 10 years, however, a great deal has been learned about conducting QWL programs and the next sections describe some of these findings.

Key Elements of QWL Programs

If one were to ask people from five different organizations to describe their QWL programs, five different images of QWL would probably emerge. In fact, it would even be difficult to comprehend why such divergent programs had the same label. Both historical factors and the complexity of QWL contribute to the diversity of QWL efforts.

QWL in the United States represents the merger of a variety of historical traditions: some domestic, some from abroad. QWL programs have made extensive use of American organizational development (OD) technologies such as participative management, survey feedback, team building, productivity gain sharing, and job redesign (Cummings and Molloy, 1977; French and Bell, 1978). They have utilized the sociotechnical system's perspective, autonomous work group technology, and approaches associated with industrial democracy that have their origins in European work (Trist, 1981). The term QWL has been applied to cooperative union–management programs that supplement collective bargaining relationships, to the comprehensive human resource management strategy underlying the design of innovative new plants (Lawler, 1978), and, more recently, to management practices such as guaranteed employment and quality circles which have been popularized by studies of Japanese firms (Ouchi, 1980; Pascale and Athos, 1981).

Given the diversity of tradition and activities incorporated under the label, it is not surprising that the term QWL has varied and sometimes contradictory meanings. The purposes and principles that form the basis for the European developments of industrial democracy are different than those that underlie the management practices developed in Japan. As the practice of QWL has matured in America, however, a moderately consistent set of objectives, values, principles, and strategies have evolved that we believe will form the central components of such programs in the future.

Objectives of QWL

The primary objective of QWL programs is to create organizations that are both more effective in delivering products and services valued by American society and more rewarding and stimulating places for employees to work.

In most cases QWL programs are begun because organizational leaders believe that they can create changes in the way their organizations operate that will better mobilize the energy and creativity of their members to meet organizational objectives, while making the organization a more satisfying and interesting place to work at the same time. QWL programs provide a vehicle for identifying and implementing these changes.

PRINCIPLES AND VALUES

The guiding element of QWL programs is a set of principles and values that provide a framework for guiding actions and changes.

The needs and rights of all individual employees should be respected.
There are many conceptions of exactly which needs and rights should be respected. Two of the most comprehensive statements on this issue have been offered by Richard Walton, N. Herrick, and Michael Maccoby. Walton discusses eight value-based categories of criteria for analysing QWL at the individual level. These are adequate and fair compensation, immediate opportunity to use and develop human capacities, future opportunity for continued growth and security, social integration in the work organization, constitutionalism in the work organization, work and the total life space, and the social relevance of work life (Walton, 1973). Herrick and Maccoby propose the four principles of security, equity, democracy, and individuation. The first three overlap with Walton's criteria, whereas individuation means recognition that different types of people grow and develop in different ways (Herrick and Maccoby, 1975).

Organizations should be redesigned in ways that simultaneously benefit employees and other stakeholders (managers, clients, stockholders, and communities).
QWL programs operate at the intersection of interests between employees and other groups. The areas of common interest are greater than is often recognized, even though different groups desire different outcomes related to QWL. For example, productivity improvements resulting from QWL programs can be of benefit to various groups. Employees may benefit from greater job security and, if some kind of gain sharing is provided, higher pay. Managers and stockholders may benefit from higher profits and greater organizational competitiveness, clients may gain from lower prices, and communities from a more secure employment base. QWL programs are designed so that all affected groups will benefit or, at least, so that none will be significantly hurt. Underlying this principle is the practical belief that change is more easily instituted when all parties gain, and that creative problem-solving is more likely when people do not feel they will be hurt by the results.

A cooperative, participative approach to problem solving and decision making is desirable.
One of the most common themes in the QWL literature is that taking participation seriously can release an untapped reservoir of employee talent for problem-solving. Most organizations are designed in ways that stifle opportunities for employee involvement, due to overemphasis on managerial con-

trol. As a consequence, most organizations fail to fully benefit from employee creativity, skill, and energy.

Change strategies need to be holistic in nature.

QWL programs are generally based on the assumption that organizations are open systems. It is generally assumed that the parts of an organizational system are interrelated, and thus the behavior of one part affects and is affected by the behavior of other parts. As a consequence, a holistic perspective toward change is needed to improve the functioning of the total organization, as opposed to improving the functioning of one part at the expense of the whole, as well as to ensure that changes become deeply rooted in the organization. It is also assumed that organizations influence and are influenced by the world around them. Organizations are not manmade islands that can safely ignore demographic and social trends, changing markets, government pressure, and other external forces. The result is that change strategies need to take into account the nature of the organization's external environment as well as its internal characteristics.

Organizations and people are imperfect but capable of learning.

Both organizations and people have the capability and responsibility for continual improvement. Sustained improvement depends on learning. Organizational learning is enhanced by the use of valid information, the development of shared understanding, and the involvement of those who are affected by decisions in the decision-making process.

These values and principles contrast sharply with the ones operating in many organizations. QWL presents an image of the way people should relate to each other and to their organization. This image offers broad, implicit guidelines for QWL programs that are linked to an image of how more effective organizations would operate. In the QWL image, the levels of cooperation, tolerance, support, and responsibility are much higher than found in most organizations today.

A variety of conflicts are embedded in QWL values. Respecting the needs of all individuals may not be possible if one person's needs can only be satisfied at the expense of others. For example, allowing employees to influence decisions may reduce the influence and centrality of some managers. Organizational needs and individual needs can conflict with individual needs for greater financial security. The critical point here is that dilemmas exist, but that QWL values stress the importance of considering and reconciling the needs of all relevant parties. Creative solutions to problems are required for QWL programs to succeed, and one of the strengths of the programs is that they provide a structure within which such solutions can be developed.

QWL Strategies

The final element of a QWL program is the strategy for change and implementation of QWL practices. Typically, QWL programs have both micro and macro strategies. The micro strategy is a general approach for creating change whenever a new QWL practice is introduced. This strategy is usually built around the principles of participation and focuses on involving affected employees in making decisions. Typically, changes will be designed and implemented by groups that represent the employees who will be affected by the changes. These groups provide the mechanisms for translating QWL values into action. The groups are generally founded with a charter that defines the domain of their activities; they are briefed on the objectives and principles that underlie the QWL program, and they are trained in appropriate areas such as problem analysis, problem-solving, and communication.These groups then form a participative structure that serves as the vehicle for translating QWL values into action.

Each of the major historical traditions in the QWL movement has its own name for such participative structures. Organization development is concerned with team building, sociotechnical systems with autonomous work groups, and Japanese management with quality circles. Innovative new plants are likely to be designed around work teams or autonomous work groups. Union–management programs may use any of these terms or others such as employee involvement group and quality of work committees.

At one time, the various labels were used in fairly distinctive ways. For example, the term autonomous work groups suggested extensive decentralization of authority, quality circles implied the use of statistical quality control methods, and quality of work committees were associated with union–management efforts. Now, however, the labels are used almost interchangeably by practitioners and by the business press.

The macro strategy of a QWL program determines the limits of the program, the timing and focus of specific interventions, the resources to be used in the program, and structures and communication channels that will be used to provide the context for program activities. The literature on organizational change contains a great many prescriptions and discussions concerning strategic choices (Beckhard and Harris, 1977; Beer and Driscoll, 1977; Nadler, 1981). Here we outline some of the key strategic choices that tend to arise in QWL programs.

How Comprehensive Will the Intervention Be?

The QWL program may be introduced throughout the entire organization or limited to particular units such as a department, a plant, or a division. Program goals of improving employee QWL and organizational effectiveness may be stated broadly enough to permit a variety of local interpretations, or goals may be defined narrowly (such as improving job satisfaction and productivity). Implementation of new practices in some areas of organizational functioning (such as the pay system) may be declared off limits, or all areas of organizational functioning may be open to change. Many different changes may be introduced at once, or the project may concentrate on one change at a time.

To What Extent Will the Intervention Be "Bottom-UP" Rather Than "Top-Down?"

QWL programs tend to be *bottom-up,* meaning that proposals for specific changes typically originate at lower levels of the organizational hierarchy. Participative structures are created partly in order to make this possible. However, programs without active support and leadership from top management usually do not survive for long. Obtaining the right balance of inputs from all parts of the hierarchy is often difficult.

To What Extent Will Participative Structures Be Distinct from the Organization's Basic Authority Structure?

In some new plants, participative groups are so integral to the authority structure that the groups plan and allocate work, help set pay levels, hire new members, and perform many other management functions. More typically, participative groups are used to supplement the existing hierarchy. In such cases participative groups can be temporary or permanent, can exist at one or several levels of the hierarchy, and can represent one or several units (work groups, departments, etc.).

What Type of Consulting Assistance Will Be Used, If Any?

Most QWL programs require consulting assistance for such purposes as diagnosing organizational needs, helping establish participative groups, providing training, assessing program effectiveness, and offering an independent perspective on future program needs. External consultants, internal consultants (employees of the organization often based in a staff department), or some combination of the two may be used.

How Will the Program Evolve Over Time?

The strategic choices made in creating a QWL program need to be reexamined periodically if the change effort is to remain viable. There is probably a tendency for programs that are sustained over a period of years to move in the direction of greater comprehensiveness, increased bottom-up change, greater incorporation of QWL structures into the existing hierarchy of authority, and greater reliance on internal consultants. In short, successful QWL efforts eventually cease to be separate programs, and instead become an essential part of day-to-day management practice.

QWL programs thus have three primary components: a set of objectives, a set of values and principles, and a strategy for change. Programs with these characteristics clearly can take many different forms. Next we point to some apparent trends in the forms taken by the U.S. QWL programs, and suggest some reasons for these trends.

TRENDS IN QWL PROGRAMS

It is not easy to identify the trends that are developing in the QWL field. Summary information on what is being done and how it is changing is not readily available. The research literature and the business press provide only incomplete reports on QWL programs being conducted, but currently represent the best available sources for determining trends in the QWL area.

Our reading of the literature points to several important trends in QWL programs. First, QWL programs do not appear to be employing any fundamentally new or different practices than in the past. Such QWL practices as participative management, job redesign, and performance-based reward systems have been studied for many years. Second, there appear to be many more QWL programs than in the past. QWL is by no means the dominant mode of management in most organizations, yet the scope of new QWL efforts is impressive by past standards. Third, many QWL programs appear to be more comprehensive than in the past, both in terms of the number of interventions used in particular programs and in terms of the scope of change within particular organizations.

Prior to about 1970, most QWL-related interventions in the United States apparently involved the introduction of a specific practice of technique in a specific location. A wide variety of interventions were studied, including survey feedback, job redesign, new pay systems, participative management, methods of conflict resolution, and many others. However, the most common intervention was probably some type of training for a relatively small group of managers. As late as the early 1970s, the literature on organizational change was characterized as insufficiently organizational in focus and excessively preoccupied with the description of management training efforts (Kahn, 1974).

Relatively few reports, even among the classic studies of this period, were concerned with interventions affecting more than a few hundred people or more than a handful of work groups or departments.[1]

Moreover, few studies prior to 1970 were concerned with multiple or comprehensive interventions, or with interventions focused on a relatively large and autonomous organizational unit (such as a manufacturing plant rather than a department or work group). The exceptions to the rule were rare, and typically qualified as landmark studies. Some of the exceptional studies concerned the adoption of interventions that were complex and comprehensive in nature. For example, Scanlon plans include systemwide changes in the pay plan, creation of a hierarchy of participative groups, and a change in management philosophy.

Similarly, autonomous work groups designed according to sociotechnical

---

[1] This generalization applies to the well-known studies of Koch and French, Morse and Reimer, the survey feedback study by Mann, the Scanlon Plan studies by Lesieur and Pickett, and the job redesign studies by Trist and his colleagues.

system principles usually entail changes in hierarchical relationships, job designs, and pay systems. The best-known early studies were conducted in a coal mine and a textile mill. In some other cases separate but related changes in several areas of organizational functioning were introduced more or less simultaneously, as in the Glacier Metals plant and the Harwood pajama factory (Jacques, 1951; Marrow et al., 1967).

Since the early 1970s, there appears to have been an increase in the number of comprehensive interventions reported in the literature. QWL programs in many organizations have evolved beyond cautious, well-contained experiments into programs aimed at changing the mainstream of management practice. The Westinghouse case (following this chapter) nicely illustrates the point. Top managers at Westinghouse view the company's QWL effort as an essential part of their business strategy—something that will infuse a wide variety of new practices into the organization in order to help it remain competitive in world markets. More broadly, we illustrate the trend we are describing by examining two types of QWL programs: innovative new plant designs and cooperative union–management programs.

The first widely reported case of a plant designed from top to bottom around QWL values, assumptions, and practices was the General Foods dog food plant at Topeka. According to one estimate (Lawler, 1978), over 100 similar plants had been built within a few years. Some companies had built more than one such plant.

The number of cooperative union–management programs has also increased sharply. Between World War II (when joint committees were mandated by the federal government) and the early 1970s, such programs were rare. Within the last 10 years, the number and scope of cooperative efforts has increased so rapidly that *Business Week* concluded:

> Quietly, almost without notice, a new kind of industrial relations system with
> a fundamentally different way of managing people is taking shape in the U.S.
> [Business Week, May 11, 1981]

Cooperative union–management programs have been created in all kinds of organizations. One review study (noted earlier) of eight pioneering projects will examine efforts in industrial plants, a coal mine, a hospital, and government agencies. Union–management QWL programs are being established throughout entire companies and even throughout some industries. So far, companies and unions in the auto, steel, and communication industries have made the greatest strides.

For example, General Motors and Ford have embarked on companywide efforts with the United Auto Workers. Joint GM–UAW experiments began in two plants during the early 1970s; the projects expanded until over 100 plants had developed joint QWL programs (Carlson, 1978). Ford and the UAW began joint employee involvement efforts later, but diffusion was more rapid. Following an initial experiment in a single plant in 1979, joint projects were created in most Ford plants by late 1981. The 1982 collective bargaining contracts between the UAW and both Ford and GM formally endorsed QWL and established union–management QWL committees throughout the two companies.

It appears, then, that there are more QWL programs today than in the past and that these programs are often more comprehensive than in the past. Why is there an increased interest in QWL among U.S. organizations?

Factors Behind the Trends

QWL programs represent a significant change in the values, assumptions, structure, and human resource management strategy of most organizations. QWL programs require a major investment of organizational resources over a period of years in order to realize the benefits of the QWL approach. Yet the payoffs of QWL programs are uncertain, as we shall see. QWL programs are the type of innovation that require what one writer has termed a "reorientation" rather than a simple "variation" in existing practices (Normann, 1971). Why have so many organizations been willing to risk changes that imply fundamental realignments in the system without the promise of predictable benefits?

Chapter 22 suggests some of the answers to this question. Westinghouse executives rather suddenly discovered that their competitive position in the marketplace was in jeopardy. They realized that the company needed to meet the challenge not only from its traditional rival, General Electric, but also from European and especially Japanese companies. Without major improvements in productivity and product quality, the financial performance and perhaps the survival of the company were threatened.

The Westinghouse case points to the crucial importance of environmental pressures in encouraging the trend toward QWL programs. Organizations usually do not move toward a reorientation in existing practice unless there is a compelling reason to do so. If the organization seems to be operating effectively, the risks of fundamental change appear too great.

The economic, social, political, and cultural changes taking place in the United States provide ample stimuli for a management reorientation. Changes in the composition and values of the workforce, the dislocations caused by the energy crisis, declining productivity rates, underinvestment in new plants and equipment, the shift toward a service economy, the loss of markets to foreign competition are discussed elsewhere in this volume[2] All of these forces imply, directly or indirectly, the need for a different human resource management strategy.

It is no accident that those companies and industries facing the greatest environmental challenges are the ones most prone to adopt the QWL ap-

[2] See Chapter 1 for a general overview of environmental trends and all chapters in Part III for specific discussions of their impact on organizations.

proach. The catastrophic decline of the auto and steel industries in recent years has led management to question its most basic assumptions, and has encouraged unions in those industries to cooperate with management in order to save jobs. The deregulation of the telecommunications industry and the breakup of AT&T have promoted major union–management QWL programs throughout the Bell system.

In other cases companies in high growth markets such as electronics and computers have turned to the QWL approach as a means of remaining adaptive to continuously changing conditions and as a way of meeting foreign competition. IBM, Texas Instruments, and Hewlett-Packard have often been cited as examples of companies making extensive use of innovative human resource practices that are related to QWL. Digital Equipment Corporation, a leading manufacturer of small computers, is also one of the leaders in the QWL field. More recently, Xerox and Honeywell have begun to make extensive use of QWL practices.Honeywell alone has in operation over 450 quality circles, involving 5% of its workforce.[3]

Whether market conditions lead to a steep decline or rapid growth, organizations in uncertain environments need to be able to respond quickly to changing conditions. Without the support and assistance of the workforce, this can be a difficult or impossible task for management. QWL programs are seen as one method of developing employee commitment to needed organizational changes.

Market pressures are not the only environmental forces encouraging the adoption of QWL programs. The Japanese success in the auto, steel, computer, and electronics markets has encouraged managers in American companies in those industries to imitate Japanese management practices. There is no doubt that the popularity of the term quality circles arises from its association with the Japanese style of management. The increasing number of reported successes with QWL programs also encourages their diffusion. Another possible cause of the increased interest in QWL programs is related to changes in the nature of business school education. During the past 10 years, the field of organizational behavior has grown very rapidly. MBA students are much more likely than in the past to be exposed to concepts and cases related to QWL.

It appears, then, that a variety of external forces are encouraging organizations in the United States to adopt QWL programs. It is interesting, on the other hand, that the experience of successful QWL programs within a given organization may have less to do with the adoption and expansion of QWL efforts than the external factors previously described. Richard Walton (1975) describes a series of cases in which "success didn't take," meaning that successful innovations were not adopted elsewhere in the same company. Isolated innovative experiments can be tolerated without affecting the system as a

[3] For a case discussion of Honeywell's ADB division, see Chapter 16.

whole, unless serious environmental threats help overcome the inertia of traditional practices.

However, it is reasonable to ask whether QWL programs really can reduce the problems that spark the creation of such programs. Put in other words, do QWL programs contribute significantly to organizational effectiveness?

EFFECTIVENESS OF QWL PROGRAMS

There is no simple answer to the question of whether QWL programs contribute significantly to organizational effectiveness. Neither QWL programs nor any specific QWL practices represent a panacea for organizational ills. There is now a number of case studies of successful QWL programs in which both organizational effectiveness outcomes and QWL outcomes for employees were enhanced; many of these have been cited earlier in this chapter. It is equally clear that many QWL programs must be considered failures (Mirvis and Berg, 1977). And, of course, many cases are a mixture of success and failure. Some indicators of organizational effectiveness may show improvement, whereas others show declines; organizational effectiveness may increase, whereas QWL outcomes decrease or vice versa. In our review of eight union–management projects, none were unequivocal successes but most showed at least some positive benefits for employees, the organization, or both.

Although the pattern of results is not consistent, we believe that enough cases of successful change have accumulated to convince any open-minded skeptic that QWL programs can significantly enhance organizational effectiveness under certain conditions. One interesting question has a less certain answer, however. That is, what are the barriers that prevent some QWL programs from improving organizational effectiveness? Almost every review of the organizational change literature and every textbook considers this question, but there is little concensus about the answer. Here we select a few factors that appears to be most important.

Inappropriate Interventions

Not all interventions are capable of influencing organizational effectiveness. For example, improvements in work place amenities such as cafeterias and recreational facilities may contribute to employee satisfaction without affecting organizational effectiveness. Edward E. Lawler has proposed that an intervention must increase employee skills, employee motivation, and/or organizational coordination and communication in order to have a favorable impact on organizational effectiveness. Situational factors play an important role, because an intervention may affect one of the determinants of organizational effectiveness in one organization but not in another. For example, a high level of automation implies the need for different kinds of communication and coordination than lower levels of automation. A diagnosis is usually required to match QWL interventions to organizational needs and conditions.

Weak Interventions

Not all interventions are equally powerful. Changes in reward systems such as productivity gain-sharing plans, and changes in the design of jobs are probably inherently more capable of favorably influencing organizational effectiveness outcomes as well as QWL outcomes for employees than many other common interventions. However, it is often difficult to implement these changes through the participative, *bottom-up* change process of QWL programs. Powerful changes are also often complex and require specialized expertise for proper design. Moreover, workers are unlikely to have experienced such changes first-hand; this makes new, complex changes seem abstract and risky. Implementing such changes in a manner consistent with bottom-up change processes is important as a means of gaining employee commitment to the changes, but requires extra time, effort, and education.

Top Management Support

One of the most frequently repeated claims in the organizational change literature is that support from the top is needed in order to successfully implement organizational changes. We believe that this claim is well founded. Top managers have and often exercise the power to block specific changes or broad programs they view as undesirable. On the other hand, top-management endorsement of a change program can also go a long way toward reducing the resistance of lower-level managers to the effort.

This does not mean that top managers need to initiate specific changes, nor does it mean that they must be personally involved with the day-to-day developments in local QWL programs. Instead, active top-management support for the values, assumptions, participative structures, and change strategy of the overall QWL program needs to be demonstrated. This implies that top managers will encourage local experimentation with new work forms and support QWL over a long period of time.

Middle-Management Resistance

In general, the middle-management levels of the hierarchy tend to be the most resistant to QWL programs. There are at least these reasons for this resistance. First, middle managers often feel that QWL programs demand interpersonal, group, and leadership skills that they have never developed. In many organizations middle managers are less likely to possess such skills than either upper or lower-level managers. Second, middle managers often believe that QWL programs increase their workload without offering them any compensating benefits. Participative groups often place costly, time-consuming demands before middle managers. Yet these managers tend to perceive that QWL programs are intended primarily to benefit lower-level employees and upper-level managers.

On the other hand, middle-management resistance is sometimes based on a direct threat to job security. Many American organizations have added whole layers of management that may actually decrease organizational effectiveness by decreasing organizational flexibility and needlessly increasing monitoring and close control of subordinates. For example, Ford has 12 layers of management compared to Toyota's seven. Since certain types of QWL interventions, such as innovative new plant designs, have involved reductions in the number of management layers, it is not suprising that many middle managers fear QWL. It should be noted, however, that most QWL programs did not lead to the elimination of middle-management layers.

Inadequate Measurement of Organizational Effectiveness

If one purpose of QWL programs is to increase organizational effectiveness, it is clear that measures of organizational effectiveness are needed to assess whether the change effort is working. Some industrial organizations and most nonindustrial organizations lack meaningful measures of productivity, quality, and other performance indicators. It is difficult to know whether QWL programs in government agencies, banks, schools, hospitals, and retail chains have made any difference in organizational effectiveness. In turn, this means that it is difficult for management to learn from its experiences with QWL and it is hard to know how to make improvements in existing programs.

ISSUES FOR THE FUTURE

As QWL programs evolve and as organizations gain more experience and sophistication in using them, new issues are likely to arise that will prove critical to their success. Although it is impossible to know for certain what these issues will be, there are some that are already emerging as important.

Persistence of Changes

Some QWL programs have been sustained for long periods of time. For example, the General Motors–United Auto Workers QWL program has continued for a decade; the Scanlon plan and other changes at Donnelly Mirrors have been sustained since the 1950s; the Glacier Metals system of works councils, begun in the 1940s, continued at least into the 1970s. However, a good deal of evidence now suggests that QWL programs often fail to survive in the long run. In a review study of eight union–management projects, we found that none persisted as joint undertakings for more than a few years, and that only about one innovation per project survived.

The impermanence of many QWL programs is a cause for serious concern, especially in light of the historical faddishness of much management practice. Research on the factors that contribute to persistence is just beginning. One general conclusion seems appropriate, however. In order to persist, changes must become deeply rooted in the day-to-day functioning of the organization, and be anchored in multiple parts of the organization (belief systems, the reward system, socialization systems, etc.). This is why the development of comprehensive QWL programs is encouraging. It is simply more difficult to abandon a complex, large-scale intervention than one that is isolated and deviant from the dominant organizational culture.

Evolution of QWL Programs

QWL programs need to evolve over time for a variety of reasons. Organizational environments change, and QWL programs need to respond to such changes if they are to continue to make a contribution to organizational effectiveness. Much of the commitment to QWL programs arises from a kind of pioneering spirit that comes with meeting new challenges. Because individuals and organizations continually learn from experience, new challenges are always available. Even if old problems are solved, new ones will arise.

However, it is not always easy to maintain an entrepreneurial spirit. Continual change is stressful and unpleasant for many people. Program leaders may leave to take new positions, creating a leadership vacuum. As the change effort goes deeper, it may threaten some who previously were neutral or supportive of the change effort. Program participants may reach the limits of their knowledge and skill in creating change and may not have a clear idea of where to go next.

Sometimes, changes are adopted that have the effect of obstructing further change. For example, the adoption of a time-off bonus plan in an auto parts factory had such an effect. Employees who finished their work before the end of the shift could leave the plant, and they became preoccupied with leaving as quickly as possible and not with creating further changes. It even became difficult to hold meetings of program committees, because different people left the factory at different times.

It is often difficult for QWL programs to stand pat for a long period of time. Unless the program evolves, changes that have already been implemented may begin to fade away.

Relationship Between QWL and Collective Bargaining

In joint union–management QWL programs the relationship between cooperative efforts and adversarial bargaining roles often becomes a major source of tension for union officials and managers, particularly at the local level.

After years of distrust and political maneuvering, both sides may be tempted to use the QWL program as a bargaining chip. This can cause a cycle of on-again, off-again support for the change effort that reinforces the distrust felt on both sides.

In addition, the tension between adversarial and cooperative processes can create problems for both managers and union officials. These problems can become particularly serious for local union leaders. Union officers at the local level tend to have less formal education and training, less experience at working in decision-making groups, and less access to staff advice and support than their management counterparts. Thus union officials tend to feel that they are at a disadvantage as members of QWL committees. Union leaders also may fear that management's real motive for initiating the QWL program is to undermine or even eliminate the union; elected officials may also be highly sensitive to charges of "being in bed with management." Managers rarely face equivalent fears. We have seen several cases in which union officers have responded to these pressures by becoming so zealous about protecting the contract and their own political position that it became difficult to adopt changes serving the interests of both management and union members.

Despite these problems, there are compelling reasons for unions to co-operate with management in QWL programs. Joint QWL efforts can provide a service for the mass of union members who want a greater voice in decision-making at work, but who often do not become involved in grievance and disciplinary proceedings. Union officers can take credit for helping to make the QWL program work, benefitting union members who do not become involved in grievance and disciplinary proceedings. Union officers can take credit for helping to make QWL program work. QWL programs are also appealing to union members in declining basic industries. These workers realize that the protection of wage and employment levels against further erosion depends on the return of their companies to fiscal health; QWL programs offer them an opportunity to contribute actively to solving organizational problems. Finally, the steady postwar decline in the percentage of unionized employees in the workforce has led some union leaders to rethink the union mission. The ability of unions to adopt cooperative approaches when possible and adversarial approaches when necessary may be attractive to some unorganized workers. We believe that these forces will continue to promote union involvement in joint projects during the next few years.

There is room for speculation about the future in the following areas. First, will unions adopt some type of QWL program internally in the future? Unions obviously face many of the same environmental demands that have led many companies to adopt QWL programs, and unions have by now received considerable exposure to QWL through joint union–management efforts. However, we know of no major union that has undertaken the task of developing itself as an organization by means of a QWL program. We would not be surprised if the United Auto Workers, the United Steel Workers, or the Comunications Workers broke new ground in this area. Purposes of an internal QWL program might be, for example, to develop local leadership skills, to improve the level of participation in local union affairs, and to improve communication and support service flows between the international level and union locals.

Second, will joint projects in the basic industries survive an economic recovery? A recovery would remove one of the major factors promoting joint programs today. Some joint efforts doubtless would remain; the GM–UAW program has survived two periods of recovery and two recessions, for example. In other cases we suspect that the persistence of joint efforts will depend upon how quickly the programs are expanded and on how deeply rooted such programs become.

QWL in the Service Sector and the Public Sector

The most highly publicized QWL efforts have occured in manufacturing. This pattern is understandable, because industry can more easily afford the investment needed to initiate QWL efforts than can most companies in the service sector and can act more quickly to adopt innovations than can government agencies. In recent years, however, QWL programs have extended to the nonmanufacturing sectors. Among the types of organizations that have adopted QWL programs are schools, hospitals, federal agencies, local governments, retail stores, hotels, and financial institutions. Although QWL programs are not as prevalent in these kinds of organizations as in some industries, the programs that have been adopted resemble those in industry. There has not yet been a great deal of research on QWL in service and public organizations, so it is difficult to know how QWL programs in such institutions need to differ from those in industry.

Effects of a Changing Workforce

There is considerable evidence of demographic and social change in the labor force. Today's employees are better educated, less frightened of authority, and more willing to sacrifice material gain for self-fulfillment and the pleasures of nonwork. More women are working than ever before. The maturing of the baby-boom generation, together with a sluggish economy, has reduced opportunities for career advancement for a large segment of the workforce.

These changes are likely to encourage the further development of QWL programs. Organizations seeking to tap the potential of their employees will not succeed as well as in the past by the use of threats, intimidation, and monetary inducements alone. Instead, managers are finding that QWL programs can provide positive incentives for employees to contribute their talents to their organizations. The QWL approach is consistent with the values of new workers; it permits employees to learn, grow, accept responsibility, and develop new skills in the course of helping to solve workplace problems.

Too Much Productivity?

As productivity increases in the economy as a whole, fewer workers are needed to do the same amount of work. Even without productivity improvements attributable to QWL programs, robots in factories and office automation threaten hundreds of thousands of jobs. It may be that workers will resist QWL changes leading to productivity improvement if they fear the loss of additional jobs. The magnitude of the threat is illustrated by a comparison in the auto industry:

> In 1980 Ford Europe, one of the most efficient western automakers, produced 1,500,000 cars and trucks with 140,000 total employees. Mazda produced 1,100,000 with only 22,000 total employees. [Miles and Rosenberg, 1982]

Indeed, auto workers in several U.S. plants we have visited already avoid productivity improvement interventions in their union–management QWL programs. Instead, these programs have focused on quality improvement, which the auto workers view as the key to increasing product demand and hence employment levels.

Management efforts to improve productivity will doubtless continue and meeting the challenge of unemployment induced by productivity increases will be important for the future of QWL programs in the United States. If employees feel that they are being asked to help eliminate their own jobs at a time when the alternatives are meager, employees may reject QWL efforts. The need for productivity improvement in American industry is real; so is the need for economic security among employees. Finding a way out of this dilemma will not be an easy task.

CONCLUSION: WHAT'S NEW ABOUT QWL PROGRAMS?

The Quality of Work Life (QWL) movement has entered an exciting and important phase. This phase has little to do with the discovery of a basically new approach to organizational change. Most of the tools and techniques used in QWL programs have been used for a decade or more. What is new is the commitment to use these methods in an integrated strategy designed to produce substantial and fundamental change in the way American organizations function. Coupled with the rapid spread of QWL programs, this means that QWL may become one of the fundamental determinants of human resource strategies in American organizations. The critical question now is whether QWL concepts will prove to be just another fad or will stand the test of time and provide the basis for developing more effective, and satisfying, methods of organizing.

CHAPTER

22

PRODUCTIVITY AND QUALITY IMPROVEMENT: THE WESTINGHOUSE STORY

Chester C. Borucki
Glenn D. Childs

Productivity and quality improvement have become a top priority concern for the majority of American industries. This is evidenced by the sharp increase in the number of quality Control workshops, seminars, and news media articles focusing on such topics as quality circles, zero-defects methodologies, acceptable quality levels, and statistical quality control. One corporation well-entrenched at the cutting edge of advances in this area is the Westinghouse Electric Corporation. To illustrate its commitment to this effort, every Westinghouse Management Council meeting since 1979 has had, as its principal theme, productivity and quality improvement. This case is designed to outline the key events and reasons leading to Westinghouse's ambitious pursuit of

The authors wish to thank Mr. Thomas Murrin, President, Public Systems Co. and Mr. Jack Springer, Director of Human Resources, Construction Group, for their valuable contribution, and Dr. Noel M. Tichy of the University of Michigan and Dr. Charles Fombrun of The Wharton School for their assistance and support in the preparation of this case.

productivity and quality improvement and to disclose the specific stategies and programs that have been developed to fulfill these objectives.

The case is presented in the following manner. The first section provides a brief overview of key events in Westinghouse history as background. The second section focuses on the evolution of the corporation's productivity and quality improvement program. The next section outlines the specific strategies and techniques Westinghouse has incorporated to attain its productivity and quality improvement objectives. Then we discuss human resources interaction with productivity and quality improvement programs. The last section summarizes the progress that has been made to date incorporating this program into operations and reflects on strategies and directions for the future.

KEY EVENTS IN WESTINGHOUSE HISTORY

The original company was formed around the genius of George Westinghouse, perhaps one of the most prolific of early inventors. For virtually all of the early decades of its existence, the Westinghouse Corporation was felt by its employees and judged by many others to be the second largest supplier of electrical apparatus in the world, following General Electric (GE). Professional and technological competition existed between Mr. Westinghouse and Mr. Thomas A. Edison who was associated with GE, from the very beginning. At that point, it revolved around the advantages and disadvantages of alternating versus direct current in commercial applications. The battle was won by Westinghouse and was manifest when the company was chosen to use its pioneering alternating current system to light the World's Fair of that period. What is paradoxical is that GE went on to become the larger of the two companies.

Westinghouse made a decisive move, a few decades later, to establish itself early on as a leader in radio broadcasting. The first successful radiocast of a commerical program, the election of Warren Harding in 1920, occurred from the Westinghouse station KDKA in Pittsburgh. This event served as the genesis of the Westinghouse Broadcasting and Cable, Inc. Group W, which for many decades had been next to CBS, NBC, and ABC as the most successful independent network. Ironically, this phenomenon repeated itself in another form 32 years later as Westinghouse became the first to telecast a political campaign, the presidential election of Dwight Eisenhower in 1952.

Early in the 1950s, Westinghouse got involved in a variety of businesses, an activity that was to repeat itself many times over the next two decades. Many of these businesses represented a significant departure from the classical apparatus business that had been the mainstay of corporate operations for over a half-century. Pioneering advancements were made in several technological areas including the design of steam turbines for the electrical utilities industry, jet research and development, and X-ray technology. Atomic research and development led to the design and manufacture of power plants for the USS Nautilus and virtually all of the Polaris-class submarines, scores of Navy cruise ships, as well as for land-based nuclear power generation facilities. The corporation's achievements during this period were exemplary. At one point in the early 1960s it was estimated that Westinghouse owned over 7000 active U.S. patents and over 9500 active foreign patents, a testimony to the extent of its inventiveness and of its involvement in research and development.

Nevertheless, the corporation suffered smartly from several events and ill-fated ventures that occurred during this period, all of which Westinghouse has been able to recover from successfully. Strikes by two unions against the corporation started in October of 1954 and continued well into the Spring of 1955, the impact of which decreased earnings by nearly 50% of the previous year's level. A satisfactory resolution was finally achieved with all but 6% of the striking employees returning to work. Another series of strikes occurred in 1963, shutting down 10 plants from a few days to 11 weeks. Again, they were successfully resolved with significant changes made in problem areas.

In the mid 1960s, Chairman Donald C. Burnham began to alter the corporate business portfolio by consciously and conspicuously launching a variety of initiatives aimed at diversification. Largely in response to President Johnson's pleas to get industry more involved in using its capabilities to help solve great social needs, the corporation ventured into low-income housing, and to a lesser extent into health care delivery systems and law enforcement. Some diversification initiatives were for more conventional business purposes. These included underseas exploration, water desalinization projects, direct mail-order businesses, a record club operation, and a French elevator company.

Though the diversification program, which extended into the early 1970s, was well-intentioned, some very serious problems resulted from this effort. The corporation suffered a precipitous drop in earnings due to losses sustained in its major appliance business, record club operations, water quality control operations, and in its French elevator subsidiary. These financial problems were further aggravated by a recession and strong inflationary pressures that pushed up the costs of raw materials.

On February 1, 1975, when Robert Kirby became Chairman and Chief Executive Officer of the corporation, he assumed leadership of a diversified organization encumbered with difficulties. He moved cautiously, initiating decisive corrective measures to change the course that Westinghouse had been pursuing. Kirby continued to trim losing operations from the business portfolio. By means of divestitures and closings, several poorly performing operations were disposed of by the end of 1975.

Rather significantly, Kirby brought to office a somewhat radical change in attitude and, in some cases, procedures. It became routine that the entire Management Committee would review in detail and collectively evaluate all new major initiatives of the corporation. Though previously there were some apparently rigorous, routine reviews of these proposals, the top Management Committee in totality was not involved in some of those decisions.

This fundamental change, though seemingly trivial, tended to unify the half-dozen top people in the corporation. Collectively, from that point on, they decided on acquisitions and divestitures, on whether to expand or contract businesses, and on the selection of general managers for business units in each group. The overall result was a "corporatizing" in a much more routine fashion than the way the organization was acting, a departure from the less participative decision-making that occurred during the Burnham administration. This mechanism has prevailed since 1975 and remains an essential element in Westinghouse's strategic planning and implementation processes.

Just as Westinghouse was making significant progress in shaping its business portfolio, an incident occurred in 1975 that again dealt a serious blow to the corporation's earnings, the impact of which is finally nearing closure. The corporation was enjoined in a series of lawsuits involving the supply of uranium of 17 public utility customers. The original contract called for the delivery of approximately 80 million pounds of uranium over a 20-year period at an average price of $9.50 per pound. Price escalations were based on industrial indices but were not keyed to changes in the market price of uranium. Unexpectedly, the market price had shot up to over four times that price. Litigations resulted from the corporation's notification to its customers that performance of the contract was excused under the legal directive of commerical impracticality. The potential financial impact of the proceedings was sizable. Experts contended that ultimate costs to the corporation would be several hundred million dollars.

Exercising jurisprudence, Westinghouse countersued, with positive results against 29 uranium producers who participated in an illegal cartel. To date the corporation has legally realized approximately $85 million from these lawsuits and has also garnered entitlements to purchase specific amounts of uranium at favorable prices in a further movement towards resolution of this issue.

Under Chairman Kirby's direction, the corporation continued to grow consistently in profitability. The acquisition of Teleprompter Corp. in 1981 strategically positioned Westinghouse as a leader in the burgeoning cable television industry and also symbolized a cautious, evaluative approach to acquisitions not well practiced a decade earlier.

Westinghouse Today

Westinghouse Electric Corporation is currently organized into four operating units and an international organization. The units are: industry products, public systems, power systems, and broadcasting and cable. Each unit is further divided into a number of strategic business units. Though the major thrust of corporate operations is in the manufacture, sales, and service of electrical equipment and components, the businesses are comprised of an array of products and services many of which are unrelated to electrical manufacturing. These include broadcasting and cable operations, community development, bottling and distribution of beverage products, and open office furniture systems. In 1981 the corporation's net earnings were $438 million on sales of $9.4 billion. Approximately 27% of total sales came from exports and goods manufactured outside of the United States. Westinghouse currently ranks thirty-fourth on the *Fortune* roster of U.S. industrial corporations.

THE EVOLUTION OF WESTINGHOUSE'S PRODUCTIVITY AND QUALITY IMPROVEMENT PROGRAM

The productivity and quality improvement strategy that was formulated and implemented in the Public Systems Company well characterizes the corporation's involvement and advancements in this area. Public Systems, under President Thomas J. Murrin, achieved a sales increase of 5.1% to $2.7 billion in 1982. This substantial gain, according to senior executives, is largely attributable to Productivity and Quality Improvement (PI) efforts.

Tom Murrin is a striking figure. A former Vince Lombardi-trained Fordham football player, Murrin gained respect and recognition in Westinghouse by successfully turning around Public Systems. Once the corporate "problem child," Public Systems was in 1975 an unpromising collection of defense electronics, soft drink bottling, real estate, and other operations that detracted from corporate profitability. Under Murrin's leadership, Public Systems has become the fastest growing company in the corporate fold. It was Murrin who was selected by Vice President and Chief Operating Officer Douglas Danforth prior to the May, 1979 Management Council meeting to chair the Productivity Committee.

From Murrin's perspective, the ground was broken for PI efforts a few years earlier. A greater awareness of radical changes that were occuring in American and worldwide markets was developing during the executive meetings of that period. The recession during the latter part of the 1970s raised concern about inflation, interest rates, and worldwide competition. Discussions were held within the executive group on how Westinghouse could continue its improved performance given these phenomena.

One important realization was that the marketplace was becoming *globalized*. Aggregations of countries, including the European Economic Community, Central and South America, and the Pacific Basin represented markets that began to compete in size and significance with the American market. Markets were no longer strictly American and imposed on foreign countries or even foreign and imposed on the United States. The ramifications were just as significant for the Westinghouse kinds of products as they were for the automobile industry.

A more startling discovery was the realization that Westinghouse was no longer number two in the world, a rank it had believed it occupied since 1886. Hitachi in Japan and Siemens in Germany appeared larger in total sales, with a number of other companies competing strongly with many of the product lines and services that the corporation offered. In Tom Murrin's words:

> We met many, many times with the Management Committee pondering these things and decided, in effect, that what we had to do basically was a much better job than we had been doing with the resources we controlled. Top management felt that it ought to be taken on as an initiative of the *highest priority,* and the mechanism for doing that was the presentation made to that year's Management Council meeting in May, 1979.

One outcome of the Management Council meeting was the formation of a Corporate Committee on Productivity, with Tom Murrin appointed as Chairman. Members of the Committee were top-ranking representatives from each of the companies and from key staff units. The Committee, endowed with substantial funding and strong support from senior management, proceeded with its mission.

Murrin accepted the PI assignment with typical zeal. A dozen subcommittees were formed on topics such as quality circles, value engineering, robotics, computer-aided information and control systems, and new plant programs. Another subcommittee was formed to help business units in the development of their own PI program.

Throughout the remainder of 1979, Murrin, accompanied by Committee members, undertook a worldwide analysis of competition and states-of-the-art in productivity improvement.

Productivity Improvement—The First Year Activities and Discoveries

After months of committee activities within Westinghouse and of studies of competition worldwide, Murrin convened senior management to report his discoveries, accomplishments, and action plans. Excerpts of his address highlighting key findings follow:

> "During the past year I was able to observe first-hand how Productivity Improvement was developing across the Corporation. I have a good feeling, a feeling that we are embarking on a decade of determination in PI. The $22 million we have committed to 84 PI projects has resulted in the organization of more than 600 Quality Circles in our plants, with more than three being added every day. Our Robotics Subcommittee is targeting 150 robots for on-line activity by the end of next year. And our Value Engineering Subcommittee is promoting techniques which may reduce costs by 30% or more. You are to be congratulated for your efforts.

At this point in his address, Murrin's tone turned chilly:

> Frankly, gentlemen, my perspective of our competitive strength is tempered with caution and concern after gazing about the boardrooms, offices, laboratories, and factories of our competition over the past year. From Fairfield to

Dallas, to Munich, to Tokyo, and around much of the rest of the world, what I see is both exciting and alarming. In particular, findings in Japan scare the hell out of me.

On the homefront, GE posted a 50% gain in their production rate from 1979–1980, increasing productivity from 2.5–6%. Their program is supported by computer-aided design, robotics, microelectronics, and advances in new plastics and materials.

Texas Instruments PI is running at about a 9.5% annual level. TI has one module of computing power per exempt employee and furthermore possesses a worldwide electronic mail and communications network capable of handling 25,000 messages daily at the extremely economical cost of four cents/message. TI projects savings alone from electronic mail for fiscal 1980 to be $31.3 million, with the largest savings of $13.6 million coming from the Management and Administration area.

Murrin highlighted advancements in Europe and Korea:

Siemens in West Germany invested $140 million in manufacturing technology in 1979, providing for a 50% increase in manufacturing process, engineering, and R&D expenditures. Siemens also uses electronic mail and may eventually become a major supplier in office automation in the 1980s. The Dutch, French, and Italians are also forging ahead in electronics and robots.

In South Korea, the Hyundai shipyard contracted for the delivery of four supertankers even before ground was broken for the shipyard. By the second year, the shipyard facilities were completed and the first supertanker was delivered on time in the third year.

The productivity results in Japan led to extensive studies of the Japanese practices. Committee members concurred that the Japanese serve as the world's current benchmark. By stressing high quality and masterfully integrating technology, people, and value engineering—plus other initiatives—Japanese industry has achieved an incomparable rate of productivity.

Toyota in 1980 produced 2700 cars per day utilizing 1.6 work days of assembly labor per car compared to Germany's 2.7 and America's 3.8 work days. Toyota had 220 robots in operation with 700 more scheduled to be added over the following three years. Robots complement the *KANBAN* system, the Japanese method of keeping inventories at their lowest possible levels by tight management of component flow. This has effectively reduced work in process by 85% with capacity built in for responding quickly to consumer volume and mix desires.

Murrin also discovered these results in an analysis of Japanese electronics and computer productivity:

1. Fujitsu, a leading computer outfit, predicts it will be the world leader in the industry by the end of the 1980s. Its overseas sales have increased by 36% accompanied by 20% PI.

2. Japanese printed circuit board production (PCB) has a productivity rate several time greater, in terms of area of board per month per worker, than Westinghouse's Baltimore facility.

Labeling typical U.S. productivity gains of 2–3% in industry as "inadequate" compared to the average 10% in Japan, Murrin cited specific reasons why Westinghouses sights could and should be higher:

1. Sony's plant outside San Diego achieved a worldwide record of 200 days of assembly line productivity without a major defect, all accomplished with a 100% U.S. labor force.

2. Matsushita recently took over a Motorola plant in Chicago, and with the same direct labor force minus 50% of the white-collar staff, *doubled* the daily rate of Quasar sets from 1000 to 2000 units. They also reduced the in-plant rejection rate from 60% to 3.8%, with a foreseeable target of 1%. Annual warranty costs reduced from a painful $17 million to $3 million.

According to Murrin:

The major element responsible for these tremendous improvements was a $20 million investment in simple mechanization aids. Matsushita gave their employees *good tools.* They planned and analyzed processes and equipment extremely carefully. Any equipment newly installed was reexamined thoroughly to make sure it was being used optimally. One hundred percent incoming inspection for components, parts, and materials was enforced, stressing *defect prevention* versus the American approach of *defect detection.* Most of their suppliers readily responded to changes in quality philosophy. The process engineers work hand-in-hand with design engineers with open lines of communication and trained from the top down through the rank and file, promoting quality awareness and an excellent employee atmosphere.

Committee members came to realize that many of the engineering concepts and practices that the Japanese employed were somewhat different than those used at home. In one instance, the Japanese engineers asked their American counterparts what their *composite yield* was. Murrin's summary of the instance is as follows:

Consider the manufacturing process involved in producing a computer terminal. If you have an array of operations that are conducted in the manufacturing process and you start with 100 units, the Japanese asked us, "How many of those 100 units go through all of these manufacturing operations perfectly, the first time?"

Not having measured this previously, we couldn't really respond. So we asked them, "Well, how many of yours do?" And they said it varies; 97.98, or 99 are representative *composite yields* of such units in a sophisticated commercial electronics plant.

As incredible as it sounds, we never measured out output in this manner. Though all these components of materials, labor hours, time, money, and space were figured into our American industrial engineering standards, we never thought to consider our *composite yield.* Studies in our plants revealed that in many of our larger operations, this figure was as low as 15%. This meant reworking, sometimes several times, the other 85% of these units.

In essence, the Japanese approached industrial engineering from a conceptually different point of view, and with astounding results, than what has been commonly practiced by American engineers for decades.

Development of Action Plans for Productivity Improvement

As a result of his explorations, discoveries, and input from committee members, Murrin formed his plan of what Westinghouse must consider:

1. Raise sights, higher PI goals can be achieved.
2. Stress quality. The Profit Impact Marketing Strategy (PIMS) shows that companies with higher quality products than their competitors are the most profitable in all business climates, even in a recession.
3. Build the Westinghouse PI program around the four components that are the secret to Japanese success:
   A. FACILITIES
      1. We must provide our employees with the best tools and equipment possible.
      2. We must emulate the best, studying the state-of-the-art here at home and around the world.
      3. We will form 12 PI subcommittees mandated to carry out this task.
      4. We will invest $2 billion in plant and equipment over the next five years to improve productivity as much as possible.
   B. MATERIALS
      1. The Japanese almost universally practice 100% incoming inspection.
      2. We must stress *defect prevention* as opposed to *defect detection.* It costs more to replace failed parts than to pay a little more for reliable ones.
      3. Westinghouse is currently sent *second line* products because they meet our Acceptable Quality Levels (AQL). Japan gets *first line.* We must upgrade our standards.
      4. We measure defects per thousand, Japan measures defects per million.
   C. TRAINING
      1. Japanese employees are trained for weeks. Each employee is taught why as well as how.
      2. The importance of quality is stressed in training.

    3. Japanese quote: "We train people, people will grow, and the company will grow with the growth of its people."

  D. METHODS

    1. Have a close liason between engineering, manufacturing, and marketing.

    2. "Value Engineering" should be a way of life in our business disciplines.

With the framework of his action plan outlined, Murrin delivered the following mandate to Senior Management Staff:

The Management Committee implemented the seed fund concept so that initial PI efforts would not be restricted by established budget constraints.

You are expected to include productivity programs in your profit and strategic plans, You should start, if you haven't already, to:

1. Describe your productivity programs.
2. Justify the necessary funding and other resources.
3. Incorporate these into all of your future profit and strategic plans.

You must be challenged and hopefully motivated by our recent findings of competitive capabilities and trends. Your mission is to:

1. Raise your PI objectives to at least 6.1% per year.
2. Expand substantially the technology, people, and value engineering efforts in your unit.
3. Greatly increase emphasis on top quality by applying proven Japanese techniques.

Though headquarters help will be available for the short term, the great majority of your funds must be justified in your respective profit and strategic plans. Your future success will increasingly depend on your PI and operating margin performance.

Thus was launched the Productivity Improvement initiative within the Westinghouse Electric Corporation.

WESTINGHOUSE PRODUCTIVITY AND IMPROVEMENT STRATEGIES

1980 was a very busy year for Westinghouse. A flurry of activity occured throughout the corporation as mechanisms were put in place to support the fundamental strategies formulated to drive the PI program. This section describes the support mechanisms and the six key strategies that form the nucleus of Westinghouse's PI effort.

In the first move of its kind ever witnessed in a U.S. corporation, West-inghouse established an executive position of Vice President of Corporate Productivity and Quality. L. Jerry Hudspeth was appointed to this position and assigned the responsibility of implementing the action plan developed by T. J. Murrin's Corporate Committee on PI.

In a second unprecedented move, Westinghouse created a Productivity and Quality Center devoted exclusively to improving productivity and quality. The center is currently staffed with approximately 300 full-time employees who are responsible for coordinating and supporting the programs at the various companies, with concentration on both blue and white-collar pro-ductivity. Also located at the center is a manufacturing technology devel-opment laboratory.

A third significant support mechanism is the Productivity Committee. It continues to oversee and administer a seed fund, now split into two separate funds, Productivity and Quality, which together totaled $60 million for the last 3½ years. Originally established to help the business units get their own productivity programs off the ground, the seed funds are now reserved for sponsoring high-risk, high-payoff projects that have potential applications in a number of corporate locations. To stimulate participation and to facilitate the process, seed fund money is available with a minimum of paperwork.

The Corporate Strategies

In mapping out the strategies that drive the PI program, the Westinghouse Management committee focused its short-range emphasis on people, tech-nology, and quality. The "strategy behind the strategies" was to begin seeding and implementing the technology which would acclerate PI momentum into the next decade. Technology, it was recognized, costs money and requires human resources in order to be implemented effectively. In contrast, people and quality programs require relatively little capital yet can potentially yield substantial returns. This positive cash flow can then be put to use in the research and development of new technologies within the corporation and in the acquisition of proven technologies developed elsewhere. Of the six fundamental strategies, the first three are coequal. They are identified and described as follows:

Improving the Management and Motivation of People

The emphasis in this first strategy is on the participative management ap-proach—getting employees involved in the identification and solution of problems. The philosophy behind this strategy, as described by Murrin is:

> Our greatest resource is our people. Treat them with respect, challenge their intelligence, appeal to their innate sense of quality—in short, encourage their full participation in your business and Productivity and Quality Improvement will likely result.

One successful instrument that Westinghouse has employed for encouraging employee involvement is the quality circle concept. "Rediscovered from the Japanese," over 1600 quality circles exist at over 200 locations involving approximately 10% or 16,000 members of the labor force with the number growing daily. Westinghouse has expanded the QC concept to include white-collar workers as well, an advancement executives feel transcends the traditional Japanese focus on the blue-collar level.

A typical Westinghouse Quality Circle consists of from 4 to 10 employees who meet one hour a week on company time to discuss ways to improve performance in their departments. Westinghouse executives believe that this minimal investment of time has paid off handsomely in literally millions of dollars of savings. But more than just savings, it has underscored the need to think and build quality products and provide quality services across the corporation.

The Introduction of New Technology in Both the Office and Factory

This strategy concentrates on providing the right tools to do the job right. A significant portion of the PI program is devoted to introducing the right tools—and best available technology—to help both white and blue-collar employees perform their job more efficiently.

Although Westinghouse is primarily a manufacturing corporation, over 50% of the employees hold white-collar positions. In Public Systems, most managers have their own personal computer and electronic mail terminal. At most locations throughout the company, telephone dictation, computer graphics, and video teleconferencing have also been installed. Most professional work stations have a standard CRT terminal or a personal computer connected to a coax data cable for linkage to corporate databases and outside vendors. Many managers and professional employees now have CRTs at home, enabling them to communicate with the data systems at the office.

Westinghouse, whenever practical, is redesigning administrative office space around the open office concept. Not only does this make more efficient use of available space, it also has been demonstrated to improve interoffice communication and to enhance worker productivity.

The corporation has also developed an extensive library of videotapes—over 200 and growing—that are used frequently for training and communication purposes. A videotape is made quarterly incorporating advancements and developments that have occurred throughout the corporation and is circulated throughout the four companies and viewed by their respective business units.

In the factory a variety of automation technologies is being introduced. The corporation is working with Carnegie-Mellon University's Robotics Institute on research work with "seeing," "feeling," and "thinking" robots.

At the Corporate Productivity and Quality Center, the advanced manufacturing group is working under a grant from the National Science Foundation on an adaptable and programmable robotic assembly system that will be capable of assembling over 400 different styles of electric motors.

Murrin believes that the key challenge facing American industry is to gain greater acceptance of robots among the rank and file and management:

> We have to get *beyond* the token robot stage and employ more robots throughout our workforce—and free our employees up to perform more intelligent work. This again, requires a commitment on the part of management and a basic attitudinal change on the part of employees.

Westinghouse also is designing what is hailed as the "Electronics Factory of The Future," under a contract with the Air Force. Expectations include a 10-to-1 reduction in production time for the manufacture of printed circuit boards, a 100% improvement in quality yield, and a 5-to-1 reduction in required manufacturing space.

Perhaps one of the most significant PI technology the corporation is implementing is one that integrates both office and factory information systems. Called WICAM, for Westinghouse Integrated Computer—Aided Management, this management tool ties office automation systems together with engineering and factory-automated systems. It is the computer in the design department talking to the computer in the engineering, and to all other computers in word processing, the financial departments, the store rooms, and on the factory floor.

Quality Improvement

This critical strategy permeates the implementation of the remaining Westinghouse PI strategies. The corporation is placing a major emphasis on quality improvement by concurrently designing *both* the product and the manufacturing process. Quality is emphasized in *all aspects* of Westinghouse business—from sales and marketing to manufacturing and shipping. The philosophy behind the quality improvement strategy according to Murrin, is fairly simple and straightforward:

> If there is top quality, all else will follow—productivity, profitability, and job security. By doing it right the first time, multiple benefits occur. Increased quality leads to increased sales, increased job security, and to cost reductions. Several years of data analysis confirm these results. In a conservative estimate of the cost-of-failure impact on profitability, for each dollar reduction in failure costs, four dollars can be added to profit margins.

This strategy also evolves from the fact that quality has become instrumental, even more so than price, in improving market share and profit margins no matter what the state of the economy may be. This is confirmed by the Product Impact Marketing Strategy data.

Statistical quality control is one successful method for monitoring quality at the manufacturing level. According to L. Jerry Hudspeth, Vice President for Productivity and Quality:

> The core of quality is to control the production process to maintain product consistency. The difficulty is determining when—and how much—to adjust the process to correct some fluctuation in the product. The more complex the operation, the more complicated the decision becomes—and the more important effective use of statistical quality control techniques become. [*Business Week,* November 1, 1982]

Application of Value Analysis Techniques

Value analysis, a highly effective technique originally applied to product redesign, has also been successfully applied to the analysis of manufacturing process, services, and organizational structures within Westinghouse. This method involves employee participation and has been demonstrated to be extremely useful with professional and management employees. Results have been cost reductions and quality improvements that have contributed to improving the corporation's competitive capabilities.

Westinghouse has successfully employed this technique to analyze an entire business, the Linguaphone operation in London. The results have been the formulation and implementation of a plan that has a potential gain of more than $5 million.

To date, several hundred managers and professionals have been trained in this method with plans for increased training throughout all business units.

Asset Management

Westinghouse has placed increased emphasis upon improving the ways it utilizes the other basic resources of its business. The focus of this strategy is on improving the use of the basic materials in the corporate businesses. These include raw materials, inventory, energy, money, and time.

One particular emphasis has been on improved inventory control, applying the Japanese "just-in-time" concept. According to Hudspeth, Westinghouse is not just considering "fine-tuning" current methods, but is advocating major change. A key objective is to "pare inventories to the bone because large inventories can cover up a lot of problems—if you can operate like Toyota with one or two hours of inventory, you clearly have a smooth operating division" (*Business Week,* No. 2763, November 1, 1982).

Slim inventories have a ripple effect in causing Westinghouse business units as well as vendors to improve quality standards. As Hudspeth states, "With minimal inventories, we can't accept a 1% Acceptable Quality Level (AQL) anymore. There are new ground rules."

Substantial gains have also been made in energy conservation in certain Westinghouse plants. Results of 40–50% reductions in energy usage have been achieved in certain plants with plans for applying these same cost-saving principles being developed for further applications to other plants in the corporation.

Transnational Production

The final strategy in the Westinghouse PI program draws from principles advanced by Peter Drucker. It involves the strategic location of manufacturing facilities, particularly feeder facilities, globally. Several direct advantages result from this strategy. Product costs are reduced, access to world markets is increased, and after-tax profitability is ultimately increased.

To date, Westinghouse has located plants in many countries around the world with multiple sites in Puerto Rico, Ireland, and Mexico.

HUMAN RESOURCE INTERACTION WITH PRODUCTIVITY AND QUALITY IMPROVEMENT PROGRAMS

A corporatewide, people-intensive program of this caliber and scope necessarily has implications for human resource management. This section focuses on interaction between the Westinghouse PI program and human resource management as exemplified through activities occurring in a group in the Public Systems Company. Also described is the strategy employed by corporate human resource management to filter the PI program through the corporation.

Accomplishing a cultural change within a large conservative company, which is essentially what the Productivity and Quality Improvement program seeks to accomplish in Westinghouse, is a very slow and tedious process. According to Jack Springer, Director of Human Resources, Construction Group (a group of business units in the Public Systems Company), there are significant barriers to change in Westinghouse:

> Consider the group, with the diversity of products and the distribution of facilities nationwide and now, even internationally. Implementing PI programs is a *tremendous* task, as well as a challenge. Each business unit is steeped in its own history and has its own environment as a result of that history, largely influenced by various management styles brought to the organization over the years through the rotation of key managers. Further, some locations have union representation, others do not. Consequently, no one single approach exists which can be generally implemented across the group.

Human resources itself had to undergo fundamental changes in role, attitude, and instrumentality to be effective in supporting the PI effort. Within the Public Systems Company, the function has decisively moved from a reactive to a proactive stance. Human resources is now operating *strategically* in the identification, evaluation, training and development, and selection of appropriate individuals for placement both within-group and within outlying business units. By realigning the focus of human resources to one supportive of strategic objectives of the Public Systems Company, group, and business units, a significant mechanism for facilitating the "cultural shift" is now in place.

Human Resources has played a key role in formulating a bottom-up and top-down strategy for implementing productivity improvement, QWL, employee involvement, and cultural change. "The thrust," states Springer, "is based on building mutual trust and respect relationships throughout the organization through meaningful involvement of employees in problem-solving and decision-making at appropriate levels." Again, with meaningful involvement and participation, employee commitment and creativity is enhanced, ultimately leading to improved quality, productivity, lower costs of products and services, and, finally, financial performance. Of course, a significant gain through employee participation and involvement is a more satisfied workforce.

The mechanism for accomplishing these objectives has been the careful utilization of the fundamental human resource tools. First, the selection process has been given careful attention. One way to effectively initiate change within an organization is the strategic placement of appropriate individuals in the proper positions. Staffing needs are matched to strategic plans, which now include the known organizational development criteria. Once individuals with appropriate management styles are placed in appropriate positions, a cohesive, interactive appraisal process occurs, monitoring their performance both formally and informally on the job. For individuals in the running for key managerial level positions, it is communicated to them through the appraisal process that they must understand and practice modern human resource management philosophies. If they do not understand and practice participative management, they are not in the running for advanced managerial positions.

The Construction Group has developed what Springer refers to as the "HOT Book." This is a program serving to identify and prepare developmental plans for outstanding professional and management employees in business units for the purpose of filling future key management positions. Autocratic people are judged poorly. The "way of the future" is to develop enablers and facilitators, not commanders. It is communicated to the individual that managers are needed who understand how to optimally utilize employees, which is through participative management. Participative managers, therefore, must be secure managers, since insecure managers tend to seek, not share, power and oftentimes refuse to share information and to work at building trust/respect relationships.

These are the appraisal criteria that are considered, along with accomplishment of business objectives, in determining both reward allocations and training and development plans. How an individual performs along these dimensions is strongly linked to his or her promotion potential within the group. The Human resource activities are interactive and integrative, with each activity having an impact on another. It is through this selection–appraisal–rewards–training and development process that the individual's career is planned and developed within the group. This sequence of activities is iterative for those individuals who demonstrate the qualities sought by the group for advanced level managerial placement.

Increased training opportunities are being provided to enhance the quality of Westinghouse people. There are several aspects to this new training focus stimulated by the overall PI program. Senior executives have been provided with an intensive, several week "executive refresher" course at Carnegie-Mellon University. Seminars focus on management issues heading into the 1990s, and graduate-level refresher courses are provided in organizational development, technology, economics, and public policy.

In-house, executive management quality seminars are now conducted to acquaint senior management with ways in which they can become visibly and effectively involved in quality improvement. Through these seminars, upper management can learn how key quality issues and actions can be incorporated into their business unit's strategic plan. They also learn how to decide on and allocate the necessary resources to support quality enhancement activities. Senior management is also taught how to incorporate quality improvement as an important element in the performance appraisals of subordinates.

For management and professionals, in-house training is underway focusing on the statistical design of experiments for quality control. "Through this training," states Murrin, "the modern handheld calculator now makes possible the successful on-the-floor use of many methods that were once left only to the statistical expert."

Additional seminars have been conducted by prominent figures in the quality profession who have been invited to address Westinghouse's top management and professional people. These include Drs. Deming, Juran, and Ishikawa, all of whom have been helpful in reorienting the Westinghouse approach to management of quality.

On the factory floor, several changes in training are occuring as well. The implementation of the quality circle approach has encouraged participative management and has been instrumental in having a positive impact on the cultural change. Corporate Human Resources is also rethinking the concept of job classifications—and who should be doing what job. The Japanese have demonstrated that worker morale, productivity, and quality can be significantly enhanced by allowing employees to perform many different jobs. "For too long," claims Murrin, "American industry has pigeon-holed our workers into tidy but restrictive job slots. A Japanese factory worker typically runs several machines—and also programs and maintains them."

Two other issues facing Corporate Human Resource Management warrant discussion. Westinghouse has had a history of union difficulties, highlighted in the first section. Remarkably, the Public Systems PI efforts in the Construction Group have been quite successful to date in circumventing union difficulties. Agreements with local unions have been reached ahead of contractual expiration dates, the success of which Springer attributes to the participative management approach currently employed in the union-represented locations. "Labor problems have been reduced because the Group had encouraged people to become significantly involved in problem-solving and decision-making." He admits it comes slowly "where the rubber meets the road"—where some managers are threatened by employees telling them how to run their business and how to improve productivity—"but when approached with facts and figures that back it up, these managers generally come around."

The second issue that presents difficulty is handling reward systems in PI and quality of work life programs. Springer concedes the day will come when Westinghouse will need to address the issue. Due to the depressed economy, foreign competition, as well as high levels of unemployment and the early stages of the Group PI and QWL effort, reward issues are currently not a significant problem. As the business climate improves, as the economy turns around, and as the group becomes more productive and profitable, these issues will become increasingly important.

In summary, both Murrin and Springer concede that the cultural change sought by Westinghouse will not occur overnight, will not occur next year, but may well be accomplished in 5–10 years. It requires people taking a new look at how to perform their jobs better. It requires managers more proficient in human resources management techniques to encourage employees to participate, both in the office and in the factory. It also takes a concentrated corporate effort and charter accompanied by distinctive, functional support mechanisms to make it work and, of, course, it takes time.

PI PROGRESS AND DIRECTION FOR THE FUTURE

Public Systems, largely due to Tom Murrin's enthusiasm, has most intensively pursued PI. These efforts have paid off as Public Systems, from 1979 to 1982, recorded a better than 7% annual increase in productivity, higher than the 6.1% corporate objective set by the Management Committee in 1979. This section of the case discloses the progress that Westinghouse has made as a result of PI efforts, discusses measurement issues associated with PI, and directions for the future viewed by Tom Murrin.

Recent 1982 results show Public Systems to have achieved higher sales and profit than in previous years, maintaining its position as the "fastest growing" high-profitability company within the corporate fold. These results are noteworthy. Two of the other three companies posted sluggish sales and diminished profits due to the effects of the depressed economy. Strongly believing the PI efforts have positively influenced sales and profitablity and that a 10% PI annual level is "reasonably attainable," Murrin cites two examples in support of his contention:

1. Westinghouse has contracted for a significant portion of the defense electronics that are incorporated in the radar and navigational systems of the

F-16 fighter plane. The recent Israeli conflict (June, 1982) with Lebanon resulted in an 80–0 score for the F-16 in aerial combat. These planes flew more sorties with faster turnaround time than any time in recorded history. The results are largely attributable to the increased Mean Time Between Failure (MTBF) of the Westinghouse electronics and, of course, the expertise of the Israeli pilots. The increased reliability of these electronics has had an impact on the increased perception of Westinghouse quality, in turn, spurring increased DOD contract work from the U.S. Government.

2. A second example demonstrates the generalizability of the quality concept. One of the Public Systems Group is involved in community development in Florida. Joe Frazier, the Executive Vice President of this group has taken to applying quality concepts to his business unit. In Murrin's words:

> Frazier began to think more and more about the importance of quality, and to study his customer's perceptions of the quality of his organization in comparison to their perceptions of the quality of competitors. Frazier's approach was much more rigorous than our original applications. He is styling and designing cities, homes, and condominiums. He has libraries of pictures that walk you, as a prospective client buying a house, up the path on the approach to a competitor's house in Ft. Lauderdale. These show you what the door looks like, what the foyer looks like, they study the hardware, the texture of the surface of the ceiling, the woodwork, appliances, etc. On the outside, you see the shrubbery, the pavement, and the whole ambiance.

> Then Frazier used the same approach on our real estate, with a qualitative difference. He incorporated the perspective of *quality* in his operations, with positive results. One could see, in comparison to competition, that certain features stood out. Their locks looked cheap, the finish on woodwork and ceilings was poor, and so forth. Frazier assumed another perspective, that of the people doing the detail design of these residences, and assertively demanding the quality called for in the specs. Full payment was withheld from contractors until the work was finished according to plan.

> Today, when you walk into one of Frazier's condominiums, the results are obvious. People say, "This *looks* like a high quality residence—this *feels* like a high quality residence." The quality approach has allowed Frazier to get higher price appreciation out of the cost of that property than the company was able to previously, and even during recessionary periods of time. The point is, improved quality does lead to improved profitability, and these efforts were inspired by our original productivity and quality studies. We can apply quality to virtually all aspects of our operations, be they manufacturing process, sales, service, or whatever.

Productivity Measurement

Certain productivity and quality improvement programs readily lend themselves to measurement. The value analysis programs, for example, incorporate statistical methods by which gains can be measured over time. Other programs, such as the quality circle program, cannot and should not be measured solely by their impact upon the bottom line of a profit statement. Other variables that must be considered, according to Murrin, include employee morale and effective two-way employee–management communications. These variables, however, are not readily quantifiable.

Collectively, these PI programs contribute to a "critical mass" that positively influences the whole corporation. To measure its productivity momentum, Westinghouse has established an overall corporate goal for PI at $6^+\%$ per year, an ambitious goal in view of the fact that U.S. manufacturing PI has been less than 1% for the last four years.

The actual measurement of productivity involvement is a complex issue. There is no satisfactory way of accomplishing a *single* measure of PI for reasons already cited. The equation Westinghouse utilizes is as follows

$$\frac{\text{Constant Dollar Value-Added Change}}{\text{Number of Employees}} = \%\,\text{PI}$$

The numerator of the equation, constant dollar value-added change, is designed to eliminate the pitfall of inflation and to avoid disturbances related to subcontracting and overtime. Murrin claims that this formula is simple, consistent, and relatively generalizable to all business units.

The shortcomings of this formula are that it is not elegant nor precise. Westinghouse has recently refined the formula so that the denominator is total employee costs—rather than employee headcount—as this correlates more closely with operating profit improvements, and provides for a more accurate measurement of PI throughout the corporation.

Directions for the Future

A normal response to the question of future plans for the corporation is "more and better of what we are now doing." However, in Tom Murrin's perspective, much more can be done than has been done or started, in terms of PI programs. The more important issue is that Westinghouse's efforts are a micro approach to PI, though admittedly, these are essential to the economic survival of the organization in the long run. What is required according to Murrin, is not only a company approach, or an industry approach, but a *national* approach to increasing PI.

At the industry level, the importance of management change must be recognized. Corporations, according to Murrin, should not be reluctant or hesitant to implement "bold and innovative changes." Training is equally as appropriate to management personnel as it is to the labor force within an organization, a philosophy put into operation within Westinghouse through the top-down and bottom-up strategies described previously.

A second related issue is the indoctrination of quality concepts and principles at all levels within the organization. Conceptually, according to Murrin, the same process must be backwardly applied to vendors, by upgrading acceptable quality levels to *first line*, and forwardly applied to the ultimate consumer, who must demand quality and *pull* it through the production process in the same manner that Westinghouse is applying to its own vendors.

"The day will come," believes Murrin, "where we will not have to rigorously practice 100% inspection, where quality standards will be an ingrained phenomena, as they are in Japan." However, to maintain global competitiveness, Murrin believes the following must be done:

Relative to government we must look at improving the fundamental incentives needed to increase the productivity of the industrial base—and reduce or eliminate the detractors. The first step is to replace the adversarial relationship between industry and government—with a cooperative one.

Industry and academe must work together to improve the training of employees so that we have a more competitive workforce. More attention must be directed toward increasing the number of graduating engineers and technical workers.

As closing remarks, Murrin's following statements are appropriate:

—We have the essential resources to meet the challenges we are facing. But we need a strategy that will allow industry, academe, labor, and government to work cooperatively and effectively. If we can successfully achieve this, I believe we'll begin to see an unparalleled flowering of technological innovation that will render a healthy United States of America again.

CHAPTER

23

THE INTERNATIONAL MANAGEMENT OF HUMAN RESOURCES

Vladimir Pucik

From a corporate perspective the dominant feature of today's world economy is the increasing globalization of market competition. Formerly isolated geographically bounded markets are being transformed, if not always into a global market, then into a set of interconnected markets where the competitive conditions in one may heavily influence the competitive outcomes in most of the others. As a result, long-term corporate strategy has to take into consideration not only the expected state of the current major markets individually, but examine and respond competitively to expected changes within a global framework. Table 23.1 presents some basic data demonstrating the increasing internationalization of markets; and the interdependence of nation-states as illustrated in the data of Table 23.2.

The globalization of market competition brings on the need to foster the development of globally oriented managers and executives. To supervise the transition of narrowly based specialists to global managers is the major strategic task facing the HRM function in many multinational firms today. Corporate staffing policies, appraisal and reward systems, as well as management

TABLE 23.1.   Global Exports in 1977 for the Largest Exporters.

Nation	Merchandise Exports (Billions U.S. $)	% of World Trade
United States	119.0	11.7
Germany	117.9	11.6
Japan	80.5	7.9
France	63.6	6.2
United Kingdom	57.5	5.6
U.S.S.R.	45.2	4.4
Italy	45.1	4.4
Netherlands	43.7	4.3
Saudi Arabia	43.5	4.3
Canada	41.4	4.1
World Total	1017.4	100.0

Source: World Bank, *World Development Report 1979* (Washington, DC: World Bank, 1979), Annex Tables 5, 8; U.N., *Monthly Bulletin of Statistics*. (New York: United Nations, May 1979), Table 52.

development programs require a significant modification of the traditional practices for this transition to be successful. At times, this process might be painful and costly. However, in the current environment, the choice facing the multinational firms is clear: either increase its global character in order to compete worldwide or give up and disappear.

The shift in focus from a single-country market to a global business perspective has had a profound impact on the corporate human resource man-

TABLE 23.2.   Stock of Direct Investment Abroad of Major Investing Countries (billions U.S. $) 1967–1976.

Nation	1967	%	1976	%
United States	56.6	53.8	136.8	47.5
United Kingdom	17.5	16.6	32.1	11.2
Germany	3.0	2.8	19.9	6.9
Japan	1.5	1.4	19.4	6.7
Switzerland	5.0	4.7	18.6	6.5
France	6.0	5.7	11.9	4.1
Canada	3.7	3.5	11.1	3.9
Netherlands	2.2	2.1	9.8	3.4
Sweden	1.7	1.6	5.0	1.7
Belgium	2.0	1.9	3.6	1.2
Italy	2.1	2.0	2.9	1.0
Other	4.0	3.8	16.8	5.8
Total	105.3	100.0	287.9	100.0

Source: *U.N., Transnational Corporations in World Development, A Re-Examination* (New York: U.N., March 1978), Table III-32, p. 236.

agement activities. Table 23.3 summarizes the implications of increasing globalization of organization structure on the human resource practices of the firm (Stopford and Wells, 1972).

In the early stages of expansion abroad the firm's international business is usually concentrated in a specialized "international" division that supervises exports, licensing agreements, and foreign subsidiaries. The role of the corporate personnel department is mostly limited to supervising the selection of staff for the new division. The emphasis is on identification of employees familiar with the corporate products, technology, organization, and culture while at the same time adaptable to constraints imposed by unfamiliar working environments abroad.

During this initial period the home-country employees stationed abroad operate as "viceroys." Their main tasks are to direct the daily operations of foreign affiliates, to supervise transfer of managerial and technological know-how, to communicate corporate policies, and keep the home office informed about relevant developments in their assigned territory. Experience with "hands-on" management as well as cultural sensitivity and adaptability are considered the necessary prerequisites for the job. The individual assignments are decided on an "as needed" basis, and crash courses in language and culture are provided for managers deemed capable of fast learning. For this purpose, a battery of selection tests was developed with the objective of identifying managers with the personality and behavioral traits most suitable for working in diversified cultural settings. Since many foreign assignments are not considered particularly desirable from the point of view of a traditional career progression in the corporation, financial incentives in the form of cost-of-living adjustments, relocation bonuses, and the like and often used to make such assignments attractive at least in the short run.

As foreign involvement increases, traditional international personnel policies limited to staffing guidance and supervision, and to administration of individualized compensation packages for expatriates gradually cease to meet the new requirements. Often, the growth in international exposure brings a transfer of the authority for foreign operations back to product divisions which than assume a worldwide responsibility. In such an environment foreign subsidiaries evolve into fully integrated parts of the corporate organization. The coordination of international activities and the formulation of strategies for worldwide markets become independent managerial functions requiring specialized expertise. The growth in foreign exposure combined with changes in the organizational structure of international operations result in an increase in the number of managerial class employees needed to oversee the contracts between the parent firm and its foreign affiliates. From the international manager's perspective, the shortage of qualified personnel makes the one-time corporate adventure a legitimate career, but this shortage may seriously limit the speed and effectiveness of foreign market penetration. Within the HRM area, the development of an international staff becomes a new imperative.

TABLE 23.3. Evolution of Multinational Human Resource Management.

Organizational Structure	HRM Function			
	Selection	Appraisal	Rewards	Development
International division	AD hoc staffing, emphasis on adaptability	Focused on technology transfer	Transfer incentive	Cross-cultural "crash" courses
Global product division	Low-level localization	Focused on communication and control	Local equity issues	Specialized international staff
Global matrix structure	Advanced localization	MBO-type appraisal	Global equity issues	Rationing of developmental opportunities
Global matrix culture	Anticipating strategy, control tool	Congruence with long-term objectives	Global opportunity structure	Global executive cadre

Not only does the transformation of the corporation into a full-fledged multinational lead to the change in focus in the HRM international activities, but the organization of the HRM function is altered as well. Originally, the HRM activities have an ethnocentric character and the policies are designed to fit primarily the experience of the home country (Vernon, 1971). Gradually, they become polycentric in nature as the multinational firm strives to adapt its HRM system to particular conditions in each locality. The expatriate employees remain under direct home-office supervision, whereas the personnel control of local employees is transferred to the subsidiaries. In the second phase, the home-office personnel staff limit their role to monitoring, and intervene in the local affairs only under extreme circumstances.

At the same time, the rising ambitions and aspirations of local employees, often coupled with pressure by foreign governments on their behalf, illustrate the necessity of awarding an increased share of managerial positions in subsidaries to local nationals (Behrman, 1970; Brandt and Hulbert, 1977; Vernon; 1971). These two factors, together with the already mentioned shortage of qualified international managers in the home country, as well as the fact that the transfer of knowhow becomes secondary to the knowledge of local business opportunities, usually result in a significant decrease of the expatriate staff in foreign operations. The function of those remaining changes considerably. As subsidiaries move towards a relative independence, the "viceroy" function is replaced with that of an "ambassador," communicating and coordinating the corporate strategic objectives with the local management. The latter are usually hired and trained locally, but they may also be recruited on the home-country university campuses and transferred to their country of origin after a relatively short training period at the head office.

The complexity of a multinational business often requires a substantial operational decentralization coupled with the need for coordination across geographical areas and product lines. The next major step in the evolution of the HRM function in a multinational firm comes when such a coordination is achieved by organizing its management structure as a matrix grid spanning across product and territorial boundaries. The emphasis is on an "MBO-type" appraisal system aiming to reconcile business objectives from each of the matrix segments which may often be in conflict because of differences in their respective contextual environments.

However, the evolution of the multinational HRM function does not come to an end, even after all the four major components of selection, reward, appraisal, and development systems are firmly established. The continuous globalization of corporate business activities together with the increased complexity of the underlying organizational structure requires a continual adjustment of the HRM system as the multinational designs its strategy to increase global market share and expand its scale.

As a corporate business becomes more and more global, the resulting complexity embedded in the multilayer matrix structure often becomes an obstacle in efficient communication and decision-making (Brandt and Hulbert, 1977). Under such conditions, the time is ripe to move away from a formal "matrix structure" to an informal "matrix culture" as the key coordination and control tool. Supporting a climate where matrixlike behavior is a natural pattern of action at the operational, managerial, and strategic levels of planning is the new task facing the multinational HRM system. Even when corporate businesses are restricted to a relatively limited geographic area, it is not easy to manage effectively the transition from a formal matrix structure to an informal matrix culture.

This is even more so when corporate business activities are spread around the globe, when the new corporate culture is to be developed not within a single national culture, but within numerous often very distinct national cultural settings.

Even more important, recently in an increasing number of businesses, the competition facing most companies has become global rather than geographically limited. To succeed in the emerging global market, the corporate strategy has to respond to global competitive conditions. Analyzing and understanding the global business environment become skills critical not only to corporate growth, but also to corporate survival.

The needs of the global business organization require a careful monitoring of conditions in the international environment and a careful elaboration of competitive strategies well in advance. This, in turn, requires the creation and maintenance of a corporate executive cadre capable of monitoring global markets, responding rapidly to emerging global opportunities and threats, as well as formulating and executing the appropriate long-term business strategies in the global context. This emerging demand for managers of global strategies cannot be met without a further strengthening of strategic HRM thinking in the corporation and their adaptation to the contingencies of multinational operations. The next section elaborates on the necessary human resource policies for multinational management.

STRATEGIC HUMAN RESOURCE ISSUES IN MULTINATIONALS

Multinational Staffing

On an operational level, the choice between staffing foreign operations with home-country or third-country nationals, or relying instead on local personnel, is often considered the key issue in multinational staffing. The section rule is based on a perceived tradeoff between the need for technical versus territorial competence in a particular location. So far, there seems to be a lack of consensus among HRM managers in multinational firms on whether technical competence is "in general" less important to the successful management of a foreign subsidiary than is the understanding of and adaptation to the local society. However, in practical terms, reliance on local management is increasing.

One of the main reasons for this development is the belief that hiring local nationals may be a reasonable defensive move, necessary to stem the potential resentment of foreign managerial dominance in the subsidary. Indeed, the delegation of authority to locals may help to satisfy the rising ambitions and expectations of many of the local employees (Bergsten et. al, 1978). Such a policy also cuts the immediate costs of staffing by the elimination of foreign transfer-related bonuses and tax adjustments, and it may be instrumental in developing a strong local management team. At the same time, the reduction in cross-national staffing ultimately leads to a reduction in the pool of managers with global rather than area-specific experience.

Because of the substantial time lag between individual staffing decisions and their aggregate impact on the experience profile of the managerial pool, many multinational firms today concentrate on developing their local management teams, and do not perceive the danger ahead of a fragmented management. Often, even when the current key executives possess formidable international experience (after all, it was they who had pushed and guided their companies in the years of early foreign expansion) the proportion of those in lower managerial ranks who could eventually match their experience is dangerously low. Although numerically the number of managers with foreign exposure is growing, there are still far too few to handle the growing demands of international ventures such as the need to recognize, in time, market opportunities and threats.

From the standpoint of building a management team capable of supervising multinational competitive strategies, the issue is not how to resolve the dilemma between technical and contextual competence. Rather, the issue is how to develop corporate human resources possessing *both* of the critical skills. Yet although some short-term and long-term tradeoffs are unavoidable, staffing decisions are still being made primarily on the basis of the current needs of the organizations without considering long-term strategic implications; or, even worse, on the basis of short-term financial expediencies, which are relatively unrelated to the nature of the business in the first place.

It is not infrequent that corporate international staffing policies are based more on tax considerations than on a long-term analysis of human resource supply as related to corporate multinational strategy. Staffing policies should not be delegated to tax lobbies. Staffing foreign operations is costly, and tax savings are welcome, but the tax effect is in the long run only a secondary constraint. In other words, few major foreign ventures ever collapse because of the high tax burden of staffing, but many are in difficulty because the parent firms are not able to assemble international management teams combining knowledge of local market conditions with technical and organizational competence.

Another area in which strategic staffing is essential to success concerns the establishment of a joint venture. Given underlying global competition, a joint venture of two independent firms will not be successful unless its continuation is in the interest of both partners in the long run. The appropriate staffing strategy calls for a staffing system doubling as a strategic mechanism of control. The objective is to obtain a sufficient amount of technical competence as well as environmental adaptiveness that would inhibit the firm to impede any breakaway action by its local partner. With this objective in mind, it is essential that the joint venture local staff be seen as permanently committed to the new operation and not temporarily assigned from the local parent. The roving ambassadors from both parent firms should be limited to the number the foreign partner can dispatch. The exchange of trainees should flow two ways, locals learning technical expertise, expatriates learning the adaptation to the area. The management trainee transfer should involve both assignments from the parent to the joint venture, as well as from the joint venture to the local parent.

The strategic implications of staffing decisions are of tantamount importance in developing local market knowhow. What happens when they are ignored can be seen in the example of United States joint ventures in Japan. Although most of these joint ventures were effective to transfer technology to Japanese partners, the American firms usually did not pay attention to developing their own potential competitive strength. Thus when Japanese partners decided to go alone, there was nothing the American firms could do but withdraw from the market. Substantial expenditures and years of hard work were lost with minimal returns.

Staffing problems of this nature are slightly less critical in the wholly owned subsidiary as the control over technology prevents the emergence of domestic competitiors, short of unfriendly spinoffs, of course. In the case of a wholly owned firm it is much more difficult to pull together a qualified labor force, as the operation has to start from zero. Although it seems natural that a wholly owned investment strategy calls for gradual growth, market imperatives often do not allow that luxury. It is, therefore, important to be able to recognize the market potential well ahead of the actual investment and prepare a sufficient number of future managerial cadres. This can be accomplished, for example, through assignments in local market research offices or training in friendly local affiliates.

The reliance on executive search and employment agencies, although a feasible short-term solution, often does not satisfy long-term objectives. First of all, the chances are high that employees will leave again. In a number of less-developed countries, as a byproduct of sloppy staffing practices of foreign multinationals, a paradoxical situation has developed. On the one hand, there is an acute shortage of middle managers capable of manning a multinational operation and having potential for further professional development, while at the same time, the market is nearly saturated with mediocre manager "cross-culture intermediaries" who peddle their skills to the highest bidder.

One approach to solving the shortage of qualified international managers is to increase the recruiting activities among foreign students at the home-country universities—a competitive advantage for U.S.-based multinational concerns, utilizing the opportunities provided by the large number of foreign students pursuing education in the United States. At the same time, many American firms still tend to recruit to fill a particular position, rather than for the corporation at large. For example, an MBA with a working knowledge of Arabic would not be considered a suitable job candidate when the only position available is in Latin America. What does not enter the staffing decision is the possibility that a year hence, such an MBA would be needed for an opening in a Middle Eastern operation now only in the planning stage.

Also, more attention has to be given to the recruiting of area specialists. After all, it is cheaper to train an area specialist internally in the intricacies of corporate finance, accounting, or marketing, than to teach an MBA the understanding of a cultural setting that goes together with fluency in foreign languages and/or with several years of living experience in the area. For example, as a result of the MBA bias in the corporate recruiting policies, graduates of many East Asian programs have difficulty finding jobs, whereas American automakers do not have even a handful of managers on their corporate staff capable of reading and speaking Japanese.

Multinational Appraisal

Several special features of globally organized businesses require a substantial modification of traditional appraisal criteria. First of all, in most international management positions, technical competence is a necessary, but not a sufficient condition for a successful performance. Cross-cultural interpersonal skills, sensitivity to foreign norms and values, understanding of differences in labor practices or customer relations, and ease of adaptation to unfamiliar environments are just a few of the managerial traits most multinational firms seek and evaluate. However, in addition to the appraisal of these basically operational and managerial-level skills, an appropriate appraisal system also has to be developed for evaluating managers on attributes associated with successful performance on strategic activities.

The successful execution of competitive global strategies require managers and executives with excellent environment-scanning abilities, familiar with conditions of business and market opportunities not in one, but in a number of countries and regions, and sensitive to the special constraints facing multinationational corporations, such as their relationship with host governments. For example, interaction with top government officials and legislators is a function reserved in the home office to the chief executive and his or her staff. In foreign subsidiaries, the same task may fall on the shoulders of managers many layers below.

The proposition that an appraisal on the strategic level ought to be focused on the congruence of current managerial performance with long-term corporate objectives is today widely accepted at least as a theory, whereas its practical application is often bogged down by the constraint of organizational realities. In what form should long-term goals be expressed to be measurable against performance? What aspects of performance should be considered?

Difficult as it is to find an answer to these two questions in a single-country environment, it is even more complicated when global operations are involved.

Given the standard practice of many multinational corporations of using arbitrary transfer prices and other financial tools in transactions between its subsidiaries worldwide as a way of minimizing foreign-exchange risk exposure and tax expenditures, the financial results recorded in the subsidiary do not always reflect accurately its contribution to the achievements of the corporation as a whole. This naturally leads to a situation where such results cannot and should not be used as a primary input in managerial appraisal.

In order to evaluate properly the subsidiary's contribution, a set of parallel accounts adjusted for the influence of financial manipulation should be maintained, or new measures of control be developed, that are less susceptible to the influence of exchange rate fluctuations, of cash-flow and liquidity management, or of transfer pricing. Another alternative is to base a manager's evaluation on the subsidiary's performance compared to the long-range goals expressed in other than profit or return-on-equity terms (growth, market share, cost of sales, etc.).

In developing the suitable mix of long and short-term objectives to be used as the framework of management appraisal on a strategic level, it is necessary to consider the implications of the following major constraints affecting strategy-level appraisal in multinational firms.

First of all, a competitive global strategy is focused on global performance rather than on returns in each of the country or regional markets. Even in a relatively competition-free environment, it can be hardly taken for granted that the sum of short-term optimal subportfolio investments leads to optimal long-term performance as a whole. The limitation of short-term local profit-maximization strategies can be seen when competitive pressure requires a multinational firm to operate and compete actively in markets where, if isolated from other markets, it would not compete. A typical case would be participation in a market where an international competitor is a dominant market leader, with an objective to challenge the competitor's cash flow through aggressive pricing policies. Although the balance sheet of this particular subsidiary might be continually in the red, by tying up the competitor's resources this strategy may allow substantially higher returns elsewhere. The difficulties in quantifying such strategies in terms of the usual ROI objectives are obvious.

Second, the volatility of the international environment also requires that long-term goals be flexible and responsive to potential market contingencies. Otherwise, the corporation takes the risk of subsidiaries pursuing strategies that no longer fit the new environment. The monitoring of relevant changes and their reflection in the appraisal process is one important area where corporate planning and HRM activities closely overlap. The volatility and fluctuations under which subsidiaries operate require precision tailoring of long-term goals to the specific situation in a given market. It is important to reconcile the need for universal appraisal standards with specific objectives in the subsidiaries. In addition, the cultural differences between home-office bound executives, regional, and local managers create another reason to fine-tune the appraisal system, as it is no longer focused on a fairly homogeneous cadre of managers.

Third, the proper monitoring of the congruence between long-term corporate strategy and activities in the subsidiary is further complicated by the physical distances involved, the infrequency of contact between the corporate head-office staff and subsidiaries management, as well as the cost of the reporting system. Although improvements in information processing technology today allow the development of sophisticated worldwide data systems, the paucity of physical contacts between managers and executives in the field and the head-office put some limitations on the latter's ability to monitor "soft" aspects of the field executive's performance (Brandt and Hulbert, 1977).

Finally, without the supporting infrastructure of the parent company, the market development in foreign countries is generally slower than at home, where established brands can support new products, and new business areas can piggyback on the means and support of other divisions. This is often very difficult to achieve in the case of foreign ventures. As a result, more time is needed to achieve results than is customary in a domestic market, and this fact ought to be recognized in the appraisal process as well.

Multinational Reward System

An effective managerial reward system should be linked to long-term corporate strategy and should anticipate changes in employees' perceptions of the value of different organizational rewards. Multinational settings make the complex task of developing such a system even more difficult; however, the fact that the corporation operates in many different environments permits the design of unique reward programs, unavailable in more conventional environments.

So far, however, as in the case of many mainly domestic firms, most multinational firms still consider rewards in purely monetary terms. In fact, although personnel systems in Japanese, American and European multinational firms are often strikingly dissimilar (Brandt and Hulbert, 1977), they all share one common problem: an inability to reward potentially promising employees with adequate career opportunities leading to more responsibility, and opportunities for growth and development. The successful managerial mix of locals, third-country nationals, and home-office employees is a goal that has so far eluded most of the multinationals. As it is natural that competition in the global environment requires the mobilization of global human resources, those companies that do succeed at it gain a substantial competitive edge. However, without a properly structured reward system in place, such global utilization of managerial skills will probably not be achieved.

Already, on the operational and managerial levels, the administration of a reward system in a multinational firm is constrained by several critical factors. First of all, the mix of home-office expatriates, third-country nationals, and local managers often serving together in a location makes it rather difficult to administer a universal compensation package. The system has to adjust equity issues within the organization with the conditions of the external labor market in countries from which individual managers are recruited, and account for cost-of-living variance as well as differences in tax treatment by respective governments. In addition, employees' expectations and what constitutes a fair and equitable compensation system might not be convergent. To maintain, in such an environment, an effective and adaptable compensation system requires careful monitoring by a highly skilled professional staff.

Today numerous multinationals have developed rather elaborate procedures to account for cost-of-living differentials between various countries, for differences in job status as well as for the necessity to provide incentives for employees to work in so-called hardship areas, such as parts of the Middle East, Africa, or Latin America. However, the task ahead is to move from transfer-incentive compensation packages to reward systems designed to elicit managerial actions in line with corporate long-term competitive strategy.

Other non monetary aspects of reward systems are also significantly affected by a multinational corporate setting. Corporate rhetoric aside, promotion lines in the vast majority of multinational firms are still defined by the country of origin. Local employees, even if hired in the home-office locations, such as the case of foreign MBAs, are recruited in the first place as potential local, or perhaps regional executives. Their subsequent experience and training would not equip them sufficiently to compete for top corporate jobs in the head office. Although there has been considerable political pressure applied on multinationals to foster the promotion of local employees within specific localities, promotion outside of a particular locale is still rare.

In such an environment it is not surprising to find that a local manager, aware of the limitation of his or her career prospects, is primarily concerned about the security and stability of the local operation only, disregarding, or paying less attention to the broader goals of the organization. It is naive to expect their commitment to long-term corporate goals in which the local managers have only a very limited control and very limited benefit. Thus in order to ensure the integration and the alignment of long-term strategy with personal goals, the career system in a multinational must be opened up.

At the same time, it happened all too often in the past that assignment to a foreign location was generally the sign of a sidetracking if not "plateauing" career. Given the importance of understanding global opportunities and global competition, foreign assignments must become a valuable reward. This can be done, if corporate promotion policies clearly indicate that global experience, rather than a temporary sabbatical, it is a necessary condition for promotion to the top of the corporate hierarchy. Again, it should be considered that this requires a very careful long-term placement plannning as positions reserved to promising home-office employees limit the number of positions needed for the reward of promising locals.

An important component of the reward system is the structuring of career opportunities. Again, the global environment provides a unique challenge to create an efficient opportunity structure as the need for country specialization has to be reconciled with the need of broader exposure for employees with an executive's potential. As already discussed, the number of American expatriates assigned overseas is increasingly limited. However, token assignment late in the managers' careers is probably not enough to fire their minds with global competitive spirit.

The usual argument against more frequent foreign assignment of home-office employees is the relatively high cost, as the typical benefit package for a middle-level executive overseas costs more than double the basic compensation. One possible answer is to select personnel for overseas assignment early in their careers, when the total compensation package is relatively low. By the time an employee is ready for promotion to an executive position, he or she has already gained valuable foreign experience and insights. The upper limits on employee selection to overseas assignment will have the additional impact of opening up managerial slots for more local employees, thus increasing the flexibility and attractiveness of their reward system. However, the variety of career opportunities in a typical multinational firm also permits the organization to offer typical career opportunities, in particular, to offer challenging lateral career transfers. The multicultural environment is, in this sense, a valuable resource that can be utilized not only to satisfy the curiosity of young and ambitious managerial trainees. It can also offer a challenge to midcareer executives choosing, or being forced, to withdraw from the competition on the main axis of the corporate hierarchy, but at the same time looking for stimulating job assignments, both from a professional and a personal perspective.

Multinational Management Development

Probably the most formidable task recently facing many multinational firms is the development of a cadre of managers and executives who have an understanding of the global market environment deep enough to enable them to survive and come out ahead.

Traditionally, most multinational companies rely in the early stages of overseas expansion on a small, but carefully selected group of managers, who after an initial exposure to domestic business, focus their careers on the operation of the company's international ventures. Although this seems to be a reasonable arrangement for a limited period of time, eventually it comes to hamper seriously the motivation, development, and retention of capable local employees. When top positions in a subsidiary are permanently blocked by rotating expatriates, the best of the local managers became discouraged, and they either resign and depart from the organization, or their willingness to make an effort on behalf of the firm begins to slacken. Over time, these disadvantages more than balance the benefits stemming from an expatriate dominance, such as ease of communication and relatively simple control structure. In addition to the internal problems, as pointed out earlier, when foreign operations begin to increase in size, the intimate knowledge of local operations may gradually become more important than communication and coordination with the parent head office. Under such conditions it is natural that a number of multinational firms begin to emphasize promotion and development of local resident managers, with expatriates shrinking in number or influence.

With the new emphasis on localization, some expatriates may prefer to become corporate "transplants" opting for limited career in the subsidiary if it is located in (for them) an attractive environment, rather than return to the home office. Others are gradually eased out of international transfers, often to the former expatriates' great relief as their family needs may call for more stability.

At that point, foreign managerial assignments usually become a "luxury item," with access limited to corporate stars (Edstrom and Galbraith, 1978). Although an exposure to unfamiliar markets, new business methods, ideas, and concepts is considered essential to the development of a well-rounded international executive, the rationing of developmental positions also has several, often overlooked, negative consequences.

First of all, the business function of a farmed-out fast-tracker is often merely symbolic, nothing more than two to three years of a corporate sabbatical. Aware that the foreign assignment is too short to provide a sufficient time to learn about the new environment and design new business strategies, as well as supervise their execution, these managers generally attempt to stay aloof of the subsidiary's daily operations. Without facing the ultimate test of the market, the incentive to penetrate the intricacies of local business diminishes. As a result, the actual experience gained by such an assignment is often much less than is perceived by the staff devevlopment planners back in the home office.

Second, development policy focused on the parent company's elite frequently neglects the grooming of local managerial talent and its integration with the parent organization. The local managers are trained to manage effectively the local operations and their exposure to the rest of the firm is limited to what they have to know to succeed locally. Sometimes they are considered for third-country transfers, for example, in order to supervise an entire region. However, opportunities for transfers to the parent company, other than for specialized training, are few and far between. As a consequence, in most of today's multinational firms, regardless of the country of origin, the composition of the top management is exclusively limited to parent-country nationals.

Third, when foreign assignments are incorporated in the development programs of high-potential executives only, the implementation of the global competitive strategy may suffer. Although it is desirable, if not imperative, that strategic premises, targets, and objectives are assimilated and adopted by the whole organization, such a condition is difficult to achieve when knowledge of global markets is not widely distributed throughout the firm.

Highly selective foreign staffing may succeed in developing corporate top bodies composed of globally oriented executives. However, their operational effectiveness will be limited if very few of home-office subordinates, lacking their broad outlook, can grasp, sharpen, and carry out their ideas.

Given the current level of technological innovations in communications, it is not too difficult from the technical point of view to develop global information networks aimed at gathering and disseminating relevant market data throughout the organization worldwide. The main constraint is the limited capacity to process and utilize such vast information flow, and the inability of many managers to interpret the incoming data correctly and early enough for use in strategy formulation and its implementation.

As a consequence, data are generally channeled to the corporate head office where such capacity is expected to be available. When the flow of information becomes centralized, the centralization of control usually follows. In situations where the competitive global environment is characterized by high uncertainty, and the opportunity of flexible response essential, such centralization may be detrimental to corporate effectiveness. Yet distribution of information flow cannot be meaningfully accomplished unless the local management possesses at least some knowledge of competitive conditions in other market areas and the executives at the head office understand enough of the detail to draw a true picture of the hole.

Worldwide management programs are the tools to build such expertise. These programs have to go beyond the simple daily operational needs focused on the checking of ongoing activities and evaluation of market opportunities. Rather, the emphasis should be on the establishment of a global strategic consensus within the organization. The basis of such a consensus lies in the knowledge of global market trends and the understanding of their competitive implications.

The necessary part of any long-term management development program aimed at future global executives is an extensive linguistic training. So far, English is the major international business language and it is quite possible to conduct routine operations around the world using English only. However, in the case of American multinationals this advantage is more like a Trojan horse. The reliance on English on the operational level diminishes the incentive to beef up the linguistic capacity of the firm and the ability to process foreign language data, so critical for timely strategic decision-making. At the same time, such companies are highly vulnerable, as English language data revealing their activities can be monitored and digested by foreign competitors at very little cost.

For example, many engineers and managers in Japanese computer companies have a sufficient command of English to enable them to follow in detail English-language trade journals or conference presentations, often a source of valuable business intelligence. In contrast, their American counterparts employ only a handful of engineers capable of following Japanese-language materials and of making the proper inference between the publicly available information and its underlying strategic significance—a task that an outside translation service is not equipped to handle.

There is no doubt that the cost of developing a cadre of global managers is high, but the cost of neglecting such a need is even higher: losing to the competitors that mastered the task. One way to reduce the cost is to shift the bulk of "global management" training to the early stages of the employees' careers. The cash expenditures needed to maintain one relatively high-ranking executive in an overseas job would in many foreign locations be sufficient to support two or even three junior managers. Early foreign assignments also foster deeper involvement in other cultures and facilitate language training for which the younger employees are generally more suited than their elders. At the same time, when global expertise is a necessary condition in selection for the top of the corporate hierarchy, foreign assignments become more attractive. Thus there is less need to pay out substantial incentive bonuses over the true cost of the transfer in order to attract capable candidates.

The shift to an early global management training cannot be effectively accomplished without a close coordination of development activities with the corporate strategic objectives. On what product lines will the company concentrate in the future? In what markets? Who are the company's future major competitors? Where are they located? What is their competitive strength? How can their weaknesses be exploited? Answers to these and similar questions examining the global competitive environment will provide guidance to the HRM staff to plan corporate development activities. In return, their long-term nature implies that the corporate strategy planners have to be sensitive to feedback from the HRM operations. Multinational management development unrelated to overall strategic objectives is generally wasteful and ineffective. Global strategy that is not accompanied by appropriate HRM development programs is unsustainable.

Contextual Factors

The evolution of strategic HRM activities in a multinational firm depends not only on global competitive conditions facing a particular firm, but also on several contextual factors reflecting the global nature of the firm's business activities. Constraints stemming from the existence of these factors have to be carefully considered and accounted for in the overall HRM strategy.

For example, in the foreseeable future, cross-national mobility will remain limited to a relatively narrow range of employees. As a result, the differences in cultural orientation between the global staff and the local staffs are likely to persist. This heterogeneity of the employee pool complicates the design and execution of an homogeneous corporatewide HRM strategy. At the same time, it would be short-sighted to limit the focus of the strategic HRM to the global personnel only. This approach would merely enlarge the gap between the cosmopolitans and the locals, already an explosive issue in a number of multinational firms. Rather, without slipping to the other extreme of insensitive uniformity, an emphasis should be given to the integration of global HRM strategy with local HRM practices. The objective is to retain the local variability within a tightly focused strategic framework. Management of this paradox is an additional task that the HRM function in any successful multinational firm of the future has to tackle.

A frequent additional source of variability in the HRM practices that has to be taken into account in the development of a global HRM strategy is the host country government and legislative environment. Legislation concerning employment conditions and distribution of authority within an enterprise vary widely from country to country and cannot be ignored. However, it would be a mistake to treat these variations as merely a troublesome constraint. Whereas getting along with the worker representatives on the board of a German subsidiary might require a cultural adaptation of the newly transferred American executive, such an exposure to different employment practices might prove to be useful in enlarging a manager's leadership-style repertoire.

From the strategic viewpoint it is also important to recognize the impact of government policies and the prevailing mode of labor management relations on the task of developing the global management cadre. As an example of the former, in many less-developed countries, although the government is willing to tolerate for the time being transfers from the parent-company home country, the "import" of third-country personnel is actively discouraged. This might often frustrate the creation of balanced and well-rounded regional executives. As for the latter, it is quite common in Japan, although totally contrary to the American experience, to look upon the company union, the ability to export Japan-focused corporate culture being one of the major obstacles.

One more note on the implication of globalization for the HRM is the order. The future managers of multinational firms will not only be more globally oriented than their counterparts today. As worldwide coordination of people becomes a critical factor affecting in major ways the outcomes of global competition, the HRM function itself will lose much of its specialist character and will become an integrated part of each and every manager's job. Thus the successful multinational firms of tomorrow will exhibit these striking characteristics: (1) the responsibility for many operational and manager-level HRM activities will be diffused globally to local and regional managers whereas (2) the corporate HRM staff will concentrate on the development of long-term human mangement strategy, closely reflecting both global competitive conditions as well as environmental variations in countries in which the corporation intends to operate.

PART IV

HUMAN RESOURCES: THE CEO'S PERSPECTIVE

CHAPTER

24

AN INTERVIEW WITH REGINALD H. JONES AND FRANK DOYLE

Charles J. Fombrun

When Reginald H. Jones retired as chairman and CEO of the General Electric Company (GE) on April 1, 1981, he left to his hand-picked successor, John F. Welch Jr., an organization widely regarded as the best-managed company in the world (*Fortune,* April 1981). With a record earnings of $1.5 billion on $25 billion in sales, profits have tripled over a ten-year period on a 160 percent increase in sales. No one doubts that much of the credit belongs to Jones.

In a conversation with Professor Charles Fombrun of The Wharton School, University of Pennsylvania, Reginald Jones and Frank Doyle (senior vice-president of corporate relations at GE) describe some of the ideas and systems that have contributed to making GE the best-managed company in the world and Jones perhaps the premier organizational statesman of the decade.

FOMBRUN: GE is particularly noted for its excellence in two core areas: strategic planning and human resources management. GE's strategic business units (SBUs) have become common parlance in the corporate world, and few companies have achieved as much sophistication in either strategic planning or employee management as GE has. How did these ideas evolve, and what kinds of systems did you put in place to link human resources management with strategic management?

JONES: Let me start with a little history to give you some background on how we got at strategic planning. We had been organized on a decentralized basis at GE from about 1951 forward—and the decentralized organization consisted of a number of departments, divisions, and groups on a line basis. There were some 200 or so of these departments, each one a distinct business enterprise. On the staff side, we were organized into what were called services. For example, there was a vice-president of manufacturing services, a vice-president of financial services, and one for employee relations—except that, as I recall, we called it employee and community relations.

Now, what would happen when a major business problem or business opportunity developed for General Electric? The operating business closest to the problem or the opportunity—whether it was a department, division, or group—would generate a proposition and a so-called business plan for the chief executive officer. The CEO, in turn, would call on the various services for counsel. Well, counsel from the vice-president of manufacturing services took a manufacturing point of view, engineering gave him a technical point of view, and marketing presented a marketing point of view. All this left the CEO with a number of memoranda—each one addressing a slice of the problem, but none taking an overall business point of view.

None of them asked things like whether the proposition fit with the mission of the General Electric Company, or whether we had the necessary resources—human, physical, or financial—given all the other problems and opportunities facing the corporation as a whole. Frankly, the CEO decided that he could not assume the burden resulting from this procedure. So, in about 1970, he created something we didn't have before: a corporate executive staff. He took three of us and said: "First, I want you three fellows to look at some of our major business problems and some of the significant opportunities available to us, and then come up with a system within General Electric that will give us a basis for doing some business planning. I'm looking for some long-range plans for this company—some vision of where we should be taking it." Our discussion focused on strategic, not tactical, planning.

Our major problem then was a confluence of three very disparate businesses, all requiring enormous investments at the same time. We were entering—or re-entering, really—the commercial aircraft engine business; we had the nuclear business, which was a real problem in those days; and we had the computer business, which was already absorbing just about every spare cent General Electric had, and was going to require very major investments. The CEO suggested that we start by looking at those businesses in considering a planning system for General Electric.

FOMBRUN: You did this in addition to your regular activities?

JONES: No, we were divorced from our normal activities. We set out on this venture by launching three major studies. The results on the study of the computer business led us to sell it because, given the other things we wanted to do, it was going to absorb too much of our resources. Study results of the nuclear business led us to make drastic changes in some of our approaches to it and put it on a more solid footing. And results on the commercial aircraft engine business led us up the road to one of our greatest successes.

At the same time, we brought in the McKinsey people and the Boston Consulting Group people to work on developing a planning system. Of course, the planning system developed then was rudimentary compared with the one we have today. But the concept of a strategic business unit evolved out of all that work. We looked at our company and said we didn't see how it would be feasible for us to develop detailed strategic plans for something like 200 business departments. We agrued that there should be a way to look at them that would pull together the businesses that were similar. So we developed a set of criteria for what came to be known as a strategic business unit.

FOMBRUN: What were some of the criteria?

JONES: Oh, such things as a distinct market, a distinct set of competitors, and a distinct mission—that is, distinct from other entities within the company. We found, for example, that a number of departments in the major appliance business—the range department, the refrigerator department, the dishwasher department, the laundry department, and so on—were really one strategic business unit because they had a common set of competitors, a common set of customers, common markets, a common mission.

So we were able to group together a significant number of entities into one strategic business unit from which we would get one strategic plan. Our first cut left us with nearly 50 strategic business units. A few were quite small—for instance one that we called our commercial equipment department, which made commercial cooking equipment sold only to restaurants and fast-food people. Their mission, their competitors, and their markets were distinct from anything else General Electric was doing. Right alongside this was an SBU several hundred times larger; it was responsible for all the white goods, yet it was just one strategic business unit. So a strategic business unit could be anything from a department right up to a division or even a group.

By grouping things in this way, we were able to spend enough time looking at strategic business plans to get a reasonable understanding of them. It required a tremendous amount of effort, even though we kept a corporate executive staff in place to review these plans—review them not from a functional viewpoint (we still had that coming to us from the former services), but from a *business* executive's viewpoint. Well, after we'd developed these strategic business plans and had begun to gain some appreciation of them, we found that, again, we were committing too much of the time of the corporate executive office— the chairman and the vice-chairman. That was when we went to the sector approach.

FOMBRUN: So the sector approach was a structural change provoked by GE's need for more sophisticated planning?

JONES: Yes. We divided the company into six sectors because although the businesses had individually distinct missions, markets, and so on, they also had a lot in common. This presented a great opportunity for all kinds of symbiotic action and planning among the businesses. To test the concept, we first set up one sector for a period of slightly more than a year—and that one consisted of all the businesses that dealt with what we called our consumer markets: businesses like small appliances, television, lamps, radios, and so on.

Again, we found opportunities to do things on a larger scale when we grouped businesses that had a lot in common than when each one handled its own affairs. In corporate advertising, for example, we found not only that we made a greater impact on the consumer, but that we could do so at considerably less expense (or could use the extra money for greater coverage) when we scheduled the advertising of the small appliances, the major appliances, televisions, lamps, and so on to get consistency. Instead of having all their advertising hit in one month, with nothing for the next month, we could get a consistent approach—

we could do some scheduling. We also found that, by George, you could get some extra mileage out of putting a small appliance on a counter when you were advertising a kitchen, instead of featuring just the major appliances in the kitchen.

The sector approach brought another dimension to our strategic planning. The real test, of course, was to classify the businesses in such a way that we could apply our available resources most effectively—focusing on those businesses that offered more profitable opportunities for the company.

Sure, we classified our businesses—but we didn't go to the four-box matrix that so many companies use: the stars, the cash-cows, the dogs, and the question marks. Instead, we went to a nine-box matrix. Some situations obviously called for a harvest/ divest decision. Some were just as obviously businesses in which you were going to make major investments for growth. In between were a lot of businesses that had to be approached with selectivity—and we graded those on the nine-box matrix, with reasonable success.

FOMBRUN: Did you try to measure your success rate?

JONES: Interestingly, after we'd been doing our strategic planning for a couple of years and trying to allocate our resources on the basis of those plans, we went back to look at our resource allocation and asked: Where did we actually spend our money? Where did we authorize appropriations? Where did we put development funds, and so on? We found that the funds had been going just where they should have been going. That is, the fellows in the upper-left corner of the matrix were getting what they wanted, and those down in the lower-right hand corner were on very short leash. In between, of course, there were gradations. And this relationship has held up ever since then: Our funds have been going where we intended them to go.

The results, over a decade, have been rather startling. When we started all this, the international activities of General Electric accounted for some 16 percent of our net income—and we knew we had tremendous opportunities offshore that we weren't capitalizing on when we went into our strategic planning. (Now, however, the situation is different. Last year the international share of our net income was up to roughly 40 percent of the total.) We knew that the utility businesses had peaked and were not going to continue with the growth we had witnessed over several decades, so we had to do some cutting back on them. The percentage of our net income that came from the electrical equipment businesses, which had been our core for many years, dropped sharply.

FOMBRUN: How far?

JONES: Let me just give you those numbers. As we started into the '70s
             the electrical core of the business—electrical equipment, sup-
             plies, and apparatus—represented 80 percent of net income. At
             the end of that decade it represented only 47 percent of net
             income. It hadn't dropped—in fact it was much higher at the
             end of the decade than at the beginning. What had happened
             was that our materials businesses, which we saw as great growth
             opportunities—our new engineered plastics, our man-made dia-
             monds, our carboloids, and the like—grew from some 6 percent
             of our net income to 27 percent ten years later. Of course, we
             knew that services in a post-industrial economy were going to
             grow and they did—moving up from 10 percent to 16 percent
             of our net. And as we strengthened our commercial aircraft en-
             gine business, our locomotive transportation business moved
             from 4 percent to 10 percent. Obviously, then, we saw our stra-
             tegic planning pay off.

FOMBRUN: Most of the implications you mention seem to leave off what
             many would consider a vital aspect of strategic planning, namely
             the human resources dimension. To what extent were human
             resources considerations included in the planning process?

JONES: I was getting to that. When we classified these businesses, and
             when we realized that they were going to have quite different
             missions, we also realized we had to have quite different people
             running them. That was where we began to see the need to meld
             our human resources planning and management with the stra-
             tegic planning we were doing. If you're going to grow a business,
             you have to provide it not only with physical resources, but with
             human resources as well. You have to have specific types of
             people running those businesses. This is where you need the
             bold entrepreneurs. When you get to the harvest/divest stage,
             you've got to have the type of management that really knows
             how to control costs, and can at the same time be looking for
             opportunities to sell off a piece of the business or to price a piece
             of the business so that it becomes more profitable. We found
             to our great surprise, for example, that some dog businesses
             which weren't yielding very much for us were more important
             to our customers than we appreciated. And when we raised our
             prices to see whether the markets would stand it—a make-or-
             break move that would decide whether we'd stay with a business
             or close it down—people responded and the businesses became
             more profitable. But, again, it took a manager who was more
             concerned with cost control than with entrepreneurship.

             Frank, why don't you explain the human resources planning

systems that we put in place to match what we were doing in strategic planning.

DOYLE: As Reg mentioned, this started with the build-up of a need for specific management and executive talent to run specific businesses—to move people with distinct kinds of personal assets into areas they were suited to. Of course, there are some who can do it all—but they are few. The second need in this regard is that when you begin to take a longer-range look at the business, you have to start taking a much longer-range view of available executive manpower and where that manpower is coming from. So the first pass focused heavily on, not human resources planning as we use it today, but where the system grew in sophistication over the decade: the manpower planning system. And most of that manpower focus was on executive and managerial manpower.

FOMBRUN: It was really the fit with the strategic plan: manpower planning as a requirement for effective strategy implementation.

DOYLE: That, I think, was the lead. But what we found, for a lot of reasons, was that the current availability of managerial manpower or technical manpower was not the total equation. There were several reasons for this. Society began to look at corporations as more than just employers. As the businesses changed more rapidly, as their life cycles altered, the external world began to penetrate the decision process—particularly in the area of human resources management. So we began to consider how to introduce the concept of human resources in conjunction with strategic thinking or strategic management planning, without going back to the days of services and narrow functional views.

The great debate of the mid-'70s focused on how to introduce a more forceful look at human resources, production resources, technical resources planning—without functionalizing the strategic planning system. That was the effort. We found that we needed to get human resources considerations introduced into the planning process at an earlier stage—because if we waited until the plans were formalized and then stepped back, the human resources decisions were already made—and a lot of them were necessarily accommodating, since they were treated as a derivative rather than a primary function.

FOMBRUN: In other words, make the human resources dimension a driving force in the formulation of strategic plans rather than consider it as an implementation issue.

DOYLE: Yes. The decision was clear-cut—that is, human resources strategic planning was not to be conducted as a separate activity.

Rather, we were going to have strategic planning with a human resources input at every stage. The reason I mention each stage is that some issues, clearly of a human resources nature, could be identified at the SBU level. For example, a business recognizing that it was moving into a heavy electronics concentration knew it would need a different mix of manpower than its ordinary systems would generate. And a business entering a harvest/divest condition knew that it might have to close plants.

The reason we then took a next-level look is that some problems representing human resources issues were generated by the cumulative impact of several discrete SBU decisions. The biggest, I think (and it also correlated with our emerging electronics issue), is that we needed to change our image on campus in view of our forecast cumulative need for electronics talent. And this was so not in terms of 1978 needs, 1979 needs, or even '81 needs—but '85, '86, and '87 needs. Knowing that our business strategies were going to take us into a different kind of manpower requirement, we began to make investments in a campus presence reflecting '86 needs rather than our '76 needs.

We also began to see that the second major effort we needed was a better quantitative fix on the external environment—to pull together such obvious things as demographics, trends in social legislation, relocation, plant closings. As we looked at what was happening both to General Electric and to the U.S. economy as a whole, it became quite obvious that a major dynamic in the late '70s and on through the '80s would arise from the emergence of new businesses and the need for old businesses to die, or be sloughed off. We had an issue that required us to start doing some early planning—on, for example, what products we put into our plants to make sure we didn't impact the community precipitously.

This planning extended even to the design of benefit plans. Everyone in American labor was demanding supplemental unemployment benefit funds. We decided to make a more modest benefit payout, but guarantee it—because our judgment was that we were going to be dealing not with a temporary layoff, but with permanent displacement. This is one of a few examples of what we did to get really structurally positioned on benefit design and campus recruiting. These are things that take a long time if you're repositioning yourself—and they require a strategic, not a tactical, effort. I think there is plenty of evidence, at least as we look internally, to suggest that those decisions are paying off handsomely for us in terms of our ability to deal with some very tough issues. And, quite candidly, these are issues with which others—the auto industry and the rubber industry, for instance—have not dealt effectively.

FOMBRUN: You started with the notion of strategic drive, followed by structural change and the need for a closer look at the human resources required to achieve strategic plans. Now I hear you stressing the operational side. Are you saying that when we start looking at the strategic aspects of the company, in arranging the portfolio of businesses, we also have to recognize the implications right down at the bottom ranks? In other words, are you making a link between the strategic level and the six-to-ten-year-out campus recruiting effort or the design of the benefits package?

JONES: A major problem facing us was our growing need for talents different from the ones we had customarily brought into the company. As we moved increasingly from electromechanical approaches, we found that the number of electronics specialists and engineers in the company was far below our needs. We knew from all the work that Frank had done how difficult it was going to be to get our fair share of new graduates. If we hadn't started working on our campus presence, we wouldn't have drawn as many as we have. But we were also faced with the need for massive retraining within the company. You just don't dismiss those electrical/mechanical engineers who worked so well for you for two or three decades and say, "Well, you're washed up." So we had to design all kinds of retraining programs, starting with the top and going on down. We've put any number of programs together in varying degrees of depth to attack this problem. This was a strategic consideration.

FOMBRUN: In other words, starting a new direction for General Electric would create human resources pressures that had to be dealt with long before any problems were manifest.

DOYLE: Right. I think the international consideration is one such pressure. When our business thinking first took us there we realized that the international opportunity was enormous. But we also knew that we wouldn't be able to manage it without a cadre of people who understood what "international" meant.

In order to direct-link a lot of our business units into international markets, we found, for example, that you had to start educating early. Sounds terribly routine—but we found, for instance, that most of our business simulations still defined *market share* in terms of U.S. markets. We had to go right through our entire curriculum and change all the business simulations we use to train our managers—change them to reflect *world market share,* as part of a world view. I don't know what the time horizon is, but I am requiring relatively young managers—those who will run the company some day—to think about business problems always in terms of world markets. Their view of business is a world view of business. Now, whether that causes our expansion or enables it, I don't know, but—and perhaps this is the most critical thing about the whole GE strategic planning system—it is a terribly tangible, useful tool of day-to-day decision making. Sometimes it has a very long-range impact.

FOMBRUN: One way to look at it is that the philosophy of decentralization put into place early in the decade, in a company that is so diversified as General Electric, required some kind of glue—and that glue or cement was put in by way of the human resources side. The training, the rotations were designed to get people used to thinking in a common way that would hold the company together. Otherwise, given the decentralization, they would all have been working with quite separate world views. Was that human resources "cement" a conscious thing at the time?

JONES: Very early in the game, following decentralization, it was the thesis that the services would act as the glue, because they had the so-called "right to look." In other words, the services could go into any operating entity of the company, see how they felt it was performing, report back, and help top management upgrade performance. But when you stop to think about it, you can see the problems inherent in that. The operating people would tend to go into their clam shell and become very, very wary of the so-called "help" from services.

The beauty of the strategic planning system was that *everybody* was party to working out where they wanted to take a given business. In other words, the operating people had every chance to say, "Here is what we want to do with this business." There was a free-form discussion with the top of the company about their plan. They always felt they were able to go right to the top to have their innings and get an audience. Then, when we would suggest to them that certain changes in the plan were in order, they tended to accept the changes more readily. And it helped that we were wiser, older heads saying things like "When we look at this from a company standpoint, it becomes apparent that we now have to complement this other business in its activities," or "We have to draw back here a little bit, because we don't quite have the funds to do that." And then they began to see that on the human resources front, because of the work we were doing companywide, we could give them the help they needed to realize their plans. In other words, we were the ones who were saying, "O.K., this is the kind of talent you need— we know where we can put our finger on it, and we can supply it." In that way, we became helpful. We weren't auditing their activities—we were boosting, assisting, and guiding, and that too has helped.

In 1974–75, when we had been running strategic planning for four or five years, I asked for a study designed to look at it from an entirely independent point of view. On a nonattribution basis, key managers all over our company at every level were interviewed—and one of the most heartwarming responses we got was in reply to this question: If the corporate executive office were to abandon strategic planning, and no longer ask you for the myriad forms you fill out every year, wouldn't you breathe a sigh of relief knowing that the "fad" was over? More than 90 percent of the respondents indicated that if strategic planning were dropped, they would continue it in the individual businesses because it had been so helpful to them.

DOYLE: When in fact we withdrew the requirement for an annual strategic plan, over 90 percent chose to recycle in order to get their results. There were no volunteers to withdraw. And it is not easy work.

JONES: It's a way of life—totally accepted.

FOMBRUN: The extraordinary thing is that GE succeeded in making it more than the paper exercise it is in 99 percent of the companies that install strategic planning systems "by the book." What made the difference at GE?

JONES: Too many so-called strategic plans are nothing more than a financial exposition of the business's so-called long-range plans. When we started out, that's what we got. Then we said, "Well, this is a financial presentation you're giving us. It's based on all kinds of assumptions as to competition worldwide—and you know, you have not tested any of these assumptions. For example, you do not have a ten-year technology plan for your business. We want to see that next year. Forget the strategic plan if you can't produce one. Give us a technology plan for your business, give us a plan that tells us what's going to evolve on the technical front in this line of business."

Then we'd say: "You've told us what you think is going to be happening with the Westinghouses, the Emersons, the McGraw-Hills—but I happen to be in Japan every year, maybe twice a year, and I know what Hitachi and Toshiba are doing. There's nothing in your plans about them. Do you realize that your largest competitor in the world is Siemens? You don't even talk about German technology in your plan."

Then we'd raise questions on markets, first bringing up the $7\frac{1}{2}$ percent growth in kilowatt-power demand year-in, year-out, decade after decade, so that the business has doubled every ten years. Then we'd say: "Here we are in 1974 now—we've had the oil shock, we aren't seeing the growth in kilowatt-hour demand, and the demands for conservation are going to aggrandize, not decrease. What's all that going to do to your market?" As you begin to ask these questions, you begin to do strategic planning. Too often, it's a paper exercise, a financial presentation of a long-range plan that somebody conjured up on the basis of a group of untested assumptions.

FOMBRUN: In studies done on successful strategic planning systems, the ones that seem to be best are very fluid and involve scenario formulation. They ask: What if such-and-so happens? They build a certain readiness for the unanticipated.

JONES: We get at that at the corporate level through an economic forecasting unit. We ask that unit to give us forecasts of the economy—not just that of the United States, but the world economy and major economies throughout the world—and to do it on the basis of differing sets of assumptions that involve different scenarios. From there, we actually rank the scenarios—giving this one a 40 percent chance, that one a 20 percent chance, and so on.

We read this in January at the corporate level and send it out at the end of January or the first part of February after it had the inputs of the corporate executive office. The SBUs then have from, let's say, the middle of February until about the first of June to put together their strategic plans on the basis of these varying scenarios and economic assumptions. Now, they're given total freedom to change an assumption made by the economic forecasting if they don't think it's going to apply. We then sit down in the summer months and go through all these strategic plans at the corporate executive office level. At the end of the summer we then give the units authorization to go ahead—either on the basis of the plan as submitted, or with changes we worked out with them. Then they are given updated information from the economic forecasting unit as the fall begins, and by November each SBU sends us the first year of the strategic plan—that is, the following year's budget in more detailed form. The second year is sketched out, but is not as detailed as the first. We review those in November, and in December we reach agreement on the budgets for the first year of the strategic plan. In January, we start all over again.

DOYLE: We also provide the planners and the human resources people on the operations side with an environmental scan of the major social, economic, and political issues that we think will have potential impact on their businesses. And if an issue is challenging enough—something that's going to be pervasive or have a cumulative impact—it becomes a formal, must-address issue.

JONES: In his unit, Frank looks at all the major social, economic, and cultural trends in society. The experts at the corporate consulting level pick out half a dozen trends that they feel are most imminent and most important to a corporation such as General Electric. They review these with the corporate executive office and, after some debate back and forth, agreement is reached. In January, at our annual meeting, we issue what we call the "corporate challenges." We say, "You now all have your budgets, you all have your strategic plans—but here are four issues that are going to be of such importance to this company as we look ahead that we want you to pay special attention to them—and we're going to ask you to give us reports on them as you come in for presentations of your plans, your budgets, your results."

FOMBRUN: How detailed are they? Are you talking about broad cultural changes or are they very statistical in terms of demographic changes, population shifts, attitudinal surveys?

JONES: The managers get a thick book that tells them everything they could conceivably want to know. Job security, for instance, was a specific challenge and each planning unit was asked to look at its current and future problems, how it tended to deal with them, and what it was going to do about them. We knew, in terms of both society and the cumulative effect of what we were doing companywide, that job security was going to be an issue. A manager might say that the issue didn't apply to his business, that his operations wouldn't contribute to it as a corporate problem—or he might say that he was right in the middle of it. The challenges are phrased rather broadly, but they require a response.

FOMBRUN: From the managers of the SBUs?

JONES: Yes. Now, at the same time, we have trained the human resources manager of the SBU in human resources strategic planning, so that we can get his input when he looks at this broader universe and we won't find ourselves limited to the top-down view of the world. So we equip these managers by giving them two things—the best of our research and the best of our education—and bringing them in early. If we don't bring them in early, we're dealing again with completed plans.

FOMBRUN: You brought up the issue of having the human resources manager trained in strategic planning. Does that reflect a decision at General Electric to get the human resources manager involved in strategic planning at the SBU level?

DOYLE: Absolutely. When we introduced the concept of resource plan-
            ning, the manager we found who was most likely not to have
            a meaningful voice in the formulation of the business plan was
            the human resources manager. So we put together quite a massive
            seminar effort at the level of SBUs plus all potential reporting
            units above the department-level SBU. We also included the
            group-level and the sector-level human resources managers. Our
            original effort covered about 150 human resources managers.

            For the first program, we taught business strategic planning—
            we didn't teach human resources strategic planning. The second
            significant exercise—a four-day exercise—involved a seminar
            that said, in effect, "All right, if you develop these kinds of
            skills, these tools, and this kind of language, what kinds of
            human resources issues emerge?" Sent back out into the oper-
            ating organization, human resources managers could then be
            more comfortable with the language of strategic planning.

            Second, they were given exercises in how to link business
            planning with human resources issues. And third, we gave them
            a body of new information that allowed them to be experts in
            an area where the operating manager may not be: environmental
            scanning. When we first estimated it as a program, we thought
            it would take five years to have meaningful impact. We had it
            in three—and the reason was that we resourced and committed
            on the front end. We got great enthusiasm from the strategic
            planning fraternity. They grabbed the opportunity to get into
            that training effort. And it worked really well.

FOMBRUN: A group of us at Columbia University have been involved with
            increasing the influence of the personnel function in the strategic
            planning process of their companies. One of the central problems
            we've found was resistance from the line—a feeling by line man-
            agement that selecting, training, and developing employees was
            their work and they didn't want to give it away. How do you
            deal with that kind of line/staff issue?

DOYLE: We didn't face that. It's true that the line manager does feel that,
            but what we want to do instead of imposing it top-down from
            a centralized human resources management function is to make
            sure that the line manager has a human resources manager of
            his own who is an integral part of his business team.

FOMBRUN: In other words, not off in a service function providing "help",
            as you put it earlier?

JONES: One aspect that we haven't discussed might help tie all this
            together. The level of management people involved is significant
            to the formulation, development, and execution of strategic
            plans. We have a vice-president of executive manpower who

reports directly to the chairman of the General Electric Company—and I can assure you, from personal experience, that the chairman spends a great deal of his time with that individual, and that individual spends a great deal of time with the key management of the organization.

Each June we sit down with top management, both line and staff, for several hours—by "we", I mean the chairman, the vice-chairmen, and the senior vice-president of executive manpower. With each manager, we go through his appraisals of all his key people in depth. We go through all of his succession planning. He has to give us succession charts for every management position in his area, and we debate with him whether these are proper selections he has made. He must look not only at people in his own units, but at people in other places all across General Electric. He can't do this without the help of his human resources planner, because that individual works directly with all the human resources planners in the system—and with people like Frank Doyle and Ted Levino, the senior vice-president of executive manpower. They know where these people are. Then we ask the manager to give a development plan for each of the promising, promotable executives working with him or her. The following year, we go back and review those same people and say, "O.K., this was your development plan. Did you realize it? Did you put him in school for X weeks at Crotonville? Did you move him to this assignment? Did you give him the coaching of this individual?"

FOMBRUN: We're talking about a group of some 250 people?

JONES: More than that, actually.

DOYLE: Two hundred and fifty to 350 would be the participating population. Then you have to look down to the up-and-coming, which brings the group to about 500. Ted Levino's organization, which is completely independent of my human resources/employee relations organization, devotes full time to that activity and acts as a highly independent agency. That pervasive requirement of a manager, to be actively involved in people development, spins out. So when I go and ask for human resources plans, and human resources work and strategies, I don't run into any value clash because the managers have all been so sandpapered through that system that they know their personal growth is stongly tied to how well they develop their people.

JONES: The people on the executive manpower staff are relatively small in number. There are probably seven or eight key people there, each of them working with a given company area under Levino, the vice-president, and they really know their human resources planners who are out there. And they know the people we're concerned with. They have great credibility because they're very independent—they're not attached to anyone but the chairman of the board. They worked directly with me when I was there. They work directly with my successor now. This arrangement, of course, avoids political problems—and nepotism if it should exist.

In the long session with each key executive on the managers reporting to them, we get into their development, their appraisal, and all of their succession planning—and we get into an identification of the most promising younger people in the company. We also get into some special assignments from time to time, such as the involvement of women and minorities in upper management. It's a terrible problem to get them into upper management because the qualified supply is limited. That takes us back into Frank's area, where we have to keep working hard on campus—by, for example, bringing them in early and protecting ourselves from all kinds of pirating.

DOYLE: This is a real problem in the engineering area. A fascinating effort—it's such an early investment—is our work on the high-school level. We've spearheaded a national consortium to get more companies interested in getting women and minority students at the high-school level qualified to go on to engineering school. This is important if you're in a technology-dominated industry or business. While we're heavily in services and a lot of other businesses, technology is an overriding need at General Electric and, I think, probably in this society. We've just seen a dramatic increase in the number of women going in and completing engineering schools. This hasn't been the case with minorities, however; they're still flowing into the independent professions rather than engineering.

JONES: Even though we've quadrupled the supply over the last seven or eight years, it's still inadequate.

DOYLE: When you talk about this whole question of planning against your future issues, some of it looks like putting your resources in so early that you wonder if you're ever going to see anything. In this case, we addressed the issue as a broader societal problem, got other people and companies involved, and then moved into more of a participant role.

FOMBRUN: You were bringing up the whole problem of identifying potential. This is really a critical thing that GE seems to do so well in terms of making sure to identify people with high potential early on and get them to invest enough in the firm to stay. So, in 20 years, when you really need that general manager or someone to head up that dynamic SBU, the entrepreneurial types have not left. What makes this work at GE?

JONES: We have a decided advantage—and that is our diversity. Quite often when someone comes off campus, that individual is really not sure about what he/she wants to do with a working life that lies ahead. The graduates can come into one of our training programs and, because these programs rotate people quite often, can go from assignment to assignment, location to location—provided they are willing. Some are married and have children, so they don't want to rotate. Trainees get a chance to look at (1) several functions of the business and (2) several very disparate types of businesses. Some have a flair for the consumer business. Others have an abiding interest in the more technologically advanced businesses, with high quotients of science and engineering. Some have a flair for getting into a given function such as communication, advertising, or public relations; with others, it may be finance. Quite often we find that someone comes in and moves two, three, four times and then catches fire—finds something that really interests him or her.

FOMBRUN: There's also the reciprocal commitment, I think, that General Electric seems to give its people—a commitment that says, "If you want to, you've got a place to stay here; we want you."

JONES: We stress one thing with all of our top management, and that's stewardship. When we talk about stewardship, we're referring to more than all of the wonderful resources this company has, and all of its responsibilities, and so forth. We emphasize stewardship for the economic working lives of our employees. So much of an employee's life is tied up with work—the individual who isn't happy in his or her working life is an unhappy individual. It's the manager's job to see that the individual has a good shot at having a satisfying work experience because the experience impacts that individual in so many ways. I'm not talking about being paternalistic—just making sure the opportunities are there. If you do that, the employees will respond.

FOMBRUN: It's hard to talk about human resources management today without citing two recent books on *The New York Times* best-seller list: one by Bill Ouchi from UCLA, *Theory Z*, and the other, *The Art of Japanese Management* by Richard Pascale and Anthony Athos. They stress the people side, the cultural nature of organizations, the participative element. And I guess they express the trend toward a "Japanesing" of American business. What do you think of it?

JONES: This must be approached with balance and perspective. I've spent a lot of time in Japan, and they're doing some wonderful things.

We were one of the very first companies to recognize this. We have productivity agreements with Hitachi, Toshiba, and Toyota in which we exchange productivity information. We're working on robots together. We recognize many of the great things they've done. But we also recognize the difference in the cultures of the two countries: Theirs is a consensus society, ours an adversarial/advocacy type of society. When you get 51 percent of the vote here, you sock it to the other guy—that's America. We're not going to change into a consensus society. We're going to move, I think, with much more alacrity *because* of our type of society.

But we've had some failings. We haven't sufficiently involved our workforce. We haven't been practicing participative activities to the degree that we should have. Frank has launched some major efforts to change this at GE. I think we've done a reasonably good job at the upper levels. I think you'd find that most of the management at GE feels that they *do* get an audience, they *do* participate in our major decisions—but we haven't gotten that down to the factory floor.

DOYLE: I think there are two things about the GE experience in this regard. The first is the question of communication—sharing knowledge about the business with employees. Way back, the General Electric employee knew more about the future and key aspects of the business, I would suggest, than was the case in any other company elsewhere in the world. Well ahead of the times, we had our foremen roundtables at which our managers talked to employees about the business in fine-grained detail, down to the lowest level of participant.

But it was a heavily top-down sharing. Listing and discussing the employee's problems didn't get into that third dimension—eliciting employee inputs regarding the conduct of the business. The Japanese, with their consensus society, have of course moved well into it. We've tried several approaches here, including a very direct mimicking of the Japanese quality circle—same training, same communications, same everything plus a whole array of adaptive devices designed to deal with fundamental cultural differences and with the fact that we were coming from a different base, a better base than most organizations have. Some things that are called quality of work life in the United States are tagged as being revolutionary—when, in fact, they are simply foremen roundtables that we've been running for 40 years.

We're doing two things: (1) broadening the base of input and training managers on how to receive that input and (2) training employees, with an emphasis on language. A lot of employees don't participate because they can't articulate their ideas in ways that can be perceived and understood by the system. We're pushing to help them become articulate. Also, we now have four, soon to be six, quite comprehensive employee profit participation plans. These include everything from a straight Joe Scanlon plan—no change, pure, back to the book—to modified devices.

I don't think the jury's in on this whole question—mainly because I don't think the Japanese have dealt with two things in their society. One is that it's aging, and the other is that it's opening up. With this aging and this opening up, some of the underpinnings of the Japanese success are going to come under heavy pressure. The worst thing for us to do would be to embrace a set of approaches that are about to unravel. I do think you have to recognize the different vitality and the different kinds of assets that an American worker has. I'm talking about that independence which can drive you crazy, that self-interest which can sometimes make you wonder whether we're ever going to get this thing together—and these are assets.

FOMBRUN: Then, too, it's hard to ignore that other element of American society—the unions, the reality of labor relations that Japan doesn't face.

DOYLE: I can't fault our major unions. They support the productivity programs, they're not wasteful, they're not obstructionist, they're vigorous advocates of the interest of the employees they represent. And relationships with unions—certainly since the '69–'70 strike, which brought everyone to their senses in that regard—have involved very little lost time. There has been a lot of good effort. Good understanding. Good communications with our unions about what's going on in our business. Here, an advocate is given time to understand where something is going—to know what's moldable and what's inevitable.

FOMBRUN: There is the anecdote of the executive officer who argued that America is in its present condition because we won the war. If we hadn't won the war, he said, we wouldn't have old technology, old plants. We'd have had our plants rebuilt for us and be in superb shape—much as the Japanese and German are. A fellow officer retorted that this would be true only if our management had been locked inside at the time of bombing! Of course, he was criticizing their short-run outlook. Actually, we've had a spate of attacks against business and business schools responsible for training financial wizards who can think only about the short run. How do you address that attack on management?

JONES: I have given a speech on this subject in which I refer to management malaise, management myopia. Now that I've retired

from the active ranks of General Electric, I have said to my peers
that I wouldn't dismiss such criticism offhand. There's something
to it. Two-thirds of the inventories of the United States are on
FIFO instead of LIFO just so we can show better short-term
results at the expense of paying higher taxes and having less
cash to invest in our business over the long term.

You can see the roots of the problem when you look at the
growing disparity between the tax depreciation we take from
our tax returns and the book depreciation we take for reporting
to our shareholders; when you look at the lackadaisical approach
to inflation-adjusted accounting; when you consider the fact that
most major corporations did the absolute minimum in terms of
delineating in their annual reports the requirements or the suggestions of FASB Statement No. 33; when you look at the decline
of R&D as a percentage of GNP; when you look at the fact that
a good deal of the R&D that we do is done for the short range,
not the blue-sky long range (it's more application engineering,
say, than it is real research). When you look at the aging of our
plant, the inadequate investment that's been made, you wonder
whether all those changes are management's fault.

How could this have happened? Sure, there is some management blame. But then you've got to step back and look at the
environment that those managers were working in over the last
decade. Compare that environment with the environment in Germany or Japan and you begin to see some of the reasons this
could have happened. We were a nation that was not the least
bit concerned with capital formation. We were more concerned
with the *distribution* of wealth than the *creation* of wealth. All of
our government planning aimed at the redistribution, not the
creation, of wealth.

When I first testified in the Spring of 1974 before the Senate
on the subject of capital formation, it was before a one-man
subcommittee. That's how interested they were in the subject.
Seven years later, I'm delighted to say that there is now a lot of
understanding of the problems of inadequate capital formation,
lagging productivity, inadequate research and development. But
it took a long time to get that across.

You've got to look also at the very different nature of the
ownership of American business versus that of Germany or Japan. A very substantial amount of the equity capital of a corporation is owned by the banks in Japan and Germany—and
not just as nominees, either. The banks actually own a great deal
of the equity capital of the industrial giants of those nations.
Those banks are inclined to be more patient. They're looking for
the long-term enhancement, the stability and security of their

investments. You also see a much higher debt quotient in the total capital structure, particularly of the Japanese companies. Again, that debt is held largely by the banking system. In Japan, the major banks are parts of the same Zaibatsu that encompasses the industrial giants.

In the United States, we've seen a decided change in the nature of the ownership and the goals of that ownership of American industry. Because we've been taxing away 70 percent of the dividends that one receives on stock in this country (though this is changing with the new tax law) our investors have become speculators, traders—more interested in capital gains that are taxed at lower rates than they are in dividends that are taxed at extraordinarily high rates. So we've seen people moving in and out of stock ownership—always seeking something that's going to move quickly to give them a capital gain. They don't want to hold the stock for much more than a year or so to get the long-term capital gain; then they go someplace else to look. When that happens you get what might be called the tyranny of Wall Street. Really, it's your investors, your so-called investors, who are looking for every quarter to be better than the quarter before. When people come under that kind of pressure, you can see how they become more short-term oriented.

I maintain that it's up to the boards of directors of these major corporations to insulate management from that short-term pressure—to see that a proper balance is maintained between short-term and long-term objectives and to compensate the management for that balanced result, not just for a quarter's result that may be achieved at the expense of the long term.

I see our major corporations today not just as economic institutions; they are socioeconomic institutions. We've got to recognize that the major corporation today has responsibilities beyond its responsibility to those in-and-out investors. That's a definite responsibility, sure—but there's also a responsibility to the employees, to the suppliers, to the customers, and to the public.

Quite frankly, corporations have failed in their responsibility to the public. The public wants value—and stability and continuity through value. If the corporations continue to fail here, then public representatives in government are going to be even more injurious to the industrial system than they have been in the past. We've just now gotten the federal government around to a little different approach to American industry. Unless we capitalize on the opportunities currently available to us, I fear for our future in this mixed-enterprise system of ours. We're charged with an enormous responsibility. We've got to recognize that the greatest asset any public corporation has today is its public franchise—that is, the willingness, the interest of the public in seeing to it that the corporation continues to exist because it is a producer of values.

FOMBRUN: The concept of the socioeconomic role of business enterprises is interesting because it links in with the political activity you were getting into. Clearly, what happens in corporations has a lot to do with what's going on in society as a whole, since most of us work in organizations of one form or another. Therefore, things like human resources systems that are put in place inside corporations help create changing attitudes and values. The criteria we evaluate people on, the criteria we reinforce, the kinds of training programs we provide, the kinds of rewards workers are given—all help create the social context.

All this leads the organization—especially a large organization like General Electric or Exxon—to say, "We have a major role to play in the national well-being." Earlier, you brought up Japan, which has a far more centralized system of control—the banks are so highly connected that they function almost as a right arm of the government. In a related but different way, we could start to think of the corporate sector in America as a matrix—a vastly complex network of relationships that serve as a guiding force for the environmental trends we were talking about.

JONES: Absolutely. About a decade ago, those of us in corporate America began to see that we really had no voice in Washington. We were going down there *after* legislation passed and complaining about it—when it was far too late.

FOMBRUN: As recently as ten years ago?

JONES: Yes, just ten years ago. We recognized that labor spoke with a monolithic voice in Washington and had enormous clout. We recognized that special-interest groups were growing up across the nation, and that they had tremendous impact on our legislators. They were saying, quite frankly, "We hold you accountable for our special interests—if you're going to get our vote, you're going to mind our special interest." Whether it was consumer groups, environmentalists, or other factions, they were there—in force—and they were heard.

Business, on the other hand, was so often after the fact, not being causative in its approach. *Adaptive* is the best word you could use for its approach, which was not even realistic. Everybody down there was focusing on his own prerogatives, with no concern about the enterprise system per se. Instead, the concern was about what that piece of legislation was going to do to this industry—its imports, exports, labor conditions, or whatever. There were a number of different groups, of course, attempting to represent business. But not one of them was able to secure the personal involvement of the chief executive officer. It was always some vice-president of the organization who attended the Chamber of Commerce meetings, or the National Association of Manufacturers, or the CED, and so on.

We decided we had to have another run at it. So we formed the Business Round Table; its membership is now some 200-strong, representing mostly the large corporations in America. The overriding requirement for participation in the Business Round Table is personal involvement of the CEO. When the policy committee meets, it's the CEOs who meet, not the vice-presidents. You can't delegate that kind of responsibility. We said, furthermore, that when it came to representing the case in Washington—whether to a senator, a congressman, a cabinet officer, or the President himself—that would be done by chief executive officers. And I think this group has made a difference. It found that, frankly, most people in both the executive and the legislative branches of government were delighted to see us—we are major employers in their districts. We have a good deal of clout in terms of things that are very important to these people. And we very quickly learned that we could get an audience.

The second thing we had to learn was that nothing was more important to a chief executive officer down there than his credibility. That meant, by George, that he had to do his homework. It also meant that whatever the position taken by the Business Round Table, it had to be one that was truly in the interest of the nation and couldn't be viewed as self-serving or self-seeking. So as we started our work, we formed task forces. We assigned half a dozen CEOs to a task force. We didn't hire a bunch of economists and professional writers. We had no paid staff to develop or write our position papers. Instead, the positions were developed by the knowledgeable people in our corporations.

I, for example, was head of the taxation task force. I had half a dozen chief executive officers with whom I worked. And I got the tax executives, tax accountants, and tax counsel of those companies together and said, "you're now our working group." They would develop position papers on all aspects of taxation. We'd bring those before our task force and have some very decided arguments about what positions we would advance. Then we would go before the 40-man policy committee of the Business Round Table with our findings and explain the position we would like to take. We would have some decided arguments there, too. Finally, we would take the positions the policy committee had agreed on and send them out to all members of the Round Table.

By means of a great deal of argument and discussion, then, we were able to achieve a more balanced perspective. Let me add, though, that there were fewer areas of conflict than we had at first envisioned. In many cases, by way of good research and ample discussion, we were able to find a position acceptable to all. There were only a few areas in which we could not get a consensus on a major position—and when we saw such an upshot developing, we set that one aside. We asked everybody to go back and talk to their people about the problems involved. The surprising thing is how few of those developed over the last decade.

DOYLE: The point of not bringing the Business Round Table's power to bear on narrow issues was a tremendous discipline. When we had interests that were narrow in the business community as a whole or the nation as a whole, we went ahead and pursued them, but without trying to bring the Business Round Table's power, influence, and resources to bear on them.

JONES: And because so many of us involved in the Round Table were involved in the labor-management group that the President had formed—going back to the Nixon, Ford, and Carter administrations—we also took the time to sit down with labor and explain our positions. It was interesting that there were areas of consensus with labor. Sure, there were areas of difference, but also areas of consensus. When we got to the matter of taxation, for example, we were able to work very closely with labor on many aspects of the tax problem. The investment tax credit was an example. We were able to get the investment tax credit in the '76 act moved up to 10 percent—a very substantial change and, in effect, permanent.

One of our greatest allies on that was George Meany, because he understood its importance. We had taken the time to show him all our research and go into it in great depth. George Meany went up on the Hill with me, and I remember that when we were in Al Ullman's office he was banging the table for a 12 percent investment tax credit. When we left Al Ullman's office I said, "George, I've never heard you more persuasive in my life." And he said, "Reg, you got some good ideas—you came up with this whole thing about inadequate capital investment and so forth several years ago. But the trouble with you is that you don't know how to sell. You go in there talking about capital formation. I'm in there talking about *job* formation. That's what rings a bell with these congressmen. Capital formation means job formation." And he was so right. This is the way you begin to develop a consensus across the electorate and get some important problems solved.

CHAPTER

25

AN INTERVIEW WITH EDSON W. SPENCER AND FOSTEN A. BOYLE

Noel M. Tichy

The year 1983 marks the 100th anniversary of the invention of an automatic temperature controller by A. M. Butz of Minneapolis. William R. Sweatt, some years later, salvaged the small firm that originally produced the heat regulators, nurtured and expanded it, then passed it on to his sons Harold W. and Charles B. Under the leadership of the Sweatts, whose Minneapolis Heat Regulator Company merged with Mark C. Honeywell's Heating Specialties Company in 1927, the corporation flourished. Known as Honeywell Inc., by 1982 its revenue had grown to $5.5 billion and its workforce to more than 94,100 employees worldwide.

Honeywell has long been an international organization; its association with Japan began in 1920. Always headquartered in Minneapolis, it is self-described as "dedicated to advanced technology and offering high-quality sys-

Reprinted, by permission of the publisher, from ORGANIZATIONAL DYNAMICS, Spring 1983. © 1983 by AMACOM Periodicals Division, American Management Associations, New York. All rights reserved.

tems and services in the fields of information processing, automation, and controls" (Annual Report 1982).

In its growth and diversification—by merger, acquisition, and internal expansion—Honeywell's history is an American classic. Harold W. Sweatt, during his tenure as chairman of the board, described his business philosophy as follows:

> While I always want to strive for perfection and never want to be satisfied with less, if I had to choose, I would prefer to settle for a little less perfection today and a little more imagination for tomorrow—recognizing that in pushing this spirit of restlessness we are bound to make more mistakes and sacrifice some immediate gains.
>
> Whatever else we may do, we must strive always to keep it fully alive—this spirit of restlessness. If we do this, if we refuse to become satisfied and content with the status quo and always strive to do better and, in the process, do a little more imagining for tomorrow—we will preserve one of our most priceless and fundamental possessions."

Tradition remains a powerful force in shaping Honeywell's culture. Edson W. Spencer, chief executive officer since 1974 and chairman since 1978, is dedicated to maintaining the restless spirit. During his term at the helm, Honeywell has continued to be an innovative, growing company with imaginative yet sound management practices.

In this interview with Noel Tichy, associate professor of organizational behavior at the University of Michigan's Graduate School of Business Administration, faculty associate at the Institute for Social Research at the University of Michigan, and member of the *Organizational Dynamics* Editorial Advisory Board, Spencer and one of the officers who report directly to him, Fosten A. Boyle, vice-president of employee relations, candidly discuss how this diversified multinational corporation approaches the future, especially the management and development of its people. They describe how Honeywell is grooming tomorrow's leaders and how human resources management philosophy and practice throughout the company are supporting the corporate business strategy.

TICHY: I would like to start with a general discussion of Honeywell's environment in the 1980s. How do you two see the business environment that Honeywell and other U.S. organizations face in this decade?

SPENCER: I would say that the whole world is going through a rather prolonged period of economic readjustment, which comes out of this recent period of excess—excess credit, excess growth, and excess inflation—and it's going to take some time to wind that down. That means that companies like ours will be going through periods of slow growth rates in the 1980s and 1990s. We may have some brief periods of high-growth rates with high inflation, but it's going to be, I think, a rather more gradual growth in the economy because people are going to conserve their capital a little better and borrow a little less then in the past. That means a much more competitive economy; it means having the personnel who can adjust to a much more competitive, slower-growth economy overall. It also means being sharp and looking in the places where you can grow faster than the total economy grows. But we have to recognize that it will be a more competitive, more difficult business environment in the next 20 years than it has been in the last 20. The second absolutely criticial thing is that since Europe and Japan have become so strong in the world economy, we can no longer just view our competititors as those across the street. We are now truly in a society in which consumers are demanding the best product at the best price and "made in the United States of America" is not necessarily something they are going to buy on that basis alone. They are going to buy because they want a product, wherever it comes from. So that means we must deal with more extensive worldwide competition than we have had in the past.

TICHY: Is the economy solely consumer-driven?

SPENCER: Call it user-, or customer-driven. Consumer-driven, sure, for video tape recorders, televisions, and automobiles obviously, but the same push from users or customers is going to apply in such industrial markets as machine tools. And even new plants and processes will come from places where they are the best and the most competitive.

TICHY: Has that change been evolving in Honeywell's thinking?

SPENCER: Fortunately, we have been abroad for many years and have always been very heavily involved in international markets, so we are much better prepared to deal with the increasing international competition than many other companies. Incidentally, a lot of our executives—I think eight out of our top dozen or so executives—have actually lived and worked outside of the United States. We are prepared for that side of it. But what we have to gear for now is to get more of the type of executives who can deal with this slower and erratic growth of the overall economy that I see coming.

BOYLE: I would add that even though we have been involved internationally, the kind of cost pressures that we have to compete with on a worldwide basis, makes it hard to get that international mentality, even in Honeywell. We still tend to operate in U.S. divisions with a U.S. mentality, and I think we have got to broaden our horizons.

TICHY: It sounds as if you assume that this is going to be an increasing trend. Let's look specifically at some of the people implications at the senior executive-level and then on down through the organization. What are the important people issues that Honeywell should consider?

SPENCER: Let me start down lower in the organization because it fits our story. About six years ago, we senior managers sat back and said: "What kind of people are we going to need in the 1980s and 1990s to manage this business? What are we going to have to do to attract them? What kind of motivation and desires are they going to have? What differences are there between their motivations and the motivations that we all have? We are all products of World War II, the job boom, and the years immediately after that, when getting work was fairly easy. Most of us in senior management are in our mid-40s and 50s. And we suddenly realized that the people we will need are, first, going to have to be trained differently; they will have backgrounds in computer science, mathematics, and engineering. And we'll need a whole new raft of skills to deal with the type of products in our high-technology business.

The second thing we realized is that we are going to shovel a lot of software. We are moving from a hardware to software company. We're moving from an electromechanical or mechanical type of product to an electronic product. We're moving throughout the whole business into computer- or microprocessor-driven systems with all the software implications that goes with it. So we will require very different skills. The old skills of the mechanical engineer, assembly-line worker, and tool-and-die maker are always going to be there, but they are going to be less important in the total picture. Well, then, suddenly somebody said "Gee, you know those people we're going to have to recruit are like our kids, more college-educated, having more finely tuned skills, probably brighter, and with many more women competing for top jobs." Then we considered what our kids are interested in: They're much more mobile, for example; they may have less loyalty to companies and more loyalty to the quality of life that they want to live. They may want to live in the Southwest or the mountains and less in the industrial heartland of the country. So we decided that we'd better start changing the way we deal with people in the company—otherwise we wouldn't be able to attract them and keep them because their desires and motivations are so different than ours were when we were their age.

BOYLE: I think we're going to have a difficult time in the 1980s getting the kind of people that Ed is talking about—that is, people who will really make a contribution in a more competitive, world-based economy. This is because if you look, for example, at electrical engineers—one of the prime technical skills we need—I think about 14,000 electrical engineers graduated in 1969. Then the number of electrical engineer graduates actually went down in the early 1970s, and this past year the number rose back to about 14,000. So we are dealing with a static supply—and with the end of the baby boom hitting the colleges, in a few years we will be fighting over not a static supply, but a decreased supply.

SPENCER: The implication is that we will need a growth business that is going to grow faster than the slow-moving averages I talked about, so Honeywell looks like a place where there is opportunity. But we are also going to have to be a place where people are going to want to work, where people will like their work, and where they will want to come and stay with us.

TICHY: On this dimension, one of the comparisons you hear a lot in Honeywell is with such companies as Hewlett Packard. Are you going to have to complete with such companies for those young people?

SPENCER: I would say that Hewlett Packard is one of a number of companies—there are many—that are younger than ours. We have an old culture; we are 100 years old. A lot of the companies we will be competing with have grown up in the last 20 or 30 years, and they've had the advantage of starting from zero and going up.

TICHY: Why is it better or easier for them not to have the hundred-year-old culture?

SPENCER: It's not better—just different. We still have the traditions of senior managers who preceded Foss and me. They have greater difficulty adjusting than perhaps we do. We have an old family heritage that we have had to come out of and over the last 15 to 20 years we have had to build a new, professionally managed business. and, you know, you don't do those things overnight.

BOYLE: You mentioned Hewlett-Packard as an example of newer electronic-type companies, but we do have similar traits in our philosophy of management and our people orientation. We tend to recruit for entry-level jobs, train, develop, and promote from within. Even in the high-growth mode we've been in, we have been able to maintain that kind of culture. We are stressing teamwork and long-term employment.

I'm not knocking other industries but if you take the banking industry, particularly commerical banking, it seems to be very competitive without much teamwork. The compensation systems, for example, seem to support the philosophy that you may not be there in a couple of years. I think those are the sorts of traits that we have avoided.

SPENCER: Take the case of Silicon Valley. We've had to adjust from a somewhat more traditional, conservative, upper midwestern way of running a business to compete for personnel with such Silicon-Valley businesses as Hewlett Packard, National Semiconductor, and Intel. Therefore, we have to swing a little bit harder and produce more quickly and faster than we are accustomed to in Minnesota, where it's more conservative.

TICHY: I assume the pressure gets put on the management at the next level above that semiconductor group. How do they have to begin to change, or how do they become different, as you begin to pump different people into the semiconductor divisions?

SPENCER: Obviously, the people who run the semiconductor divisions for us have to deal with the semiconductor world. But their bosses, who probably aren't products of the semiconductor world, have had to learn how to do things in that world and be willing to adapt and be flexible and to adjust to different reward schemes, different lifestyles, and so on, and I think they've done it rather well.

TICHY: If you start moving up the ladder and you start thinking of executives who can manage Honeywell in the future, are they going to be different—given the world view you have—and if so, how?

SPENCER: Well, I think obviously they are going to have to be able to cope with the technology changes. They are going to have to cope with a higher speed of change in technology, product, competition, and marketing than perhaps most of us did in our younger days. They are going to have to cope with this different motivation of the younger people they will be hiring in the 1990s and the next century. They're going to have to be able to deal with a global competitive environment. And I think it requires a broader-gauge person who is trained in a broader way perhaps than a lot of our managers of this decade and the previous two decades.

TICHY: Do you see it changing, or are you in the process of changing the way in which you develop senior managers over the next decade?

BOYLE: We have worked hard on development strategy over the last three years. In a company as big as Honeywell, you can run almost any kind of development program two or three times a year and get 25 people to come to it. But we try to match our development strategy with the training constituencies at various levels in the organization. We put together a model in which we split the workforce into five levels, starting with nonsupervisors and going all the way up to vice-president; within each level there are four stages of development. We compare development programs with this model to see where the duplications are, where the gaps are and, in general, to take a more strategic approach to our development efforts. That leads to a core curriculum of courses and a supporting curriculum for all management levels. We have also brought a new corporate conference center on line to assist in our development efforts. Now development, from my perspective, takes place about 80 percent on the job, 10 percent through the coaching and mentoring of one's supervisors or peers, and probably 10 percent in a classroom setting. However, classroom training is a powerful catalyst. I think classroom training sets a tone and pulls the other development efforts together. We are doing some further study in terms of job development and relationship development and the way in which we might put that down on paper and communicate it to the organization. We're still looking at how to develop people more effectively and efficiently and how to get the best leverage for the dollar that is spent. But we still have a lot of work to do on this.

SPENCER: Let me expand on Foss's answer with a couple of specific examples of what we are doing to add meaning in this area. We established a human resource department four years ago. Until that time Foss had had a fairly typical personnel career—labor relations, compensation, division personnel involvement, corporate staff work, and so on. At that time the corporate personnel department became the corporate employee relations department, obviously symbolic of a change in attitude towards the function. Though it didn't change a lot of things internally, it was a signal to people. Then Foss went from that very traditional personnel development plan to become the first director of the human resource department. It was a training place where Foss could expand his scope and understanding of this whole process of developing people. That's what we all felt the company had to do and, of course, he moved from there into corporate vice president of employee relations, reporting directly to me.

TICHY: That was part of this whole plan to focus more attention on human resources?

SPENCER: Right. The human resources department became the vehicle for implementing the kind of concept that we evolved—the change in motivation and the openness in dealing with people.

TICHY: How do you make this happen? Is it those on the line that make this happen? A struggle in many organizations and perhaps in Honeywell is getting the line's cooperation. This is a significant part of their job. How is this transition happening at Honeywell, and what are some of the successes and problems you still have to overcome?

SPENCER: I think it depends on the attitude that is created by those of us in senior management and whether the chief executive can maintain a nonpolitical, open, easy environment between himself and the people who work for him. Those who work for him who are

smart and observant and who agree on the concepts (if they disagree differences are talked out) are going to transmit that in the
way they deal with the people who report to them, and it's going
to go on down through the organization that way. It's probably
a lot easier for a 40-year-old executive to do that than it is for a
60-year-old executive. And there are some of our senior management who struggle with this, but recognize it and push it in their
organizations. There are others, though, who just can't adapt to
it, so the process doesn't go at the same rate of speed throughout
the whole organization; I think it's fair to say that in some of our
divisions and groups, it moves rather slowly. There is still a tendency to be too authoritarian, to be too protective of one's turf.
And we just have to find ways to break that down.

TICHY: How do you monitor or manage that?

SPENCER: I guess I don't monitor it. The chief executive of this company
            doesn't monitor. He knows his people very well; he's talking to
            them and travels among them frequently. All of us travel a lot
            and get our hands directly on the operations. We have a pretty
            darn good feel of where it's working and where it isn't; the com-
            munications in this company are pretty good. I think we in senior
            management can see rather quickly where more change is needed
            and work with those people to help improve their attitude toward
            this new managing style and try to implement it a little bit better.

BOYLE: I think we have to keep in mind that, first of all, changes in an
            organization's climate and culture are long-term, and they do take
            a long time to develop. People really measure you in terms of what
            your actions are and what you do, not what you say, so senior
            management has to set the tone. In a larger organization there are
            some symbols that you use. Ed developed some principles, both
            an operating set of principles and then later a employee relations
            set of principles. We have been trying to disseminate these widely
            over time. In addition, we have undertaken some special things
            in the last two or three years. Jim Renier (current vice-chairman,
            former president at Honeywell Control Systems) and his staff have
            taken up the subject of management climate and culture, looking
            at what are we now and what should we do about it. Then some
            of his bigger groups took up the same issue themselves, so there
            have been some special efforts like that. But change comes through
            people viewing how people manage the business and what they
            stand for; that's how you implant a strong culture into the line.
            In some cases, a true change in climate will require the replacement
            of the managers involved.

TICHY: Are you beginning to hold people more accountable at senior levels
            for their ability to develop people?

BOYLE: We hold them accountable, but I'm not sure we hold them any more accountable today than we did ten years ago. It's just that we're looking for different results from them because we're looking for a different approach to management, perhaps, than we did ten years ago. We still have what we started in 1969, high talent reviews and review of EEO results and promotions. We do this in great detail, all the way up to the top of the company.

TICHY: Does the development review process provide a vehicle for changing Honeywell's culture?

SPENCER: Whereas I might work out problems almost daily with the people who work for me—we interact all of the time—the development review process lies in the way in which the chief executive and the employee relations vice-president and the vice-president in executive development get their hands on a broader perspective and can ask lower-level people directly what they are doing.

TICHY: How does the development review process relate to the strategic planning process at Honeywell?

BOYLE: Well, our strategic planning process involves a mid-year review that is essentially a five-year look at marketing, research and development, and strategic sorts of issues. Then we have a year-end review, which is a three-year financial plan that really turns more into next year's financial plan. All of the divisions come forward to corporate twice a year.

The development review is not part of these strategic reviews. Now we have a human resources planning process that we are pushing very hard to support the divisional employee relations departments. We want the divisional employee relations director to be a full member of the general managers' team and help in developing the strategic reviews. Any significant human resources issues that fall out of that planning process should be brought forth to corporate management at the time of the strategic review. The development reviews take place division by division; we roll up division reviews in the first quarter and then group reviews by midyear and then go on to corporate reviews. Ed finally takes them to the personnel committee of the board in September. So the two processes are not together. Now, certainly, some companies will argue that's wrong. I think if we were to submerge the development process into the strategic-planning process we would lose some of the people-evaluation aspects that we get by separating them.

SPENCER: On the other hand, they come at the same time of the year, so that at the same time I'm reviewing a long-range strategic plan for all of these operating units in the business, I'm also going through the personnel-development plan and it's very easy to see if the two are out of sync.

TICHY: So when you're going through the strategic plans you're conscious of the manager's plan for people resources? Then, if the manager's business plans are out of sync, you will do something about it or raise questions?

SPENCER: Oh sure—for example, ten years ago a great deal of interest suddenly arose throughout the organization in developing the type of people who can use integrated circuits in our products. Answers to questions we asked in the talent reviews made it apparent that we didn't have enough integrated-circuit designers in the company. So we started a crash program to go out and train and hire integrated-circuit designers.

TICHY: Do you see more linkages between the business strategic-planning process and the talent-review process in the future—or are you satisfied with the way they are positioned now, looking ahead over the next five years?

SPENCER: I'm very satisfied. The two processes are complementary: We use the talent reviews to raise questions that come out of the strategy reviews to be sure we've got the people we need. Then, in the strategy reviews, we make sure we ask the question, "Have you got the people to do that?" We get a *yes* or *no* and then see that any needs are addressed accordingly in the talent-review process.

BOYLE: I think that if top management and management at all levels consciously make the linkage, it works fine. You have the best of both worlds.

SPENCER: There is another thing that helps it work. Foss, as the vice-president of employee relations, sits in on all the strategic-planning meetings and all of the operations-planning meetings. It's his job, really, to remind me if there are places that, in his opinion, we are not doing what we should be doing.

BOYLE: That is a significant advantage over the way we were organized before. It was very hard to ask the vice-president of employee relations to have a strategic orientation about some of these things and make sure we are covering the bases when, in fact, the vice-president was not involved in the reviews.

TICHY: Let me raise an issue—the role of staff and line, especially in the human resources area. I guess at one end of the spectrum might be the view that staff is not to be seen; they're overhead; they'll get in the way. At the other end of the spectrum is the view that they're an integral part of the management team who should be actively involved. Which is it at Honeywell?

BOYLE: I think we've made some progress on the line-versus-staff issue. I think effective companies have to operate as a team. I don't think the staff should lose sight of the role that is essentially to support operating management to get the job done. On the other hand, I suppose, Honeywell is like any other company: I've been in situations where I felt certain portions of the company regarded the staff as a necessary evil rather than a productive portion of managing the business. But I do think we've made some progress. It's because of the signals that we have had at the top, where the use of the staff is different than it was before. We have been able to upgrade our staff. After all, you have to bring something to the party before you're really accepted, and we have made some progress on that.

SPENCER: Hopefully, everybody in the organization and line management observes that Foss sits with me in all of these meetings and is part of our monthly management committee, and therefore would look on their own employee relations director as having the same relationship with them as Foss has with me. And I think in most parts of the company it works that way. Where it doesn't work that way, many times it's not the organization's fault; it's because you don't have a good enough person or the right fit between the line manager and the staff manager.

TICHY: One of the comparisons I've heard made in Honeywell is between the financial staff and other staffs. The financial staff is characterized as a positive strong force. It's seen as having more of a team relationship with the line than, for example, employee relations. How do you see this?

SPENCER: The objective is to have all of our corporate staff departments function the way the financial department has for a very long time, and our corporate controller has been in that job or a job very similar to it since 1969. He had also been a controller in many different operating units in the business before that. A lot of the people in the controller's departments are people he brought in, trained, and moved around. The objective, though, and we're doing this in employee relations increasingly, is that every employee relations director in a line-operating unit of the company should realize that his promotion depends on two things. First, and most important, is satisfying his boss—doing the right things and meeting objectives that he and his boss agree on. When the time comes for promotion, we're going to see that every person also has to be approved by the corporate vice-president of employee relations so that he has his hand into the overall quality, development, and the training of the employee relations department.

TICHY: I assume the controller's organization has to balance service and control. How does that get worked out in the human resources area?

BOYLE: I think that the financial community has a little more leverage in their ability to control and get acceptance from the line departments. There are several accounting standards that must be met.

It's not a question of saying, I think you should do it this way because you'll end up with a better situation; however, that happens many times in employee relations because you are dealing with intangible things. With the controller's organization, it's usually a question of these are the rules, and this is what we are going to do about the situation. But I think the objectives are exactly the same. You have to have the right roles. There's a role for the corporate employee relations department, and in a couple of the big groups we have group-level employee relations departments. If they play the right role, we can all help support the divisions in the right way—not get in their way, not set up barriers, but in fact help them get their job done. We have sorted out many of these turf-and-role questions, and we're working very hard to make sure we have the right kind of people with the right kind of relationships to the line in employee relations.

TICHY: I see a two-way street there. It puts pressure, if you move in a direction that you're talking about, on the professional quality of the employee relations staff—to be able to play that role by going to those meetings and adding value to them. How do you look at the challenge of developing an employee relations function that can take on some of these new tasks and think more in business terms than had been historically true for employee relations people?

BOYLE: That is a challenge. Employee relations, looking back over 20 years, has changed a great deal. It used to be labor relations as the king of the hill, but the labor movement is in trouble. Our company is now more generally made up of salaried technicians, engineers, and so forth. Labor relations is still important, but many other factors have come into the picture. The field is changing as a result of all kinds of legislation passed over the last 20 years. ERISA legislation, EEO legislation, OSHA legislation, and so on have had an impact on employee relations. Practitioners have to be aware of this legislation and know how to effectively deal with the issues created by it. More change is occurring as we face this whole area of motivation and culture, and how you get people involved in changing management styles. It is a different sort of thing; it's much more psychologically based and it requires different kinds of skills. To some degree I think we have to bring new people into employee relations. We have done that at various levels in Honeywell over the last few years, although we're still developing and promoting from within as our main course of action. However, there are certain departments in which we do need specialists who can provide assistance to divisions. We can't afford specialist expertise everywhere, so one role of corporate is to provide some special expertise not present in the divisions.

TICHY: As a teacher of M.B.A.s, I can't resist exploring your views on the role of M.B.A.s in the employee relations field at Honeywell as well as some of your broader views on M.B.A.s in other areas of Honeywell. I've gotten interested in training M.B.A.s who have interest in human resources/employee relations careers. Now some companies, such as EXXON, have shifted rather dramatically by putting primarily M.B.A.s into the employee relations function, while other companies wouldn't touch an M.B.A. with a ten-foot pole for that function. My question is, where do M.B.A.s fit or not fit into the employee relations area at Honeywell?

BOYLE: Our company has not hired M.B.A.s in large amounts. By that I mean that we haven't had a program requiring that we go to prestigious M.B.A. schools and take X number of people a year. We have hired a few M.B.A.s and we have a number of people who come to work for us and then get M.B.A.s, either at night or in some cases through a day-a-week program that permits them to continue to work full time. So we've not been, traditionally, an M.B.A.-oriented hiring company. I don't think we've been M.B.A.-oriented in the employee relations field either. We've hired several people with master's degrees in industrial relations out of schools like the University of Minnesota and other schools that have the speciality, and hopefully we'll do more of that with Michigan. I don't have any bias toward an M.B.A. not being able to do the job. I think a bright person with a degree who has a strong interest in the field is a good bet. Most of our recruiting is still geared to the industrial master's programs that are, in many cases, aligned with business schools.

TICHY: There is an interesting issue here. An argument can be made that in order to change the human resources role, to be more active in the business-planning process, and to deal more actively with finance, marketing, and production, an M.B.A., which is a generalist degree, would help. What I hear you saying is that such a business generalist doesn't fit with the major part of your strategic plan.

BOYLE: No, I'm not saying it doesn't fit. As I understood it, the question you asked was whether we have an active program to hire M.B.A.s into the employee relations field. Since we don't have an active program for M.B.A.s in general, we don't have one for employee relations. I think an M.B.A. can fit very well into employee relations, and I think a broad background, a generalist background is very, very helpful. You tend to get quite a spectrum of capabilities in employee relations anyway. A lot of people who are now in employee relations started in production control in Honeywell. Because we hired people with various degrees in production control it seemed to be a spawning ground for people who later transferred into employee relations, and many of them stayed there. We also get people coming out of sales and from other disciplines.

I think that to be effective, people in employee relations have to be members of the team that's managing the division or the group or the corporate area—and that means that they have got to know something about the total aspect of the business. Transferring into the function after initial hiring may be the best way to obtain this knowledge.

SPENCER: Let me give you a different perspective on the M.B.A.s. My own attitude has shifted somewhat over the years; maybe it's because I have a son who has an M.B.A. I used to feel that the M.B.A.s 10, 15, 20 years ago wanted to get ahead very fast. They thought they had extra credentials, and that they were therefore a little better perhaps than people who weren't quite as well-equipped. Frankly, we found their impatience to get ahead caused a problem about three years down the road after they suddenly realized that they weren't moving fast enough.

We developed a general attitude of being cautious about hiring M.B.A.s, but my own view of that has changed. I'm not sure it's changed broadly throughout the company, but today most M.B.A.s will hopefully have had work experience between their undergraduate years and their M.B.A. degree. When they get their master's degree it says to me that this person has learned what the world of work is like and has decided that he or she wants to make a career in business and has been willing to invest two years and all of that money to hone skills to a higher degree. Today we should be perhaps a little more aggressive with M.B.A.s because the level of maturity is quite different than it was when we got them right out of college. Broad exposure to finance and manufacturing and other functions is pretty good. I must say that I would lean toward M.B.A.s who have worked, who have honed the tools of marketing and manufacturing and technical things, more than toward those who want to be financial wizards.

TICHY: That's interesting, I started teaching M.B.A.s in 1972 at Columbia, and I was there until a year and a half ago. I watched them change over the years. I share some of your views. I think part of the change is based on shifts in the criteria for those who come to a business school. There is also a more realistic view of the world that we live in. They are harder-working now than they were ten years ago, by far.

SPENCER: I do not have as high regard as perhaps some people do for those with the straight undergraduate business degree who then go out to look for a job. The reason is that I think people in their undergraduate years ought to broaden themselves as much as they possibly can, and if they have made a decision not to be a scientist or an engineer or a doctor, they should start out early in their careers by maybe learning how to read and write properly by taking English and literature courses, as well as some mathematics. Everybody ought to take mathematics; it is absolutely essential. If a person wants to get a business degree, he or she ought to do it at the graduate level rather than the undergraduate level. It's that breadth of experience in the educational process that develops the long-term employee or senior manager who is better than somebody with a very narrow focus such as that of the undergraduate business major, in my opinion.

TICHY: Let me pick up on that theme and ask you, in an autobiographical way, to look at your own development as a manager and to explain how that process provides lessons for developing the manager of the future. What were your development experiences and what things contributed to your ability to perform your current role?

SPENCER: I would say that the most important element in my education and understanding of broad things—people relationships and historical relationships and a whole lot of things that have been indirectly very useful as I progressed up the management ranks of the company—was two years of graduate school at Oxford in political economics and philosophy. Because it was in a European country, I was absorbing a whole different culture, which I think was extremely helpful. Obviously it also got me started on my internationalization. The second thing that had a very profound effect was five years of working in Japan. It's not that the Japanese do everything so well, but they do have a way of building a consensus towards a common objective that is extremely useful and helpful. Some of the things that we are trying to do within our company and many other American companies today is to share objectives, to get people to agree on the objectives, and then to go out and get it done. The Japanese have been doing that for centuries, and they do it very effectively in business as well.

TICHY: When in your career did that experience come?

SPENCER: In the late 1950s and early 1960s—about 15 years ago. It was after I had about ten years of work experience. First, I spent five years with Sears, five years with Honeywell, five years in Japan, and then fifteen years here in upper management.

TICHY: Were there any other developmental experiences that were significant, as you look back over your career?

SPENCER: I was lucky because in foreign assignments you get a very broad experience; you're there alone, thousands of miles away, and you have all of the functions reporting to you—operations engineering, selling, employee relations, and public relations, and so on. So you get a much broader experience much earlier when you run a foreign affiliate than when you have to run a very large U.S. division. Unfortunately, we can no longer send as many young up-and-coming American executives abroad as we could 20 years ago to run foreign affiliates for experience, because we now have very, very capable foreign nationals running those affiliates. What we have to do is look for the people who might be the general managers of the future and be sure that in their early thirties they are being tested. By the time they are 35 or 40, we know whether this person can become a division general manager, group vice-president, and so on.

TICHY: How do you create those conditions for testing?

SPENCER: One way we've done it is to create small business ventures; instead of folding business opportunities under a great big division, we create a venture and put a venture manager in charge of it to test their abilities. It's a small unit but it presents a broad range of responsibilities, as opposed to a narrow functional responsibility in a huge venture.

TICHY: There was a *Wall Street Journal* article in July on Jack Welch's views on what General Electric (GE) has to do to succeed over the coming decade. He contends that the kind of world that GE wants to be able to successfully compete in will need to increase the entrepreneurial behavior of its management. To do that Welch says GE is going to have to create more testing conditions that provide managers with more opportunity to take risks and fail, but fail in a way that does not cost them in their careers and/or disrupt the organization. Thus they can learn from their experiences. Are there any parallels in this for Honeywell?

SPENCER: I agree completely with what Jack says. I think we've been fortunate because most of our companies have relatively small, self-contained units. We probably have 30 different self-contained businesses in those parts of our business that we identify as the control businesses, in which people can have that broad responsibility. We break the bigger units down into ventures and nonventures and we take the nonventures and break their managers down into program managers and product-line managers, both of whom have a very broad responsibility. It's been quite different in the computer business. We're competing with a rather monolithic major competitor; hence we tend to try to drive things in that direction. Now we're in the process of trying to find ways to break that business into smaller, more manageable units.

TICHY: What happens in Honeywell if you fail as a manager? Different corporate cultures deal with failure differently. On one end of the

spectrum you find companies where, if you fail once, that's it—
while there are others where if you fail, you go into the penalty
box for awhile and then you work your way out of the penalty
box. What happens in Honeywell?

BOYLE: I don't think it's good to fail in any organization. However, much
obviously depends on the mistake that causes the failure. I think
that we are tolerant of failure at Honeywell. To give you an example, we have this promote-from-within philosophy that permeates the culture. We do not let people go—long-sevice
employees for example—without giving it a lot of thought. The
group vice-president has to sign off on termination of any employees with 15-or-more years of service. So if you look at what
we stand for, there is certainly a permanence about this organization that's part of the culture. Now I would say that we're
tolerant of failure, but I would also say that we are very intolerant
of factors that go into that failure that involve things like integrity
of the individual, compromising organizational principles, and similar matters. If it's straight risk that was taken, I think we are
somewhat tolerant.

SPENCER: I've also felt that in some cases, people failed because we put them
in a job they couldn't do. We have a greater responsibility in that
case. Obviously, if you take the person out of that job, the person
might get mad and walk out the door. On the other hand, I've
always felt that if a person fails because he's in over his head, we
should give him another chance at something within his capacity—
and if he can't do that, either, then we have to find a way to help
him out the door. Both Foss and I are saying that a great deal
depends on why that person failed and whether he failed as a
result of our fault. If that's the case I want to make sure he gets
another chance. If he fails because he comes up short on integrity
or judgment and it's not a case where a legitimate risk-taking
situation hasn't worked out, then it's another issue.

TICHY: Let me ask another kind of philosophical question: That is, where
on the spectrum you would place yourself in terms of viewing
human assets as fixed-versus-variable assets. Some corporations
prefer one over the other. For example, IBM makes a big thing of
full employment and thus treats the people more as fixed assets.
Where do you come out on that?

SPENCER: My immediate reaction is that all people are variable assets because
they change, and move around, and get promoted; they are not
anchored in cement. They are all variable assets to be dealt with
accordingly, as they can be changed and developed and promoted
and moved.

TICHY: What about laid off?

SPENCER: My attitude toward that is very clearly that a company has to do what is needed to be competitive; if it has to reduce employment to be competitive, or if it has to reduce old skills that can't be retrained and hire new skills, it must have the freedom to do that. Even IBM has had layoffs and early retirements. I don't know of any American company that's immune. It would be marvelous to say we have fixed, full long-term employment, and nobody is ever out of a job. But if we are comparing our situation with Japan, we must take into account the fact that Japanese companies have a very large number of young women who are temporary workers and can be laid off, and companies also have a great ability to off-load their unemployment on their subcontractors. It's not quite what the propaganda makes you think it is.

BOYLE: I don't think we do anybody a service if we have a policy that doesn't permit us to react to the business situation. However, we are trying to involve more of our employees in managing the business and we're asking them to share the objectives that we have. The more we do that, the more employees will say to us, "Well, you may have to lay off people, but you should not look at it as the only or the first way to cut costs." We have had some layoffs, but I'm hopeful that as the business goes up we can introduce some buffers that will lessen the impact of layoffs in another down cycle. It's going to take some time and some thought.

TICHY: *The Wall Street Journal* this morning (November 3, 1982) discusses the layoff of 1,800 people on the computer side of Honeywell. How do you face that kind of difficult situation and minimize the damage to those who stay in the organization? It is happening right now.

SPENCER: One thing to do is to look at each one of those people as an individual and try to recognize his or her other strengths and weaknesses and find other places in the division where they can be placed. That's the first thing. The second thing is to transfer them to jobs in other parts of the company. And the third thing you do is to help them find opportunities with other companies.

BOYLE: I think what we also try to do is be as candid as we can in terms of why we have to take the action and the numbers of people involved, and to provide the best outplacement help possible.

SPENCER: But you know the thing that I think we should never lose sight of, in any business, is that our success as a company is going to depend on our ability to be competitive and make profits, to grow and expand the business, and to offer more employment opportunities. Therefore, if from time to time we get soft, we get fat, we get lazy, we get noncompetitive, or we have market conditions that turn against us, then we have to take action to bring the costs and number of people in line.

TICHY: In Europe they have legislation that changes the degrees of freedom in terms of doing that. How would you deal with that whole issue of employment—the role of private sector versus government? Coming from Michigan I constantly wonder about the issue, and what happens to the auto industry where several hundred thousand hard-working souls are permanently out of jobs. Who does what with those people?

SPENCER: First, talking about the problem of maintaining employment levels outside of the United States, in most countries that I am familiar with you *can* reduce your payroll. It's just that there are legislative costs of doing it as opposed to the negotiated costs of doing it in this country. Where you are involved heavily with the government, my experience has been that it's very difficult, but if the facts are laid on the table you can get the support of the government to go ahead to adjust your workforce to the size you need to be competitive in the business. It's a lot tougher, it takes longer, and it cost more outside the United States than it does in the States.

TICHY: Taking a more philosophical, societal view, what are your thoughts about how that problem should get managed or will get managed in the United States?

SPENCER: I've been observing and reading more about people, paying more attention to the issue of structural unemployment, and I think that in this country and in western Europe we are going through a dramatic change in the skills that society needs in the future. It gets back to the question that we discussed much earlier about what kind of people we need in Honeywell in the 1980s and 1990s. Unfortunately for a lot of people who have devoted their careers to working hard on the assembly lines in automobile factories, the steel mills, and the mines in northern Minnesota, there is going to be less of a demand for those kinds of skills and that kind of experience.

That places a great responsibility on society and on government to try to find ways to retrain those people, to provide unemployment compensation for those people, and to assist those people in moving to other parts of the country. In a large, diverse country like ours, it's a difficult problem. The Japanese have handled this problem very well because although they at one time dominated the world export market for textiles, now they are a huge importer of textiles. A lot of their textile workers were moved into shipbuilding and the steel mills. As those industries become more mature, a lot of people are beginning to move into automobiles and into electronics. One of the things that really tells the tale is this: I read an article in the Japanese newspaper recently about how the automobile industry in Japan is not going to be competitive in the later part of the decade on a world basis and therefore they had begun to think now about what type of opportunities can be created in the later part of the decade for automobile workers who will no longer be needed on the assembly lines.

TICHY: Does this create a societal problem for Japan?

SPENCER: Yes. But being homogeneous, and having that strong link between business, education, and government, they're better able to handle the problems and work toward common objectives to solve those difficulties than we are in our diffuse and larger society.

TICHY: What roles does Honeywell play in this big, diffuse society?

SPENCER: I think the more important role that Honeywell can play is to run its business very well, to be in growing markets, and to need more people to meet our competitive edges than we hope we have with product lines that are expanding the sales line. That's the Number One thing.

TICHY: Let me get back to the challenges of the 1980s. If you look at the world you have laid out for Honeywell, and the kind of environment you are going to be struggling with, what are the major people-related challenges or hurdles that you see out in front of you?

SPENCER: I think one of the most critical things we have to do within this company is to develop opportunities in the upper levels of management for minority Americans and female Americans. All of our statistics on equal employment are very, very good in a statistical sense, but we have not done as good a job as we should in getting these people into the upper levels of management. Why do I say that's a responsibility that we look upon as a challenge? First of all, because in a societal framework, it's a necessary thing, but also because there is a lot of skill there. You have got to take those people who have just as much skill as white males because we are going to need those skills in the future, and there is a whole resource out there in female employees and minority employees that we can tap to fill the needs of the future. So that's one challenge that I see out in front of us that has both a self-serving motive and a societal motive to it.

BOYLE: I mentioned earlier the availability of technical people. Recruiting the right kind of technical people in sufficient numbers will be a challenge.

SPENCER: There is a third area of challenge that I see in front of us. Increasingly, this competitive world needs a very productive workforce. As you know, productivity has been a theme in the company. It relates again to the attraction and the motivation of the type of intelligent people that we are going to need to run this business.

But we have to work on the sharing of objectives, the quality circles or quality of work life movement at lower levels in the organization, the openness of communication between all levels of people in the business from the top management on down because that is what I think is the key to creating more productive companies. Productivity, like quality, is an attitude, and there are lots of tools you use to get productivity and to enhance the attitude of people toward wanting to do their job better. You have to create an atmosphere in which people can say, "Yes, I do want to do my job better and here's the way I can do it. I'll go tell my boss about it."

TICHY: Staying on that theme, one observation I have in looking at Honeywell is that there is probably as much innovative, people-oriented activity going on in Honeywell in terms of quality circles, development, and programs addressing these very issues as there is in any other company in the United States. One worry I have in looking at all of this activity is whether it will get institutionalized five years from now. Will it have been looked back on as an interesting time when a lot of activity went on, such as 700 quality circles, but which somehow all faded away? The questions that I have is, how do you ensure that it all becomes a way of operating rather than a bunch of programs?

SPENCER: I think there's a risk at the lowest level of the quality circle that it can fade away because people are getting kind of tired of it; they have run out of things to talk about. What you have to do on that level is to rejuvenate it every once in a while. If you find that it is running out of gas in some part of the company, you go back in and rejuvenate it. New ideas come from new people who are involved. This can be done, and I think it will be done.

I don't think the company is going to change the approach to the whole subject of productivity and quality and getting the people involved in things. That's becoming too much ingrained in the way we do out business. Unless they add a new chief executive who felt very differently about this than I do, and hence the people who work for him feel differently than those who work for me, I don't think that is going to change. Again, we go back to the first thing we talked about: the driving force to keep it from changing is probably not the chief executive or upper management—it's the driving force of the type of people we've got to have in this business and what they want to do to stay working productively at Honeywell.

BOYLE: We talked about the workforce as being brighter and better educated. Their expectations haven't changed in any revolutionary sense, but they have been changing and the expectations of the new managers are different from those of the old ones and they wouldn't want to manage people in the old way. I recognize what you are saying. I think there are a couple of things that could make it fade away, and one would obviously be a leadership change at the top. Now you're seeing a lot of activity because of the demonstrated commitment of the corporation starting at the top and working down. There probably is too much activity in some areas—too much of it being of a program nature, but I don't think that's adverse. I think if it's important to the company and important to the people up and down the line who work for the company, then it will become institutionalized. I think we are on the right track.

SPENCER: There is a risk in going too far; as I have said many times, don't ever forget who the boss is. I don't mean just me—I mean all the way down the line—because you have to make decisions to get things done, and consensus and group discussions are fine but somebody has got to say every once in a while, this is what we are going to do. Let me just say I don't want anybody to think that I'm not attentive to the need to run the business in that way, so I remind people about it every once in a while.

TICHY: On the issue of institutionalizing things, is there an effort being made to examine the kind of the personnel systems that support the organization similar to the way you are selecting people, developing them, appraising them, rewarding them, that may need modifications with this new kind of workforce and this new focus on productivity?

BOYLE: Yes, we're thinking about some of those things. In fact, this year we have a couple of gain-sharing pilot plans in the reward area that we started. I think that in a large, decentralized company you have the luxury, if you will, to try certain things. In a big company I don't think you want to change reward systems without some analysis and testing. In terms of development, I think I've covered the kind of things that we are trying to do to tie the development systems into our efforts in quality-of-work-life and productivity themes.

TICHY: How about appraising people? Is the quality-of-work-life effort, and the attention paid to those issues becoming a part of the formal appraisal?

BOYLE: I wouldn't say it's part of the appraisal process. We have all kinds of different appraisal systems, but I think it's done more indirectly than directly if you get right down to it.

TICHY: Is that something that should or will be happening more, as you look out over the next few years?

BOYLE: I think that if you look at what's happening and what we are trying to do, this will come kind of naturally. People will get appraised and rewarded for elements such as how they are involving the workforce in managing the business, because that will just become a natural part of the appraisal criteria. Ed, what do you think? Do you anticipate or think it's desirable or not to begin to build that into the formal appraisal process?

SPENCER: It's hard to put a quantitative number on those kind of things. I don't want people to be evaluated on how many quality circles they have, because you get a lot of quality circles and no quality. But I do think we evaluate people on a subjective set of goals and objectives as well as on things like affirmative action, community involvement, and long-term development of management talent, and this is one very good way. Certainly it ought to be in the objectives, because then it becomes a talking point between the boss and the employee and at least when they go through the appraisal process, they bring that subject up and they focus on what progress is being made.

TICHY: Let me end by asking each of you to discuss your leadership roles. Given the challenges and the things that you say Honeywell needs to accomplish over the next few years, how do you view your own leadership roles on people issues?

SPENCER: I think the chief executive should take very seriously how he can raise his own attitudes and his own relationships—not only to those who report directly to him but to those who see him or hear about how he gets along. I frankly am sometimes surprised at the influence the chief executive can have on an organization. It's a great deal more than people write about. Most of us, very humbly don't wish to acknowledge that fact, but nonetheless the chief executive's tone, his integrity, his standards, his way of dealing with people, his focusing on things that are important or not important can have a profound impact on the rest of the organization. What I am saying is that the way the chief executive and senior managers of the company conduct themselves as individuals has a more profound impact on how other people in the company conduct *themselves* than anything else that happens. When people don't fit that culture, either they shouldn't come in the first place, or they will find they are not welcome.

TICHY: How does that consciousness then translate into some things that you may specifically do or not do?

SPENCER: Well, let me take a little thing that I think is very important. I didn't start this at Honeywell; I obviously learned it from the people who went before me—two generations of managers before me. That is, going to other people's offices when you want to ask questions rather than calling everybody to come to your own office, and doing things orally rather than asking for memos and then writing memos back. Those are little things but it requires a personal contact to work in that way—and that, in turn, can have impact on this whole subject that we are talking about.

BOYLE: I think that one of the leadership goals for corporate employee relations is to be looking at those things out in the longer range that will have an impact on the organization and at least suggest to management that we ought to examine these areas. If we make decisions not to do them, fine, but we definitely need a long-range, strategic orientation in our work. The other thing we need is an orientation that something can get done. A lot of times staff departments say management won't buy that, or that's not going to happen. I think it's important for those in leadership positions in employee relations to be doers, to be able to say either we are not going to do that and forget about talking about it, or work on those things that have possibilities. You want to work on the things that have payoffs for the organization.

TICHY: Is part of your role that of being devil's advocate for senior managers on things you see regarding people?

BOYLE: I'm sometimes a devil's advocate when I press Ed on employee relations matters. For example, his view is different from mine on the expansion of the bonus programs that we have. Yet he is willing to listen to a proposal this year to examine the subject further, and we had some examination of these issues last year. In this position you have to be a devil's advocate.

TICHY: Ed, is that how you see Foss's job?

SPENCER: Yes, sir, absolutely.

TICHY: Which, if I understand, must be an historical shift in terms of the role that employee relations has played.

SPENCER: The role has been expected of employee relations but I think different chief executives relate differently to the department, and perhaps because I'm so conscious of employee relations needs today as being different from those of the past, it may be a more important department in my mind than it was in those of my predecessors to whom it was a labor relations and compensation department. It's an evolution that is going on in most companies.

TICHY: Let me wrap up with one kind of leadership issue; that is, how do you manage the succession issues? I'm not focusing just on your succession, but also on the succession of key people in the organization. At GE, for example, there was attention to the competitive dynamics in a succession process for chairman Reginald Jones's position. An effort was made to try to manage that process. Instead of having one winner and six losers, Reginald Jones worked three winners and four losers so as to get teamwork at the top. It struck me as a unique approach to looking at succession issues in trying to tilt the scale toward more teamwork at the top by not making the competition pyramid into such a win/lose situation. I'm wondering how succession issues are philosophically viewed in Honeywell—again, not just specifically around the CEO spot. The pyramid gets small at the top and you often have more capable people than slots. How do you manage that very difficult task?

SPENCER: I guess my own philosophy of it is a little different from the one you cited. In the first place, I do agree that you have to have teams of people running divisions or groups or companies; the world is too big and complex for one person to have to run a division and make omnipotent decisions. So, therefore, as you evolve leaderships and divisions and on up, you find people who can fit together as a team and some who can't, and those who can't tend to have to move on to some other environment to see whether they can fit into some other team. There is a law of natural succession in the business at all levels. Pretty soon you find that among peers people are looking to one that is a little stronger, a little more of a leader.

It isn't a question of pitting people competitively against each other, it's just the natural strengths and weaknesses of individuals, and the needs of the business at a given time that determine whether it's a market need, a financial need, or a technical need. Somehow it will be recognized pretty clearly that so and so deserved the job as division manager and most of the other people recognize that too. We have not had in this company, fortunately, many cases where one person has been promoted and several other people quit because they felt he shouldn't have gotten the job. We feel we've done a pretty good job—not only because we can look down and see who the best people are, but also because people down below seem to help us as a natural thing to do.

TICHY: In that situation, what do you see as the CEO's role?

SPENCER: To keep asking, prodding, and suggesting moves, suggesting promotions for people who come up looking like pretty good people. Out of it all, for each job there always seems to be one person who is a little better than everybody else.

TICHY: Historically, has it worked out so others end up accepting the promotions?

BOYLE: The proof of the pudding is that we have not yet had a lot of people either leaving or sitting in the organization and being dysfunctional or destructive in terms of what they are trying to do. A lot of that goes back to the framework of what kind of company we are and what we stand for—what our culture is. We tend to be more teamwork-oriented.

REFERENCES

Abowd, J. N. and H. S. Farber. "Job Queues and the Union Status of Workers." *Industrial and Labor Relations Review*, 1982, **35**, 354–376.

Adams, J. S. "Inequity in Social Exchange." In Leonard Berkowitz (Ed.), *Advances in Experimental Social Psychology*, Vol. 2. New York: Academic Press, 1965.

Agenold, M. "Swedish Experiments in Industrial Democracy" in L. E. Davis and A. B. Cherns (Eds.) *The Quality of Work Life* (Vol. II). New York: Free Press, 1975.

Aldrich, H. *Organizations and Environments*. Englewood Cliffs, NJ: Prentice-Hall, 1979.

Alfred, T. "Choice in Manpower Management." *Harvard Business Review*, 1967.

Averitt, Robert. *The Dual Economy* New York: Norton, 1968.

Bandura, A. *Social Learning Theory*. Englewood Cliffs, NJ: Prentice-Hall, 1977.

Barker, R. G. and P. V. Gump. *Big School, Small School: High School Size and Student Behavior*. Stanford: Stanford University Press 1964.

Beckhard, R. and R. Harris. *Organizational Transitions*. Reading, MA: Addison-Wesley, 1977.

Beer, M. and J. W. Driscoll. "Strategies for Change." In J. Richard Hackman, and J. L. Suttle (Eds.), *Improving Life at Work*. Santa Monica, CA: Goodyear, 1977.

Behrman, J. N. *National Interests and the Multinational Enterprise*. Englewood Cliffs, NJ: Prentice-Hall, 1970.

Bell, D. *The Cultural Contradictions of Capitalism*. New York: Basic Books, 1976.

Bergsten, C. F., T. Horst, and T. H. Moran. *American Multinational and American Interests*. Washington, DC: Brookings Institution, 1978.

Berger, C., C. Olson, and J. Boudreau. "A Facet Satisfaction Model of Union Job Satisfaction." Unpublished paper, Krannert School of Management, Purdue University, 1982.

Brandt, W. K. and J. M. Hulbert. "Communications and Control in Multinational Enterprise." In Warren J. Keegan and Charles S. Mayer (Eds.), *Multinational Product Management*. AMA Proceedings, 1977, pp. 119–146.

473

Brett, J. M. "Why Employees Want Unions." *Organizational Dynamics*, 1980, **9**(2), 47–59.

Burroughs, J. D. "Pay Secrecy and Performance: The Psychological Research." *Compensation Review*, 1982, **14** (3), 44–54.

Business Week. "Re-industrialization of America," June 30, 1980.

Business Week. "Concessionary Bargaining," June 14, 1982.

Business Week. "Will the Slide Kill Quality Circles?" January 11, 1982, 208–209.

Business Week. "Can John Young Redesign Hewlett-Packard?" December 6, 1982, pp. 74, 76, 78.

Campbell, J. P., M. D. Dunnette, E. E. Lawler, and K. E. Weick. *Managerial Behavior, Performance, and Effectiveness*. New York: McGraw-Hill, 1970.

Carlson, H. C. "G.M.'s Quality of Work Life Efforts," *Personnel*, 1978, **54**(4), 11–23.

Cummings, T. G. and E. S. Molloy. *Improving Productivity and the Quality of Work Life*. New York: Praeger, 1977.

Carnazza, J. *Succession/Replacement Planning: Programs and Practices*. Center for Research in Career Development, Columbia University Graduate School of Business, New York: 1982.

"Casting Executives as Consultants." *Business Week*, August 30, 1982, 46–51.

Chamberlain, N. W. and D. E. Cullen. *The Labor Sector*, 2nd ed. New York: McGraw-Hill, 1971, p. 227.

Cooke, W. N. and F. A. Gautshi, III. "Political Bias in NLRB Unfair Labor Practice Decision." *Industrial and Labor Relations Review*, 1982, **35**, 539–549.

Chandler, A. *Strategy and Structure*. Cambridge, MA: Harvard University Press, 1962.

Chandler, A. *Strategy and Structure: Chapters in the History of Industrial Enterprises*. Cambridge, MA: M.I.T. Press, 1962.

Crozier, M. *The Stalled Society*. New York: Viking Press, 1973.

Crystal, G. S. *Executive Compensation*. New York: AMACOM, 1978.

Davis, S. and P. Lawrence. *Matrix*. Reading, MA: Addison-Wesley, 1979.

Deal, T. E. and A. A. Kennedy. *Corporate Cultures*. Reading, MA: Addison-Wesley, 1982.

Devanna, M. A., C. Fombrun, N. Tichy, and E. K. Warren, *Study of Human Resource Management Issues in Strategy Formulation and Strategy Implementation*. Working Paper. New York: Strategy Center, Columbia University Graduate School of Business, 1981.

Devanna, M. A., C. Fombrun, and N. Tichy. "Human Resources Management: A Strategic Perspective." *Organizational Dynamics*, Winter 1981 51–67.

Devanna, M. A., C. Fombrun, N. Tichy, and E. K. Warren. "Strategic Planning and Human Resource Management." *Human Resource Management*, 1982, **21**(1), 1–17.

Devanna, M. A. *Male Female Wage Gaps: A Look at MBA Careers a Decade Later*. New York: Center for Research in Career Development, Columbia University, 1983.

Diesing, P. *Reason in Society*. Westport, CT: Greenwood Press, 1968.

Drucker, P. *Management: Tasks, Responsibilities and Practices*. New York: Harper & Row, 1973.

Drucker, P. *Managing Turbulent Times*. New York: Harper and Row, 1979.

Ellij, B. R. *Executive Compensation—A Total Pay Perspective*. New York: McGraw-Hill, 1982.

Edstrom, A. and J. Galbraith. "The Transfer of Managers as a Coordination and Control Strategy in Multinational Organizations." *Administrative Science Quarterly*, 1977, **22**.

Edwards, R. *Contested Terrain: The Transformation of the Workplace in the Twentieth Century*. New York: Basic Books, 1979.

Etzioni, A. *An Immodest Agenda*. 1982.

Foulkes, F. and H. M. Morgan. "Organizing and Staffing the Personnel Function." *Harvard Business Review*, 1977, **55**, 142–154.

Financial World. "Hewlett Packard: The Program Works." April 1979, **148**, 34.

Fisher, R. and W. Ury. *Getting to Yes: Negotiating Agreement Without Giving In.* Boston: Houghton Mifflin Company 1981.

Fiske, D. W. "Two Worlds of Psychological Phenomena." *American Psychologist,* 1979, **34,** 733–739.

Flynn, J. and R. Niven. "Second Thoughts on Manpower Cuts," in *International Management,* September 1982, 51–53.

Fombrun, C. and N. Tichy. "Strategic Planning and Human Resource Management: At Rainbow's End." In Robert Lamb, ed., *Competitive Strategic Management.* Englewood Cliffs, NJ: Prentice-Hall, 1984.

Fombrun, C. "An Interview with Reginald Jones." *Organizational Dynamics,* Winter 1982.

Fortune. "America's Most Admired Corporations." 1984, **109** (1), 50–62.

Foulkes, F. K. and H. M. Morgan. "Organizing and Staffing the Personnel Function." *Harvard Business Review,* 1977, **55,** 142–154.

Freedman, A. *Managing Labor Relations,* New York: Conference Board, 1979.

Freeman, R. B. "Job Satisfaction as an Economic Variable." *American Economic Review,* 1978, **68,** 135–141.

Freeman, R. B. "The Effect of Unionism on Fringe Benefits." *Industrial and Labor Relations Review,* 1981, **34,** 489–509.

Freeman, R. B. and J. L. Medoff. "The Impact of Collective Bargaining: Illusion or Reality?" In Jack Steiber, Robert B. McKersie, and D. Quinn Mills (Eds.), *U.S. Industrial Relations 1950–1980: A Critical Assessment.* Madison, WI: Industrial Relations Research Association, 1981, 47–48.

French, W. L. and C. Bell. *Organizational Development.* Englewood Cliffs, NJ: Prentice-Hall, 1978.

Galbraith, J. *Designing Complex Organizations.* Reading, MA: Addison-Wesley, 1973.

Galbraith, Jay. *Organizational Design.* Reading, MA: Addison-Wesley, 1977.

Galbraith, J. and D. Nathanson. *Strategy Formulation: Analytical Concepts.* St. Paul, MN: West Publishing Co., 1978.

Galbraith, J. and D. Nathanson. *Strategy Implementation: The Role of Structure and Process.* St. Paul, MN: West Publishing, 1978.

Gayle, S. and L. Gray. "Ten Best Places to Work." *Black Enterprise,* February 1982, **12,** 37.

Geertz, C. *The Interpretation of Cultures.* New York: Basic Books, 1973.

Gilmore, T. "A Collective Process for Coping with the Demise of a Work Group." In Hirschhorn and MBSC Associates *Cutting Back.* San Francisco: Jossey-Bass, 1983.

Ginzberg, E. *Good Jobs, Bad Jobs, No Jobs.* Cambridge, MA: Harvard University Press, 1981.

Greiner, L. "Evolution and Resolution as Organizations Grow." *Harvard Business Review,* 1972, **50** (4), 37–46.

Grinyer, P. and S. J. Bazzaz. "Corporate Planning in the U.S." *Strategic Management Journal,* 1981, **2**(2).

Hall, D. T. *Careers in Organizations.* Pacific Palisades, Ca., Goodyear Publishing, 1976.

Hall, D. T. and F. S Hall. "What's New in Career Management." *Organizational Dynamics,* 1976, **5,** 17–33.

Hall, D. T. and B. Schneider. *Organizational Climates and Careers.* New York: Academic Press, 1973.

Henderson, B. *Henderson on Corporate Strategy.* Cambridge, MA: Abt Books, 1979.

Herrick, N. Q. and M. Maccoby. "Humanizing Work: A Priority Goal of the 1970's." In L. E. Davis and A. B. Cherns (Eds.), *The Quality of Work Life; Vol. I: Problems, Prospects, and the State of the Art., Vol. II: Cases and Commentary.* New York: Free Press, 1975.

Hirschhorn, L. and MBSC Associates. *Cutting Back.* San Francisco: Jossey-Bass, 1983.

Hirschhorn, L. "Revealing and Concealing in the Retrenchment Process." In Hirschhorn, *Cutting Back*. San Francisco: Jossey-Bass, 1983.

Hofer, C. and D. Schendel. *Strategy Formulation: Analytical Concepts*. St. Paul, MN: West Publishing, 1978.

Jacques, E. *The Changing Culture of a Factory*. London: Tavistock, 1951.

Jennergren, P. "On the Design of Incentives in Business Firms—A Survey of Some Research." *Management Science*, February 1980, 180–201.

Kahn, R. L. "Organizational Development: Some Problems and Proposals." *Journal of Applied Behavioral Science*, 1974, **10**, 485–582.

Kanter, R. M. *Men and Women of the Corporation*. New York: Basic Books, 1977.

Kanter, R. M. "The Middle Manager as Innovator." *Harvard Business Review*, July–August 1982.

Kanter, R. M. *The Change Masters*. New York: Simon and Schuster, 1983.

Kaufman, H. G. *Professionals in Search of Work: Coping with the Stress of Job Loss and Underemployment*. New York: John Wiley, 1982.

Kay, E., H. H. Meyer, and J. R. P. French, Jr. "Effects of Threat in a Performance Appraisal Interview." *Journal of Applied Psychology*, 1965, **49**, 311–317.

Kerr, S. "On The Folly of Rewarding A. While Hoping for B." *Academy of Management Journal*, 1975, **18**, 796–783.

Kimberly, J. R., R. H. Miles, and Associates. *The Organizational Life-Cycle*. San Francisco: Jossey-Bass, 1980.

Kochan, T. A. "How American Workers View Labor Unions." *Monthly Labor Review*, 1979, **103**(4), 23–31.

Kotter, J. P., *The General Managers*. New York: Free Press, 1982.

Lasch, C. *Culture of Narcissism*. New York: Warner Books, 1979.

Latham, G. P. and L. M. Saari. "The Application of Social Learning Theory of Training Supervisors through Behavioral Modeling." *Journal of Applied Psychology*, 1979, **64**, 239–246.

Latham, G. P. and K. N. Wexley. *Increasing Productivity Through Performance Appraisal*. Reading, MA: Addison-Wesley, 1981.

Latham, G. P., K. N. Wexley, and E. D. Parsell. "Training Managers to Minimize Rating Errors in the Observation of Behavior." *Journal of Applied Psychology*, 1975, **60**, 550–555.

Lawler, E. E. "The New Plant Revolution." *Organizational Dynamics*, 1978, **6**, 2–12.

Lawler, E. E. *Pay and Organizational Effectiveness: A Psychological View*. New York: McGraw-Hill, 1971.

Lawler, E. E. *Motivation in Work Organizations*. Monterey, CA: Brooks/Cole, 1973.

Lawler, E. E. *Pay and Organization Development*. Reading, MA: Addison-Wesley, 1981.

Leighton, A. *The Governing of Men*. Princeton, NJ: Princeton University Press, 1945.

Levinson, H. "Criteria for Choosing Chief Executives." *Harvard Business Review*, July–August 1980, 113–120.

Locke, E. A. and G. P. Latham. *Goal Setting: A Key to Productivity*. Englewood Cliffs, NJ: Prentice-Hall, 1983.

Lorange, P. *Corporate Planning: An Executive Viewpoint*. Englewood Cliffs, NJ: Prentice-Hall, 1980.

Lorange, P. and R. Vancil. *Strategic Planning Systems*. Englewood Cliffs, NJ: Prentice-Hall, 1977.

Lorsch, J. (Ed.). *Handbook of Organizational Behavior*. Englewood Cliffs, NJ: Prentice-Hall, 1983.

Lorsch, J. W. and A. Allen, III. *Managing Diversity and Interdependence: An Organizational Study of Multi-Divisional Firms*. Boston, MA: Harvard University, Graduate School of Business Administration, Division of Research, 1973.

Magenau, J. M. and D. G. Pruitt. "The Social Psychology of Bargaining: A Theoretical Synthesis 1." In Geoffrey M. Stephenson and Christopher J. Brotherton (Eds.), *Industrial Relations: A Social Psychology Approach*. New York: Wiley, 1979, pp. 197–199.

Mahler, W. R. and W. F. Wrightnour. *Executive Continuity: How to Build and Retain an Effective Management Team.* Homewood, Illinois Dow Jones Irwin, 1973.

Marrow A. J., D. G. Bowers, and S. E. Seashore. *Management by Participation.* New York: Harper and Row, 1967.

Marshall, S. L. A. *Men Against Fire.* New York: William Morrow, 1947.

Meyer, H. H. "The Annual Performance Review Discussion: Making it Constructive." *Personnel Journal,* 1977, **56**, 508–511.

Michael, D. *Control Without Bureaucracy.* London: McGraw-Hill, 1979.

Miles, R. E. and H. R. Rosenberg. "The Human Resource Approach to Management: Second Generation Issues." *Organizational Dynamics,* Winter 1982, **10**, 26–41.

Miller, E. L., E. H. Burack, and M. Albrecht. *Management of Human Resources.* Englewood Cliffs, NJ: Prentice-Hall, 1980.

Mitchell, D. J. B. *Unions, Wages, and Inflation.* Washington, DC: Brookings Institution, 1980.

Mirvis, Phil and D. Berg (Eds.). *Failures in Organizational Development and Change: Cases and Essays for Learning.* New York: Wiley-Interscience, 1977.

Mobley, W. H. *Employee Turnover: Causes, Consequences, and Control.* Reading, MA: Addison-Wesley, 1982.

Montgomery, C. A. "The Measurement of Firm Diversification: Some New Empirical Evidence." *Academy of Management Journal,* 1982, **25**(2).

Murray, T. "Silicon Valley faces up to the People Crunch." *Dun's Review,* July 1981, **118**, 60.

Nadler, D. and M. Tushman, "A Diagnostic Model for Organizational Behavior." In J. R. Hackman and E. E. Lawler, *Perspectives on Behavior in Organizations.* New York: McGraw-Hill, 1977.

Nadler, D. "Managing Organizational Change: An Integrative Perspective." *Journal of Applied Behavioral Science,* 1981, **17**, 191–211.

Nadler, D. "Managing Transitions to Uncertain Future States." *Organizational Dynamics,* Summer 1982, 37–45.

Nealy, S. "Pay and Benefit Preferences." *Industrial Relations,* 1963, **3**, 17–28.

Neufeld, M. F. "The Persistence of Ideas in the American Labor Movement: The Heritage of the 1830's." *Industrial and Labor Relations Review,* 1982, **35**, 207–220.

Newman, W., E. K. Warren, and J. Schnee. *Process of Management,* 5th ed. Englewood Cliffs, NJ: Prentice-Hall, 1982.

Nixon, R. *The Real War.* New York: Warner Books, 1979.

Normann, R. "Organizational Innovativeness: Product Variation and Reorientation." *Administrative Science Quarterly,* 1971, **16**, 203–215.

Ouchi, W. *Theory Z: Meeting the Japanese Challenge.* Reading, MA: Addison-Wesley, 1980.

Pascale, R. and A. Athos. *The Art of Japanese Management.* New York: Warner Books, 1981.

Pelz, D. and F. Andrews. *Scientists in Organization.* New York: Wiley, 1975.

Peters, T. and R. H. Waterman, Jr. *In Search of Excellence: Lessons from America's Best-Run Companies.* New York: Harper & Row, 1982.

Pfeffer, J. and G. Salancik. *The External Control of Organizations.* Englewood Cliffs, NJ: Prentice-Hall, 1977.

Phillips, J. and A. Kennedy. "Shaping and Managing Shared Values." McKinsey Staff Paper, December 1980.

Reypert, L. J. "Succession Planning in the Ministry of Transportation and Communications, Province of Ontario." *Human Resource Planning,* 1981, **4**, 151–156.

Rogers, E. and R. A. Rogers. *Communication in Organizations.* New York: Free Press, 1976.

Roth, L., M. A. Devanna, *A Career Development Study.* Unpublished paper. New York: Center for Research in Career Development, Columbia University, 1983.

Ruane, B. "A Quantitative Evaluation of an Employee Relations Function." *The Career Development Bulletin,* 1982, **3**(2), 6–11.

Rubin, M. "Communities Coping with Natural Disasters." In Hirschhorn et al., *Cutting Back.* San Francisco: Jossey-Bass, 1983.

Rumelt, R. P. *Strategy, Structure and Economic Performance.* Cambridge, MA: Harvard University Press, 1974.

Salschneider, J. "Devising Pay Strategies for Diversified Companies." *Compensation Review,* 1981, 5–25.

Sandver, Marcus H. "South–Nonsouth Differentials in National Labor Relations Board Certification Election Outcomes." *Journal of Labor Research,* 1982, **3**, 13–30.

Servan-Schreiber, J. J. *The Global Challenge.* 1980.

Stein, B. "Organizations in Trouble: Two Vignettes." In R. M. Kanter and B. Stein, *Life in Organizations.* New York: Basic Books. 1979, pp. 387–400.

Stopford, J. R. and L. T. Wells, Jr. *managing the Multinational Enterprise.* New York: Basic Books, 1972.

Taylor, A. "Layoffs and the Problem of Discrimination." Working Paper, Management and Behavioral Science Center, The Wharton School, University of Pennsylvania, 1983.

Taylor, Sir H. *The Statesman.* Cambridge, MA: Heffer and Sons, Ltd., 1957.

Thune, S. S. and R. S. House. "Where Long Range Planning Pays Off." *Business Horizons,* August 1970.

Thurow, L. *Zero-Sum Society.* New York: Basic Books, 1980.

Tichy, N. M., C. J. Fombrun, and M. A. Devanna. "Strategic Human Resource Management." *Sloan Management Review,* Winter 1982, 47–61.

Tichy, N. M. *Managing Strategic Change.* New York: Wiley, 1983.

Toffler, A. *The Third Wave.* New York: Morrow, 1980.

Trist, E. L. "New Directions of Hope: Recent Innovations Interconnecting Organizational, Industrial, Community, and Personal Development." *Regional Studies,* 1980, **13**, 439–451.

Trist, E. "The Evolution of Sociotechnical Systems as a Conceptional Framework and as an Action Research Program." In A. H. Van de Van and W. F. Joyce (Eds.), *Perspectives on Organization Design and Behavior.* New York: Wiley, 1981.

Tushman, M. and W. Moore. *Readings in Managerial Innovation.* Boston: Pitman, 1982.

Tushman, M. L. and R. Katz. "A Longitudinal Study of the Effects of Boundary Spanning Supervision on Turnover and Promotion in Research and Development." *Academy of Management Journal,* September 1983, **26**,(3).

Vernon, R. *Sovereignty at Bay: The Multinational Spread of U.S. Enterprises.* New York: Basic Books, 1971.

Vetter, E. *High Talent Manpower.* Ann Arbor, MI: University of Michigan, Graduate School of Business, 1967.

Vetter, E. The Nature of Managerial Planning. *Management of Human Resources.* Englewood Cliffs, NJ: Prentice-Hall, 1980.

Vroom, V. *Work and Motivation.* New York: Wiley, 1964.

Walker, J. W. "Evaluating the Practical Effectiveness of Human Resource Planning Applications." *Human Resource Management,* 1974, **13**(1), 19–27.

Walker, J. W. *Human Resource Planning.* New York: McGraw-Hill, 1980.

Walton, R. E. "Quality of Working Life: What Is It?" *Sloan Management Review,* Fall 1973, 11–21.

Walton, R. E. "The Diffusion of New York Structures: Explaining Why Success Didn't Take." *Organizational Dynamics,* Winter 1975, 3–22.

Walton, R. E. "Establishing and Maintaining Commitment in Work Organizations." In *The Organizational Life Cycle.* J. Kimberly, and R. H. Miles and Associates (Eds.), San Francisco: Jossey-Bass, 1980.

Warren, L. "The Role of Human Resources in Strategic Planning." *Career Development Bulletin,* Columbia University Graduate School of Business, 2(4), 1981.

Wellbank, H.L., D.T. Hall, M.A. Morgan, and W.C. Hanner. "Planning Job Profession for Effective Career Management and Human Resources Management." *Personnel,* 1978, **55,** 54–64.

Wellington, J.K. "Management Succession at Arizona Public Service." *Human Resources Planning,* 1981, **4,** 157–167.

White, Michael D. "The Intra-Unit Wage Structure and Unions: A Median Voter Model." *Industrial and Labor Relations Review,* 1982, **35,** 565–577.

Wexley, K. and G. Latham *Increasing Productivity Through Performance Appraisal.* Reading, MA: Addison-Wesley, 1981.

Whyte, W. F. (Ed.). *Money and Motivation: An Analysis of Incentives on Industry.* New York: Harper, 1955.

NAME INDEX

SUBJECT INDEX

485